After They Closed the Gates

After They Closed the Gates

JEWISH ILLEGAL IMMIGRATION TO THE
UNITED STATES, 1921–1965

Libby Garland

The University of Chicago Press CHICAGO & LONDON

LIBBY GARLAND is assistant professor of history at Kingsborough Community College, the City University of New York.

The University of Chicago Press, Chicago 60637
The University of Chicago Press, Ltd., London
© 2014 by The University of Chicago
All rights reserved. Published 2014.
Printed in the United States of America

23 22 21 20 19 18 17 16 15 14   1 2 3 4 5

ISBN-13: 978-0-226-12245-8 (cloth)
ISBN-13: 978-0-226-12259-5 (e-book)

DOI: 10.7208/chicago/9780226122595.001.0001

Library of Congress Cataloging-in-Publication Data
Garland, Libby, author.
After they closed the gates : Jewish illegal immigration to the United States,
1921–1965 / Libby Garland.
pages cm
Includes bibliographical references and index.
ISBN 978-0-226-12245-8 (cloth : alkaline paper)—ISBN 978-0-226-12259-5 (e-book)
1. Jews, European—United States—History—20th century. 2. Immigrants—United States—
History—20th century. 3. Illegal aliens—United States—History—20th century.
4. United States—Emigration and immigration—History—20th century. 5. Emigration and
immigration law—United States—History—20th century.   I. Title.
E184.354.G37 2014
304.80973—dc23
2013029157

♾ This paper meets the requirements of ANSI/NISO Z39.48–1992 (Permanence of Paper).

CONTENTS

ACKNOWLEDGMENTS

In the course of writing about people who resorted to counterfeit documents and adopted personae in order to slip past national borders, I found myself thinking a lot about how the modern world has produced some very strange ideas regarding individual identities, as well as about the ways that people represent themselves in order to conform to such notions. The persona of the "author" may be one of the strangest of such invented individual identities. There is something odd about putting one's name by itself on the front of a book, as if research, writing, and publishing were not a collective enterprise—intellectually, logistically, financially, and emotionally.

It turns out, for example, that being able to pay the rent is generally a prerequisite for producing a book. I am grateful to the following for providing financial support for my research and writing: the Jacob Rader Marcus Center of the American Jewish Archives in Cincinnati, the Feinstein Center for American Jewish History in Philadelphia, the University of Michigan Rackham School of Graduate Studies and the Program in American Culture, and the Professional Staff Congress–City University of New York Research Awards program. Thanks go, too, to the faculty and administrators at Kingsborough Community College for their support of my work, particularly to my department chair, Fran Kraljic, and to the department administrator, Cindy Adelstein.

No historical researcher can get very far without the help of archivists and librarians. My thanks go to all those at the American Jewish Archives; the American Jewish Committee Archives; the American Jewish Historical Society; the American Jewish Joint Distribution Committee Archives; the Immigration and Naturalization Historical Reference Library; the Leo Baeck

Institute; the Manuscript Division of the Library of Congress; the National Archives in New York City, Chicago, and Washington DC; the Western Jewish History Center; and the YIVO Institute for Jewish Research, who helped lead me to wonderful material. The librarians at the New York Public Library's Jewish Division, especially Faith Jones, Roberta Saltzman, and Michael Terry, were always particularly helpful in finding elusive publications and providing answers to obscure questions about Jewish history.

The heart of this study consists of stories and documents that do not belong to me. I thank those people who shared their family stories with me for this project: Joan Friedman, Sidney Rabinovich, Ester Reiter, Ethel Seid, and Martin Stein. I am grateful, as well, to the many people whose often painful encounters with US immigration law produced the sources that now reside in archives and libraries, which I have drawn from throughout this book. I thank, too, all those students and friends whose stories about their present-day experiences of migration—though I do not quote them in these pages—profoundly shaped my understanding of the personal stakes, risks, and hopes entailed in such encounters with the immigration system.

Studying and thinking are activities that happen as much communally as they do solitarily, and so I am lucky to have found myself surrounded by smart, creative, and hardworking people throughout my years working on this project. During the time I spent at the University of Michigan, I was part of an especially vibrant intellectual community; I thank the staff, faculty, undergraduates, and graduate students in American Culture and History for their energy and communal ethos. Particular thanks go to Gina Morantz-Sanchez, Anita Norich, David Scobey, and Terry McDonald for their thoughtful criticism and scholarly insight.

In New York, I have been equally surrounded by intellectual vitality. Colleagues at Basic Books, Big Onion Walking Tours, CLAL–The National Jewish Center for Learning and Leadership, and the Gilder Lehrman Institute of American History, besides being important mentors and friends, provided me with perspectives on the practices of research, writing, and history from outside the world of academia that made me think in new ways about all these things. In particular, I would like to thank Justine Ahlstrom, Tim Bartlett, Jim Basker, Stephen Bottum, Shari Cohen, Michael Gottsegen, Glenda Johnson, Jo Ann Miller, and Robert Rabinowitz. Teaching, too, has meant learning to engage in new ways with my subject. My students at the School for Democracy and Leadership, the College of Staten Island, Hunter College, and Kingsborough Community College always brought into our classes passionate opinions, provocative questions, and a breadth of personal experience that pushed me as a teacher, a researcher, and a writer. My colleagues at these institutions also have taught me a great deal about what it means to write for and talk with others about history. In this regard, I would like particularly to thank Rick Armstrong, Jhumki Basu, Nancy Gannon, Dan Gelbtuch, Kevin Kolkmeyer, Eddie Pessutti, Rick Repetti, Sarah Schwartz, Jacob Segal, Michael Spear, Eben Wood, and Joanna Yip.

I also thank the many patient, smart people who have read this project in all its various stages and provided thoughtful, detailed feedback. This book would not be a book at all, of course, without the editors and other staff of the University of Chicago Press. Robert Devens took the project on and worked with me to reshape it; and Russell Damian and Tim Mennel were enormously helpful in getting me over the finish line. Elissa Park provided tactful, smart copyediting; Mary Gehl oversaw the book's production. All were encouraging, steering me and the manuscript with grace, intelligence, and patience through the long process of publication. Thanks go as well to the two anonymous readers for the press whose input aided me along the way. I appreciate, too, the chance to have published some of my ideas as articles. Portions of chapters 3 and 4 appeared in somewhat different form in Libby Garland, "Not-quite-closed Gates: Jewish Alien Smuggling in the Post-Quota Years," *American Jewish History* 94, no. 3 (September 2008): 197–224. Chapter 5 appeared in somewhat different form in Libby Garland, "Fighting to Be Insiders: American Jewish Leaders and the Michigan Alien Registration Law of 1931," *American Jewish History* 96, no. 2 (June 2010): 109–40.

In New York and beyond, Ruth Abusch-Magder, Jay Arena, Charlotte Brooks, Tamara Mose Brown, Katherine Chen, Jessica Cooperman, Huey Copeland, Marni Davis, Holly Dugan, Deborah Gambs, Howard Garland, Sylvia F. Garland, Idana Goldberg, Marion Jacobson, Rebecca Kobrin, Erica Lehrer, Kate Masur, Vanessa May, Carmen Menocal, Alex Molot, Cheli Morales, Leslie Paris, Josh Perlman, Jane Rothstein, Jordan Schildcrout, Alix Schwartz, Tracy Sivitz, Eliza Slavet, Jonathan Soffer, Nikki Stanton, Stephen Steinberg, Nick Syrett, Michael Terry, Amy Wan, and Grace Wang read parts of the manuscript and offered ideas for improvement. Tom Klug graciously shared his own expertise and sources on alien registration. Eckart Goebel bears the responsibility for getting me to return to this project after a hiatus. There are some people who have worked with me on so many drafts and talked so often about the ideas in this book that whole sections of this work came about in collaboration with them, and anything that might be elegantly or intelligently formulated in those sections is very likely their doing: Tamar Barzel, Alisa Braun, Beth Dill, Jen Fronc, Eric Goldstein, Margie Weinstein, Karen Miller, Glenn Perusek, and

Annie Polland. Many of the people who have read my work over the years and given me their thoughts about it are scholars whose own works in progress I have had the good fortune to read and discuss. The opportunity to see other people's work develop is as valuable as having a circle of skilled and caring readers, and this project evolved very much in conversation with those who have shared their writing with me. Any errors in this book are, of course, solely mine.

There are also many people who have provided me with hospitality, meals, humor, perspective, and other forms of caretaking and respite without which scholarly writing, and life in general, would be intolerable: Beatrice Aranow, Max Belkin, Alison Clark, Grit Dielmann, Laura Fink, Aura Fuentes, Jose Fuentes, Mira Geffner, Volker Gläser, Lisa Goldblatt, Alex Jones, Anne P. Kühl, Dan Lederman, Daryl Maeda, Robin Michals, Eric Mitchell, Fulvio Montagna, Mary Murray, Spencer Neyland, Jon Nichols, Said El Omari, Ishtiaq Omer, Stephen Powter, Sundeep Rangan, Alex Seiffert, Yumi Selden, Robert Silver, Rose Silver, Melita Smilovic, Sabrina Spatari, Julie Subrin, Tobias Tunkel, Rebecca Vollmer, Stephanie Werhane, Debra Wilson, Miki Yamashita, Kritika Yegnashankaran, and Joscha Zmarzlik. I would also like to thank the swimmers and coaches of Red Tide, who taught me that writing is an endurance sport, and without whose early-morning camaraderie I would likely long ago have given up the academic enterprise.

Deep thanks are due to my family, whose interest, love, and support—which I have relied on my whole life—have made all my work possible. I thank my grandparents, Asna Finkelstein, Saul Finkelstein, Sylvia M. Garland, and Max Garland, for their many years of generosity, and especially my grandmother Sylvia M. Garland for sharing so many stories from her own life. My sister, Miriam Garland, has been a steady source of never-judgmental encouragement and humor. My parents, Howard Garland and Sylvia F. Garland, have always been walking proof of the pleasure that can be found in a life of teaching, questioning, and learning. Their delight and pride in my academic work, from grade school to the present day, has often made me feel it is all worthwhile.

Finally, I would like to thank Jacob Fuentes and his daughters Heavenly Fuentes and Faith Fuentes, who—despite my boring habit of spending vacations and weekends typing away by myself in library basements—have unwaveringly supported my work on this book. The extraordinary way the three of them have taken me into their lives, offering what seems to be an infinite supply of warmth and love, has helped me understand more deeply what it means to be welcomed and just how precious an experience that is.

INTRODUCTION

On February 11, 1928, the SS *Iroquois* had just completed the short voyage from Havana to Miami when US immigration inspectors detained one of the ship's Jewish passengers. This traveler's documents identified him as thirty-two-year-old Sam Weisstein, born in Poland but now a naturalized citizen of the United States. The inspectors found it suspicious, however, that Weisstein could not explain how he had obtained his papers. After close interrogation, the man confessed that he was not Weisstein but Chaim Josef Listopad, a Jewish carpenter born in Mlawa, Poland. Listopad was not a US citizen and had never even been to the United States. He had bought the papers in Havana just two weeks earlier, paying fifty dollars to a Jewish stranger wearing a white tropical suit and straw hat. Listopad might not have made this purchase had he known that the Bureau of Immigration in Washington, DC, already had a thick file on the real Samuel Weisstein, whom they had long suspected of smuggling Jews from Warsaw to the United States for profit.[1]

In 1921 and 1924, the US Congress passed radically nativist legislation decreeing that most immigration would henceforth be strictly limited according to nation-based quotas. The controversial new laws drastically limited the number of Europeans allowed to legally enter the United States, especially from southern and eastern Europe, and made permanent an already existing near-total ban on Asian immigration. Consequently, these laws fueled an extensive underground of illegal immigration from Europe, a phenomenon that has gone largely unexamined in scholarship on this era.[2] After the laws' passage, many eastern European Jews, desperate to escape ongoing postwar economic and political crises, did what Chaim Josef Listopad did: they entered the nation illicitly. Some sailed into the port of New York City with fake German passports bought in Berlin. Others came into Florida from Cuba, hidden with Greeks and Chinese in the holds of boats loaded with contraband liquor. Still others crossed the nation's land borders surreptitiously, coming into Vermont from Canada by car or into Texas from Mexico by foot. *After They Closed the Gates* tells the story of this Jewish illegal immigration, exploring the experiences of immigrants who entered the country illicitly. The book also investigates the responses that government officials, Jewish organizations, alien smugglers, and immigrants' families had to this new, unsanctioned flow of people across US borders.

There are two intertwined questions at the heart of this book. The first concerns the social history of the restrictive 1921 and 1924 laws themselves. What did these laws actually mean for people's lives at the time? Historians have tended to take the unprecedented immigration laws at face value, attending to the letter of the laws while leaving their day-to-day workings largely unexamined.[3] Law, however, does not exist solely in the province of legislative debates, statute books or judicial decisions; it also plays out through lived experience. The letter of the law, though a crucial part of the historical record, cannot capture all the law's implications, consequences and meanings. *After They Closed the Gates* argues that the meanings of the new immigration legislation of the 1920s emerged not just from the text of the laws themselves, nor even solely from their enforcement and administration by government actors. Rather, the laws' meanings were created, over the course of many years, as a result of the actions of lawmakers, other government officials, political and aid organizations, alien smugglers, and migrants themselves. All these groups, in different and competing ways, helped define the reality of immigration under the quota regime. Although the new legislation did rewrite the rules governing the nation's literal and metaphorical borders, those rules were far from simple to implement. The history of Jewish illegal immigration during the era of immigration quotas, a dramatic episode in American Jewish history, serves also to reveal a larger story about US immigration policy, that is, the extent to which the reordering of the nation's boundaries in the quota era happened in an uneven manner with much confusion and contention.

The book's second question concerns "Jewish illegal aliens." We know in retrospect that Jews, like other European ethnics, ultimately escaped the category of "illegal alienness"—despite their history of smuggling and illegal entry—in a way that, for example, Mexicans have not. The way this happened is less well understood, yet in its twists and turns this story offers compelling insights into the contingent nature of citizenship, belonging, and American-ness. This book traces the process through which Jews came first to be associ-ated with, and then to be uncoupled from, illegal alienness. The second part of this process—the "de-illegalizing"—entailed vigorous political efforts on the part of American Jewish citizens. As the history of these efforts indicates, in the era of the quota laws, American Jewish citizens, new arrivals, and would-be immigrants alike shared a more complex relationship to the United States than scholars have fully grasped. In exploring the fault lines of that relationship, this book also sheds new light on the connection between the quota laws of the 1920s and modern conceptions of the illegal alien.[4]

REEXAMINING THE "CLOSING OF THE GATES"

The history of Jewish illegal immigration during the quota era forces us to reconsider and refine a central narrative of twentieth-century American and Jewish history, a narrative we might call the story of the "closing of the gates" to European immigrants. The history of illegal immigration during this period makes it clear that the effects of the quota laws, though dramatic, were not as straightforward as historians have suggested. The gates did not simply close. Rather, the new laws produced a great deal of debate and uncertainty about immigration law enforcement and government power, the meanings of legal and illegal immigration, and the boundaries between Americans and aliens.

The quota laws have long served as a sharp dividing line in the historiogra-phy of European ethnics in the United States. The passage of the permanent quota law in 1924 has stood as the end of the great epic of European mass im-migration, inaugurating a time when European ethnics, cut off from homeland cultures, became increasingly concerned with their relationship to the nation around them. Historians writing about the post-1924 period have often fo-cused on European ethnics in their American context, as workers, voters, and consumers coming to identify more fully with a national—and white—culture.[5] For the most part, the literature of American Jewish history follows this same pattern, taking up the question of immigration and immigration policy again only in connection to how these became matters of public concern after Adolf Hitler came to power in 1933.[6]

In part, the use of the quota laws as a historiographical boundary line reflects the demands of the historical discipline. Historians tell narratives about change over time; we need events that mark the beginnings and ends of these narratives and distinguish one era from another. The quota laws have functioned as just such markers. As is demonstrated by their undeniable demographic impact, it is true that in many ways the quota laws represented a historical turning point for European immigration in general and Jewish immigration in particular. In the twelve months before the passage of the 1921 law, 805,228 immigrants were recorded as having entered the United States legally, 119,036 of them Jewish. In the year after the 1924 law took effect, 294,314 immigrants entered legally, of which 10,292 were Jewish.[7]

Even beyond their statistical impact, the laws were revolutionary in the realm of American immigration policy. They represented an unprecedented effort by the US government to control the nation's geographic and demographic borders. The quotas, which were explicitly based on the understanding that foreigners from Asia as well as southern and eastern Europe presented political, racial, and cultural threats to the United States, were an attempt on the part of lawmakers to render a precise, nation- and race-based formula for American unity. The 1924 law frankly declared it a national priority to exclude Asians, and to add only so many from Lithuania, so many from Russia, and so many from Italy per year. The effects of this approach to immigration policy proved enduring. The quota laws remained basically unchanged for four decades, and many of their underlying ideas, including the necessity to put a quantitative cap on immigration and to guard the nation against potential threats posed by incoming foreigners, remain central to public discourse and government policy. Certainly, then, these laws fundamentally shifted the nature of international migration and the tenor of domestic immigration policy.

Although scholars have long acknowledged the significance of the immigration quotas, little investigation has been made into the actual workings of the laws and scant attention paid to the laws' meanings for the range of historical actors whom they affected. Looking at the official data generated after the quota laws, it is easy to see why historians have not written much about European immigration during these years. Such data, as noted above, reflect plummeting numbers of entering immigrants and thus strongly seem to suggest that the quota laws accomplished their aims. *After They Closed the Gates* makes a case for expanding the historical record of quota-era immigration policy to include more of people's actual experiences with the law.[8] The implementation of the quota laws entailed the mobilization of a vast government apparatus: consuls regulating and limiting the issue of visas, inspectors making judgments about immigrants at ports and borders, investigators tracking down illegal entrants, and bureaucrats tabulating statistics and producing reports. To develop a fuller understanding of what the laws meant in real life, we need to consider on-the-ground details of migrants' encounters with this government apparatus. In reality, the new immigration laws *happened* in a great variety of ways and places—indeed, every time a migrant did or did not succeed in entering the United States anywhere along its vast borders or through any port. As this book makes plain, such encounters are illuminating to historians, allowing us to witness both the power of the law and the limits of its efficacy.

The law *happened* in other ways as well, beyond the interactions between those enforcing it and those purportedly subject to its enforcement. Law may define the terrain upon which the meanings of legal regimes are constructed, but those meanings are never defined unilaterally. Rather, they evolve out of the often conflicting understandings, experiences and actions of all those engaged in the realms described by the law.[9] Focusing on the lived experience of the quota laws illustrates this dynamic by showing us the laws through the "wrong" end of the historian's conceptual telescope, so to speak. For the actors at the time, whichever side of the law—or the ocean—they were on, the effects of the law were not a done deal. In its wider sense, as an ever-shifting landscape of causes and effects, US immigration law during the era derived not only from the doings of lawmakers and state officials but also from interactions among state actors, political and aid organizations, smuggling rings, and individual migrants and their families. To draw a rich and detailed portrait of this historical landscape, I draw both on the scholarly tradition of "bottom-up" social history—examining the stories of ordinary people—and on more state-centered approaches.[10]

New laws always open up realms of noncompliance and criminality. Focusing on Jews in Europe and the United States, this book explores several key junctures at which the new immigration restriction regime was hotly contested. The laws' passage did not stop European Jews from wanting to come to the United States, nor did it prevent their US relatives from wanting them to come. Conditions remained terrible in Europe for many years after World War I. Jewish communities across eastern Europe, in particular, were in desperate straits, impoverished, politically precarious, and financially overwhelmed by the needs of Jewish refugees displaced by the war.[11] Under the circumstances, many European Jews were determined to emigrate to the United States, and rather than preventing them wholesale from entering the country, the quota laws prompted some of them—with the aid of smugglers—to develop the most efficacious illegal means of doing so.

Much can be learned about both the workings of US law and the experiences of Jews during this era by examining this underside of the US legal system, as well as by exploring the reactions of the US government, the American Jewish community and Jewish individuals and families to the violation of US law by Jewish migrants. The project of constructing a history around people who were set on evading detection is, of course, a challenge. The migrants and smugglers at the core of my story wanted to stay under the record-keeping radar, as the government officials who authored many of the records I have used knew very well. Just as it is impossible today to know the precise numbers of people who entered the United States illegally, or exactly who they are or where they are from, so it is impossible to know precisely how many Jewish and other immigrants entered the country illegally in the era of the quotas. Nevertheless, newspaper articles, government hearings and reports, the records of Jewish aid and political organizations, fiction and memoirs, and the recollections of family members of migrants provided me with rich evidence of the global scene of illicit Jewish migration to the United States during the years after the quota laws' passage. My best estimate suggests that Jewish illegal immigrants during the years between 1921 and 1965 numbered in the tens of thousands, possibly higher. In the early years, almost all these immigrants seem to have come from the large Jewish communities of eastern Europe, which had been the source of the great Jewish immigration to the United States in the late nineteenth and early twentieth centuries. Later, with the rise of the Nazi regime, they were joined in their attempts to immigrate illegally by Jews from Germany and Austria. Italians came illegally in what were likely comparable numbers; Greeks, Czechs, Poles, Russians and other Europeans also immigrated in violation of the law.[12] These figures are, by the measures of our own day—when the legal and illegal flows of people are at a historical high—relatively small. At the time, however, the upsurge in European illegal immigration mattered beyond the migrants who came illicitly into the nation. Illegal European immigration during the quota era mattered to government officials, to activists on all sides of the immigration issue, to alien smugglers, and to would-be immigrants and their families. The historical record makes it clear that whatever the actual tally of immigrants evading the new laws, European illegal immigration became an issue that aroused both public and private conflicts and anxieties.

My study considers how such conflicts and anxieties played out in regard to Jews. The shift in US immigration law played a crucial role in reshaping the global Jewish scene, and thus this study serves as a window onto the new forms of Jewish identity, community, and migration that developed in a post–World War I world. In turn, the Jewish stories on which I focus illuminate the formation of a modern American politics in which control over the national and ethnic demographics of immigration became paramount. At the same time, these stories highlight the logistical and conceptual difficulties inherent in such efforts at state control. The quota laws grew out of a widespread belief that some kinds of foreigners should be kept out of the nation, and out of a certainty that these groups could be recognized, counted, and stopped from entering. Strategies of illegal immigration that Jewish migrants employed—forgeries, disguise, and surreptitious entry—challenged these fundamental premises. That is, Jewish illegal immigration demonstrated that it was not entirely possible either to secure national borders against the "undesirable people" whom the laws were intended to keep out, or to sort desirable immigrants from undesirable ones or aliens from citizens. Jewish migrants, as a heterogeneous group coming from many countries and speaking a range of languages, particularly confounded the categories of ethnicity and nationality on which the quota laws were based.

Jews were not the only immigrants to defy the new US laws; indeed, in this book the stories of Jewish illegal immigrants mingle with those of other immigrants who entered the nation illicity, including Asians and non-Jewish Europeans. But there are several reasons I have focused on Jews. As one of the largest groups arriving in the United States during the mass immigration of the twentieth century's first decades—only Italians came in greater numbers during those years—Jews were in the spotlight of the debates that produced the quota laws and often came under public and governmental scrutiny afterward, when illegal immigration was on the rise. Moreover, Jewish communities in the United States and abroad were particularly well organized around migration issues and thus were important actors in the interpretation of and conflicts over official immigration policies. American Jewish groups, drawing on the considerable resources of a community established by earlier, mostly German Jewish immigrants, were, more than any other ethnic group, in the forefront of immigration activism in the United States from the late nineteenth century all the way through the post–World War II period, when their efforts helped get the quota system abolished. The fierce battles of American Jewish groups both to advocate for Jewish immigrants and to safeguard their claim to the loyal Americanness of Jewish communities during the quota era illuminate the pressures that nativism exerted on ethnic communities in the United States, as well as the possibilities for resisting such pressures. American and European Jews were also well represented in the international underground of alien smuggling, as they were in other arenas of organized crime. The interactions of Jewish individuals and organizations—legal and illicit—with the laws and the officials writing and enforcing these laws, then, provide an important window on the quota-era politics of immigration. Furthermore, the diversity of Jewish experiences with migration in this era conveys just how complex the implementation of the US quotas proved to be. The doings of established American Jewish leaders, international Jewish smugglers of aliens, and struggling Jewish migrants abroad, as well as their families in the United States, all shaped the ways that US immigration law played out in reality. Because Jews were also coming from and through so many different places, tracing the history of Jewish illegal immigration also demonstrates the kaleidoscopic range of places in which the US immigration restrictions were being enacted and contested: the action of this book is set not only in the American contexts of New York, El Paso, Miami, and Detroit but also abroad in Warsaw, Berlin, Toronto, and Havana.

These facts, however, speak to more abstract issues that make Jews significant actors in a history that is, in many ways, a counterstory to the existing metanarrative of American immigration history for this era. With their long diasporic history, ever extended by new imperatives to leave the places they had settled, Jews had forged complex webs of connection across geographic divides and continued to do so in the era of the quota laws, as migration remained a central Jewish concern. Moreover, Jews were a people with a historically fraught relationship to nation-states. Indeed, they were often legally thwarted in their efforts to prove their fealty to the states in which they lived. Stateless, geographically scattered, linguistically and culturally diverse, they frustrated (or were scapegoated as undermining) grand projects of defining national and ethnic identities. As heirs to this history, Jews formed a challenging case vis-à-vis the quota laws, to the vexation of the US government. Furthermore, as an international community with ties that spanned many countries, Jews found themselves at cross-purposes with the efforts of the United States and other nations to harden their borders during the post–World War I era. Thus, Jews—both migrants and the families and organizations that aided them—to some extent provided a counterforce to those state efforts, however unequal in power. Therefore, a study of illegal immigration focusing on Jews presents us with a unique mandate, as well as a valuable opportunity, to keep in play the tension between the macrohistory of the law—its successful program of drastically reducing immigration—and the counterhistory represented by stories that don't fit the standard narrative.

EMERGENCE AND DISAPPEARANCE OF JEWISH ILLEGAL ALIENS

In June 1930, the assistant US attorney in Miami sent a letter to the attorney general in Washington, DC, regarding the case of Chaim Josef Listopad, the Polish Jewish migrant who tried to enter the country in February 1928 using the naturalization papers of alien smuggler Samuel Weisstein. Charged with violating the law for his attempt at illegal entry, Listopad was released on a $3,000 bond; the record does not indicate who put up this money on his behalf. Sometime afterward, Listopad disappeared. The immigration inspector in charge at Miami had conceded to the US attorney's office that "I have heard nothing of his whereabouts and it is my opinion that the chances of his being apprehended are very remote." In light of this challenge, the Florida authorities agreed that the case should be dropped. After this there is nothing more on Listopad in the government file.[13]

Listopad's disappearance speaks to the second question that I address in this book. As an illegal immigrant who ultimately eluded capture and who vanished from the official record, Listopad evokes that erasure of Jewish illegal immigration from our historical consciousness upon which I remarked at the outset. The history of Jewish illegal immigration begs the question of how that erasure has happened—in other words, *why* Jewish immigration to the United States is so rarely associated with illegality in scholarship or in current discourse. Indeed, the phrase "Jewish illegal alien" sounds downright strange, for the idea of the "illegal alien" has become strongly identified in the United States with other groups, notably Mexicans. I would like to suggest two possible reasons why "Jewish illegal alien" has such an odd ring to it. The first is the strong communal and historiographical investment in what we might call "the narrative of the good European immigrants" of the late nineteenth and early twentieth centuries—the story of those who came by ship, worked hard in the nation's booming industries, became naturalized, and worked their way up the socioeconomic ladder. For the most part, historians of Jewish and other ethnic communities have treated their subjects with admiration and respect. Indeed, for many historians, myself included, immigration history is a project connected to family histories; thus, it is natural that historians should be sympathetic to their subjects. Those subjects, having often escaped from violence, poverty, and oppression, seem only due such a humane approach. By contrast, in our contemporary context, illegal aliens are not widely celebrated as heroic resisters of oppressive regimes. The most negative views in circulation today paint them as racial, linguistic, cultural, or religious outsiders who become criminals by breaking US immigration law, and among them are some who threaten the fundamental well-being of the country. This notion of illegal aliens does not fit our collective historical image of those earlier, "good European" immigrants, helping to explain why scholars, for the most part, have not looked at historical sources on Jewish immigration with illegality in mind.[14]

However, the uncoupling of Jewishness and illegal immigration status was also the result of a complicated historical process that began while the quota laws were still in force. Not least important in this process were the strenuous political efforts of American Jews themselves, who feared being associated with illegal immigration precisely because they sometimes *were* so, as we shall see. American Jewish leaders, for example, responded to the increase in Jewish illegal immigration by walking a fine line between insisting on Jews' inherent law-abidingness and advocating for less stringent application of the quotas. They lobbied for clemency in individual cases, pleading that many of the Jewish immigrants caught violating the new laws were not criminals, but rather were decent people who were suffering great hardship, and thus deserving of leniency. Meanwhile, these leaders also battled against measures they saw as criminalizing immigrants and ethnic communities more broadly, such as legislative proposals to register all aliens in the country, and the government's increasing use of deportation as a punitive measure.[15]

However, although Jews protested the discriminatory nature of US immigration policies, they often avoided making common cause during the quota era with groups such as Chinese or Mexicans, who were widely regarded as unassimilable racial outsiders during these years.[16] This stratagem points to the ways in which the success of American Jews' struggles to dissociate themselves from the specter of the "illegal alien" relied, at least in part, on their ability to assert themselves as whites. Unfettered access, as whites, to naturalization, along with other kinds of political and financial resources, also contributed to American Jews' eventual success in these efforts.

As noted earlier, scholars have pointed to the decades after the quota laws' passage—before, during, and after World War II—as a time when European immigrant communities became more fully established as whites, as Americans, and as citizens. The path to this position of belonging, however, was rocky in some particular ways historians have not yet captured. Jews' escape from a permanent association with illegal immigration is at the crux of this story. That escape, which spanned several decades, illuminates in detail the ways in which the quota era served as a crucible for contemporary notions of legal and illegal immigration, aliens and Americanness.

After They Closed the Gates starts by reexamining the quota laws themselves. Chapter 1 explores the laws' genesis, considering the social and political forces of the late nineteenth and early twentieth centuries that ultimately produced the quotas. That era saw an increasing national anxiety around the political, biological and cultural dangers posed by immigrants, particularly the "new immigrants" from southern and eastern Europe who came in great numbers during those years. Concurrently, the federal government took ever stronger measures to control immigration. The race science of the era, which declared southern and eastern Europeans, along with Asians, to be unassimilable foreigners, combined with the nationalistic fervor of World War I and widespread antiradical, anti-immigrant sentiment to set the stage for the nation's grandest experiment to date with immigration restriction and control. But this chapter argues against a historical view of the quota laws that takes at face value their seemingly precise ethnic formula for controlling immigration. Indeed, the laws reflected confusion rather than certainty about classifying groups of people from around the globe. Understanding this confusion, in turn, lets us understand how illegal immigration could operate in this era. Though the laws were predicated on the idea that there were sharp divisions among races and peoples, in practice it was hard for officials to know who was who, especially when immigrants entered the country with forged papers or in disguise.

Once the quota laws were passed, individuals and communities both in the United States and abroad were confronted with new kinds of decisions and problems. The next three chapters trace the rise of Jewish illegal immigration through the experiences of different Jewish networks and migrants. Chapter 2 examines how established Jewish organizations confronted the legal conundrums posed by the new laws. Specifically, it examines Jewish leaders' responses to the illegal immigration of Jews over the Mexico–Texas border and to the plight of Jews stranded in Europe with US visas rendered defunct by the Immigration Act of 1924. The quota laws posed new dilemmas for American Jewish leaders, pitting their desire to operate in solidarity with Jewish migrants against their need to be regarded as law-abiding Americans. Moreover, there were a number of gray areas that remained in the laws themselves. Jewish leaders exploited this lack of clarity in their efforts to shape the regime of US immigration law as best they could. Whenever possible, they sought to engage in a strategic balancing act in which they tried to argue the cases of Jewish migrants without seeming to encourage or condone any lawbreaking on the part of those migrants.

If legitimate Jewish communal organizations were deeply concerned by the possibility that the quotas would spur some Jewish migrants to become illegal immigrants, however, there were other groups that saw the quota laws as a business opportunity to be seized. Chapter 3 investigates the underground of Jewish organizing around migration, namely the profit-driven world of Jewish alien smuggling. Like the legitimate Jewish organizations, smuggling rings sought to shape the ways the quota laws functioned in reality. The chapter demonstrates that there was a symbiotic relationship between government mechanisms of enforcement and smuggling networks. Each provided the other with a reason for being, and each shaped the strategies the other used to achieve its goals. Tracing the emergence of this underworld, moreover, sheds light on how the very act of migration increasingly came to be associated with criminality during this era, helping to create a national conception of the dangers posed by "smuggled aliens."

Next, the book turns to an examination of illegal immigration from the perspective of the Jewish migrants themselves, whose own ideas about the US quotas played an important role in shaping what those laws meant to people on the ground. Chapter 4 examines Jewish migrants' experiences with illegal immigration in the years following the quota laws, experiences that show the extent to which illegal immigration to the United States was embedded in a long and complicated set of interactions between individuals and the newly established international regime of national borders and identity documents. Moreover, looking at individuals' migration stories broadens the frame of reference beyond US law, as well as beyond the moment when migrants entered the United States illegally. This approach also demonstrates just how unclear the boundaries between legal and illegal migration could be from the point of view of individuals and families struggling to make the best choices in the chaotic, dangerous world of post–World War I Europe. This chapter also examines the underworld of disguise and temporary "passing," in which illegal immigrants participated when they were smuggled into the country. Such masquerade challenged the fundamental categories of the quota laws even as it relied on them.

Ultimately, however, Jews, like other European immigrants, did not remain associated with illegal immigration. Chapters 5 and 6 explore the political processes that help produce this shift. Chapter 5 turns to the issue of internal "border control" in the United States during the 1920s and 1930s. It investigates the battles over alien registration laws requiring all nonnaturalized foreigners to register with the government. Jews from a range of organizations consistently opposed these laws and led the fight against their passage and implementation. This chapter, which focuses in particular on the fate of a state alien registration law passed in Michigan in 1931, argues that Jews ultimately escaped the specter of illegal alienness in part through their own political efforts in the face of such controversies.

During and after World War II, both US policy and the landscape of international Jewish migration underwent a profound transformation. The Holocaust, the establishment of the State of Israel, the Cold War, postwar American prosperity, and the rising tide of the American civil rights movement all served to recast debates about race, immigration, and law. Chapter 6 traces the ways in which these forces, along with ongoing American Jewish activism, helped redefine the relationship between Jews and US immigration law, and indeed helped complete the process of severing the official association between Jews and illegal immigration. The incorporation of "refugees" into US law, which was in large part a product of Jewish activism on behalf of those displaced by World War II, played a role in this process. This language helped to validate—in however grudging a fashion—the claims that European migrants in particular had on the nation. So, too, did the increasing attacks on the quota system, which came to be seen after the war as an embarrassing legacy of a racist past. In 1965, President Lyndon B. Johnson signed the bill that finally dismantled that quota system, thereby unmaking the law that had helped produce Jewish illegal immigration in the first place. Less publicly, US immigration policy was quietly working to create paths to legitimacy for European immigrants who had entered illegally, with officials waiving deportations and granting changes of immigration status. During this same postwar period, meanwhile, illegal immigration increasingly came to be defined as nearly synonymous with Mexican immigration, a starkly racialized equation, which, in turn, helped erase the history of the illegal European incursions of the prewar period.

Finally, in a brief epilogue, I examine how the subject of the book resonates today. In many ways, our current moment represents a focus on borders and national security that harks back to the 1920s. The daily papers are full of ongoing conflicts, local and national, over control of borders and migrants. They are full, too, of stories that suggest the human stakes involved. Border control has always been an elusive goal, whose pursuit has profound effects on individuals, communities, and the nation at large. Whatever policies are implemented in the coming years, an appreciation for this dynamic will remain central to the unfolding history of immigration.

CHAPTER 1

Building the Apparatus of Immigration Control

On May 19, 1921, President Warren Harding signed the Emergency Quota Act into law. This law did something altogether new: it established numerical limits on immigration in the form of nation-based quotas pegged to the ethnic composition of the US population. The law decreed that "the number of aliens of any nationality who may be admitted . . . to the United States in any fiscal year" would be limited to 3 percent "of the number of foreign-born persons of such nationality resident in the United States as determined by the United States census of 1910."[1] Some immigrants were allowed to enter without being counted against national quotas, including government officials, business travelers, tourists, minor children of citizens, or anyone who had resided for a year in a Western Hemisphere nation before coming to the United States. Chinese immigrants were still excluded by law, as they had been since the Chinese Exclusion Act of 1882. Immigrants from the "Asiatic barred zone" also were defined in the Immigration Act of 1917, which encompassed much of Asia.

The immigration quotas were made permanent, and considerably smaller, in the Immigration Act of 1924. The 1924 act applied quotas to immigration from everywhere except, as in 1921, those from the Western Hemisphere. This time, however, the law decreed that the annual quota of each nationality would be limited to only 2 percent "of the number of foreign-born individuals of such nationality resident in continental United States as determined by the United States census of 1890."[2] Moreover, it expanded Asian exclusion by barring all "aliens ineligible for citizenship" (only foreigners deemed white or of African descent could naturalize) from immigration.[3] It was thus designed to virtually eliminate Asian immigration and reduce to a tiny stream the flow of "new immigrants," meaning those from southern and eastern Europe who had been arriving in the millions during the first decades of the twentieth century, who had only small representation in the census of 1890. Under these new quotas, only 2,248 immigrants would be permitted to enter annually from Russia, 5,982 from Poland, and 3,845 from Italy. By contrast, the system favored the "traditional" immigrant-sending nations of northwestern Europe: Germany, for example, was allotted 51,227 quota slots, and Great Britain and Ireland a combined 62,574. Altogether, the law established a cap of around 164,000 quota immigrants each year from more than sixty different countries.[4] The law further declared that by 1927 a new formula for the quotas would be established. There would be a cap of 150,000 immigrants per year, with each nationality being allotted the percentage of that total equal to the proportion that this nationality represented in the 1920 population of the United States—excluding black and Indian peoples—either by birth or by descent.

These new laws were a grand experiment in statecraft and social engineering. They attempted to codify a precise formula for American unity. They applied to European immigrants, albeit less harshly, a nation- and race-based principle of exclusion similar to that which had been pioneered with Asian immigrants. The quotas were calculated to stem the influx of the poor "racial stock" that nativist activists and lawmakers argued made up the recent immigration from southern and eastern Europe, which they contended posed a grave threat to the physical and civic fitness of the nation. The quotas were intended, as well, to keep out dangerous "Bolsheviks" and others who might foment political unrest, types deemed to be overrepresented among the newer immigrants. The laws also represented a major turning point in federal control over immigration. They broadcast a deep official unease about the permeability of the nation's borders and produced unprecedented state efforts to reify those borders and exert new forms of control over them. They constituted, moreover, a baldly judgmental ranking of the peoples of the world, as well as a bold assertion of US power over the movements of people from around the globe.

Yet the quotas did not serve as an impermeable wall around the United States. A great many people were still coming and going legally across the nation's borders. Immigrants from the Western Hemisphere, including Mexicans and Canadians, were, as noted, not limited by the quotas; immediate family members of US citizens, including naturalized ones, were also exempt from the quotas. Additionally, there were all those whom the laws' architects intended, but failed, to keep out. Indeed, the laws set the stage for the emergence of European illegal immigration on a large scale, because implementing them—distinguishing illegal immigrants from legal ones before, during, or after their entry into the nation—proved devilishly complicated from the start. In other words, the quota laws, in attempting to clearly define legitimate immigration in new ways, perpetuated the very difficulties that they were intended to address.

As the federal apparatus of immigration policy, law, and enforcement expanded in order to combat these difficulties, it was faced with a moving target. "Legitimate" immigration proved murkier than the quota legislation's authors had hoped; that murkiness also had far-reaching consequences. One of those striking consequences constitutes this book's primary subject—the emergence and subsequent "disappearance" of Jewish illegal aliens during the quota era. That story, which threw into stark relief the challenges of immigration policy for both government officials and Jewish communities at the time, now serves as a powerful means for tracing the changing nature of the federal apparatus of immigration policy, as well as its inconsistencies and contradictions. Four intertwined aspects of immigration policy played out in particularly significant ways on the national stage and were ever-present in the story of Jewish illegal immigration as it unfolded after the quota laws. Each of these policy aspects had its roots in political and social processes in the nineteenth and early twentieth centuries; thus, this earlier period merits examination.

The first aspect of immigration policy considered here is the development of a national discourse around immigration as a threat to the nation's political, moral, economic, and racial vitality. The Immigration Act of 1917, whose provisions remained in effect after the two quota laws were passed, provides a lengthy catalogue of the personal attributes that defined would-be immigrants as inadmissible. In so doing, the measure conveys the range of public anxieties that attended immigration by the first decades of the twentieth century, when immigration was at an all-time high. It also furnishes a kind of capsule history of the federal government's ongoing efforts to address those anxieties by screening newcomers. The law's remarkable list of those types of immigrants deemed inadmissible included the following:

> Idiots, imbeciles, feeble-minded persons, epileptics, insane persons; . . . persons of constitutional psychopathic inferiority; persons with chronic alcoholism; paupers; professional beggars; vagrants; persons afflicted with tuberculosis in any form or with a loathsome or dangerous contagious disease; persons certified by the examining physician as being mentally or physically defective . . . ; persons who have been convicted of or admit having com-

mitted a felony or other crime or misdemeanor involving moral turpitude; polygamists . . . ; anarchists and similar classes; immoral persons and persons coming for an immoral purpose; contract laborers; persons likely to become a public charge; . . . persons whose ticket or passage is paid for by any corporation, association, society, municipality, or foreign government, either directly or indirectly; [and] stowaways.[5]

Beyond decreeing the nation's official unwillingness to admit those foreigners who were judged to be lacking mentally, morally, physically, politically, or financially, the 1917 law also described the enormous Asian "barred zone" from which immigrants were not to be admitted.[6] The sprawling list of unwanted traits reflected the categories of prohibited immigrants that had accrued since the early days of federal limitations on immigration in the late nineteenth century (which, in turn, grew out of earlier state and local efforts to control immigration). The law also augmented those limits, most notably by extending the earlier ban on Chinese immigration to cover much of Asia and by adding a ban on "aliens over 16 years of age who are unable to read some language or dialect."

Although this list nowhere mentions them specifically, Jews, along with other suspect groups, figured prominently in the history of US immigration policy's evolution. Heavily represented among the "new immigrants" of the late nineteenth and early twentieth centuries, Jews were often explicitly invoked as evidence of the problems of mass immigration during the debates of that era. American Jews played a significant role as political actors in those same debates, drawing on the expertise and resources of a well-to-do community already established in the nation. Jewish activists thus entered the quota era with a great depth of experience in the realm of immigration and an awareness of the difficulties of pressing their case with the US government and the American public.

A second crucial aspect of immigration policy that emerged in this era was a growing demarcation between legal and illegal immigration, as well as an attendant focus on regulating points of entry at seaports and land borders. In the latter part of the nineteenth century, as federal laws began to decree who was allowed to enter the country and who was not, the nation grappled with this distinction for the first time. Chinese who entered the country in violation of the Chinese Exclusion Act of 1882—an unprecedented measure to deny entry to an entire group of people—were the first major objects of public consternation about illegal immigration. Government officials and the public at large also reacted anxiously to the breach of borders by other immigrants, including Jews,

Italians, Lebanese, and others who entered the country surreptitiously to avoid increasingly stringent rules about immigration. Concerns about the illicit immigration of Chinese and other immigrants were entangled from the start with the elusive nature of the problem. For one thing, tracking immigrants' entry into a country with lengthy land borders and coastlines was daunting; for another, even at regulated entry points, distinguishing illegally from legally immigrating individuals proved more complex than lawmakers imagined when they were crafting the legislation. The quota laws were intended in part to redress these problems, but, in many ways, served to make them more complicated. As we shall see, the confusion over illegal and legal immigration played out dramatically for Jews after the quota laws were passed.

The third characteristic aspect of the US immigration policy that developed in the late nineteenth and early twentieth centuries was the way that policy both reflected and contributed to the growth of a strong federal state. In particular, the creators of immigration policy came to rely on those bureaucratic practices of record-keeping, identification, and classification that proved essential to the exercise of state power throughout the modern world. Benedict Anderson calls these tools—such as maps and censuses—the "grammar" of state power, a "classificatory grid" meant to illustrate and enable state control over identifiable, discrete, and countable groups of people.[7] James Scott, similarly, has described the way emerging nation-states used such methods to render populations "legible" and thus possible to monitor and control.[8] The years of policy debates that ultimately produced the quota laws entailed enormous amounts of data gathering and analysis, and the laws themselves demanded acts of classifying and quantifying on an order that had not been seen before.

Such official efforts to classify and regulate immigration were part of larger struggles to manage difference in a multiethnic, multiracial nation. The precision implied by the law's mathematical formulas, however, was belied by a vast confusion about the nature of racial, national, linguistic, and religious identities both at home and abroad. All these were theoretical categories that in practice were never easy to pin down. Jews, as a group that confounded neat systems of classification, proved especially vexing to such state projects. For their part, American Jewish activists closely followed government schemes to define both citizens and aliens, and they sought to shape the process when they could.

A final aspect of US immigration policy that bears consideration here is that policy's relationship to international shifts in state responses to migration. As Aristide Zolberg has observed, understanding the development of a restrictive US immigration regime purely as a product of nativism—a domestic affair—obscures the extent to which that regime grew out of a kind of global immigration-control "arms race." As the economic and demographic forces of globalization fueled an enormous upsurge in migration toward the end of the nineteenth century, the world's wealthier countries, including the United States and European nations, sought to control the flows of people across their borders more tightly. Despite accompanying rhetoric that cast border control both as integral to national sovereignty and as unilaterally established and enforced, these individual nations' policies in fact were enacted in relation to each other. If one national government moved to control migration, others had to respond in kind, lest unwanted immigrants flood the still unrestricted countries. Even once they were inside a nation's borders, immigrants of this era faced newly erected barriers to citizenship. Official efforts to control borders thus extended to the legal and metaphorical boundaries of nations as well.[9]

Jews were central to international debates over migration control, just as they were to domestic ones. Indeed, in Europe, Jewish migration frustrated—and produced—state efforts to regulate the admission of newcomers. The westward migration of eastern European Jews during the late nineteenth century, widely regarded as a dangerous invasion, spurred some countries to implement exclusionary policies specifically targeted at Jews.[10] Jewish communities in the receiving nations mobilized their political and economic resources to help prevent those policies from becoming yet harsher, but much like the Chinese, Jews were still widely viewed wherever they went as an undesirable, unassimilable, alien element.[11] Jewish and other Americans were well aware of the negative reception that eastern European Jews met in other nations. Jewish participation in struggles over the direction that US policy should take, as well as that policy itself, must then be seen in international context.

FROM STATE TO FEDERAL IMMIGRATION CONTROL

Contrary to a longstanding narrative of US immigration history, immigration was not entirely free or unregulated during the first century of the nation's existence. Neither was admission to the national polity. Debates over the entrance and incorporation of foreigners were intertwined with efforts to define the nation from its inception.[12] In 1790, the fledgling US Congress passed a law stating that only "free white persons" were eligible to naturalize, thereby linking the notion of US citizenship both to race and to economic status.[13] Soon afterward, the 1798 Alien and Sedition Acts (repealed two years later) gave the president power to deport aliens and also stipulated a longer waiting time for naturalization.[14] In 1819, the federal government passed laws regulating the conditions on passenger ships; it began to track immigrant arrivals in the same year.[15] The international slave trade was also at issue from the nation's beginning. The Constitution mandated that Congress could not ban the importation of slaves until 1808; after that, of course, it did so.[16]

These measures trace a longstanding federal interest in the matters of immigration and the acquisition of citizenship. However, until the latter part of the nineteenth century, states and localities took the lead in efforts to control immigration, often with the help of charitable agencies. As immigration climbed sharply during the middle decades of the nineteenth century, state governments, particularly of those states with major seaports such as New York and South Carolina, sought to regulate the admission of foreigners. Following accepted ideas about undesirability that dated back to the colonial era, state legislatures passed laws excluding criminals, people with contagious diseases, or those who might need public charity.[17] In Manhattan as of 1855, for example, Castle Garden, at the island's southern tip, became a processing center for newly landed immigrants. Inspectors there attempted to screen newcomers for contagious illnesses and the likelihood that they would become a burden on public charity. Measures to control people's movement were not limited during this era to addressing migration across the nation's borders. In the South, the mobility of both slaves and free black people was sharply curtailed; northern states, too, tried to limit the influx of African Americans from other states.[18]

In the middle decades of the nineteenth century, lawmakers who sought to screen out "undesirables" were responding in part to public pressure. Immigration, urbanization, and industrialization brought with them mounting social and political unease, especially in heavily immigrant cities of the Northeast and Midwest. Anti-Catholic nativist sentiment, for example, was intense. Irish Catholic immigrants, who began arriving in great numbers during the 1830s and 1840s, faced accusations of disloyal allegiance to a foreign power, namely the pope. Urban political corruption—especially the herding of new arrivals to the polls—was another concern. Anti-immigrant forces contended that utterly lax and inconsistent naturalization policies were at the heart of such practices and that the waiting period for citizenship should be lengthened by many years.[19] For a brief period in the 1850s, the anti-Catholic, nativist Know-Nothings who made these arguments garnered a good deal of political support.[20]

Although such developments demonstrate that the anti-immigrant movement was a significant element in public discourse, until the late nineteenth century the movement had little staying power and no government force supporting its demands. The burgeoning industries of the Northeast and the newly acquired lands in the West created high demand for an influx of cheap labor. The Democratic Party, which came to depend on immigrants as an important part of its electoral base, also served as a counterforce to restrictionist arguments. Powerful commercial and political interests thus stood arrayed against any impulses toward major national regulation or restriction of immigration.[21] Nor was there yet the bureaucratic infrastructure to implement immigration restriction on a national scale. Until the late nineteenth century, when the federal government took on a much expanded role in American life, immigration control remained decentralized and minimal. No federal bureaucracy yet served a mandate to focus on immigration, and no congressional committees devoted themselves to the issue. Neither federal nor state authorities rigorously collected data or demanded documentation from individuals traveling into or out of the country. Moreover, any existing controls pertained only to seaports; land borders, as yet, played almost no role in any efforts to control the movement of people.[22]

However, by the latter part of the nineteenth century, Supreme Court decisions indicated that the judiciary understood the regulation of immigration to be under the federal government's jurisdiction. In 1876, the court ruled in *Henderson v. Mayor of the City of New York* that state laws levying a per-passenger tax on ship-owners transporting immigrants violated the constitutional right of Congress to regulate commerce. States depended on this revenue to fund their immigration work, and the Supreme Court's decision made difficulties for those local authorities and agencies charged with overseeing immigration, especially in New York, the nation's busiest port. It seemed clear that the federal government would have to either provide funds or take over the operation of processing immigrant arrivals. More broadly, the decision also decreed the state regulation of immigration to be unconstitutional. All signs pointed toward the need for more federal involvement.[23]

In 1875, meanwhile, Congress passed its first law restricting immigration. Addressing two central fears about the contemporary upsurge in immigration from China, the Page Act banned the importation of unfree "coolie" labor and prostitutes.[24] This law signaled the start of new federal action on immigration matters. Interestingly, as John Torpey observes, the historical moment at which the federal government began in earnest to seek control over immigration across its borders coincided with the government's affirmation of its citizens' right to move freely within the nation.[25] In other words, the post–Civil War era, which was a period of national consolidation, expanded citizenship, and growing state power, also ushered in the federal government's early efforts to draw more sharply the line between the inside and the outside of the nation, as well as between citizens and foreigners.

CHINESE EXCLUSION

During the later decades of the nineteenth century, several developments contributed to a massive shift in US immigration policy, helping to ensconce nativist politics more firmly in the center of the national debate and restrictionist legislation in the nation's legal code. One of the most crucial new social forces to affect immigration policy was the fierce anti-Chinese movement, the first successful push by nativists to exclude undesirable aliens and the beginning of the federal government's full involvement in immigration restriction. The federal law that outlawed most Chinese immigration and the federal apparatus established to try to enforce that law proved to be models for the later quota legislation and its enforcement.[26]

Ironically, the Chinese immigration that ultimately faced popular backlash and federal prohibition was originally encouraged by the US government during the 1860s as a valuable new source of labor.[27] But the same 1868 treaty between the United States and China that guaranteed that Chinese workers might immigrate freely to the United States also stipulated that these workers had no right to become naturalized citizens, thus ensuring that they would remain political and social outsiders.[28] Twelve years after that agreement, the nation officially reversed course, first with an 1880 treaty allowing the United States to limit Chinese immigration whenever it might be judged counter to US interests and then with its landmark immigration restriction law, the Chinese Exclusion Act of 1882.[29]

The anti-Chinese policies of the United States reflected an international trend during this era toward curtailing Asian immigration, which white-dominated governments and bodies politic throughout the Pacific world treated as a threatening invasion. Australia, South Africa, New Zealand, and Canada implemented laws hardening their borders against Asians.[30] Although they were similar in intent and together represented a broad international shift, such sweeping national policies also grew from distinctly local and regional power struggles. In the United States, a complex blend of labor, racial, and party politics in California produced what would become a nationwide agitation for Chinese exclusion. During the course of the Chinese exclusion movement, national tensions—post-Reconstruction battles over race and citizenship, as well as power struggles between labor and capital—played out on political terrain particular to the country's western region. Led largely by a coalition of white (and white ethnic) working men who feared the consequences of competing with a labor force they regarded as imported and indentured, the frequently violent and always volatile anti-Chinese agitation produced legislative successes on the state level and culminated in the passage of the federal Chinese Exclusion Act. The anti-Chinese movement had progressed from regional to national scale without meeting much resistance from the wider public or from legislators. The alignment of white laborers against western capitalists, and against the Chinese they employed, reflected economic and racial dynamics particular to the region. However, the sentiments invoked by the western anti-Chinese movement resonated around the nation. Virulent anti-Chinese racism was commonplace in northeastern and southern cities as well as in western ones. Few public voices expressed sympathy for the Chinese or contested the notion that they could never become good Americans in the ways that other immigrants could. The anti-Chinese movement emerged forcefully on the national scene through such vehicles as the policies of the conservative, craft-oriented American Federation of Labor (AFL) and the warnings of the press and nativists in Congress.[31]

The work of administering Chinese exclusion played a critical role in making immigration control a central component the federal government's mission, and indeed it made such control part of the nation's self-definition. As Lucy Salyer has shown, the energy with which Chinese immigrants—and Chinese American citizens, many of whom ran into difficulties when they tried to reenter the United States after traveling—argued their immigration cases before the courts ultimately created a body of judicial precedent that defined aliens as people with different rights from citizens, even though the Chinese were successful in much of their litigation. This new demarcation represented an important shift in legal thinking, from more flexible nineteenth-century ideas about the rights of residents, in general, to the keen distinction between citizens and aliens that came to characterize modern immigration law. At the same time, such litigation—and the ongoing public perception of Chinese as immigrants who were problematic and hard to control—helped spur government actors into constructing a powerful immigration bureaucracy, which was able to rule on immigration matters independently from the power of the courts.[32]

The anti-Chinese agitation, the increasing wielding of state power against a group of immigrants, and those immigrants' contestation of such power also helped solidify a national understanding that there was a critical link between sovereignty and controlling migration across national borders.[33] Indeed, Chinese exclusion in many ways helped *produce* those borders. Before 1882, immigration control, to the extent that it existed at all, was geared toward seaports and not land borders. After the passage of the Chinese Exclusion Act, however, as Chinese began to enter the United States via Mexico and Canada, authorities

turned their attention to stemming illegal immigration across those land borders.[34] Enforcement efforts included increasing personnel to inspect and, after
1904, patrol the border. Although such measures were largely ineffectual, they
nevertheless represented a new official attention to land borders as key sites for
implementing immigration law.

Chinese exclusion entailed a new projection of US power abroad, as the
United States attempted to make Canada and Mexico cooperate with US efforts to exclude Chinese.[35] Furthermore, the project of enforcing Chinese exclusion involved the invention of entirely new bureaucratic methods on the
part of the state. Exclusion was a sweeping attempt to bar immigrants according to race, but it also provided for numerous exceptions: merchants, students,
tourists, and those who were citizens by virtue of their birth in the United
States. To police these individual distinctions, the federal government instituted new forms of documentation, inspection, and record keeping.[36] The era
of Chinese exclusion thus also saw the emergence of illegal immigration practices—smuggling, forgery, and fraud—that challenged state efforts to control
national borders and the flow of people across them. Government authorities
found themselves for the first time encountering on a large scale the challenge
of distinguishing immigrants who were allowed to enter the country, such as
citizens, merchants or students, from those who were not.[37]

TOWARD GENERAL IMMIGRATION RESTRICTION

The passage of the Chinese Exclusion Act in 1882 coincided both with an
upsurge in European immigration and with the passage of the first generally
restrictive federal immigration legislation. Drawing on earlier state and local
regulations, and prodded by frustrated state authorities who wanted to see
the federal government play a greater role in immigration matters, Congress
voted in favor of a law that same year decreeing that convicts, lunatics, idiots,
and persons who could not "care for themselves without becoming a public
charge" would henceforward be barred from entering the nation when they
arrived at its seaports. The law authorized states to enforce the measure and
levied a fifty-cent head tax to fund the associated administrative expenses.[38]
This legislation bore little resemblance to the radically xenophobic Chinese
Exclusion Act of the same year. Yet the federal government's opening of these
two legislative fronts—which would meet in the twentieth century with the
passage of the quota acts—reflected a common project to centralize immigration control.

This project moved to the forefront of public debate during the final decades of the nineteenth century, as the nation grappled with the massive changes wrought by accelerating industrialization, urbanization, and mass immigration. During this era, for example, there was growing alarm about the connection between immigrants and political and labor radicalism. The late 1870s and 1880s were tense years in the struggle between capital and labor. With the financial panic of 1873, unemployment skyrocketed. Upheavals such as the great railroad strike of 1877—in which many of the strikers were immigrants—rocked the country and provoked fears of all-out class warfare fueled by immigrant laborers (the recent example of the 1871 Paris Commune made the possibility of a workers' revolution seem more real).[39] Then, in May 1886, during a spate of workers' strikes demanding eight-hour workdays, a bomb went off in Chicago's Haymarket square, killing or gravely wounding a number of police officers. Public condemnation followed swiftly. Newspapers denounced the barbaric foreign anarchists who had supposedly committed the act. Six German immigrants and one English immigrant, along with one native-born American, were convicted of the crime, though without clear evidence. All but one of the defendants were sentenced to death.[40] Meanwhile, even as public fears of immigrant labor radicalism mounted, labor organizations such as the AFL expressed a different fear, namely that the huge streams of cheap immigrant labor would undermine workers' efforts to hold their own against capital. Labor unions now mobilized against European immigrants some of the same arguments white workers had used in their campaigns against the Chinese.[41]

During this same period, some of the immigrants from around the world who now faced new strictures on their entry at seaports did the same thing that Chinese who were banned from immigrating did: they sought alternative means of entry. Throughout the 1880s, inspections at seaports remained relatively lax for non-Chinese immigrants, the new federal legislation notwithstanding. (By the decade's end, for example, New York City's Castle Garden had only two inspectors to process the thousands of immigrants who passed through each day.[42]) Even so, the media and government officials noted increasing numbers of such immigrants coming over the Canadian and Mexican borders in order to avoid inspections. Not technically illegal for non-Chinese, since the regulations implemented by the general immigration law of 1882 applied only to seaports, this cross-border immigration was clearly designed to circumvent that law's restrictions, particularly on the admission of paupers.[43] Land borders remained sparsely regulated and guarded for several decades to come, but this new mode of immigration—along with the illicit Chinese traffic over the same borders—nevertheless served to draw the nation's attention to those borders and to the difficulties involved in controlling immigration.[44]

In the 1890s, Congress passed laws that both added to the categories of banned immigrants and strengthened the bureaucratic apparatus of immigration. The Immigration Act of 1891 decreed that polygamists, those with a contagious disease, those who had been convicted of any crime "involving moral turpitude," and those whose immigration was "assisted" (a measure aimed at contract laborers, also prohibited by earlier laws) were no longer admissible. Unlike the 1882 legislation, the 1891 act was not limited to seaports, but rather applied to any entry into the nation. The law also established a federal immigration bureaucracy, providing for an office of a superintendent of immigration within the Treasury Department (this would later become the Bureau of Immigration).[45] Meanwhile, the federal government made plans to take over the immigrant-screening operations of the nation's major seaport in New York City. In 1892, a federal immigration station opened at Ellis Island.[46]

The new restrictions on immigration and general anti-immigrant feeling grew in tandem. During the late nineteenth century, nativist politics became a major force on the national level. The economic depression of the 1890s served to intensify the antiforeigner backlash sparked by the Haymarket affair of 1886. The founding of the Boston-based Immigration Restriction League (IRL) in 1894, spearheaded by a group of young, elite Harvard graduates, such as attorneys Charles Warren and Prescott Hall, professor of climatology Robert DeCourcy Ward, and several prominent philanthropists, gave the movement clout and institutional staying power, as well as political savvy and significant influence in the highest governmental circles. These men were dismayed by what the 1890 census revealed to be a change in the national origins of arriving immigrants. They saw the rising tide of the "new immigration" from eastern and southern Europe as a profound threat and called for legislation to bar "elements undesirable for citizenship or injurious to our national character."[47] They disseminated their views widely via lecture and print—newspapers all over the country received their impressively credentialed literature—and had an important inside line to Congress via the newly elected and staunchly restrictionist Bostonian Republican Senator Henry Cabot Lodge. The main remedy they pushed for was a literacy test, in which arriving immigrants would have to prove that they could read in their own language. The IRL and its supporters saw such a test as a good way to keep out the less desirable classes, particularly from eastern and southern Europe, where educational opportunities were limited. In 1896, Congress obliged by passing a measure requiring immigrants to pass a literacy test, but President Grover Cleveland vetoed the bill. Only in 1917 would the literacy test become part of US law.[48]

Although the immigration restriction movement of the 1890s did not yet have enough momentum to translate its aims into permanent policy, the IRL and its allies were successful in garnering a good deal of support for restriction. The turn of the century, however, saw a lull in anti-immigration activity. The ebbing of nativist sentiment coincided with the surge in national confidence that followed the United States' triumph in the Spanish-American War. The widespread Progressive spirit of reform, moreover, with its faith in the human capacity for change, engendered optimism about immigrants' ability to blend into American society. Also important in fostering a more benevolent attitude toward immigration was the easing of the economic depression of the mid-1890s, which quieted simmering resentments and removed flashpoints for social tensions. The strong economy served as a counterweight to persistent anxieties about foreign people within the nation's borders and, increasingly, abroad, as the United States moved into the imperialist arena.[49]

Even amidst this lull in anti-immigration sentiment, however, forces gathered that would ultimately lead to a more robust nativist politics. At the turn of the century, social commentators, academics, and politicians fretted over the woes of an increasingly urbanized society. The popularity of reformer Jacob Riis's 1890 book of photos and essays exploring New York's immigrant neighborhoods, *How the Other Half Lives*, reflected Americans' contradictory stance toward immigration during this period. One of the more widely read examples of a genre of exposé-cum-travel-narrative, the book illustrated the need for better laws governing housing, labor, and sanitation, even as it also reflected the native-born public's combined fear of and fascination with seediness, grunge, and decay in immigrant quarters of the city.[50] Meanwhile, the prospect of the "closing of the frontier," as historian Frederick Jackson Turner had put it in a speech of 1893, along with the fact that ever more of the population no longer lived in rural areas but in urban ones, struck many contemporary observers as cause for alarm. Without the safety valve of "empty lands," unrest seemed to threaten. Corrupt, industrial cities were growing ever bigger, teeming with the "new immigrants" of southern and eastern Europe—Italians, Poles, Jews, and others (by 1910, e.g., about 20 percent of New York City's population and 10 percent of Chicago's were Jewish).[51] Immigrant neighborhoods were seen as breeding grounds for poverty, disease, and criminality. Italians and Jews, as the largest and most visible of the new groups, were particular targets of public blame, as well as of rising discrimination and violence.[52] Both groups seemed to many observers to exhibit strong tendencies toward poverty and criminality. A neighborhood like New York's Lower East Side, densely populated with Jewish and Italian immigrants, with a heavily trafficked red light district where prostitutes, pimps, and gang members operated openly, struck many as the epitome of the problems that new immigrants brought with them. In 1908, New York City's police commissioner, Theodore Bingham, went so far as to state that Jews were responsible for more than half the city's crime—an unfair accusation that greatly alarmed American Jews even as it must have confirmed the suspicions of many city residents.[53]

Rising anti-immigrant sentiment and the concurrent push for immigration restriction was a galvanizing force in American Jewish politics. Among the groups that came in for particular condemnation by restrictionists, Jews emerged as a major voice in national debates over immigration. In the late nineteenth century, for example, a number of left-leaning Jewish unionists mounted a vocal argument within the labor movement against both anti-Chinese and more general anti-immigration measures, clashing with their fellow labor activists who supported immigration restriction as a proworker measure.[54] On the other end of the American Jewish social spectrum, the American Jewish Committee (AJC), a rights organization founded in 1906 by prominent American Jews, predominantly of German descent, developed an extensive expertise on immigration issues. Along with a number of Jewish immigrant service organizations, the AJC would become one of the most respected and effective groups working in the field.

Starting around the turn of the twentieth century, the intensified fears about the depravity of immigrants both fueled and was fueled by a new discourse about race, emerging from the natural sciences and making its way forcefully into social debates. The rise of Mendelian genetics gave new urgency to older understandings of the social implications of Darwin's theory of evolution, underscoring the importance of heredity; respected natural scientists began to argue that these processes defined human behavior, as well as the workings of the animal and plant worlds. Even as scientists of the natural world turned their attention to analyzing the social worlds of human beings in terms of heredity—or, as was often the case, in terms of "race"—the burgeoning fields of the social sciences, such as psychology and anthropology, focused on human behavior in relation to the newest scientific theories of nature. Scholars from both the natural and social sciences thus looked for distinctive traits among groups that they could attribute to race. The new and influential science of eugenics, in particular, made the link explicit. Eugenicists argued for the importance of preserving the "best" racial strains and warned of the danger of inferior "stock" and race mixing.[55] All these developments fed discussions of immigration as a dangerous racial problem, one linked to the unchangeable biological nature of those coming to the United States. Many scholars made such anti-immigration arguments explicitly, contending that Jews, Slavs, and Italians were of a lower racial order that threatened to pollute the nation's racial stock. Meanwhile, elites such as those individuals in the IRL seized on such scientific wisdom and worked to publicize and capitalize upon it.[56]

Meanwhile, lawmakers continued to expand the national apparatus of immigration control. In 1903, Congress passed a comprehensive immigration law that reaffirmed earlier regulations and added some new ones. The head tax was raised, the entry of immigrant anarchists was banned—a reaction to the 1901 assassination of President William McKinley—the period of time within which aliens could be deported was extended, and immigrants were now required to undergo health inspections before embarking for the United States.[57] In 1907, Roosevelt brokered a "Gentleman's Agreement" with the Japanese government, which henceforward pledged to keep Japanese laborers from emigrating to the United States. In that same year, Congress passed yet another immigration act, which raised the head tax once again and established a commission to investigate immigration.[58]

CLASSIFICATION AND DOCUMENTATION

The increasingly influential social sciences contributed in other ways to the nativist project, in particular by contributing to the development of official approaches to immigration control. The quota laws of 1921 and 1924 rested on a faith in the power of classification and documentation, as well as a belief that these were essential tools in governing. Such ideas reflected evolving notions of governance. The gradual growth of the immigration bureaucracy over the course of the late nineteenth and early twentieth centuries—new legislation, the establishment of the Bureau of Immigration, and the apparatus of Chinese exclusion—was part of the expansion of a bureaucratic, administrative state that relied heavily on statistics and other practices drawn from the social sciences.[59] In 1902, for example, the government established the Bureau of the Census as its own agency, the most ambitious and sophisticated collector of national statistics anywhere in the world.[60] Meanwhile, spurred by movements to reform and rationalize government, state and city governments replicated such efforts on a local level. Across both local and federal institutions, the US government expanded and professionalized its scope and operations.

Like other government agencies, the Bureau of Immigration sought to implement state-of-the-art methods of data gathering and processing.[61] The bureau's reports from the century's first two decades contain hundreds of pages of tables laying out details on newcomers: data on how many immigrants were admitted; on how many were excluded and why; and on immigrants' country of origin, occupations, race, age, health, geographic distribution, sex, criminal activity, progress toward naturalization, and more. The official effort to develop finely tuned categories to track immigration reveals much about the underlying assumptions that the state, as well as the American society at large, held about which attributes of immigrants (and people more generally) were perceivable, measurable, and of relevance to the nation's well-being. The political debates those categories engendered, in turn, reflected and fueled battles over the place of immigrants and other groups in a rapidly changing society.

"Race" often stood at the center of such debates. As racialist thinking moved to the fore in discussions about immigration, state actors saw a new imperative in better documenting what were understood to be the racial characteristics of immigrants and immigrant communities. Yet, there were no simple approaches to this task, since the meanings of race were then, as now, an elusive mix of indefinable and seemingly self-evident. What relationship, precisely, the concept of race had to the streams of foreigners arriving in the nation was a question that vexed contemporaries, much as it has vexed historians since.[62] Many Americans might believe that they knew what race was and what differences the term denoted, but it was difficult to pin down such concepts in policy. Indeed, the effort to capture the meaning of immigrants' racial identities was embedded in a wider set of controversies over the meaning of race in twentieth century America. Race was a complex, controversial, multiple and changing set of legal, scientific and social understandings of human difference, determined at the same time and often in conflicting ways both locally and nationally, in courts, censuses, legislation, and social practices. "Ethnicity" had yet to emerge as a widely used category of analysis; "race" thus did the conceptual work of referencing simultaneously national, linguistic, and hereditary differences.[63] The "new immigrants" from Europe were, for the most part, generally not considered by white Americans as racially "other" in the same ways that African Americans or Chinese were, although sometimes Italians, Slavs, Jews, and other suspect immigrants were indeed explicitly compared to both groups.[64] In any event, the extent to which the difference represented by the "new immigrants" mattered for the well-being of the polity and was racially, biologically defined permeated debates over immigration policy.

American Jews had a complicated relationship to the notion of race, as well as to the notions of nationality and peoplehood with which the idea of race were entangled during early twentieth-century debates over immigration.[65] As as result, Jews found themselves at odds with official attempts at racial classification during this era. American Jewish leaders' tussles with the US government over immigration authorities' new classification system demonstrate their discomfort with assumptions underlying the state's bureaucratic methods. These clashes help illuminate, as well, the government's commitment to its practices of gathering and sorting data on immigration, whatever conceptual difficulties were entailed.

There were many groups whose status as race or nationality was hard to delimit. Italians, Brazilians, and Syrians, for example, all proved vexing in this regard. However, Jews struck other Americans, and each other, as a group that especially troubled such efforts at classification. Both Jews and others debated extensively who Jews were racially, ethnically, and nationally.[66] Such questions regarding Jews had emerged with particular vitriol in Europe with the rise of nation-states and had more recently become central to debates around Zionism within the Jewish community.[67] These debates carried over to the US context. Were Jews a race or a religion, or both? Were there "real" connections—ties of blood, of belief, of loyalty, of a shared past or future—among them, domestically and internationally, that made them a people? In the nineteenth century, Jews in the United States had found the concept of a Jewish race useful and meaningful, for it allowed them—as a small and relatively homogeneous community—to define themselves simultaneously as a people apart and as Americans. Racial otherness, as self-defined, could be a powerful unifying force. But with the start of the mass immigration of eastern European Jews and the rise of an immigration restriction movement steeped in racialist thinking, American Jews saw reason to back away from a racial self-definition.[68] Racial distinctiveness had come to mean that a group occupied a fixed place in the biological hierarchy that modern eugenicists described. Many American Jews around the turn of the twentieth century feared that, in the eyes of the government and the American public, a notion of racial Jewishness would serve to define Jews as inferior and as permanent outsiders, much as they were understood to be in the European nations from which many of them came.[69]

From the point of view of immigration officials charged with keeping accurate records on the composition of newcomers and immigrant communities, Jews were of particular concern and not only in regard to questions of race. The concern arose in part because, along with Italians (who were classified as northern or southern Italian), Jews represented the majority of the "new immigrants." Additionally, however, Jews highlighted the limitations of the older practice of tracking immigrants largely on the basis of their geographic origin. Jews were noteworthy for being one of the groups that crossed national boundaries most often. That is, while Armenians immigrated in significant numbers from Russia as well as Turkey, and Poles came from Germany, Austria-Hungary, and Russia, Jewish immigrants arrived from all over Europe, north to south and east to west: Austria-Hungary, England, France, Germany, Romania, Russia, and Turkey. [70]

Early measures to revamp the government's classificatory apparatus met with little objection from Jews or anyone else. In 1899, the Bureau of Immigration began to classify arriving immigrants by "races or peoples," as well as by country of last permanent residence. [71] In large part, the decision to add the new category reflected the fact that among the "new immigrants" the relationship between geographic origin and group identity was complex. The immigration of the late nineteenth and the early twentieth centuries, particularly from the geographically sprawling empires of Russia and Austria-Hungary, was more diverse than earlier immigration in terms of what was described at the time as linguistic, national, and racial identity (and today would be more likely understood as linguistic or ethnic identity). As a federal commission on immigration would later explain in discussing the 1899 shift in record keeping, "according to Bureau of Immigration statistics, as many as 12 different races, all indigenous to the country, are represented among immigrants from Austria-Hungary, while people of 7 distinct races come from Russia." [72] Despite the determination on the part of federal authorities to capture accurately the complicated demographics of immigration, the relationship between race and nationality was not much clarified by the awkward official formulation "races or peoples." As Matthew Frye Jacobson observes, this phrase reflected the confusion inherent in the government's emerging classificatory system. Who were races, who were peoples, and what was the difference? Or was everyone—Armenians, French, Hebrews, and Northern Italians—both? [73]

The new classificatory system did catch the attention of the American Jewish press. It also found at least one vocal opponent in the person of Simon Wolf, a prominent Washington attorney who advocated with lawmakers on behalf of Reform Jews. Wolf protested the inclusion of "Hebrew" on the list on the grounds of religious liberty. He argued that Jews were a religious rather than a racial group and the only religious group to be listed in government data. However, Wolf's protest garnered little interest among American Jews; neither did a similar effort he made in 1903. [74]

Six years later, however, American Jewish community leaders became much more concerned about the issue of the government's classification of

Jews. This time, a number of rabbis and secular Jewish activists joined Wolf in an organized protest against the government's use of "Hebrew" as a category in its immigration data. There were several reasons for this change of heart. First, the federal government had launched an important new initiative that gave American Jews pause: the Dillingham Commission, the committee formed in 1907 to study immigration. The commission's work marked a milestone in the US government's commitment to scientific documentation of immigrants, including race-based analyses. As a political compromise that arose after restrictionists once again failed to legislate a literacy test, the commission was established under the leadership of Senator William Dillingham, Republican of Vermont and chair of the Senate's Committee on Immigration.

The group's work was a major undertaking. Funded with a one million dollar appropriation, the commission spent four years conducting a vast study of immigration, publishing the results of its research in forty-two volumes.[75] The Dillingham Commission itself pointed out that, with the exception of the census, its report was the largest effort at information gathering that the government had ever undertaken. The report's scope was enormous. Altogether, the report included original data on more than three million people about "patterns of immigration from Europe; conditions in the European countries from which the immigrants were drawn; the position and economic status of recent immigrants in the United States, including their occupations, residential patterns, levels of assimilation, and incidences of incarceration for pauperism, insanity, or criminality; the fecundity of immigrant women; and conditions in cities."[76] The report also included a volume titled *Dictionary of Races or Peoples*, which was intended to be an exhaustive compendium of the most up-to-date definitions of the world's groupings and definitive proof of biological differences among the different types: for example, between southern and eastern Europeans and the older "stock" that made up earlier streams of immigration. The report did concede that such differences apparently faded over time in the United States, thereby pointing to an important difference in the understanding of "race" when applied to European immigrants and when it was used in reference to those of African or Asian descent, whose biological characteristics were thought to be immutable.[77] Nevertheless, throughout the report, the racially distinct "new immigrants" came out in a most unfavorable light—described as of measurably inferior intelligence and much less likely to assimilate into American society. The report strongly recommended, on the basis of its data, the enactment of restrictive immigration legislation, including a literacy test and nation-based quotas. The report's data, conclusions, and recommendations met with great favor among immigration restrictionists and provided an important reference point in the immigration debate for years to come.[78]

In addition to becoming alarmed at the discriminatory implications of the work conducted by the Dillingham Commission, American Jews had observed anti-immigrant sentiment and the push for restriction growing stronger during the century's first years. Moreover, the Bureau of the Census was proposing to add European races to the census of 1910, meaning that the census would use the classificatory system pioneered by the Bureau of Immigration instead of classing European immigrants as simply "white," as had been the practice.[79] American Jewish leaders' confidence was also deeply shaken by the 1909 decision by the Department of Commerce and Labor to classify Syrians as "Mongolians" and thus render them, as Asiatics, ineligible to naturalization. They feared that Jews—like Syrians, widely understood to be of Middle Eastern ancestry—might also be classified as Asiatics.[80] The activism of Simon Wolf and other Jewish leaders, including New York City attorney Louis Marshall of the American Jewish Committee, helped defeat the proposal to change the census. Marshall was also instrumental in arguing court cases that restored Syrians' right to naturalize as white persons.[81] The use of racial classifications in the government's immigration documentation, however, was more entrenched. Led by Simon Wolf, American Jewish leaders mobilized around the issue. The Union of American Hebrew Congregations (the nationwide association of Reform Jews), the fraternal organization B'nai B'rith, and the American Jewish Committee worked together to publicize the issue among American Jews. They also took their argument to the Dillingham Commission, whose investigation was ongoing.

American Jews did not succeed in their bid to get the commission to change the practice of classifying Jews as a race in immigration data. Lawmakers and government officials had never been receptive to Simon Wolf's argument on this issue. The State Department, for example, detailed its own—and other nations'—longstanding usage of race when speaking of Jews.[82] The Dillingham Commission noted that dictionary definitions and, more damningly for Jewish leaders' purposes, the early twentieth-century Jewish scholarly compendium, the *Jewish Encyclopedia*, identified Jews as race.[83] In any case, the category "race," as one census official had observed in reference to the matter some years earlier, could have various meanings, not all pejorative. Jews, he wrote, were clearly a community of bloodline, so why did they object to the notion of race?[84] Moreover, government officials contended that the racial classification as used by the Bureau of Immigration had more to do with accurately tracking the arrival and fortunes of the foreign-born than with placing Jews permanently into some lower spot in the domestic racial order. In other words, according to these officials, "race," when applied to Jews, was not intended to imply an unchanging, separate status on the level of the separation of white from nonwhite peoples. W. W. Husband, secretary of the Dillingham Commission (and future Commissioner General of Immigration) wrote to the assistant secretary of commerce and labor in 1908 that he had done his best to convince "a prominent Hebrew" (likely Wolf) that there was little need for concern on the matter:

> I . . . called his attention to the fact that beyond the second generation the Commission made no reference to races except in the case of Orientals, negroes and American Indians, but that the American-born children of American-born parents were designated as Americans, whether the race of their forefathers was Irish, Italian, Bohemian, Hebrew or any other race except those specially mentioned above.[85]

The classification "Hebrew" remained in place in official immigration data.

It is important to note that even within the American Jewish community there was no consensus on the matter of race. Many American Jews—particularly Zionists—objected to the argument that Jews did not constitute a race. For them, this amounted to a denial of Jewish peoplehood, which notion lay at the core of their belief in the need for a Jewish nation. An assertion of Jewish peoplehood, in their view, was a powerful answer to Jewish outsider status rather than a cause of it. In part because of this dissension, American Jewish leaders dropped the battle over the role of racial classification in immigration statistics.[86] Yet, their broader uneasiness about Jews' place in immigration policy and law remained and would become more urgent and widespread in years to come.

TOWARD THE QUOTAS: WORLD WAR I
AND ITS AFTERMATH

World War I transformed the public debate about immigration and immigration policy itself, as it did so many aspects of American life. In the years before the war, nativists' racialist critiques of immigration had shaped the public discourse but had not succeeded in broadly reconfiguring policy. This failure was due at least in part to the Progressive era's characteristically strong faith in immigrants' abilities and their tendencies to assimilate. Organized antirestrictionist activism, such as that pursued by American Jewish groups, thus met with a measure of sympathy in and out of Congress. During the war, however, international and domestic developments shifted the public discourse and helped set the stage for the postwar developments in immigration policy. "One hundred per cent Americanism," the national call to unity during wartime, was shorthand for a frankly nationalist and xenophobic ideology that permeated politics on all levels of national life. Despite the vast number of immigrants serving loyally in the American armed forces, wartime brought about a spike in nationalism and, relatedly, in the fear and suspicion of foreigners, many of whom were now seen as potential internal enemies. Unnaturalized foreigners from Germany or any of its allied lands were decreed "enemy aliens." Germans, still the largest immigrant group nationwide, were hit particularly hard by antiforeigner sentiment, whether or not they had been naturalized.[87] German Americans were suspected of being foreign spies and were sometimes victims of nationalist violence; German newspapers were banned by localities across the country; and the teaching of German language in public schools met with sudden protest.[88]

The literacy test idea, which had originally been proposed decades earlier, had always been intended to keep out the "undesirables" of eastern and southern Europe rather than the immigrants of western Europe. Nevertheless, the intense anti-German feelings aroused by the war helped lend the immigration issue new urgency. It was no coincidence that it was during the war, with its frenzied climate of antiforeigner agitation, that the literacy test, which had been narrowly defeated several times already, finally passed, as part of the comprehensive Immigration Act of 1917. This law, following the precedent set by earlier immigration acts, also raised the head tax on arriving immigrants, added new categories to the list of excludable aliens, and expanded the scope of Asian exclusion to India and beyond by instituting the "Asiatic barred zone" described earlier.[89] Given the precipitous decline in transatlantic immigration during the war, there was scarcely the opportunity to implement the law with European immigrants until much later, but the legislation signaled a significant shift toward broad-based restriction.

Wartime also saw a major change in the government's practices of identifying and tracking individual immigrants. Even before the advent of a modern reliance on data, the government had long gathered some kinds of information on foreigners entering at ports, such as that required in steamship passenger manifests, which included immigrants' names, ages, and occupations.[90] It was not until the World War I period, however, amidst a climate of heightened concern over the threat outsiders posed to national security, that the United States became part of what John Torpey describes as the modern "international passport system"—that international system of labeling all individuals in force today, without which people cannot cross national borders legally. The war was a turning point in this regard internationally. In Europe, for example, wartime meant that migrants and foreigners were being regarded with newly anxious scrutiny. All over the continent, identification requirements were introduced or revived after a period in which such controls had generally declined.[91] The United States also at this moment came to regard its borders as crucial sites of control over national security. Foreigners might be dangerous spies; it was important to know who was coming in and out. As of 1918, immigrants entering the United States had to show a passport with a visa issued by a US consul certifying that the alien was admissible.[92] Immigrants, in other words, now had to be "documented."[93]

After World War I, international migration—indeed, foreignness itself—was still regarded with distrust both in the United States and abroad. In Europe, where newly defined nation-states were replacing sprawling, multiethnic empires, states displayed less tolerance than did earlier regimes for the flow of people across borders. Within those borders, governments insisted on more rigid, ethnic definitions of national membership that rendered foreigners unwelcome and native minority populations foreign.[94] Jews, despite the hopes of those who had pressed hard at the Paris Peace Conference of 1919 for minority rights in the new postwar Europe, met with both official and popular prejudice.[95] In the United States, meanwhile, the official sense persisted that incoming foreigners required high levels of scrutiny. The wartime passport and visa requirements for entering aliens were maintained after the armistice.

Many Americans also feared that the unprecedented upheavals of World War I would spur masses of "undesirable" people to flee chaotic, postimperial eastern Europe and its new nationalistic states. The US government's response, ultimately, was to place new barriers to entry into its own newly nationalistic state: the Immigration Acts of 1921 and 1924. The powerful forces driving this change were both domestic and international. In the years immediately after the war, anti-immigration political pressures continued to mount. The literacy test proved less of a barrier than it would have been had it been enacted when first proposed; literacy rates throughout Europe were rising. Jews, in particular, were not screened out by the literacy test to the satisfaction of the measure's original proponents, both because of their higher literacy rates than other groups from southern and eastern Europe and because of an exemption from the test for victims of religious or political persecution, a policy for which Jewish groups had successfully pushed.[96]

The war had shifted public sentiment toward nationalism and nativism so sharply that there was now widespread support for more restrictive immigration laws.[97] Meanwhile, the Russian Revolution, in combination with massive labor and racial unrest at home that exploded particularly fiercely in 1919, also contributed to the demonization of foreign radicals.[98] The "Red Scare" of 1919–20—in which Attorney General Mitchell Palmer, with the cooperation of local authorities, went on an unprecedented sweep of immigrant communities looking for foreign radicals to deport—was an event of relatively short-term duration.[99] However, anxieties about "Bolshevism," anarchism, and radicalism remained strong long after the Palmer raids. Furthermore, just as the depression of the early 1890s had galvanized anti-immigrant sentiment in the United States, a national economic slump now intensified public alarm about a potential rise in undesirable European immigration. As a key piece of evidence for the argument that this was an impending danger, advocates for restriction noted that the number of Jews arriving in 1920 had shot up dramatically.[100] In December 1920, the Committee on Immigration of the US House of Representatives cautioned fellow lawmakers that American Jews themselves were pointing toward an impending deluge:

> The flow of immigration to the United States is now in full flood. The need for restrictive legislation is apparent. . . . Members of the committee . . . found by far the largest percentage of immigrants to be peoples of Jewish extraction. . . . The committee has confirmed the published statements of a commissioner of the Hebrew Sheltering and Aid Society of America made after his personal investigation in Poland, to the effect that "If there were in existence a ship that could hold 3,000,000 human beings, the 3,000,000 Jews of Poland would board it to escape to America."[101]

The report further included warnings from Head Consul Wilbur Carr, whose intelligence from the field included items such as the following: "The great mass of aliens passing through Rotterdam at the present time are Russian Poles or Polish Jews of the usual ghetto type. . . . They are filthy, un-American and often dangerous in their habits."[102] In the face of such reports, arguments for tighter immigration restrictions met with broad public support. Labor, for example, in the form of the AFL, now advocated vigorously for suspending immigration altogether.

Meanwhile, the political alignments that had traditionally countered the forces of immigration restriction were coming apart. Jewish and other ethnic groups continued to fight against proposals for more restrictive immigration laws, speaking out in public forums and publishing their views in articles and books. The American Jewish Committee, the Hebrew Sheltering and Immigrant Aid Society (HIAS), the United Hebrew Trades, and others all testified before Congress against immigration restriction. (Indeed, Jewish groups were so heavily represented in congressional hearings that they may have confirmed their opponents' suspicions that immigration was a particularly "Jewish cause."[103]) Some industrial leaders also continued to advocate for open immigration. But increasing numbers of businesses were willing to do without foreign immigrants, their need for cheap labor partly sated by the entrance of women and black southern migrants into industrial jobs during the war. When Congress shifted to Republican control in 1919, Congressman Albert Johnson of Washington, who brought to his job a history of antiradical activism and anti-Japanese sentiment forged in his experiences at home, took on the chairmanship of the House Immigration Committee. In 1920, Congress debated bills that would stop all immigration. By comparison, the 1921 Emergency Quota Act, which introduced the quota system, was, relatively, a gentle compromise. Even the Immigration Act of 1924, with its much more restrictive provisions, was a compromise between those favoring a complete bar to new immigration and those who saw such measures as too extreme.[104]

The quota laws represented a triumph for those who argued that immigration needed to be subjected to overall numerical limits (in addition to being regulated in terms of immigrants' characteristics), an idea that continues to structure immigration policy to this day. It was also a victory for those who wanted immigration controlled on the basis of race, with reference to the eugenicist theories of racial hierarchies. The almost total ban on Asian immigration, as well as the severe limitation of immigration from eastern and southern Europe, would, it was hoped, help ensure the nation's racial good health in years to come. This triumph was tempered, to some extent, by the fact that quotas were assigned on a national, not racial, basis—that is, they defined the number of people who could enter from Poland, not the number of ethnic Poles who could enter. Some contemporaries argued that the quota system should also be figured according to racial categories within national ones. This argument seems to have arisen largely because the nation-based system did not limit Jewish immigration as much as a race-based system would have done. In early 1924, for example, as Congress debated proposals for the new quota law, South Dakota's Republican Senator Thomas Sterling introduced an amendment that would have divided each national quota into subquotas based on race. His argument, in other words, was that no racial group should be allowed quota slots in numbers disproportionate to its representation in that nation's general population. The senator conceded openly that this measure was aimed at Jews, whose representation in the immigration from Poland, Romania, and Russia far exceeded the proportion of Jews in the population of those places. He insisted, however, that his logic—which was essentially the same as those behind the quotas—was only fair.[105] This proposal, however, was never adopted. In any event, many of those convinced of the general inferiority of the "new immigration" hoped that the national quotas provided a screening system that would be nearly as effective as one explicitly based on racial groupings, given that the places from which immigration would be eliminated or most curtailed were the ones from which the groups deemed most inferior were coming. The law also had the advantage that the system it established could be argued to be treating all the nations subject to quotas equitably by applying the same standard to each.[106]

Even though the quotas were not calculated according to race, the 1924 act also served as a victory for those committed to a racialist vision of the nation in that it mandated a national genealogy project—an accounting of European "blood" since the nation's founding.[107] The initial phase of the 1924 act would implement restrictions based on the proportion of people of each nationality present in the census of 1890. As mentioned earlier, however, this was only a short-term plan. Ultimately, the quotas were to be reckoned by cataloguing the nation's whole white population, as determined by the 1920 census, by descent, and giving nations quotas relative to their representation in this national family tree.

The Immigration Act of 1924 was also a dramatic turning point in the US government's commitment to make documenting and tracking individual immigrants central to its immigration control efforts. The law attended to the question of documentation in detail, refining and expanding the already formidable paper requirements for immigration. The text of the law conveys a sense of the extent to which the new system demanded that all individuals provide detailed documentation on themselves. Section 7, for example, explains the process by which immigrants now had to apply for a quota visa:

> In the application the immigrant shall state (1) the immigrant's full and true name; age, sex, and race; the date and place of birth; places of residence for the five years immediately preceding his application; whether married

or single, and the names and places of residence of wife or husband and minor children, if any; calling or occupation; personal description (including height, complexion, color of hair and eyes, and marks of identification); ability to speak, read, and write; names and addresses of parents . . . ; port of entry into the United States; final destination, if any, beyond the port of entry; whether he has a ticket through to such final destination; whether going to join a relative or friend, and, if so, what relative or friend and his name and complete address; the purpose for which he is going to the United States; the length of time he intends to remain in the United States; whether or not he intends to abide in the United States permanently; whether ever in prison or almshouse; whether he or either of his parents has ever been in an institution or hospital for the care and treatment of the insane; (2) if he claims to be a non-quota immigrant, the facts on which he bases such claim.[108]

In addition, each immigrant had to provide two photographs of him- or herself, along with "two copies of his 'dossier' and prison record and military record, two certified copies of his birth certificate, and two copies of all other available public records concerning him kept by the Government to which he owes allegiance."[109] The "documentedness" of immigrants now extended far beyond passports and ship manifests. Aristide Zolberg has usefully observed that the 1924 law formalized a "remote control" system by which the United States' control over the migration process began abroad, long before immigrants set out on their journey.[110] This is true, but the new system also meant that there was now a complicated international web of people and institutions that any one immigrant had to navigate in order to obtain the documents and permissions required to enter the country—shipping companies; various levels of US bureaucracy (the consulates, run by the State Department; officials of the Immigration Bureau, working out of the Labor Department); local and national authorities in other countries; and relatives and friends at home and abroad.

The international impact of the Immigration Act of 1924 was also felt in other ways. A number of nations protested that the law interfered with their own right to regulate emigration. As many who objected to the laws had predicted, Japan, despite the fact that Japanese immigration had long been curtailed under the Gentlemen's Agreement of 1907, expressed outrage about the provision that banned Asian immigration. Such objections, however, had little impact. To the contrary: the US law would become a model for other nations, serving as an evidence of the need to control and document immigration and offering model mechanisms by which to achieve this end.[111]

PERSISTING DISORDER

The quota laws were an unprecedentedly ambitious attempt to impose order on and exercise control over phenomena that were necessarily disorderly: the migrations of vastly diverse people from all over the world who were coming to the United States in a multitude of ways for a multitude of purposes. The quota laws have been regarded as a clear-cut historical transition—a definite "closing of the gates" of the United States—in part because the quota formula they codified appears to be so mathematically well defined. However, these acts of seeming specificity, and the mechanisms of documentation and control that they relied on, could not fully contain the confusion that reigned regarding how to classify, sort, and identify immigrants. Indeed, these uncertainties in part allowed for illegal immigration; although the laws were predicated on the idea that there were sharp divisions among races and peoples, and between foreigners and Americans, it was hard even for experienced inspectors to tell who was who when immigrants entered the country with forged papers or in disguise, which many did. This confusion came back to haunt the US officials charged with the law's implementation.

Nor were the outcomes of the law—the power the law had over individuals, families, ethnic networks, organizations, or communities—ever fully predictable. As the new legislation came into force, Jews abroad and in the United States would discover that its foundational concepts, which seemed clear-cut on paper, were still very much in flux. Jews' unique relationship to national belonging, their vexed relationship to shifting notions of race, and the multinational nature of their immigrant cohort made them key actors in the drama of defining the meaning of the quota laws.

CHAPTER 2

American Law, Jewish Solidarity

El Paso, Texas, January 1921: Rabbi Martin Zielonka was in his study at Reform Temple Mount Sinai when four visitors arrived unexpectedly. They were, it turned out, Jewish illegal immigrants. Their presence alerted Zielonka to a situation that alarmed him: eastern European Jews were illegally crossing over the Mexico–Texas border. The immigrants, desperate to escape the ongoing havoc of eastern Europe but unable to obtain the necessary documents, had apparently taken this circuitous route to the United States on the advice of steamship agents in Europe. Shipping companies, mindful of impending American immigration restrictions, were promoting Mexico as a "back door" to the United States. Jews who chose to try this route were sailing from Spain or the Netherlands into the Mexican port of Veracruz, then going north, most hoping to get to relatives in the United States. Not all succeeded in evading American authorities. Nine Jewish immigrants had landed in the El Paso jail alone and others elsewhere in Texas. There was at least a shipload more somewhere in Mexico, and hundreds of other Jews on the way to Mexico from Europe, all bound for the United States.[1]

June 1924: a hundred and twenty-seven delegates from forty-five American Jewish organizations sequestered themselves for a day-long conference in New York City's Hotel Astor. Labor unions, women's groups, and civil liberties organizations were all represented; attendees included immigrant activists, social workers, and distinguished second-generation lawyers. The occasion that brought this eclectic crowd together: the quotas, made permanent by the newly passed Immigration Act of 1924, had stranded thousands of eastern

European Jews at ports in Europe and elsewhere. The law had rendered the US visas that these would-be immigrants carried invalid, their steamship tickets useless. The United States did not want them to come, the countries where they were—France, England, Latvia, and Greece, among others—did not want them to stay, and the war-ravaged countries they had fled, such as Soviet Russia, did not want them back.[2]

The immigration laws of 1921 and 1924 forced the American Jewish establishment—rabbis, social service agencies, and advocacy organizations—to contend with the havoc these measures caused for Jews trying to immigrate to the United States. The situations of Jewish migrants caught in geographic liminal zones, such as the Mexico–US border and European ports, vividly thematized the complex gray areas the new restrictive immigration regime produced. None of the people who understood themselves as representatives of the American Jewish community wanted to be seen as breaking US law, or as supporting immigrants who did. Legality and illegality in the face of the new laws, however, proved not to be clear-cut categories. As American Jewish leaders forged communal responses to the immigration crises the laws produced, they found that the new immigration laws generated a number of not-yet-decided questions open to political debate. Did entering the country illegally make someone a criminal, or was there room for leniency? Should possession of a US visa entitle someone to enter the country even if the immigration quota was decreed full? Could migrants' plights serve as leverage for protesting the laws' unjustness? American Jewish leaders proceeded cautiously on such issues. They advocated for migrants with the government to the extent that they felt they could while still respecting US law.[3]

Some scholars have depicted American Jewish groups as simply resigned to the immigration quota laws, especially after 1924, but that is not the case.[4] American Jewish organizations did not mount a full-on assault on US immigration law during the 1920s, but none of the leaders working on immigration issues, however cautious, were merely reacting passively to the laws as if they were set in stone. Rather, these leaders were active and vocal participants in shaping how the laws were put into practice. Rabbi Zielonka, for one, came to share government officials' goal of stemming illegal immigration over the Mexican border, but he pursued this aim by different means and for different reasons. For their part, the immigrant advocates who became involved with the cases of Jewish migrants stranded after the 1924 law urged lawmakers and officials to interpret the law as liberally as possible. Through all their efforts, American Jewish leaders fought to ensure that any Jewish immigration that took place would be perceived as—and would be—legal and "desirable," whether that meant forestalling Jewish attempts to enter the country illicitly or persuading lawmakers to broaden the parameters of legal immigration under the quota laws. This was frustrating work. American Jewish leaders often clashed with each other, their constituents, and their international counterparts over how to understand and approach questions of law and policy. Nevertheless, they persevered.

If American Jewish leaders attempted to define what the quota laws would mean in practice, those laws also reshaped the parameters of American Jews' relationship to the nation. The issues of peoplehood and citizenship in the era of the modern nation-state had always been complicated for Jews. Could Jews be worthy citizens of the nations in which they resided or did they have dangerously divided loyalties? This essential question about Jewish membership in modern polities was famously crystallized by the turn-of-the-century Dreyfus affair. The doubts about Jews' divided loyalties both persisted and were recast by the era's major developments, including the upheavals of World War I, the Russian Revolution, the battles over minority rights in postwar Europe, and the new urgency with which Jews were taking up the Zionist cause.[5] In many ways, the United States was the most liberal toward Jews of the modern nation-states. Still, American Jews during and after World War I did not feel themselves to be immune from the pressure to prove their capacity for loyal citizenship. This was especially true during and after World War I, when the nation's "Americanism" fever cast suspicion on all immigrant communities.

The quota laws produced their own dilemmas about legitimacy, loyalty, and responsibility for those leaders who saw themselves as spokespeople for the American Jewish community. Jews around the world hoping to reach the United States were suddenly caught in the gears of the new US laws. However committed American Jewish leaders were to aiding Jewish immigrants, those leaders were in a difficult position. The pull of Jewish solidarity conflicted painfully with the requirements of American law. Furthermore, these leaders had to figure out how to advocate for immigrants in a hostile nativist political climate while still insisting on their own unimpeachable Americanness. American Jews were aware that the necessarily international nature of immigration issues—which often involved multilingual communications, multinational partnerships, and transatlantic financial transactions—made it both difficult and imperative to prove that they were rooted firmly in American law and society. Similarly, accusations that American Jewish groups pursued illegal immigration activities made it essential to maintain above-board reputations, especially challenging in an era when theories of an international Jewish cabal were widespread.

The new immigration legislation was also a turning point in American Jews' relationship to Jews elsewhere in the world. The laws shifted the terms under which international Jewish solidarity could operate. Jewish organizations in the United States and elsewhere had long been engaged in work with international Jewish communities, and all the American Jewish actors discussed here believed that what happened in the world of international Jewish migration was their concern. They understood the dire situation that European Jews were facing. The war had made refugees of hundreds of thousands of Jews across the continent. Tens of thousands had been killed by the violence wracking eastern Europe, where the new regimes that emerged after the destruction of empires were hostile to their Jewish populations.[6] Exactly what to do about the difficulties in which Jewish would-be-immigrants abroad found themselves as the immigration quotas came into force was less clear. To what end could and should national and international Jewish networks be mobilized? To what extent could American Jewish organizations now hope to intervene effectively with states on Jews' behalf? Those Jews trying to enter the United States after Congress passed the new immigration laws were trapped between and among states in a no-man's land of national belonging at the very moment at which the United States sought to make its national borders more rigid—indeed to a large extent because of this shift toward harder American borders. The nation-states of postwar Europe, too, were defining and guarding their borders during this era as never before. American Jewish leaders aiding Jewish migrants risked clashing with their own government as well as others.

American Jews did choose to continue their immigration-related work, in large part from a strong sense of connection to Jews elsewhere in the world. But even as such work was a statement of American Jewish commitment to other Jews, it also highlighted—indeed, exacerbated—the fault lines and tensions among Jews, both in the United States and internationally. In other words, American Jewish immigration work made it painfully clear just how fractured were the national and international Jewish communities. Disagreements among American Jewish groups about whether advocacy for migrants should entail mass meetings or quieter, behind-the-scenes diplomacy highlighted differences in political culture between recent eastern European immigrants and more established Jewish Americans of largely German descent. As Jewish organizations worked to maintain international migration and communication networks, tensions among national and international headquarters, branch offices, and regional actors spoke to the disjunction between local, national, and international Jewish communities.

As they threw themselves into the difficult immigration issues produced by US law, American Jewish leaders had to balance competing commitments to their constituents, to Jews abroad, and to US law. Through their legal and organizational efforts, they helped define what those laws would mean for Jews—and others—inside and outside the United States. At the same time, however, as the quota laws remade the landscape of immigration and US borders, these leaders also came up against the limits of their activism on behalf of, and of their identities as part of, a global Jewish community.

AMERICAN JEWISH ORGANIZATIONS AND IMMIGRATION

American Jewish organizations were among the most visible and best organized of the American ethnic, religious, and other civic groups involved in immigration issues. Those groups that aided and advocated for Jewish immigrants participated in the culture of vibrant associationalism that characterized American Jewish life in the late nineteenth and early twentieth centuries, as it did American life more generally. These organizations ranged from the official bodies of the various religious denominations to secular fraternal organizations to left-wing labor groups; from local groups to national ones; and from immigrant aid societies based on hometown ties to Zionist organizations that supported Jewish settlements in Palestine. Synagogues, schools, camps, hospitals, newspapers, and cemeteries were only some of the institutions such American Jewish organizations fostered.

The diversity of American Jewish organizations reflected the different stages and origins of Jewish settlement in the United States. The older groups had their roots mainly in German Jewish immigrant communities established in the mid-nineteenth century.[7] The International Order of the B'nai B'rith (IOBB), founded in 1843 as a secular fraternal order, was one such organization. By the twentieth century it had grown into one of the major national Jewish service organizations.[8] The American Jewish Committee, founded in 1906 by a small group of prominent Jews, became one of the most important voices for the civil rights and liberties of American Jews.[9] As more eastern European Jews established themselves in American society, they launched their own organizations, such as the Hebrew Sheltering and Immigrant Aid Society (HIAS).[10]

During the peak era of European immigration, many Jewish groups worked to aid immigrants. Though sometimes they struggled over turf, they also cooperated with each other as well as with non-Jewish groups like the YMCA and the Immigrants' Protective League to provide new arrivals with temporary housing and information, help with transportation, and other services. They also coordinated with their counterparts abroad, such as the German Jewish organization Hilfsverein der Deutschen Juden (Aid Association of German Jews). The best known among the Jewish groups was HIAS, headquartered in New York and with active branch offices in cities including Philadelphia and Boston. The National Council of Jewish Women (NCJW) had a Department of Immigrant Aid that focused on the needs of women immigrants; along with HIAS, the NCJW was one of the select group of aid agencies allowed to have permanent representatives posted at Ellis Island.[11] The IOBB, for its part, increasingly focused on providing social services in immigrant communities toward the end of the nineteenth century. Local initiatives within immigrant communities also provided newcomers with a network of mutual aid and other social services.[12] Meanwhile, Jewish organizations, most notably the American Jewish Committee, engaged in political work against restrictive immigration laws, as well as in legal and political advocacy on immigrants' behalf.

American Jews made such work a communal priority for several reasons. In an era when a large percentage of Jews in America were either foreign born or the children of foreign-born parents, immigration was a central concern of organized Jewish life.[13] Moreover, Jewish communities in the United States had no foreign government to advocate for them the way other groups did; instead, they had to represent themselves.[14] While other groups also organized to provide a range of mutual aid and other services for immigrants, Jews could draw from a rich set of financial and political resources represented by the older, more established segment of American Jewry, and the philanthropic will of successful, prominent Jewish businessmen, such as the bankers Jacob Schiff and Felix Warburg, to ensure stable funding.

What might have been deemed a thriving, diverse Jewish civic sphere struck some contemporaries as fractured and fragmented.[15] The Jewish institutional landscape was so complex that Jewish leaders frequently expressed despair over what they saw as a lack of ideological and organizational unity among the nation's Jews. Further complicating this lack of organizational unity were divisions of religious observance; Reform, Conservative, and Orthodox communities disagreed over the fundamental role of religious practice in daily life. Despite various attempts at creating organizational entities that could claim to speak for the nation's Jews—to Jews themselves, to the press, to the US government, and to the international diplomatic community—no group ever came to represent American Jews at large.[16]

Indeed, the question of immigration, both because of and despite its urgency for many American Jews, was often at the heart of divides among them. While Jews from across the range of class, national, and religious backgrounds in the United States often expressed the idea that they were connected to each other, divisions along the lines of relationship to Old World and New could run deep. Eastern European Jewish newcomers and the more established Jews, many of largely German descent (often distinguished in contemporary and historical sources by the New York City descriptors "downtown" and "up-town," though these divisions among Jews both mattered and differed across the nation) struggled with differences in political culture, language, religious practice, and economic status. They often regarded each other across gulfs of misunderstanding, accusing each other—in the context of Yiddish and English newspapers, organizational scuffles, and personal correspondence—of being overly patronizing or uncouth, conservative or radical, respectively. The older community's philanthropic, educational, and "Americanizing" activities on behalf of their eastern European immigrant coreligionists were often met with resentment and mistrust. Meanwhile, such developments as trade union-ism, Socialism, and Zionism, which had devoted and vocal followings in the immigrant communities, worried the more established American Jewish com-munities, who feared that their own status and respectability were put at risk by association. Even by the 1920s, as eastern European Jews began increasingly to assume positions of leadership in social service and other organizations formerly run by the wealthier segment of American Jewish society, tensions persisted. American Jews felt both bound to and divided from each other and Jews elsewhere. They saw their fates as interconnected and yet different, their interests as linked and yet sometimes at odds.

The immigration-related dramas that developed after the quota laws' pas-sage reveal these complicated dynamics at a moment of both domestic and international flux. With World War I, the equation of Jewish power and re-sponsibility had changed. During and immediately after the war, the orga-nized American Jewish community found itself taking the lead in international Jewish affairs for the first time, as European Jewish communities struggled with the physical and financial devastation around them. The Joint Distribu-tion Committee (JDC), an umbrella group created during the war to coordi-nate and administer the American Jewish funds raised for Jewish communities overseas along with HIAS, instituted and vastly expanded their international work during these years, raising large sums of money from Jewish communi-ties across the United States to fund their efforts.[17] Meanwhile, American Jew-ish groups—dissension among them notwithstanding—played an integral role in advocating for both European Jewish minority rights and the Zionist cause at the Paris Peace Conference in 1919.[18]

The postwar triumph of American immigration restrictionists, against whose legislative proposals Jewish groups had fought hard, was a blow for American Jewish leaders. It was obvious that the quota laws would reshape Jewish demography and culture in the United States, although it was unclear exactly how.[19] Also evident was that the new laws would put substantial barriers between American Jews and their European counterparts. However, the immigration quotas did not lead Jewish groups to disengage from international Jewish issues in general or immigration issues in particular. Faced with the new US immigration laws, American Jewish organizations such as the JDC, HIAS, and NCJW worked harder to create and manage channels through which people, news, and money could flow. They disseminated information about the new laws' complexities, worked with consulates and shipping companies to process visa and passport applications, and transferred messages and remittances from the United States to Europe.[20] Within the United States, they, along with non-direct-service organizations like the American Jewish Committee, sought to mitigate the impact of these laws, lobbying the Departments of Labor and State to halt deportations and lawmakers to expand the parameters of nonquota admissions.

American Jewish groups, however, did not react in unified fashion to the issues of legality and illegality raised by the new immigration laws. Rather, American Jewish leaders' responses to these laws—their political and aid strategies, public statements, and fundraising—were forged amidst a morass of organizational politics and charged personal interactions. Organizations tussled, for example, over complicated questions of spokesmanship. Determining which leaders spoke for whom could be fraught, especially when it came to advocating for Jewish communities with Congress, the White House, or the courts. Activism on immigration issues was thus intertwined with inter- and intraorganizational politics.

External pressures also affected how Jewish groups arrived at their policies and practices. The national climate of nativism and anti-Semitism that intensified during the 1920s was the constant backdrop for all organizational decision making. In the early years of the decade, virulent attacks on "the international Jew" in Henry Ford's *Dearborn Independent* and the rapid political rise of the Ku Klux Klan were among the most alarming developments for American Jewish leaders.[21] Many colleges and universities instituted quotas to limit the number of Jewish students, which, while never as harsh as the *numerus clausus* that kept Jews out of European universities, seemed to echo immigration restrictionists' focus on excluding undesirable Jews.[22] Other forms of social discrimination during this era, such as those in housing and employment, seemed equally ominous signs that, for Jews, American acceptance was in short supply.[23] In this context, those Jewish groups operating in the field of immigration found themselves on particularly difficult ground. They were invested in the very things that seemed suspect to the government and American public: international connections among Jews and the tasks of helping Jews from elsewhere enter the United States. Consequently, preserving the image of American Jewish respectability and safeguarding the reputations of their own organizations were of paramount importance.

As American Jewish organizations, particularly HIAS, the NCJW, and the JDC, moved increasingly into the international arena, their situation—and their relationship to US law and government—became more complicated. In certain ways, the chaos of postwar eastern Europe created new opportunities for them to play meaningful new roles in aiding Jews abroad. There was an administrative vacuum in the arena of overseas migration work once the war ended. American Jewish organizations provided valuable help to the overwhelmed US consulates, faced with long lines of would-be immigrants. HIAS, for example, took over some of the tasks of consuls in Poland, providing space and advice for prospective Jewish emigrants seeking to fill out visa applications. HIAS also successfully made a case for letting visa applicants show correspondence from their US-based relatives as evidence that they had family who would care for the them on arrival in the United States, in lieu of official affidavits to that effect, since such documents often went missing in the unreliable transatlantic mail.[24] Jewish groups also began to handle the logistics of transatlantic finance, transmitting enormous amounts of private dollars from Jews in the United States to their relatives on a not-for-profit basis.[25]

But such international activities also made Jewish organizations suspect. Indeed, reports of immigration groups' activities abroad, especially those of Jewish groups, fueled nativist arguments to pass the quota laws. HIAS, for example, made enemies among American financiers with its nonprofit remittance work, which bankers felt was cutting into their potential business. They went so far as to accuse HIAS of breaking banking laws by banking without a license.[26] US authorities, for their part, frequently believed Jewish organizations to be on the wrong side of the law. Most commonly, they suspected that Jewish groups were illegally funding immigration. In 1921, for example, in the months leading up to the passage of the quota laws, American consuls sent various reports to their superiors in Washington indicating that HIAS and lesser-known organizations were conniving to get European Jews to the United States. "Although I am not able to present convincing evidence that Nuchow violated the Immigration

Laws," wrote the American consul from Cologne in early 1921 with reference to one Jewish American working with Polish Jewish migrants in Germany, "nevertheless it seems that his activities should be further investigated."[27]

Jewish organizations found themselves repeatedly battling such accusations. Louis Marshall, a prominent New York City attorney, president of the American Jewish Committee, and one of the most active leaders in Jewish affairs both domestically and abroad, took up the issue at the highest levels of government with his characteristic vehemence. "There is not a shadow of truth in the suggestion that [HIAS] has directly or indirectly been engaged in the violation of any provision of our Immigration Laws," Marshall wrote the secretary of labor in 1921. "It is a charitable organization pure and simple . . . It has never supplied any money for the purpose of enabling immigrants to come to this country." Rather, he contended, HIAS labored in Europe to keep immigrants informed, help them avoid scams as they exchanged currency, facilitate their applications for passports and visas, and provide any "other legitimate service that is needed by helpless men, women and children who have been the football of fate during the agonizing days of the great conflict from which they have been the sufferers."[28] Not only were HIAS's activities not illegal, he argued in another letter to the secretary of state, but in fact, "the society has rendered great assistance to the American Consulates and has simplified their task. It receives no compensation for the services rendered and is a philanthropic institution in the best sense of the word."[29] Such indignation notwithstanding, allegations of wrongdoing exerted pressure on Jewish organizations involved in immigration issues to be extra scrupulous in their work. "We must," Louis Marshall wrote to HIAS president John Bernstein in 1921, "seek to outdo any other part of the American people in strict observance of the law and in avoiding even the appearance of irregularity."[30]

The suspicions directed at HIAS and other groups reflected the government's perennial distrust of Jewish organizations. They also stemmed from the reality that the desperation and disorganization prevailing in eastern Europe after the war created opportunities for shady business of various kinds. The uncertain terrain of responsibility for financial and administrative dealings with immigrants in postwar eastern Europe made for accusations of lawlessness all around. This dynamic was intensified by the passage of the quota laws, which left plenty of room for illegal, entrepreneurial schemes that capitalized on people's desperation to immigrate to the United States: bribery, document counterfeiting, and human smuggling. Despite Jewish groups' protestations of their legitimacy, US officials remained suspicious and continued to scrutinize the operations of Jewish organizations.

The mistrust was mutual, fostered by the chaotic climate of postwar Europe. Those working with American Jewish organizations in Europe believed that US officials there often behaved unethically. The passport law of 1918 decreed that every immigrant entering the United States needed a passport with a visa issued by a US government representative in that immigrant's native land—a wartime measure originally intended to keep out anyone deemed a threat to national security. The law remained in effect after the war, however. Russian Jewish immigrant journalist Reuben Fink, writing for the *Nation* in 1921, reported that Jews were enraged that American consuls were arbitrarily rejecting Jewish visa applicants. He added, too, that some consuls illegally extorted money from prospective immigrants in exchange for visas.[31] Jewish groups also accused steamship companies of selling tickets to Jewish would-be immigrants without regard to whether those customers would ever be allowed to get to a port or embark on a ship. In 1922, a HIAS worker in Europe cabled the organization's New York headquarters that steamship companies were responsible for mass arrests of Jews who had arrived on the Russian border with prepaid ship tickets but without the papers necessary to satisfy Russian law. The telegram read:

> Many arrested spent months jail untold suffering. For heaven sake warn our people in America not buy prepaids and write their relatives in Russia not budge until they can travel legally. Steamship companies profiting by collecting this blood money for prepaids. Have seen things in Latvia that convicts some steamship companies of action that is little short of murder.[32]

American Jewish leaders trying to devise strategies to address the situations that Jewish migrants faced in the new era of restrictive US immigration policy had significant resources. They had a rich web of national and international organizations. They had expertise in the fields of social work, immigrant aid, and legislative advocacy. They had experience working both internationally and domestically. The quota laws, however, posed new challenges.

JEWS ON THE MEXICO–US BORDER

For Rabbi Zielonka, himself an immigrant from Germany, deciding what to do about the surge in Jewish illegal immigration over the Mexico–US border was not easy. The four eastern European Jewish men who made their way into his study in January 1921, seeking help after crossing the border illegally, impressed him. Zielonka reported that they were "exceptionally splendid specimens with good educations."[33] However, he knew that by law they should be deported and worried that the specter of Jewish illegal immigration would prove damaging for American Jews. He wrote a hasty letter to a colleague, seeking counsel. "I am in a quandary," he confessed to Rabbi Henry Cohen of Galveston, Texas. "My heart goes out to these boys who have come from a literal Hell and yet, as an American citizen, my first duty is towards this country and its laws. I do not want to be an informer on them and yet, I realise that they are . . . simply adding to the immigration unrest in our own land. What would you do," he asked Rabbi Cohen, "if you were in my place?"[34]

From 1907 to 1914 the Gulf of Mexico port city of Galveston had been the focus of American Jewish organizational efforts to redirect a portion of Jewish immigration through Texas, with the aim of countering urban congestion in the Northeast and of stemming increasing public resentment of Jewish immigrants. Rabbi Cohen, who had lent his efforts to this experiment, was regarded as an authority on Jewish immigration.[35] "I know how you feel," he replied to Zielonka a few days later. "When any of our immigrants were returned to the port whence they came by process of law, I had a sleepless night, I can tell you." Nevertheless, Cohen stressed that Zielonka's choice was clear: "Your first duty is towards the country and its laws."[36]

That Zielonka was so torn about what to do reveals both how urgent he felt the immigrants' situation was and how morally ambiguous their violation of immigration law seemed to him when he first encountered it. Ordinarily, the rabbi had a reputation as a hardcore advocate for law and order. After being ordained by Hebrew Union College (the Reform Jewish rabbinical seminary) in Cincinnati, where he grew up, he served a short stint in Waco. He came to El Paso in 1900 to serve as rabbi for its fledgling Reform congregation. Zielonka found the border city a tough frontier environment—"a pioneer city," he said later, "where everything was free and easy and where life was not taken very seriously."[37] El Paso was famous for its vices, especially its thriving red-light district; Progressive-era reformers tried in vain to bring the city to heel.[38] Zielonka shared these reformers' sensibilities. Throughout his El Paso career, he endeavored to be a civilizing force.[39] From his pulpit, he preached against gambling, sensationalist journalism, and racy movies; he worked with a local citizens' organization battling for tighter regulation of drinking, gambling, and guns. Even in his own Sunday school, he was known for being authoritarian and unforgiving.[40]

Even so, Zielonka was moved by the immigrants' predicament. He knew that they were coming from war-torn regions characterized by poverty, violence, and persecution of unwanted minorities. Zielonka also understood that the immigrants had experienced a long and difficult voyage and harrowing trip north, that they were hoping to get to loved ones, and that they were broke. Ultimately, however, he came to agree with Cohen. The law was the law, and Jewish immigrants, however desperate, should not break it. He feared, as he explained to Cohen, that the immigrants would not only be jeopardizing their own futures in the country if they entered illegally but also be endangering "the good name of American Jewry."[41] That is, Zielonka believed that Jewish illegal immigration would not remain a local affair. Rather, it would have national consequences for American Jews, who would be seen as guilty by association. Zielonka held to this conviction over the years that followed and acted accordingly. He did his best to stop the flow of Jewish illegal immigrants over the Mexican border into the United States.

In his desire to help Jewish immigrants while remaining within the confines of US law, Rabbi Martin Zielonka is representative of other Jewish organizational leaders to whom Jewish illegal immigrants turned for help. Local chapters of the NCJW in Florida and California, for example, also found themselves facing the delicate problem of aiding Jews who had entered the country in violation of US law.[42] But Zielonka played a particularly important role on the issue, becoming the national point person on all things connected to Jewish migration to and from Mexico. Moreover, his location is significant. El Paso, a city of eighty thousand tucked into the western corner of Texas, with a Jewish population of only around two thousand in 1921, might seem an unlikely site for examining Jewish immigration history.[43] Scholars of American Jews have tended to focus on the larger centers of Jewish settlement—New York, Chicago, Los Angeles. El Paso, however, was one of the places cast suddenly into the spotlight as the US quota laws remade the terrain of international Jewish migration. It was also a place where the nation's border, and who and what crossed that border, had an immediate and daily significance. Jewish illegal immigrants were thus entering into a drama with both national and regional resonance.

The Rio Grande had long demarcated a region in which the question of boundaries was complicated, shifting, and ever-present. The Mexico–Texas borderlands had a history of contested sovereignty; it was a place where Mexicans, Anglos, and African Americans coexisted in a patchwork of economic and social relations. Nobody living in El Paso could be unaware of the border. Ever since the city's boom in the 1880s, when the railroad lines linking it to major Mexican and US cities were completed, El Paso had served as a major border-crossing point for goods and people.[44] Indeed, El Paso flourished because of the strong social and economic ties linking the Mexican and American sides of the border, and the city depended on the easy flow of people from one side to another.

As the previous chapter noted, however, the nation's southern border came under new scrutiny in the late nineteenth and early twentieth centuries as the federal government increasingly sought to control immigration. There were reports of European and Middle Eastern immigrants, including Jews, Italians, Hungarians, Greeks, and Lebanese, sneaking over the border because they could not meet the new, stringent health or financial requirements of the law.[45] US authorities were most concerned about the border crossing of Chinese immigrants, largely banned from immigrating to the United States since 1882. Extensive smuggling networks evolved to facilitate the movement of Chinese into the United States, and Chinese communities on both sides of the border aided immigrants by providing money, lodging, and information.[46] This illicit immigration along the Mexico–US border grew larger after the turn of the century, when the United States persuaded Canada to cooperate with its enforcement efforts by allowing US authorities access to Canadian territory and passing its own restrictive legislation. Mexico was more resistant to such pressure and thus came to be the easier route for immigrants evading US law.[47]

Immigration officials were concerned by the ways that immigrants used cross-border routes to subvert US law, and they pushed for greater enforcement measures, arguing that alien smuggling and the phenomenon of illegal entry—particularly by Chinese immigrants—posed a threat to the nation's security. Indeed, guarding the border against unwanted immigration became tightly linked during these years to the definition of national sovereignty.[48] Nevertheless, the Mexico–US border remained porous to people traveling in both directions during the early twentieth century. Despite stepped-up patrols and more thorough inspections at crossing points, the southern border was too enormous to guard effectively. Moreover, the movement of people across the border—the heavy seasonal flow of Mexican agricultural immigrants and the busy daily traffic of local commuters—was essential to the region's economy. The Mexico–US border as a political dividing line had become more salient in theory, but in practice the region around El Paso and elsewhere along the Rio Grande continued to function as an integrated whole.

Still, the events of the first decades of the twentieth century threw the political meanings of the boundary between the two nations into sharp relief. During the Mexican Revolution, El Paso residents had front-row seats for spectating hostilities across the river; revolutionaries, meanwhile, smuggled arms through the city into Mexico. In 1912 and 1913, thousands of Mexicans fled across the border to El Paso in order to escape the violence in Chihuahua.[49] After fighting spilled over the international border into New Mexico, the United States sent its own forces into action. By 1916, much of the US army and the entire National Guard were stationed along the Mexican border, with more than fifty thousand National Guard troops in El Paso alone.[50] World War I intensified the nation's focus on the border. In early 1917, Germany's foreign minister cabled his government's representative in Mexico, proposing a Mexican alliance with Germany. In exchange, Germany would help Mexico regain lands it had lost to the United States seven decades earlier, including Texas, Arizona, and New Mexico.[51] The cable, intercepted by the British and widely published in the American press, heightened fears of enemies invading from the south and indeed helped spur the United States to declare war in April 1917. During the war, the military presence in El Paso grew even greater, as Fort Bliss became a center for troop mobilization. Wartime immigration legislation also served to highlight the border as a crucial site for safeguarding national security. The comprehensive immigration law of 1917, which raised the head tax on immigrants and imposed a literacy test intended to keep out those deemed undesirable by the government, led to higher levels of inspection and enforcement. In 1918, Congress passed its emergency wartime measure requiring that every immigrant have a passport, followed by another measure requiring all "hostile aliens" to get permits for either departures or entries into the nation.[52]

The decade after the war saw a further transformation of the border's image in the public mind. When the passport law was made permanent after the war, the function of the border as a checkpoint was further institutionalized. With the advent of Prohibition in 1920, the Mexico–US border also came to mark the boundary between wet and dry, and border crossing in both directions became a way for Americans to evade the ban on alcohol. Businesses sprang up on the Mexican side to meet the American demand for drink. American tourists flocked to El Paso in order to go have a good time in Ciudad Juarez, whose main street was rumored in the 1920s to have the densest concentration of saloons in the world. Liquor bootleggers, too, crossed the El Paso border to stock up on liquor, sometimes winding up in gun battles with the area US Customs officials.[53]

During the 1920s, the Mexican border's association with illegal immigration also became fixed permanently both in the national imagination and in official practice. By the decade's end, Mexican immigration itself—for so long a central aspect of the region's existence—was being increasingly criminalized. Curiously from the vantage point of the twenty-first century, however, when the link between the Mexican border and illegal Mexican immigration seems self-evident, this latest phase of the border's evolution was spurred in large part by US authorities' reactions to Europeans' illegal immigration during the years after the quota acts. When the first quota law came into force in 1921, government authorities were cautiously confident that they had learned how to control illegal Chinese immigration through Mexico (although Chinese immigration in fact continued). They were only beginning to express concerns about Mexican immigration itself, which had for so long been part of the local landscape, and so integral to the regional economy, that it was largely unregulated.[54] The history of Jewish illegal immigration from Mexico to Texas provides a window onto this era of the border's transformation. It also serves to highlight one stage in the larger effort American Jewish activists made to keep Jews from being associated with illegal immigration.

Once Zielonka made up his mind that Jewish illegal immigration needed to be stopped, he took action. Three weeks after he wrote to Rabbi Henry Cohen of Galveston for advice, Zielonka set out for New York City. He hoped to convince the leaders of national Jewish organizations there that the phenomenon of Jewish illegal immigration from Mexico threatened the good standing of all American Jews. He urged sending social workers to Mexico to convince Jewish migrants to remain there. The New York leaders, however, were cool to the idea. Events on the Texas border in early 1921 did not strike them as urgent. They were more concerned with lobbying against the impending immigration restrictions and coordinating massive relief efforts for Jews in the war-devastated communities of eastern Europe. Some, like Felix Warburg, prominent banker and chairman of the Joint Distribution Committee, worried that stationing a Jewish social worker in Mexico might backfire politically. "The non-Jewish world," he feared, might "proclaim that we have placed a worker there to overcome the American Immigrant Restrictions."[55]

It is not that Jewish organizational leaders had never considered Mexico of interest. The issue of Jewish illegal immigration in potentially great numbers through Mexico to the United States was new for them, but the issue of Jewish immigration *to* Mexico was not. The question of whether European Jews should view Mexico (with a Jewish population by 1921 estimated at under ten thousand) as a land where they could settle had long caused contention both in the international Jewish community and among American Jews.[56] In the late nineteenth and early twentieth centuries, Jewish groups had considered several proposals—none of which they pursued—to undertake large-scale settlement of eastern European Jews on Mexican land. American Jewish groups would return to the issue of Mexico in months and years to come, exploring whether it could serve as an alternative destination for Jewish migrants unable to enter the United States. At the moment, however, they were not interested in acting on Zielonka's ideas. In the end, the New York leaders agreed only that American Jewish groups would cable their workers in European ports to discourage would-be immigrants from attempting the Mexican route.[57]

Zielonka, however, did not see this as a sufficient communal response to the new problem of illicit Jewish border-crossing and persisted in organizing to address it via other means. After returning to Texas, he brought the issue to the spring regional gathering of the International Order of B'nai B'rith (IOBB), in which he was active. With the support of other Texas rabbis and Archibald Marx, a New Orleans contractor and second vice president of the IOBB, Zielonka convinced the IOBB to fund his plan, which was more ambitious than the one he had pitched to the New York leaders. He wanted to help stop Jewish illegal immigration to the United States by making Mexico itself a viable permanent home for Jewish migrants.[58] Over the next several years, he devoted enormous effort to this project. The IOBB helped Zielonka establish a lodging house in Mexico City, where new arrivals received food, medical care, employment advice, and assistance in contacting relatives in the United States. Moreover, IOBB workers made sure to meet every steamship that came into Veracruz, so as to impress upon arriving migrants the dangers of smuggling into the United States and to urge them to remain in Mexico. "Beware of friends who insinuate that they can smuggle you to the American side," read one Yiddish handbill the IOBB distributed to Jews disembarking in Veracruz.[59]

Yet, despite Zielonka's success at launching his Mexico project, it was not all smooth organizational sailing along the way. The IOBB got into scuffles with other Jewish groups over turf and strategy. Archibald Marx became incensed in the summer of 1921, for example, when HIAS decided to investigate the Jewish situation in Mexico after all. "HIAS has mailed a lengthy report to Jewish Press taking credit for what has been done and absolutely ignoring us," he cabled Zielonka on August 30. A few days later he composed an angry letter to HIAS:

> I seriously criticize your Committee [on Mexico] for the wanton waste of money in going to Mexico when you knew that others were there . . . Imagine my surprise when I learned on my return home that the Hias . . . had sent your committee there without advising the President of our Organization who is a member of your Advisory Board of your plan and that your organization had not even taken the trouble to ask what we had done so as not to come in conflict with our work.[60]

At the same time, however, it was clear that HIAS's intercession with the federal authorities on behalf of the Jewish illegal immigrants was probably helpful. Zielonka pointed out to Marx that the Department of Labor, at least in part in response to HIAS's advocacy, agreed that it would allow a hundred fifty Jewish illegal immigrants to return to Mexico instead of deporting them to Europe, which meant that they would not lose the right to enter the United States legally in the future.[61] Perhaps, Zielonka even suggested, "this may give us a clue for the division of labor in this work, leaving the Washington end and the New York end to the other organization."[62] Tensions over organizational relations regarding Jews in Mexico never disappeared, but a division of labor of sorts emerged over time. By the end of January 1922, the president of the IOBB wrote to Marx that, despite some recent "stormy correspondence" with HIAS president John Bernstein, "Mexico now seems to be recognized as our field." In fact, as of 1926, the Emergency Committee for Jewish Refugees, a coalition of Jewish organizations that included HIAS and that was formed to aid the Jewish immigrants stranded by the 1924 quota law (and discussed below), entered into agreement with the IOBB to subsidize its work in Mexico.[63] Tensions aside, the funding agreement suggests that in the end, Zielonka succeeded in making his point to the larger American Jewish organizational community: the work in Mexico was worth doing. Not, however, because most American Jewish leaders believed European Jews should immigrate to Mexico—indeed, the Emergency Committee's commissioned report strongly emphasized that Mexico was too "backwards" to be a good destination for European Jews.[64] Rather, they could agree that Zielonka's Mexican Bureau's work was important because European Jews were crossing the Atlantic in the hopes of reaching the United States. Like Zielonka, leaders of American Jewish organizations believed strongly that it was imperative to keep Jewish illegal immigration from becoming a large-scale phenomenon. Helping Jews in Mexico was crucial to preventing their illegal immigration to the United States.

For their part, government officials in El Paso and Washington paid close attention to the situation. The quota laws reflected the belief that strictly limiting immigration of the less "desirable" races and groups was essential to the nation's well-being. Authorities were thus alarmed at the breach of its borders by those undesirable people. In June 1923, the Bureau of Immigration supervisor in charge of the El Paso district reported that "the number of European aliens arrested in this district annually increases, and the prediction is made that the situation . . . will grow worse instead of better."[65] Officials often expressed particular suspicion of Jewish immigrants, in part because of their longstanding conviction that Jewish agencies were illegally assisting immigration to the United States. In May 1922, for example, the US consul in Antwerp warned the secretary of state that "large convoys of emigrants are forwarded by Jewish relief societies or by steamship agencies directly to Rotterdam or to Liverpool," where they were embarking for Veracruz.[66] Of course, the quota laws were the cause of the sudden influx of Jewish immigrants across the Rio Grande. Although Congress did not pass the quota legislation until May 1921, news of the potentially closing gates had reached Europe earlier, as did the rumor that Mexico was an easy back door into the United States.[67]

The strategy of coming to the United States through Mexico, however, often turned out to be harder than Jewish migrants hoped, even before the quota law went into effect. The new passport requirement, for example, proved to be an obstacle for many young Jewish men who, having fled military service in Poland or Russia, were unable to obtain proper passports from authorities in their home countries. Undocumented, they resorted to surreptitious entry or forgeries. Twenty-six-year-old Naftoli Lederman from Poland, for example, tried to cross into El Paso in early 1921 with a fake passport bought in Berlin. The document was, Zielonka reported, a rather "cheap imitation," with Lederman's photo placed sloppily where the original had been. It aroused the suspicion of US officers on the border, who detained Lederman.[68]

Yet, as Zielonka discovered when he began questioning jailed immigrants, the notion of the permeable border remained an effective marketing ploy for European steamship companies even after the first quota law passed in 1921.[69] Zielonka speculated that foreign governments, too, saw the border as a business opportunity. Issuing papers to immigrants was an easy way to raise revenue. "In Germany," he observed, "the respective consulates of the newly formed governments and republics in eastern Europe have made a tremendous source of income from issuing passports to whomsoever seeks one." Moreover, "the Mexican consulates in Berlin and the port cities of Europe"—who knew perfectly well, he observed, that the migrants were only using Mexico as a waystation to the United States—"are inducing immigrants to sail to Mexico . . . with the sole purpose of receiving a fee of ten dollars a visa."[70]

Throughout Zielonka's efforts to address the issue of illegal immigration, he had to navigate complicated legal issues that even government authorities were hard-pressed to know how to handle. A case Zielonka described as "not different from a great many that come to my attention" illustrates the confusion that the new laws and the resulting Jewish illegal immigration caused among American Jewish communal leaders.[71] It also suggests the range of actors that could get involved in any given case and the challenges Zielonka had in trying to get community leaders elsewhere to fall in line with his own ideas. It is the case of one Shaya Petlin, a young Jewish man who set out, probably some time in 1920 or early 1921, from Poland with his two sisters. All three planned to come to the United States to join their third sister, a Mrs. Mayerson of Dayton, Ohio. Petlin's two sisters arrived safely in Dayton. He himself fared worse. German authorities in Berlin detained him on account of his Polish passport, which was bogus. When he left Germany, it was for Mexico, not the United States as per the original plan. He arrived in June 1921, just as the US quotas came into force, and stayed in Mexico for two months. His worried family in Dayton heard nothing from him until August, when he sent a letter to his sister from jail in El Paso. He had been caught trying to cross the border.

Mrs. Mayerson appealed to the Dayton Jewish Federation for Social Service. This organization, in turn, contacted Zielonka on the advice of Dayton lawyer and IOBB member Sidney Kusworm, asking for his help. It was urgent, they explained; the family was "terribly wrought up." Kusworm added his appeal to theirs. He knew the Petlin case was part of a larger phenomenon of a rise in Jewish illegal immigration. As an IOBB brother, he also knew both that Zielonka was active on the issue and that "many perplexing situations . . . present themselves on account of our co-religionists who are attempting to get in the United States."[72] Kusworm expressed confusion about the legal ins and outs of Petlin's case, as well as apprehension about encouraging the family to do something unlawful. "[Petlin] has written his relatives here for $1000.00," he explained to Zielonka: "He can get out . . . if he pays that sum. I believe this is in the nature of a bribe, and of course if that is the fact, I would not countenance it for a minute." He asked Zielonka to investigate the case and report back to him whether there was any legal way to get Petlin permanently into the United States. He concluded his request by reiterating his desire to stay above the law, saying, "I know that you would not countenance any underhand methods and I certainly feel the same way about it."[73]

In his reply to Kusworm, Zielonka expressed none of the ambivalence he had evinced earlier, perhaps because he thought that sharing such sentiments would be counterproductive. Zielonka wrote to Kusworm that there was no need to investigate further. The situation was clear: Petlin was in the wrong. "I have little if any sympathy with these men who are involving the good name of the American Jewry and who are accomplishing little if anything for themselves," the rabbi wrote, adding, "They are warned against such procedures whenever we get in touch with them." Money, he told Kusworm, would be of no use. "There are some smugglers along the border and there are some attorneys on the border who will make such rash promises," he explained, "but who are unable to make these promises good after they have received their pay." Protesting the arrest was useless, too. The only possible strategy to aid the family, Zielonka said, was to lobby to have Petlin returned to Mexico rather than deported to Europe.[74]

Zielonka had not entirely settled the matter, however. Petlin was released from jail on bond provided by his family and allowed to go to Dayton for a temporary stay. He was, as Zielonka had hoped, granted permission to return to Mexico in lieu of getting deported to Europe. This meant he could potentially enter the United States legally at a later date. But Kusworm and his partner R. B. Shaman, who was serving as Petlin's lawyer, again wrote Zielonka for help navigating the quota laws. They were still uncertain about the boundaries of legality and illegality. "We are rather anxious to know just what crime he is charged with," Shaman wrote, "and what the usual outcome in such a case is. Of course," he added, perhaps unintentionally echoing Zielonka's own language, "we have no sympathy with men who commit these crimes, realizing as we do that they injure the cause for which we are putting forth great effort. Nevertheless, we . . . will have to do the very best we can."[75] Kusworm, for his part, inquired of Zielonka whether there was any way Petlin might legally remain in Dayton. He would not become "a public charge," Kusworm assured the rabbi, invoking one of the main reasons immigrants had been excluded or deported in past years. Petlin's sister was willing to put up a bond for him for the long term. Petlin himself wanted to find employment. "It would seem a shame," wrote Kusworm, "to have him deported." In fact, Kusworm had clearly come to think that perhaps what Petlin had done did not constitute illegality at all. He suggested that the facts of the case might prove Petlin's innocence. "He claims that when he was in Warsaw," Kusworm explained, "he paid some money for a visa of his passport but that the man who took the money turned out to be a fraud, and therefore he came under honest intentions but was taken advantage of in the old Country."[76]

Zielonka was adamant that the origins of Petlin's invalid visa were irrelevant. "He was caught," the rabbi pointed out, "smuggling himself into the United States," which meant that an order of deportation would probably follow. If Petlin had been in possession of a legal passport with proper visas and had presented himself for inspection by immigration officials at the border but been refused entrance, then it would have been possible to appeal to the State Department and possibly have Petlin admitted on bond.[77] As it was, however, Zielonka maintained, the best case scenario remained Petlin's return to Mexico.

Zielonka may have simply been motivated by the desire to be practical. In March 1921 a number of Jewish immigrants arrived at Ellis Island from Poland with fake passports they seem to have acquired in good faith. They were deported despite the intercession of the American Jewish Committee and HIAS.[78] Zielonka likely knew this and thus decided that Petlin had little chance of finding merit in official eyes. At times, however, Zielonka seems to have resolved his initial ambivalence by deciding that illegal immigration was clearly wrong. "As an American I have little sympathy with the men who are arrested on the border for endeavoring to enter illegally," he wrote Kusworm in one letter, adding sternly, "As a Jew I have still less sympathy for them. It is not a question," he insisted, "as to whether the law is right or wrong, the fact remains that it is the law of our land and as such it must be obeyed."[79] Indeed, he expressed the notion that border crossing itself was evidence of guilt. "The very fact that [Petlin] came via Mexico," Zielonka informed the Dayton contingent, "instead of the nearest and quickest port, New York, is evidence that he could not have legally entered at the other port."[80]

Still, Zielonka continued to view illegal immigration as qualitatively different from other forms of lawbreaking. He conceded to Shaman that Petlin had "committed no crime from an ethical standpoint." He also saw most of the recent Jewish border crossers as different from immigrants deemed excludable under the older laws—paupers, prostitutes, anarchists, and others. He took a stand to this effect in 1925, when he wrote the secretary of labor on behalf of a young woman named Riva Zarecas, who had been apprehended for crossing the border illegally. "The county jail," Zielonka wrote, "is no fit place for a decent young lady to be confined, for she is confined with dope fiends and women of that character. I know that she has broken one of the laws of this government but she has not broken a moral law and she ought not be confined with moral lepers."[81] Zielonka's description of Zarecas as "a decent young lady" who had broken no "moral law" implied that she was no prostitute or drug addict, but rather a respectable young woman who made an unfortunate choice.

In contrast to his inclination to intervene for illegal immigrants whom he found to be deserving, Zielonka was absolutely unwilling to advocate for Jewish border crossers who seemed legally suspect in ways beyond their mode of immigration. An example is Percy Menkin, who was arrested in Marfa, Texas, in 1925. Menkin's uncle, a rabbi in Lebanon, Pennsylvania, contacted Zielonka to ask for his assistance in the case. He also contacted HIAS and at least one other rabbi in Texas, who then forwarded his appeals to Zielonka.[82] Menkin, Zielonka informed HIAS, did not deserve help with his case. The young man had apparently tried several times already to enter the United States from Canada, where he had spent time in jail, and he had admitted to the immigration authorities (though not, it seems, to his uncle the rabbi) that he was a long-time member of the radical Industrial Workers of the World, one of the groups targeted in the government's deportation sweeps of 1919. The authorities described Menkin to Zielonka as "one of the meanest customers" they had come across.[83] "You realize . . . ," Zielonka wrote his colleague in Dallas, whom Menkin's uncle had also tried to enlist in his nephew's cause, "that we cannot be over-enthusiastic in seeking help for this man."[84] In addition to disapproving of the young man's radicalism, the rabbi thought Menkin's immigration history suggested unapologetic recidivism. "Even if he was returned to Mexico he probably would try to get in again," Zielonka wrote. Nevertheless, even though Zielonka refused to advocate for Menkin, he was willing to extend to him the same material charity other Jewish cases were shown. While in jail, Menkin received, as Zielonka informed the man's anxious uncle, "a pair of pants, three pairs of socks, two suits of underwear, a shirt, a cap and a complete shaving outfit, consisting of soap, razor, etc."[85]

Zielonka's notions of legality and morality, as well as his ideas about who merited aid, shaped his own practices of advocacy and doubtless influenced the actions of many others who worked with him on the Mexican Bureau project or turned to him for advice on immigration matters. However, his views did not always mesh with those of other American Jews. In spring 1921, for example, government officials in Texas noticed with dismay that Jews, such as those of Laredo's IOBB Lodge, were posting bond for Jewish illegal immigrants; Zielonka also found himself at odds sometimes with family members of illegal immigrants. The rabbi did encounter Jewish families who disapproved strongly of their relatives' plans to immigrate illegally to the United States. But family members could also feel otherwise. In 1923, for example, Shaya Petlin's sister Mrs. Mayerson returned to the offices of the Dayton Jewish Federation for Social Services "beside herself with grief and worry," according to the agency's report, after Petlin had run into trouble on the border again. She was unapologetic for her brother's border hopping. She knew it was illegal but refused to see it as criminal. "She says," explained the letter from the agency's staff person to Zielonka, "her brother is guilty of no crime excepting the wish to come to his family."[86] Zielonka had to contend with such communal responses as he dealt with individual cases. His view of legality did not always prevail within American Jewish communities, any more than the IOBB's warnings to Jewish immigrants in Mexico guaranteed that they would not attempt to smuggle themselves over the US border. This fact, in turn, may have pushed him to taking a particularly hard line when advising other American Jews what to do about illegal immigration.

There are some provocative absences in the extensive documentary record Rabbi Zielonka left. The larger story about immigration in this region remains invisible in these sources. One would never know from his correspondence and reports, in other words, that, while European immigration at the Mexican border helped shape the popular vision of the border as synonymous with illegality, it was *Mexican* immigration that was becoming the most contentious border-related issue, as noted earlier. During the late nineteenth and early twentieth centuries, US officials never exerted much effort in trying to control Mexican immigration. Although a new head tax and literacy test were instituted in 1917, Mexicans—who provided much-needed labor—were exempt from these measures until after the war.[87] After the war, big southwestern agricultural and industrial employers, long dependent on Mexican labor, fought successfully to keep Congress from including the Western hemisphere in the quota system. Mexicans were, they argued, seasonal migrants who returned regularly to Mexico and thus not threatening to American society as were other "inferior" immigrants. Thus, no numerical restriction was placed on Mexican immigration.

By 1921, however, the official processes of immigration over the Mexico–US border had changed, as authorities now subjected all immigrants to the head tax and literacy test. The quota laws, moreover, had ushered in a new era of immigration control. Officials now srcutinized all immigrants' documents more carefully. Accordingly, more Mexicans opted to enter the United States illegally so as to avoid the expensive and onerous process.[89] Meanwhile, many contemporary lawmakers, government officials, and anti-immigration activists found it unacceptable that immigration should continue so freely over the nation's southern border. Over the course of the decade, immigration restrictionists pushed hard for extending the quotas to the Western Hemisphere.[90] Many contended that Mexican immigration was at least as racially and culturally undesirable as Jewish, Slavic, or Italian immigration, if not more so.[91] By way of compromise between the wealthy southwestern employers and the restrictionist camp, the US government adopted indirect means of trying to limit Mexican immigration, urging American consuls in Mexico to be sparing in issuing their visas. This, together with the stricter controls at the border itself, spurred more Mexicans to cross the border illegally. Meanwhile, the Border Patrol, which in its early years had focused on apprehending Europeans, by the last years of the decade increasingly turned its attention to Mexicans. Apprehensions and deportations of Mexicans who entered illegally increased rapidly.[92] By 1931, when the IOBB's Mexican Bureau ceased its work, there was still significant concern about illegal European immigration over the Mexican border and elsewhere. However, the Mexico–US border had clearly become a place where the phenomenon of illegal immigration seemed linked primarily to Mexicans themselves. This shaped perceptions not only of Mexican newcomers but also of Mexicans throughout the Southwest, who were viewed by Americans as trespassers on land that had historically been part of Mexico.[93]

Zielonka, involved for many years in the affairs of his border city and in immigration matters, doubtless grasped that the meaning of border crossing was changing. He certainly must have followed the debates over immigration in Congress. The presence of the Border Patrol and the stepped-up scrutiny of border crossers, as well as the gradual criminalization of Mexican immigration, would not have escaped him. His investment in maintaining the appearance of Jewish immigrants, and American Jewish communities, as conscientiously law abiding, was forged in this context. For Rabbi Zielonka, the stakes in dissociating Jews from illegal immigration must have become vividly clear. Jewish immigrants—and the Jewish communities to which they came—should not share the fate of Mexicans in the United States.

STRANDED JEWS

The mood was reportedly grim on that June day in 1924 when the hundred twenty-seven representatives of Jewish organizations gathered in the Hotel Astor to consider the plight of the thousands of Jewish migrants stranded in Europe by the new immigration quotas. "All hearts were heavy with grief," reported the Yiddish daily *Forverts* (Forward) in its front-page coverage of the conference. "All heads bowed under this new misfortune that has befallen the Jewish masses across the ocean. Speaker after speaker declared this the biggest crisis for Jews in centuries."[94] Conferees labored to formulate strategies. By the day's end, they had formed the Emergency Committee on Jewish Refugees (ECJR), to be headed by Louis Marshall. The JDC, HIAS, and the NCJW were to play leading roles on the ECJR, and the other Jewish organizations present that day agreed to be a part of it as well.[95] For the next few years, the ECJR worked to get the visa-holding migrants out of limbo. It negotiated with the United States and other governments to admit the migrants and sent delegations to research feasible alternative destinations for them, such as Mexico.

At some level, the plight of the exiled, persecuted Jews whom the ECJR planned to help was familiar in a mythic sense, a match for the old image of

Jewish diasporic wandering. The migrants' situation was also familiar from more recent reports of Jewish war refugees' hardships. Nevertheless, the stranded migrants' situation also reflected a historic shift in the meaning of Jewish migration. American Jewish organizations understood that the Immigration Act of 1924 fundamentally altered the dynamics of international migration and that Jews abroad would suffer. As the National Council of Jewish Women observed in a newsletter article about the crisis, "America has unwittingly invented a new kind of misery."[96] The 1921 temporary quota law was harsh, but even in the three years of its operation 1,539,371 immigrants, 153,232 of them Jews, were able to enter the United States legally.[97] The quotas established by the Immigration Act of 1924 were much smaller than those implemented by the earlier law, and this time the restrictions were permanent. Those waiting abroad for what they had hoped would be the annual "opening of the quota" were in trouble.

The stranded migrants, caught by the new law between Europe and the United States were, at one level, a humanitarian disaster. At another level, their predicament became a collective question mark for American Jewish leaders, who were forced by the situation to grapple in new ways with their roles as part of an international community. The plights of the Jewish migrants who were being kept from completing their journey from Europe to the United States highlighted the ways that the difficulties immigrants encountered with US law were being pushed abroad. From American Jewish leaders' perspective, what united the situations of these Jews trapped in Bremen, Hamburg, Cherbourg, Southampton, Rotterdam, Danzig, Constantinople, and Riga was that all these people were poised to leave for the United States but could not. These port cities abroad became, ideologically speaking, quasi-American border zones. This shift complicated questions of responsibility and strategy for American Jews advocating on behalf of Jewish migrants.

The group of stranded migrants whose cases the ECJR took up represented a gray area, a liminal realm of "in between" legality created by the new law. Indeed, their predicament called into question the very meaning of "immigrants" and "legality." What and who, precisely, was a legal immigrant? It is telling that the stranded migrants appear in the committee's records under an array of terms. They are variously referred to as refugees, transmigrants, emigrants, immigrants, stranded emigrants, stranded immigrants, and aliens. This proliferation of terminology suggests how complicated it was to pin down these migrants' relationship to the United States or other nations. It was unclear, in other words, whether they were most defined by their homelands, their strandedness, or their intended destination. It was unclear whether they were potential illegal immigrants or, by contrast, essentially legal immigrants marooned abroad by a legal technicality. Jewish organizations advocating for these migrants were on strange legal ground. Any argument on their behalf had to be conducted somewhat in the realm of hypotheticals and questions without precedent: if the US government made an exception for this group, what might the implications be for the administration of the new law? Should the visas that the migrants already held entitle them to passage to the United States? Was the US government itself in a kind of violation of papers?

Although such issues were different from those Zielonka faced in his work with illegal immigration over the Mexico–US border, the ECJR also confronted similar problems, too. Like Zielonka, the American Jewish leaders who responded to the issue of the stranded migrants saw it as vital not to run afoul, or appear to run afoul, of US law, however much they disagreed with that law. Rather, they tried to craft an advocacy strategy based on taking a compromise path between protest and accommodation, a strategy that would remain key for them in their work on Jewish migration issues throughout the interwar years. But just because the ECJR was walking a fine line in its challenge to US authorities does not mean that its efforts were insignificant. The numbers of migrants involved were relatively small, but their case took on symbolic meaning. The history of the ECJR demonstrates the intense efforts that Jewish leaders devoted not only to aiding Jewish migrants in trouble but also to trying to define the meaning of Jewish immigration in the era of restrictive quotas. Those American Jews working on the stranded migrants' cases sometimes privately expressed their misgivings about those migrants' choices, characters, and intentions. Publicly, however, American Jewish leaders argued that the stranded migrants should be seen as legal, deserving, future American citizens. Whatever happened with the migrants themselves, their predicament proved an opportunity to contest some of the assumptions about Jews that underlay the quota laws.

The crisis of the stranded migrants had its roots in earlier events: it was the international version of a recurring problem that the 1921 quota law had caused, a problem on which many American Jewish organizations had cut their teeth on the issue of quasi-illegal immigration. The 1921 legislation specified that a maximum of 20 percent of the quota for a given country could be filled each month. In the years between 1921 and 1924, this policy led to an absurd situation. Subject to fines for each immigrant deemed ineligible to enter, steamship companies were anxious not to arrive with a shipload of immigrants above the quota. At the very end of each month, ships packed with immigrants hovered outside the ports—especially New York City, but elsewhere as well.

At midnight on the first of the month, the ships made a mad race for shore so as to get their cargo into the United States within the quota. Inevitably, this led to administrative confusion.[98] Thousands of immigrants, including Poles, Hungarians, Greeks, and Jews, ended up in a legal limbo as a result of arriving too late, sometimes by only an hour, for the month's quota. Controversy arose as to whether such immigrants should be excluded and returned to the ports from which they had come. Along with other immigrant advocates, Jewish groups argued that, by lobbying lawmakers and bringing court cases, these immigrants should be allowed to stay.[99] They contested the notion that these late arrivals made the immigrants excludable. In other words, American Jewish leaders fought to define all these arrivals as legal and thus admissible, despite the fact that the new law might seem to decree otherwise.

The American Jewish Committee's Louis Marshall, for example, argued that the government's policy was not only arbitrary and unfair, but illegal. In December 1921, he wrote to the secretary of labor in defense of six hundred immigrants from Poland who had arrived in New York at the end of November, after the month's quota had been filled. It was an outrage, he insisted, that "people who sought lawfully to come to the United States, who were provided with passports and visas, who are presumptively able to comply with the requirements of the Immigration Law, are condemned to deportation, simply because they entered the port a few days or a few hours before other people who arrived subsequent to the 1st of December at the same port." This, he argued, could not be said to reflect the will of the American citizenry or the intent of lawmakers. "I believe that I sufficiently understand the American people and their representatives in Congress," he wrote, "to venture the assertion that nobody who voted for the Act of May 19, 1921, ever contemplated so monstrous a consequence as that which has been asserted in the ruling of Mr. Husband [the commissioner general of immigration]. It is contrary to common sense and fair play."[100]

Moreover, Marshall pointed out, the law was being applied differently to people who came in different months, which ran counter to the principle that laws applied equally to all. "Under precisely the same circumstances as those to which I have called your attention people who arrived in the latter part of October were admitted and their admission was charged against the quota for November. Why, then," he asked, "should not the same rule apply now?" Indeed, he argued:

> The very fact of admitting the latter has brought about the result of crowding out those who arrived in accordance with the quota assigned for that

month. And yet Mr. Husband is seeking to charge these unfortunate men, women and children with negligence because they left Poland to come to the United States in reliance upon their passports and visas, upon the information given by the Department of Labor.[101]

The outcomes of court challenges indicate that the judiciary sometimes agreed that the administration's position on these late-arriving immigrants was of questionable legality. In at least one instance, a test case brought on behalf of a Greek immigrant in this situation was decided for the government.[102] However, another ruling in 1923 determined that government miscalculations of the quota meant that detained immigrants—at least those who had not already been deported—must be allowed to enter the United States.[103]

The authorities were put on the defensive by the swirling controversy. They often seemed confused or ambivalent themselves about the boundaries of legal immigration. On a few occasions, they simply relented, admitting aliens at least temporarily.[104] At other times, they claimed that in fact it was the limits of their power that kept them from making determinations in the immigrants' favor. They agreed with immigrant advocates that immigrants who came in excess of the month's quota might not be criminals. Rather, these immigrants were unfortunate casualties of the impersonal workings of the law passed by Congress. But by the same token, the law stood, and there was nothing the officials charged with enforcing the law could do. In a letter to Congressman Emmanuel Celler of New York, who had written in support of admitting the immigrants in question, the assistant secretary of labor expressed this position:

> The Department fully understands that no fault attaches to these aliens because of their arrival in excess of quota. . . . I am very sorry that so much hardship must come to these people, and wish that I could see my way clear to alleviate it, but the law being what it is it is quite impossible for the Department to issue instructions to permit these several hundred aliens to land merely because it was through no fault of their own that they did not arrive here earlier.[105]

Despite the efforts of Jewish and other ethnic organizations, many of the immigrants who arrived in excess of quota during these years were deported.

The 1924 law produced similar controversies, but these were even more complicated. The law's effect was to move such issues into the international arena, from US ports to ports abroad. This is not to say that the law clarified questions about legality and immigration status on the domestic front, but rather that it pushed these questions onto European territory as well. Indeed, many of those Jews stranded in European ports during 1924 represented a backlog of the earlier law, either because they had been among those sent back since 1921 as excess quota immigrants or because they had never been allowed to embark for the United States in the first place, but had instead been waiting in the ports for months or years for the quota to open. The internationalization of immigration conundrums was also a consequence of the fact that the 1924 law made Europe into a theater of what Aristide Zolberg has dubbed "remote control" US immigration policy operations.[106] When legislators crafted the legislation, they sought to eliminate the monthly chaos in American ports and ensure that all arriving foreigners would be thoroughly prescreened. The 1924 law thus specified that investigation and inspection of immigrants, along with the granting of visas, would now be in the hands of US officials abroad, rather than a matter to be handled at Ellis Island or other American points of entry.

All this combined to produce the situation in the early summer of 1924 that brought Jewish organizations to their meeting at the Hotel Astor: a migratory traffic jam as the law tightened. In the United States, Jewish organizations were bombarded with queries about what to do for relatives overseas.[107] Abroad, Jewish migrants became desperate at the news of the new regulations, besieging aid organizations and American consulates with requests for help getting to the United States.[108] American Jewish leaders agreed that the situation was dire enough to call for an organized, public, collective response. The ECJR they formed was an umbrella group. Its letterhead reflected the range of organizations included officially, but in practice it was led by those groups most experienced in dealing with Jewish immigration and European Jewish communities: HIAS, the NCJW, the JDC, and the American Jewish Committee. A small executive group met regularly in New York to coordinate fundraising efforts, investigations, and disbursal of funds. The committee became involved with Jews stranded in Cuba as well as those in Europe, and in 1926 began to fund Zielonka's Mexican Bureau. The work with Jewish migrants in Europe, however, engaged the bulk of the committee's energies.

Louis Marshall served as the group's chair and, as on so many issues, became its most public spokesperson. He was articulate, respected, knowledgeable, and well connected in high government circles and the Republican Party, and the operations of the ECJR were very much shaped by his particular ideas about strategy, Jewish obligation, and activism. Those operations were carried out on various fronts. The committee set out to raise money from American

Jews, employing expertise honed during the war. In September 1924, it announced its goal at a fairly modest (compared to Jewish organizations' vast wartime fundraising efforts) but still substantial figure of half a million dollars. The committee expressed the hope that American Jews would "offer the hand of cooperation to those unhappy homeless Jewish brothers and sisters . . . whose need is an inescapable summons to duty on the part of all American Israel."[109] It sent out letters to Jewish leaders nationwide, pleading the urgency and magnitude of the migrants' cause: "Of all the tragedies that have overtaken our people since 1914," the letters said, "this is one of the worst . . . Won't you . . . respond quickly . . . so that this new chapter of Jewish agony will end?"[110]

Meanwhile, the committee tried to determine solutions to the migrants' problems. Against the possibility that the United States would refuse them entry, the committee explored other prospects: repatriation to the migrants' home countries, for example, or visas to Canada, Argentina, or Mexico. Simultaneously, the committee lobbied Congress to admit those migrants who held US visas. Marshall crafted his arguments for this option cautiously. If the ECJR sought to persuade American Jews at large that the migrants were helpless brethren suffering from a crisis of massive proportion, Congress, Marshall believed, needed to hear a different message. The Congress that had passed the 1924 law was in no mood to be generous toward the very eastern Europeans it had voted to exclude.

In forcefully written letters to lawmakers and in Congressional testimony on behalf of a resolution to admit the migrants, Marshall made his case. He appealed to lawmakers on humanitarian grounds. "What will become of these people if they are not admitted to the United States?" asked one Congressman during Marshall's testimony. "God knows," Marshall answered, adding, "Nobody can prophesy what will happen, except there is one certainty, speedy death."[111] At the same time as he impressed upon lawmakers the issue's urgency, however, he also argued that the number of migrants was so small as to be "quite unimportant," an unfortunate loose end left in the "twilight zone" of an administrative error, namely American consuls' act of issuing visas that the United States would no longer recognize. The United States should do the honorable thing: "clear the books" of these errors.[112] Such action would not, he implied, change or undermine the fundamental structure of the new law. Furthermore, he argued that these migrants, with their "pioneer spirit" and "exceptional intelligence and excellent character," had the potential to become exemplary Americans.

Marshall also argued that Congress should address the stranded migrants' situation because the issue was a specifically American one, caused by a contradiction the US government had created by issuing visas and then passing a law that invalidated those same visas. The migrants stuck in Europe possessed legitimate papers. Marshall conceded that visas did not guarantee admission to the United States, but his arguments implied that that they did represent a stamp of honorary Americanness and were an indication that representatives of the US government had already deemed the migrants worthy of admission—that the migrants were, then, really potential Americans in transit. The visas might not exactly signify a legal obligation on the part of the US government, but they did, Marshall argued, signify a "moral" one.[113] Furthermore, Marshall emphasized his own standing, and that of other ECJR members, as American citizens. "[W]e feel," he told the Congressional committee, "that we have a right as American citizens to come here and say that there is an obligation" to admit the migrants.[114]

In his lobbying, Marshall also took care to describe the migrants in terms that resonated with contemporary American arguments about the importance of an activist approach to social welfare. Rather than argue, for example, that the migrants were a persecuted ethnic minority in their homelands, he stressed that the migrants were members of families torn asunder by the new law. Admitting them to the United States would not be detrimental to the nation but would actually strengthen the American social fabric by reuniting families. Marshall also invoked American social reformers' warnings about the ill fates that could befall young girls left on their own, pointing out (though he avoided the charged term "white slavery") that the young female migrants "are exposed to every moral danger."[115]

Emphasizing the migrants' identities as family members and helpless young women also served to de-emphasize the migrants' identities as potential workers. Immigrant family members might strengthen the social fabric, but immigrant workers, labor groups who had lobbied hard for restriction had argued, were cheap labor who undermined American workers and should be excluded. Moreover, casting the migrants as families, not workers, and underscoring their citizenship potential had racial implications in the context of battles over restrictive immigration policies. As chapter 1 noted, the 1924 law applied to southern and eastern Europeans, albeit in less drastic form, group-based immigration restrictions of a sort that had until then been reserved for Asian immigrants, whom white workers had fought to exclude as un-American "coolie labor." Asian immigrants, considered unassimilable, were denied the right to become American citizens, and—in a legislative catch-22—Asians were then excluded from immigrating on the basis of being nonnaturalizable. Marshall's argument was thus an oblique (though not necessarily conscious) act of distancing Jewish immigrants from the category of inadmissible Asians.[116] That Jewish labor groups like the United Hebrew Trades and the Amalgamated Clothing Workers Union were part of the ECJR likely added some credibility to Marshall's argument, as did, no doubt, the fact that Samuel Gompers, head of the powerful and restrictionist American Federation of Labor, came out in favor of admitting the stranded migrants.[117]

This is not to say that such arguments and language were purely strategic or purely in the service of a cynical public relations effort. Internal correspondence and policies make it clear that committee members really did worry about the migrants as divided families and women in danger.[118] And when Marshall's rhetoric implicitly grouped eastern European Jews with whites, he was not inventing this identification for lobbying purposes. The committee's internal reports suggest an understanding of Jews as unambiguously European and also as "white," at least in the sense of being deeply different from Asians, Africans, and indigenous North Americans. Mexico, for example, struck committee investigators as too racially primitive for Jews, inhabited as it was by "illiterate, impoverished indigenes who are without any desire to accommodate themselves to what we term western civilization."[119] In a similar vein, the NCJW's Cecelia Razovsky, who was on the ECJR's subcommittee to investigate Cuba, noted that the hard labor of cutting sugar cane there was suitable for Chinese and Negro laborers but not for European Jews.[120]

Government officials were not convinced either of the stranded migrants' deservingness or of the trustworthiness of the American Jewish activists lobbying on the migrants' behalf. The ECJR's efforts elicited mixed reactions from the US government. Some officials expressed deep suspicion. Assistant Secretary of Labor E. J. Henning, for example, wrote to the secretary of labor that he had thoroughly investigated the situation. He claimed to have attended the "International Hebrew Conference on Emigration and Immigration" in Rome during the summer of 1924. (There was in fact a conference of international governments convened by the Italian government, which Henning attended in his official capacity.) He reported that he was lobbied there on behalf of the migrants, whom he described as "more than eighteen thousand Jews" with passports and visas.[121] Henning, whose characterization of the conference as "International Hebrew" and inflation of the number of Jewish migrants involved suggest the central and negative role he ascribed to Jewish organizations in the international migration arena, was convinced the migrants themselves were to blame. "One great cause that brought about this situation," he wrote, "is the feeling in so many countries in Europe that the United States is common property of all the world, and that all the world has a right to come here and, accordingly, they refuse to take seriously the provisions of our law or the warnings issued by us."[122] Henning particularly resisted the idea that reuniting families was a central issue for the migrants. Family members had enough preference under the quota, he thought, to ensure that they would be reunited quickly, and thus the family bonds to which Marshall and other advocates for the stranded Jewish migrants alluded were largely fictional. There "is much complaint," he wrote, "because at times cousins several times removed, uncles, aunts and distant relatives cannot come to each other. Careful investigation has shown that these distant relatives knew very little of each other in the country of their birth and rarely lived in the same communities."[123]

According to Louis Marshall, others in the government, including President Coolidge and William Husband, the commissioner general of immigration, expressed more sympathy toward the stranded migrants. Indeed, Marshall believed that the congressional resolution to admit the migrants came close to passing. Restrictionists in Congress, however, wanted to make passage of the resolution contingent on the success of an extremely harsh deportation bill. This, Marshall observed, "would have led to a worse tragedy than the one which we were seeking to ameliorate."[124] Thus outmaneuvered, supporters of the resolution never succeeded in getting it passed.

Legislative activism on the migrants' behalf was a very different enterprise than actually aiding them. The migrants' cases were far less straightforward than Marshall and others made them out to be in their public appeals. Symbolically, they might be worthy future citizens of the United States trapped by an unjust glitch in US law, but, in actuality, they were caught up in a welter of international complications. Marshall and the ECJR, in appeals to fellow Jews and to lawmakers, described the migrants as a unified group with a common problem. As all the American Jewish organizations involved quickly realized, however, the stranded migrants' situations varied widely from city to city and from case to case. Indeed, the range of problems was so complex, the migrants so geographically dispersed, and the news from Europe so jumbled that for the first several months the members of the ECJR themselves found it difficult to get a picture of the situation clear enough to let them figure out whom they would help and how. "America has been informed about the number of emigrants in Europe differently by different sources," the Joint Distribution Committee's Bernhard Kahn told leaders of European Jewish organizations in February 1925, when they met to discuss the ECJR's work.[125]

Once the organizations pooled their information, a clearer picture of the situation emerged. The demographic snapshot the committee used in its publicity efforts was somewhat accurate. The migrants were indeed in dire straits. The records indicate that many did have US visas, and that many were wives, young women, and children headed to male relatives in the United States. But this was not the whole story. Throughout fall 1924 and early 1925, the ECJR invoked round figures of eight or ten thousand Jewish migrants stuck in ports.[126] In early 1925, however, the JDC's Bernhard Kahn wrote from Europe to give his colleagues a detailed report of the migrants' plight. He divided what he calculated to be about seven thousand Jewish migrants into two groups. There were about thirty-five hundred who actually seemed to have obtained American visas before the 1924 law rendered these defunct (some of these were people who had made it to the United States after 1921 but been sent back due to the monthly quota). There were another thirty-five hundred who had never gotten visas and thus, given the new quota law, were much less likely to obtain them now. The first group, he explained, was further subdivided into two categories: those who had already reached port cities such as Bremen, Southampton, Danzig, and Constantinople, and others who were not actually in ports, but rather in "transit countries," in cities such as Warsaw, Berlin, and Kishinev. The status of the second group—those without visas—was similarly complicated. Half consisted of those "on the borderline between emigrants and refugees," who had long been trying to get visas to the United States. The other half consisted of what the organizations saw as the most pitiful but the least likely to ever reach the United States, people "who have fled Russia and taken refuge in the neighbouring countries, without knowing what they would finally do in these countries."[127]

In other words, although ECJR lobbying and publicity efforts glossed over such distinctions, this was not simply a great stream of migrants holding US visas. Furthermore, not all the migrants were "merely" dependent family members—wives, children, and girls. Detailed records from the German ports of Bremen and Hamburg, which the German Hilfsverein der Deutschen Juden provided the ECJR, show that many migrants were in fact traveling in complete family groupings.[128] Moreover, some of the migrants were young working men on their own, similar to those turning up on the Mexico–US border, though apparently with the right kind of papers—real or fake—to allow them to travel the more usual route.

It is understandable that the ECJR did not mount a fundraising or political campaign based on the complications the law caused for European

Jewish migrants and the organizations that tried to help them. This would not have helped Louis Marshall make his argument, for example, that the US government bore a moral responsibility to admit the stranded migrants. On the ground, however, such complexities mattered. After all, the migrants' legal status was as much a matter of where the migrants were at the moment as of their relation to the United States immigration law. In other words, legal status was a category that had to be calculated in an international context. Migrants in different places and positions were in a range of relationships to different nations' laws. Indeed, some were better off than the ECJR suggested, thanks to certain countries' laws. In certain places, for example, the law required shipping companies for which migrants held tickets to pay for those migrants' upkeep—this was the case in Germany, Holland, and England. And in some locations, such as Antwerp, migrants were granted permission to work for money, while in others they could not. Depending on the law where they were, then, some migrants were more destitute, and thus more dependent on aid from relatives or organizations, than others.

In Latvia, for example, where many of those Jewish migrants with US visas were clustered, the organizations' tasks were made more complicated by local regulations that rendered the migrants marginal and left them little legal recourse. In a 1926 report on the situation, the JDC's Werner Senator explained that the shipping companies in Latvia were not required to pay for the migrants' room and board. On the contrary, the migrants, required to stay in and pay for lodgings run by the shipping companies, were racking up debts they had no way of paying. Even migrants who obtained new visas under the 1924 act were being held back from departing if they had unpaid debts to the shipping companies.[129] Moreover, the migrants in Latvia were subject to a tax of five dollars per person per month. "In case this tax is not paid, the emigrants are threatened with expulsion to Russia," Senator explained.[130] To make matters more complicated, as Senator pointed out, that very tax was due to a contract Jewish organizations had brokered with Latvia on behalf of migrants, many of whom had come to Latvia from Soviet Russia to get visas because the United States, having broken off diplomatic relations with Russia in 1917, had no consul in the USSR. The migrants—or "transmigrants," as they were called in this case, given their intention to stay in Latvia only long enough to get their visas—had been crossing the border surreptitiously, breaking laws of both the Soviet Union and Latvia, and Jewish organizations stepped in to convince the Latvian government to let them remain.[131]

Just as the migrants' legal relationships to the United States and the countries where they were stuck varied, so too did their relationships to a third set of places, namely, those to which migrants might consider going next. Repatriation presented legal difficulties for all those migrants, for example, who had left the Soviet Union without passports and thus were in violation of the law there.[132] And meanwhile, despite some initial hope that Argentina and Canada might take many of the migrants, both destinations proved difficult. The French branch of the international Jewish Colonization Association (ICA), which had a history of helping send Jewish migrants to Argentina, hoped that "all healthy persons able to perform hard work" among the stranded migrants—except single women—would be permitted to go there. In the end, however, the Argentinian government decreed that only certain categories of people, such as "agricultural laborers, electrical engineers, [and] mechanic[s]" would be admitted.[133] Canada, meanwhile, was denying visas to the stranded migrants because of an agreement with the US government. "These emigrants," Senator reported the Canadian government reasoned, "could not be considered bona fide emigrants; rather are they looked upon with suspicion, using Canada only for the purpose of crossing the borders to the States illegally."[134] Thus, the migrants' desire to come to the United States was regarded as itself a potentially criminalizing force. Ironically, this logic ran exactly counter to the argument Louis Marshall tried to make when he pled the case of these worthy would-be pioneers to the US government.

The migrants' situation thus produced difficult questions about the migrants' legal status vis-à-vis multiple nations. This aspect of their predicament also raised difficult questions about American Jewish responsibility. Poised in international no-man's land, these European Jews needed advocacy and aid, but whose? Which of the international Jewish communities and organizations should be responsible for which of the migrants? Marshall and the ECJR argued forcefully to American lawmakers that the migrants represented a particularly American problem. Behind-the-scenes discussions, however, suggest that in practice American Jewish leaders were much less sure what their responsibilities should be toward Jews abroad affected by the new laws, starting with the stranded migrants, the group most on the front lines of this issue. The cases of the stranded migrants presented more international problems, for example, than the ones Zielonka faced in his work with the IOBB Mexican Bureau. It was hardly practical to imagine working on the issue unilaterally.

From the European Jewish organizations' perspective, meanwhile, the stranded migrants were part of a much larger problem of hundreds of thousands of displaced Jews in difficult straits around eastern Europe. Mindful of the European Jewish groups' preoccupation with the larger refugee crisis around them, Bernhard Kahn felt obliged to explain the ECJR's position to the leaders of the various American and European Jewish organizations with whom he met in Berlin in February 1925. "In my opinion," he told them, "we can reckon with American help for *only* those people suffering through the harshness of the American law—those whom have been done an injustice by America, so to speak." That is, American Jewish leaders wanted to be responsible primarily for those Jewish migrants entangled most directly with the US quota laws.

Even regarding the European Jews stranded by the change in US law, however, American Jewish organizations felt that the burden should not be theirs alone. From the beginning of the crisis, the Americans, even while they hoped Congress and American Jews would step in with legislative and financial support, also wanted European Jewish groups to accept some of the moral and fiscal responsibility for the migrants on their territory. In a lengthy letter to the ICA in September 1924, Louis Marshall said as much. "[The migrants] are not in the United States; nor is it possible, to our great regret," he wrote, making no mention of the prospect that there might be a Congressional remedy for the crisis, "that they can come to our country because of our recent immigration laws, which have made that impossible." Marshall wrote that American Jews had "done all in their power to maintain the open door and . . born cheerfully and without complaint whatever burden was attendant upon immigration. It is, however," he argued, "as much the concern of the I[CA] and of the various Jewish organizations of France, England, Belgium and Germany, as it is that of American Jewry."[135]

But transatlantic cooperation among Jewish organizations proved difficult. Despite the talk of international Jewish solidarity so crucial to the ECJR's resolution and fundraising appeals, the American groups felt constantly stymied by the Europeans' internal turf wars. "My investigation on the emigration question was delayed by the jealousies of different societies in Europe," reported Bernhard Kahn from Europe in early 1925.[136] The American organizations found the ICA, in particular, unreliable at best. Communications about the group were filled with exasperation. "We have been trying for some time past to ascertain the precise facts relating to the sending of immigrants to Canada and the relations of ICA to that work," wrote Marshall in one acerbic letter in 1924, "and we must confess that the more we investigate the situation the more confusing it is."[137] Even worse than the ICA's vagueness about its negotiations with Canada were the rumors of its involvement in illegal activities connected with the stranded migrants. In fall 1924, the New York–based Yiddish paper *Morgn zhurnal* (Morning Journal) reported that the ICA was likely trafficking in Canadian visas that it had secured for Jewish immigrants in Romania.

The trafficking appears to have been in fact carried out not by officials of the ICA but rather by an intermediary between the organization and someone indirectly connected to the Canadian Department of Labor. Nevertheless, to Marshall the affair suggested a dangerous sloppiness. "I have been very greatly disturbed by rumors . . . with regard to the methods pursued in connection with the admission of Jewish immigrants into the Dominion," he wrote the ICA sternly. "The effect of all this has been to interfere greatly with the collection of funds which our Committee is seeking to raise in order to help the refugees and to add to the difficulties and embarrassments under which we are laboring."[138]

Despite these frustrations, the ECJR decided it was wisest to coordinate as closely as possible with the European organizations, and indeed to turn over to these groups as much of the work with the stranded migrants as they could handle. In July 1925, the ECJR joined with the ICA and the Emigdirect (an umbrella group of eastern European Jewish aid organizations, funded by HIAS), to form the United Evacuation Committee (UEC), the international version of the ECJR. The ICA was included because in France it was the premiere organization involved with Jewish migration, though it continued to disappoint. The inclusion of the Emigdirect, meanwhile, a group decidedly more grassroots in nature than the aristocratic ICA, helped maintain the appearance that the UEC was a collective and not merely a top-down effort. "[T]he coordination of the staffs of the two organizations with those of a third 'democratic' organization offered certain advantages," explained Senator in his 1926 report: "[P]ublic opinion was appeased by it, and the absolute impartiality of our work, through closest cooperation with European Jewry, was assured."[139]

This new arrangement did not end the tensions between American and European organizations as they tried to collaborate on migration-related matters. Given the dire finances of postwar Europe's Jewish communities, the UEC was largely funded by the Americans—80 percent of the money came from the ECJR and 20 percent from the ICA. Even having retained a good measure of fiscal control, however, the ECJR remained exasperated with the European organizations, indeed expressing suspicion that they might be corrupt and mismanaged, and thus echoing the very accusations against which the American Jewish organizations often had occasion to defend themselves. Sometimes the Americans' notions of European mismanagement reflected the gap between the standards that the larger, more professional American organizations saw themselves as upholding and the more erratic, personal operations of the smaller-scale European groups. Senator, for example, explained that those organizations in charge of the UEC worried that the groups in eastern

Europe would use funds for purposes other than those for which they were earmarked. "In order to carry on its work systematically and keep close supervision over the local committees" so that they would not do this, he wrote, " . . . members of the managing board and its inspectors [which included himself] undertook regular visits to the different harbors and countries in question."[140] As the American Jewish leaders reflected on the work of the UEC in summer 1926, their assessments of the multinational partnership were mixed. They were disgusted, for example, with the ICA's inability to follow through on its promises. "When one remembers the very haughty attitude that ICA took at the discussion in reference to the foundation of the Evacuation Committee," Bernhard Kahn wrote, "and compares their big words of that time with the results of today, I must confess that not many of these words have turned into actualities."[141]

The difficulties American Jewish leaders had in trying to get European groups to take some responsibility for the stranded Jewish migrants were compounded by similar struggles with Jewish communities at home. Press coverage, the eagerness of the large array of Jewish organizations to be represented on the ECJR, and much of the correspondence with the committee suggests that there was a good deal of public concern about the migrants among American Jews. After all, many Jews in the United States had relatives and friends still in Europe eager to join them. Whether these loved ones were among the migrants in question, their fate hung in the balance as well, and the ECJR's success with the stranded migrants could augur well for American Jews' ability to advocate for European would-be immigrants more generally. Despite Marshall's assertion in a letter written to a US senator in February 1925, however, that he knew "of nothing that has so greatly stirred up the Jewish people of this community as has the plight of these unfortunate immigrants," the ECJR ran into resistance to their fundraising efforts.[142] However sympathetic to the stranded migrants' cause, American Jewish communities were laboring to meet their own institutional needs, long put on hold during wartime outpourings of money to aid European Jews. In fall 1923, Marshall reflected on this fundraising fatigue in a letter to the prominent New York Reform rabbi Stephen Wise: "Every community seems to have a drive of its own and is apparently dealing with local problems action on which, owing to the pressure of the War Relief campaigns, was deferred." He noted that the Jews of Philadelphia, Pittsburgh, and Chicago had all turned toward local fundraising efforts, and that many more communities were trying to fund synagogues and Jewish centers.[143]

The fact that American Jewish leaders sometimes failed to coordinate with each other also undermined their efforts to raise money for the stranded Jewish migrants. Even when local American Jewish communities were eager to contribute to the migrants' cause, they could be confused about the roles and responsibilities of the different—and indeed overlapping—national American Jewish organizations involved. One concerned Jew in Peoria, for example, wrote to the ECJR saying that he was hoping to send a few hundred dollars from the community within the next week. However, he added, it was hard to keep track of who was raising money for what. "It has been hard to explain to our people the reason for this fund," he wrote, "as a collector for the Hebrew Immigrant Aid Society has been here within the last month and left the impression that his collections would cover the subscriptions to this fund."[144]

Indeed, intrapersonal and intraorganizational tensions plagued the American Jewish leaders working to address the stranded migrants' situations. Louis Marshall clashed with local activists even when they agreed that the stranded migrant crisis demanded the immediate attention of American Jews. Marshall had little patience when he saw Jewish organizations duplicating each other's work, functioning at cross-purposes or making each other's efforts—or, especially, his—look uncoordinated. In a sharp letter to the president of the International Order of B'rith Abraham (a Jewish fraternal organization), for example, he reprimanded that group for "issuing broadsides with regard to legislation on the subject of the stranded refugees." He was also angry that "a committee representing your organization has gone to Washington and has made itself quite numerous there, without regard to our plans or to what we had done or were doing." American Jewish organizations taking responsibility for the stranded migrants through supporting the ECJR as Marshall ran it was a good thing; organizations taking these matters into their own hands, Marshall believed, was not. "Permit me to say," he wrote caustically, "that I regard such conduct as absolutely disloyal. Apparently there are some people who are more interested in seeing their names in headlines than in accomplishing any good." Furthermore, Marshall equated this organizational encroachment on what he considered his own territory with the work of the political enemy. It was ill-conceived and ill-coordinated independent action like this, he fumed, that had sabotaged the efforts of more experienced organizations that had managed for so long to keep restrictive immigration policy at bay. "If your organization had made one-tenth of the effort to raise funds to help our cause that it has in upsetting the plans of those who know what they are about, it would have been of some use, but, true to form, it is merely doing mischief.

A Jewish equivalent of the Ku Klux Klan," he finished dramatically, "is no better than one under the leadership of the Imperial Wizard."[145]

In another instance, Marshall had a sharp exchange with a Jewish busi-
nessman in Chicago who wrote to the American Jewish Committee about his
efforts to circulate a petition on the migrants' behalf, which he then presented
to Congress. Marshall, angered, warned that such independent local efforts
would jeopardize the ECJR's work. "While I fully appreciate the philanthropic
spirit which has induced your action," he wrote the Chicagoan, "you will permit me to say that it has been ill-advised. The entire matter of immigration is
of the most delicate nature and . . . calls for expert knowledge." The man wrote
back that he resented Marshall's "imperialistic orders," but Marshall remained
adamant.[146]

At times these clashes also reflected a sense among Marshall and some of
his colleagues that the activism of some segments of the American Jewish community only served to damage the public image of Jews. The Chicago busi-
nessman may have been correct that Louis Marshall liked to be in control. But
his dispute with Marshall also reflected a disagreement over political methods
that profoundly divided American Jews, perhaps on no issue more intensely
than immigration. The American Jewish Committee, though it saw itself as
speaking for American Jews at large, relied heavily on behind-the-scenes efforts to influence domestic and international policy and believed in only the
most cautious uses of publicity. While public mass meetings and petitions
were favored by the left-leaning Jewish groups that included more foreign-
born Jews, Marshall and his colleagues were generally for a more top-down
version of activism. They found the more vocal methods of immigrant Jewish
groups unseemly at best, and harmful at worst, for they feared that public to-
do only gave restrictionists extra ammunition. Marshall went so far as to argue
that it was certain Jews' indiscretion that clinched the victory for immigration
restrictionists, as he did in this letter:

> The greatest difficulty that has been encountered in the efforts to maintain
> the traditional policy of America toward the immigrant has . . . resulted from
> ill-considered statements made by various Jews; such as those credited to
> Rabbi Schmellner to the effect that whoever can come from Europe to the
> United States is anxious to come here, or as the editor of a Yiddish newspa-
> per put it before the Senate committee, with disastrous effect, if there were
> a ship which could carry the 3,000,000 Jews of Poland all of them would
> come to the United States. That was enough for the anti-Semites and the im-

migration restrictionists as a justification for placing upon our statute books, first, the Quota Law, and now, the Immigration Act of 1924.[147]

Even Marshall's radio address about the stranded Jewish migrants, which aired in the fall of 1924, represented a compromise between public protest and private, individual action, as the American Jewish Committee's Harry Schneiderman explained in a general letter about the broadcast. Marshall had declined invitations all over the country, the letter said, because "we do not want to give this effort the semblance of a campaign. . . . No national conference or public meetings are being scheduled for this appeal." The radio show, he explained, was designed to achieve maximum impact with minimum appearance of public agitation. The hope was that Jews would gather in small groups of influential leaders instead: "May we ask you to call a meeting of leading Jews in your city at the home of one of your members who possesses a radio set and 'listen in' on Mr. Marshall's address? We feel certain that if the members of your community would hear Mr. Marshall's message you will have no difficulty in raising the amount allotted to your community toward the $500,000 fund."[148]

Just as Marshall saw some American Jews as complicit, in a sense, in producing the restrictive immigration laws, so he and his colleagues did not always regard the stranded Jewish migrants as totally blameless for their own situation. This attitude followed in part from the role Marshall and the other Jewish leaders were playing. The American Jewish organizations working with the ECJR were acting as professionally as possible, in accordance with the ideals of social service and modern theories of social work. In their desire to "liquidate" the problem of the stranded migrants, as they put it in their internal reports, they found themselves interpreting situations quite differently than those migrants did. The organizations were interested in effecting the movement of large groups of people, rather than in the individual desires of particular people. The migrants were cases, and each case needed to be considered as part of a larger problem. Sometimes this approach made for a clash of wills. Even as the Jewish groups worked on the migrants' behalf, they sometimes saw the migrants as unruly and unreasonable. Werner Senator, for example, expressed vexation at the ways the immigrants tended to interfere, as he saw it, with the organizations' tasks. The organizations often met with resistance when they urged migrants to go somewhere other than the United States—something the organizations were working hard to make possible at all by negotiating intensively with the governments of Canada, Mexico, and

Argentina. Migrants with old American visas were especially reluctant to give up their chance at the United States. "It is of course rather difficult," Senator admitted, "to persuade someone to choose a new country of destination when he has only another six or nine months to wait."[149] This, he complained, "proved a check to our work."[150]

Senator had even less sympathy for those the ECJR labeled refugees—the group of stranded migrants without old visas, who thus had a much smaller chance of getting to the United States in the foreseeable future—who did not accept visas that the UEC managed to procure. His theory of "migrant psychology" was a cynical one. He noted that there were many cases in which migrants who had "implored the committees to transport them to Palestine, Canada, or Argentine" later refused to go there when the visas came through. "Why?" he asked rhetorically: "The answer may seem strange, but it is true. The facility of getting a visa reduces its value in the eyes of the emigrants."[151] Senator suggested that such obstinacy was symptomatic of inertia and moral decline among migrants, wrought by their situation. In the case of refugees he saw this as particularly true: "The past six to seven years of suffering and restlessness," he wrote, "together with the loss of the financial support of relatives, had made them lose all moral balance."[152] In other words, European Jews' experiences with migration chipped away at their morality until their capacity for gratitude toward Jewish aid workers got too small and their sense of legal entitlement to the welcome of foreign nations too strong.

Finally, despite Marshall's assurance in his lobbying efforts that the migrants were "law-abiding" people, it was clear to those working closely on the issue that this was not necessarily the case. Many of the migrants, after all, had long been in violation of various laws, governing military service or border-crossing. American Jewish organizations wanted to emphasize to lawmakers and the public that the Jewish migrants were not criminals. Nevertheless, among themselves they admitted that Jewish lawbreaking happened elsewhere in the process of migration and that the stranded Jewish migrants might well be inclined to break US immigration laws. "The people that may consent to go to Mexico or Cuba," wrote Kahn to Marshall in February 1925, "will have the vague hope that in the near future they may be able, legally or by stealth, to cross the American frontier."[153] Indeed, Kahn was skeptical that it was at all advisable to send any migrants to these places for precisely this reason. In private, in other words, American Jewish leaders acknowledged that Jews abroad were liable to violate any nation's efforts to control migration, and that for would-be immigrants, obeying US law was less a priority than was getting where they needed to go.

Despite all the difficulties and quarrels, however, the bulk of the migrants' cases were eventually solved to at least the partial satisfaction of Marshall and the ECJR. Some of the migrants were able to hang on for two or three years where they were, with the aid of the various Jewish groups, until they finally received their new visas to the United States. Others went to Argentina, Mexico, Canada, or Palestine, again with the help of Jewish organizations. A few returned to the places from where they had come.[154] As late as July 1927, a number of migrants remained marooned in ports, but the American groups wound down their organized efforts on the migrants' behalf after withdrawing from the UEC in late 1926.[155]

JEWISH AMERICAN STRATEGIES FOR CONFRONTING THE QUOTA LAWS

The histories of American Jewish leaders in the early years of the quota regime demonstrate the extent to which the new immigration laws left open questions about their meaning and implementation. The cases of the Jewish immigrants from Mexico and the stranded migrants in Europe were only two of the thorny situations that emerged in the wake of the quota laws. Yet, these cases demonstrate some of the major implications that the quota laws had for American Jewish leaders. First, leaders sought to distance themselves and their organizations from any association with illegal immigration. They did not want to risk being seen as fostering or supporting the violation of US law in any way.

Second, both Zielonka's story and that of the ECJR also show how American Jewish leaders developed a strategic approach to the workings of the quota laws. After World War II, American Jewish groups would come to fight fiercely for the admission of Jewish refugees and to overturn the quotas. Before the war, however, Jewish leaders expended little effort on what struck them then as the hopeless task of getting rid of the quotas altogether. Instead, they generally pursued a policy of cautious but law-abiding resistance, advocating for Jewish migrants around the laws' margins. The strategies they pursued, while not a wholesale attack on the restrictive immigration regime, nevertheless had significant impact. American Jewish leaders sought to mitigate the effects of the laws on individual migrants or particular groups of immigrants and to define legal immigration as generously as the law allowed. During the 1920s, for example, American Jewish groups played an important role in the efforts to convince lawmakers to broaden the category of immigrants who were admissible without regard to quota limits. They also brought cases to court that challenged certain aspects of the laws' administration and provided assistance and advice for individuals slated for deportation.[156] Jewish groups' efforts to push immigrants toward naturalization were also part of their strategic response to the laws, given that relatives of US citizens were more likely to be able to immigrate outside the limitations of the quota. They also fought to keep new laws they perceived as anti-immigrant from being passed, such as laws further limiting immigration, or those mandating universal alien registration (an issue explored in chapter 5).[157] In their efforts to fight the legal system on its own terms, the approach American Jewish leaders took to the quota laws was similar to that of the Chinese immigration activists whose legal battles during the era of Chinese exclusion have been chronicled by Lucy Salyer. Indeed, as she points out, Marshall and his colleagues had been involved in some of the legal struggles to combat the harsher aspects of Chinese exclusion; thus, the fact that they carried such strategies into the new era of restricted European immigration is not surprising.[158]

Finally, on an international level, Zielonka's work in Mexico and the eventual withdrawal of American Jewish groups from the work of the UEC both illustrate another key strategy that American Jewish leaders employed to counter the effects of the immigration restrictions during the interwar years. While they never disengaged from immigration issues, these leaders also came to see one of their main goals as helping European Jews stay where they were, because they believed this was European Jews' best option. During this period, for example, the JDC poured an enormous amount of resources into working on reconstruction projects to help make Europe a viable place for Jews to remain.[159] Similarly, like Zielonka, the JDC also turned to efforts to help European Jewish immigrants make new homes elsewhere. Such work in Palestine during the interwar period carried the greatest symbolic meaning, of course, and received the most funding of any such resettlement projects. However, other places also garnered attention from American Jews, including Mexico, Cuba, and elsewhere. Thus, the same laws that made it impossible for many Jews to come to the United States at the same time spurred the internationalization of American Jewish aid work. In retrospect, the fate of European Jews during the Holocaust makes American Jewish organizations' efforts to reconstruct European Jewish communities seem especially tragic, but in the 1920s this could not have been foreseen.

CHAPTER 3

Smuggling in Jews

In 1925, the US Bureau of Immigration sent Inspector Feri Felix Weiss on an undercover assignment to Havana, Cuba. His mission was to investigate the business of smuggling aliens into the United States.[1] Many of the aliens who were immigrating illegally were eastern European Jews; others included Italians, Greeks, and Chinese. In much the same way that liquor bootlegging exploded after Prohibition began in 1920, the alien smuggling business mushroomed in the wake of the new immigration quotas of 1921 and the even harsher ones of 1924.[2] The bustling international port of Havana, already a center of rum-running activity, became equally important as a hub of alien smuggling. Just two hundred miles from Miami, with plenty of shipping traffic linking it to US ports, the city offered easy access to the Gulf and Atlantic coasts of the United States.[3]

In Inspector Weiss the Bureau of Immigration had engaged someone with considerable qualifications. Weiss had served for more than a decade as an immigration inspector in the port of Boston, an experience he detailed in a three-hundred-page book published in 1921.[4] Moreover, he was passionate about his work. A Hungarian immigrant who had arrived in the United States in 1896, Weiss was fiercely patriotic toward his adopted homeland, as well as a staunch supporter of the idea that its borders must be defended against incursion.[5] His book, *The Sieve, Or, Revelations of the Man Mill, Being the Truth about American Immigration* was dedicated "to all who believe in AMERICA FIRST!" and it railed against what Weiss saw as the scourge of unfit and subversive immigrants making their way into the country.[6] When the Bureau of Immigration hired Weiss in 1925, he traveled to the Florida coast and then on to Havana, working long hours for pay he considered much too low, in order to crack the methods of the smuggling rings that operated there. For several months, he and a colleague prowled the grungiest districts of Cuba's largest city, chatting up the questionable characters they found at seedy bars in the early morning hours. Weiss's vivid, almost daily reports to the bureau show Havana to have been a center of the organized, international network of smugglers who turned the US quota laws into profit. The city was just one among many alien smuggling centers that the US government wanted to know about; alien smuggling was a multinational business. Samuel Weisstein, for example, was the smuggler with whose naturalization papers the Polish Jewish carpenter Chaim Josef Listopad (whose tale is told in this book's introduction) attempted to enter the country in 1928. Weisstein was a US citizen based in New York who worked with his colleagues not only out of Havana but also out of Leipzig, Breslau, Paris, Danzig, Pinsk, Warsaw, and Tampico.

To assess the history of the alien smuggling that flourished in this era is to confront the quota system's fundamental instabilities. The quota laws, and the complex mechanisms by which they were implemented, reflected the government's efforts to control the nation's physical and demographic boundaries. These laws were predicated on the belief that it was crucial and possible to control the flow of people over national borders, and to distinguish between desirable and undesirable peoples and between aliens and American citizens. In other words, the quota laws attempted to define and regulate a new set of relationships among migration, identities, and the state. The alien smuggling system both profited from this new set of relationships—exploiting immigrants' need to pass through or avoid US government inspection in order to enter the country—and defied it. Indeed, the system existed in the gaps between how these relationships were perceived by the state and the quite different ways they might be lived in reality, where distinctions among legal and illegal routes, immigrants, and documents could be the cause of much confusion. The rise of alien smuggling challenged not only the practicality of the quotas but also their logical foundation, as smugglers made financial hay out of the fact that the boundaries of geography, identity, and law were far from clear in practice. The smuggling system, like any black market, also mirrored the legal system it subverted. Did the state demand papers from migrants? Smugglers provided forged or black-market papers. Did the state implement penalties to make steamship companies comply with the laws? Smugglers used their own boats and ports, operating with their own rules and fees.

Smuggling rings both deliberately used and evaded the ethnic pigeonholing that formed the basis of the quota laws. Like established aid organizations, rings were often ethnically based in terms of clientele and personnel, as long as it suited their bottom line. They were often, however, ethnically mixed, defying authorities' expectations about how ethnic networks functioned. Smugglers also exploited the notion that it was possible for the government to define and track individual immigrants by means of rigorous bureaucratic documentation and oversight. Every official act of documentation proved to be a potential opening for smugglers to create convincing false identities; every moment of official scrutiny proved to be a potential opportunity to turn authorities' assumptions about immigrants' identities into blind spots that allowed those immigrants to slip into the nation. The history of Jewish alien smuggling thus reveals the elusive nature of national and ethnic identities during this period, when enforcing immigration law depended on the ability of US officials to sort immigrants into the proper categories of ethnicity and national origin.

The history of Jewish alien smuggling also illuminates a key stage in the emergence of modern ideas of "illegal alienness." One reason historians have assumed the efficacy of the quota laws may be that they have not tended to consider European immigration to the United States in connection with illegality. However, the very act of immigration came to be increasingly associated with "criminality" during this era in part because of widespread defiance of the quota laws by immigrants from Europe—both Jewish and non-Jewish. This defiance, and the notions of criminality it engendered, helped shape US policies and public understanding about immigration and "illegal aliens."

THE RISE OF JEWISH ALIEN SMUGGLING

Because both alien smugglers and immigrants entering the nation illegally were necessarily invested in remaining "undercover," few stories of successful alien smuggling ever made it into official archives or were recorded in first-person accounts. Nevertheless, significant traces of the smugglers' activities remain, captured by the government and journalistic investigators who took an interest in their doings. These sources demonstrate that Jewish smugglers and immigrants played integral roles in the growing underground world of illegal immigration. In part, this simply reflects Jews' ongoing desire to come to the United States. Only Italians immigrated in greater numbers during the first decades of the twentieth century, and thus the large Jewish immigrant enclaves that had formed in the United States in the late 1800s and early 1900s remained important destinations for European Jews even after the quota laws were implemented. The centrality of Jews to the story of illegal immigration in the years after the quota acts also reflects the fact that, by the time the United

States passed its new immigration laws, there was already a well-established tradition of Jews crossing national borders illegally.

Thus, smuggling networks were already in place that could expand to meet the demand created by the US laws. In the late nineteenth and early twentieth centuries, *ganvenen dem grenets*, Yiddish for "stealing [over] the border," was a common mode of getting from Tsarist Russia to Germany en route to the ports of Hamburg or Bremen. Migrants risked the illegal crossing because the official Russian documents required for the journey were prohibitively expensive and difficult to obtain.[7] All over the region, dubious characters offered their services to those who sought to cross borders clandestinely. "There were 'agents' who arranged the journey," recalled one Jewish migrant who made the journey in 1893, "bribed officers and soldiers of the frontier forces, and sometimes also swindled the poor Jewish emigrants . . . People usually crossed the border illegally on Saturday nights, because the senior officers were then otherwise engaged, usually celebrating, and the 'agents' could deal more easily with the junior officers and other ranks."[8] During and after World War I, when many Jews in eastern Europe were fleeing violence, economic devastation, and political upheaval, they continued to cross borders, often without regard to legality. Indeed, national boundaries and regimes in the region changed so often during this period that those borders were not always clearly demarcated.

As noted in earlier chapters, a cohort of Jewish immigrants—along with Chinese, Japanese, Lebanese, Greeks, and Italians—also entered the United States illegally via the Canadian or Mexican borders during the late nineteenth and early twentieth centuries, as tighter US immigration restrictions led some people to try the nation's "back doors." By the 1920s, then, smugglers representing all these ethnicities had long offered illegal immigrants their services.[9] Thus, those Jews who sought to migrate to the United States in violation of the US quota laws were following an established pattern. Yet, even while the new US laws fueled an existing smuggling industry, they also reshaped this underground scene in unprecedented ways. Jewish alien smugglers were among those whose trade flourished and expanded in the years after the quotas became law. Jewish illegal immigration to the United States in the quota era was a much bigger, more organized, and more financially complicated business than the long-running business of intra-European Jewish smuggling, or the earlier illicit traffic of European Jews over US borders. The 1924 immigration law, in particular, by instituting a "remote control" system in which the entire process of inspecting immigrants and issuing visas took place abroad, pushed alien smugglers to internationalize their operations in new ways.[10] Moreover, this business now posed a more vital challenge to the US government, which by passing the quota laws had made immigration and border control more central to its national sovereignty than ever before.

After the passage of the quota laws, US authorities noticed that European alien smuggling was on the rise. "The smuggling of aliens from Cuba in small schooners headed for nearby points in Florida has assumed alarming proportions," Joseph Wallis, the assistant commissioner of immigration in New Orleans, reported to his supervisor in 1923.[11] Later that spring, when William W. Husband, the commissioner general of immigration, filed his annual report with the secretary of labor, he emphasized that the business was expanding in response to the high demand. "[A] most troublesome development of the year," he wrote on the report's first page, "has been the growing tendency of inadmissible European aliens to attempt to enter the country surreptitiously, which in turn appears to have led to increased activities on the part of professional smugglers engaged in the business of assisting such aliens to enter over the land and water boundaries."[12]

Government officials in the Departments of State and Labor energetically set about tracking alien smuggling. They seem to have taken seriously all reports from the field—from individual consuls abroad, self-described patriots, and even anonymous correspondents such as the one who wrote in 1924 to Ellis Island officials about Joseph Rubinsky, a notorious smuggler who worked with Samuel Weisstein and who, like Weisstein, was a naturalized citizen from Poland loosely based in New York City.[13] The letter claimed that Rubinsky was "fixing up emigrants with folks passports and visas." The writer warned that "a great bunch" of people with these false papers had already left Warsaw and were all headed to New York.[14]

Legislatively, too, the federal government signaled its intent to enforce immigration law. Alien smuggling was clearly defined as criminal in the immigration laws of 1917 and 1924. The Passport Act of 1918 similarly defined providing aliens with false documents or transporting them surreptitiously into the country as serious crimes, punishable by fines and jail time.[15] In 1924, Congress established the Border Patrol to help with enforcement along the nation's land borders.[16] In 1925, Congress granted immigration officials extensive power to arrest without warrants aliens illegally entering the country, and to search any vessel, train, car, or other vehicle suspected of transporting aliens. Moreover, because the Supreme Court had decreed in their 1916 decision in *Lew Moy v. the United States* that aliens were "entering" the nation up until the moment they reached their final destination, officials were authorized to carry on their hunt for law violators not just at the border but throughout the nation.[17]

Despite periodic reports of government success in breaking up rings, however, enforcing the laws remained an uphill battle. Each new layer of state apparatus the government deployed to regulate migration—for example, consular bureaucracy and additional document requirements—spurred a matching level of sophistication in the smuggling industry.

Estimates of the overall volume of business—that is, how many aliens actually came into the United States via smugglers' channels and how much they paid—varied greatly. Hard data were elusive. "The exact number of bootlegged immigrants is not known," explained a *New York Times* article in May 1924, shortly before the 1924 quota act was passed, adding, "they have been estimated from 17,000 to 200,000 a year."[18] Figures provided by the American consul in Havana in 1932 suggest that something on the order of thirty-one thousand Europeans, about eighteen thousand of them Jews, may have smuggled in through Cuba alone in the years since the quotas.[19] Prices varied over the years, depending on the location and method of entry. Fifty dollars or less could buy a quick trip across the Canadian border, but a forged visa from Poland ran from five hundred to a thousand dollars.[20]

Smugglers' ongoing activities throughout the interwar years indicate that the business never stopped being profitable. Feri Weiss, for example, estimated that the alien smuggling trade, at an average payment of two hundred fifty dollars per migrant, generated two and a half million dollars a year in Havana.[21] "It's such easy money," Weiss was told by an informant who was trying to explain why there seemed to be an infinite supply of smugglers in Cuba's largest port city.[22] Others in the business echoed this assessment. It was "the easiest thing on the pike" to smuggle aliens from Havana into New Orleans, Tampa, or Mobile, the smuggler John Gelabert promised a new associate of his in 1925, assuring him that he had been doing it without incident for several years.[23] As such evidence indicates, the efforts of the United States to control global flows of people were never entirely successful. Even as they managed immigration to some extent, the new laws also helped to produce and nurture new forms of international criminality.

ALIEN SMUGGLING IN "ETHNIC CRIMINAL" CONTEXTS

It is a historical irony that the rise of alien smuggling, rather than generate doubts about the efficacy or logic of the new laws, served to reinforce the very suspicions of ethnic criminality that had helped nativist immigration policy triumph in the first place. Contemporary American observers—journalists, activists, and government officials—understood the phenomenon of the newly flourishing alien smuggling rings in several broader contexts, all of which were laden with ethnic associations. To the US government, the smuggling business was one branch of the world of organized crime, which loomed large in the American imagination during these years, making national headlines, inspiring fiction and films, and commanding the attention of government mob busters.[24] Organized crime was perceived to be a profoundly ethnic world; in fact, the most powerful and notorious mobsters came from the large urban communities of Italians and Jews: Al Capone, Lucky Luciano, Louis Lepke, Meyer Lansky, Arnold Rothstein, Dutch Schultz, and Bugsy Siegel.[25]

Immigration authorities regarded alien smugglers as criminals of this ilk: members of sinister ethnic networks committed to subverting government authority for profit. In 1931, Assistant Secretary of Labor Murray W. Garsson went so far as to opine that alien smugglers were "lower than Al Capone's gangsters at their worst."[26] In particular, both government authorities and the press drew connections between the alien smuggling business and the organized liquor bootlegging occasioned by Prohibition, a business in which Jewish mobsters figured prominently. In 1927, Commissioner General of Immigration Harry Hull reported that "the bootlegging of aliens has grown to be an industry second in importance only to the bootlegging of liquor."[27] It seemed to some of those studying European alien smuggling that the industry was, as one 1925 article in the strongly nativist *Saturday Evening Post* put it, "as well organized as its twin brother, the rum-running industry, to which, indeed, it bears a strong family resemblance in its methods and leadership. They might, in fact, be called the Roughstuff Twins."[28]

Though such comparisons may sometimes have been couched in melodramatic language, they had some basis in reality. Alien smuggling may not have been central to the business schemes of the major crime bosses, but many alien smugglers apparently got their start in rum running. Some switched from the trade in alcohol to the trade in aliens. "Indeed," wrote an immigration inspector at Port Huron, Michigan, to a colleague in Detroit in 1924, reflecting on the booming alien smuggling racket across the Canadian border, "the smuggling of aliens has become so profitable that one or two rum runners, according to information at hand, have abandoned the rum game and have taken up the smuggling of aliens."[29] From Havana the following year Inspector Weiss reported that steamship captains who found rum running too difficult were instead loading up on aliens.[30] One incentive to make this change in merchandise was that human "contraband" required no investment and the aliens were sometimes gullible enough to pay up front. This move allowed the most un-scrupulous smugglers to conclude the business deal by simply dumping their human cargo overboard.[31]

Often traffic in contraband alcohol and aliens, as well as narcotics, went together. Smugglers liked to hedge their bets. Those who smuggled liquor, reported a US immigration officer in Montreal, often chose to "augment their probable profits by having one or more aliens ride with them as passengers, suitable compensation to be made upon safe arrival of the latter in some interior point in the United States."[32] Meanwhile, those who were primarily smugglers of aliens sometimes carried small supplies of dope or liquor as "insurance." "The smuggler of aliens," Weiss reported to the Bureau of Immigration from Havana, "carries a few casks or extra big bottles of liquor which he drops when the boat gets to a certain marked location, and it is picked up later by the ac-complices, especially in case the aliens cannot be landed. These bottles full of Bacardi rum or other select stuff, especially Whisky, pay at least for part of the trip if the aliens do not pay."[33]

Indeed, the alien smuggling business was jump-started by the fact that the bootlegging infrastructure—boats, personnel, and meeting places provided by seedy bars in ports and urban centers—was already in place. The US gov-ernment, meanwhile, whose individual agencies each had their own jurisdic-tions, was stymied by the flexible relationship between rum running and alien bootlegging. In 1927, for example, J. L. O'Rourke, chief border patrol inspec-tor of the Buffalo, New York district went before Congress to urge "coordi-nation of the immigration, prohibition and customs service in the interest of efficiency."[34]

As an often brutal traffic in vulnerable people, alien smuggling was also associated by many observers with a second context: the international traffic in prostitutes, known in the racially loaded terminology of the day as white slavery. For several decades before the passage of the immigration quotas, prostitution had been the primary focus of public and governmental con-cern about illegal human traffic. Jews were often implicated in the sexual traffic in women both as organizers and prostitutes and thus already were connected in the minds of authorities and the public at large with human smuggling.[35] In the early quota years, despite its apparent decline (especially in the United States), white slavery continued to be a pressing issue for activ-ist leaders and governments around the world.[36] Indeed, authorities some-times mistook one sort of smuggling for the other, as when alien smuggler Joseph Rubinsky was arrested in 1924 by Breslau police on charges of white slaving.[37] But the connection was not always fanciful: just as liquor bootlegging and alien smuggling often went hand in hand, the traffic in women was intertwined with alien smuggling more generally. Daniel Lewis, a half-Jewish, half-Cherokee informant in Miami, told government authorities in 1922 that in the apartment upstairs from the restaurant in which he worked, a Jewish alien smuggler named Jacob Lauton was hiding Jewish prostitutes.[38] Inspector Weiss in Havana claimed that several houses there "contain girls . . . of Italian, Hungarian, Slav, Jewish, and other races" who were "practicing prostitution" and "probably trying to come to the States clandestinely."[39]

Finally, journalists and government officials also noted that smugglers of European aliens borrowed methods pioneered by smugglers of Chinese, almost completely barred since 1882 from immigrating to the United States. As mentioned earlier, a number of sophisticated smuggling networks along the nation's northern and southern borders had long done good business getting Chinese immigrants into the country. Chinese alien smuggling via Mexico, in particular, intensified in the first decades of the twentieth century, and US immigration authorities' early efforts to control that region had developed in direct response to this growing traffic.[40] Government officials remained concerned about Chinese illegal immigrants during the years after the quota laws were passed, and a division of the Bureau of Immigration dedicated exclusively to the issue of Chinese immigration continued to function throughout this era. However, the business of smuggling European aliens had to some extent supplanted the Chinese traffic. This may have been partly because crackdowns on Chinese rings had been effective. Reports also indicate that those in the business sometimes preferred taking European cargo even when there was a demand for travel by Chinese immigrants. Apparently, Chinese immigrants found it too risky to make part of their way on their own. "It is more profitable for the smugglers to handle European aliens than it is to bring in Chinese," New Orleans Assistant Commissioner of Immigration Joseph Wallis explained in 1923. "Europeans may be landed at some isolated point on the coast and left to look out for themselves. Chinese agree to pay much larger sums to be smuggled into the country, but payment is contingent upon safe delivery at some inland point or Eastern city."[41]

All these contexts, then—organized crime and liquor bootlegging; Chinese illegal immigration; and the traffic in women—shaped the public and governmental view of European alien smuggling in general and Jewish alien smuggling in particular. Each served to create a kind of template for public and governmental anxiety. When government agents began to notice the increase in alien smuggling, there was already an existing set of anxieties about the trespassing of national borders by smugglers, especially those seen as racially or ethnically different. There were, in other words, several existing ominous narratives within which alien smuggling could be understood.[42] The phenomenon of European alien smuggling built on and complicated the challenges these other forms of criminality posed to government control over state borders. Thanks to the black market created by the quota laws, illicit border crossing became bigger business and more elusive than ever before.[43]

ETHNIC AND TRANSETHNIC NETWORKS

Jewish smugglers were not the only ones prominent in the business of transporting illegal European immigrants. Nor were Jewish immigrants always the group of illegally entering aliens of greatest concern to the public or to government agents charged with enforcing immigration laws. Nevertheless, government officials did their best to track the ethnic demographics of illegal immigration, seeing such information as critical to decoding and combating the smuggling scourge. Authorities were well aware that many of the smugglers and smuggled immigrants were Jews, and made note of this fact as they did of other smugglers' ethnicities. A Florida customs collector reporting to his superiors at the Treasury Department in 1922, for example, took care to specify that some of the smuggling in his region had a particularly Jewish character. "Last week a man very prominent in Hebrew circles informed this office that he had been approached by a fellow Hebrew who informed him that he had arranged to bring in a large number of co-religionists into Tampa," he wrote. "During the past year," he added, "there have been at least three parties of Hebrew immigrants illegally in the country intercepted in this state."[44] Even when authorities already knew definitively that someone was Jewish, reports might emphasize the fact. In 1925, for example, Investigator Feri Weiss sent his employers a description of the notorious Jewish smuggler Dr. S. J. Jamieson: "Short, stout, weighing about 200 lbs; wears moustache; hair sprinkled with gray; decidedly Jewish type face."[45] Elsewhere, Jewish smugglers are described in stereotypically negative ethnic terms such as "shrewd" or "swarthy."[46]

Such attention to smugglers' and immigrants' Jewishness reflects authorities' expectation that smuggling would be organized along ethnic lines. Contemporary observers generally assumed, in the words of one newspaper article on alien smuggling from Canada, that "an Italian smuggler will help an Italian across, a Jew will help one of his brethren across, and so on."[47] This fit American ideas of how ethnicity worked—namely, the belief embedded in the quota laws themselves that ethnic identities were distinct, recognizable, and durable, and that these identities predictably shaped the behavior of individuals and groups.

Certainly, smuggling rings were in part ethnically specific networks. Jews, for example, seem to have dominated the alien smuggling trade from places such as Poland and the Soviet Union, the countries from which most Jewish immigrants were coming during these years. But the alien smuggling rings also reflected the ethnically mixed world of global migration, running counter to the ideas about ethnic distinctiveness that undergirded the quota laws. Unlike established Jewish groups working on migration issues, such as the Hebrew Sheltering and Immigrant Aid Society and the National Council of Jewish Women, illegal rings had no particular mandate to serve their fellow Jews. Jewish smugglers, though specializing in eastern European Jewish clientele, also were willing to take money from other migrants trying to reach the United States and to work in concert with non-Jewish colleagues. Conversely, although Jews entering the United States illegally often did so with the services of Jewish smugglers, who could speak their languages and were more likely to win their trust, they also paid Mexicans, Cubans, Canadians, and others to get them in, often in the company of Greek, Chinese, Irish, Italian, and other immigrants. Whatever the actual demographics of alien smuggling, contemporaries persisted in imagining smuggling as a necessarily ethnic activity—even though it was evident that both the smuggling scene and ethnic identity were more complicated than such assumptions indicated. One of Weiss's Havana informants, for example, thought the investigator would be surprised by the news that "now they are mixing all kinds of races together on these trips—Jews, Huns, Slavs, Italians and Greek, and some Syrians and Chinks."[48]

Sources often suggest the difficulties that authorities had in keeping track of smugglers' ethnic origins, however much they wished to do so. Such evasion was, after all, what smugglers did professionally. Just as smugglers provided others with false identities to evade the immigration laws, they also slipped in and out of ethnically marked identities for their own purposes. The following passage, from a government report on the Florida smuggling scene in 1922, reflects this kind of slippage:

These men are named A. Goerlich (a Hungarian) who is now in Havana [and] . . . a German by the name of Hans Huspal but better known in Havana as "H Rosebaum," he hangs around with a fellow named Izenberg at that address, Izenberg is commonly called "Bismark." And the other man of the combination is a [J]ew by the name of "Fox" who is now in New York City and can be located by watching Rosebaum or Izenberg. . . . On or about July 1ˢᵗ, 1922, "Fox" showed Informant a passport answering his description in every particular except his hair, Fox's hair being black and the passport calling for blonde hair. Fox had his hair on his head, hands, and arms bleached with peroxide and ammonia, paying a certain party . . . $5.00 to do the job.[49]

The author does not speculate about why a German smuggler might find it advantageous to go by a Jewish name, or why someone named Izenberg would be known as "Bismark," or why the passport of "Fox" called for blonde hair. He does, however, convey the game of ethnic musical chairs smugglers could play.

In sum, the smuggling rings in which Jews were involved were both ethnic and transethnic. Smuggling networks exploited both the reality of ethnic identities and the permeability of ethnic boundaries. Their history serves as a commentary on the extent to which ethnic identities could be persistently fluid even as, and perhaps more importantly because, the new immigration laws tried to define them precisely and contain them.

GEOGRAPHIES OF ALIEN SMUGGLING

In the history of Jewish immigration to the United States, and of European immigration more generally, certain places loom large: Hamburg, Bremen, Liverpool, New York City. Most of the millions of immigrants who came to the United States in the hundred years before the immigration quotas arrived via the shipping companies that operated between the great European and American ports. As important urban centers and transport hubs, these places continued to figure in the new world of European illegal immigration after the restrictions of the immigration acts of 1921 and 1924. The history of smuggling networks also illuminates, however, a more complicated geography of migration than scholars have tended to describe. The field of immigration history has often been more focused on people's experiences at the points of departure and arrival than on the contingencies of the journey.[50] However, the complex, shifting geography of alien smuggling networks, which spanned multiple places and adapted to the needs of the moment, merits as much attention as the places immigrants left behind and settled. Given that the problem to which smuggling addressed itself was how to get people from one place to another, the history of alien smuggling casts a spotlight on the processes of migration itself. For many migrants, the smuggling business shaped the means by which people got from one place to the other, the places through which they traveled, and the decisions they made about where to go next and how to get there.

Moreover, an examination of the geography of alien smuggling demonstrates the fragility of national efforts to control borders. Such efforts, as we have seen, were a central feature of the international system that emerged after World War I, as many nations sought to define and police their geographic and demographic boundaries. The quota laws were the US version of this political turn. Smuggling, however, challenged the very premise that a nation could control migration across its borders. Alien traffickers did not merely lack respect for the inviolability of national borders. Rather, they profited from the gap between how national borders worked in theory and in three-dimensional, full-scale reality.

Smugglers sought out clientele wherever people in transit clustered, and thus many of Europe's large urban centers became integrated into the circuits of illegal migration. In eastern Europe an enormous population displaced by the war was on the move. This massive upheaval, which US-based relatives, friends, and Jewish aid organizations saw as a disaster, appeared to smugglers as a huge market waiting to be tapped. In Warsaw, long lines of people waiting outside the magistrate's office and the American consulate ("from early morning to late evening," as one Jewish immigrant later recalled) hoping to procure passports and visas constituted an obvious pool of potential customers.[51] In Berlin, smugglers approached would-be immigrants in consulates and the offices of shipping lines, offering to help them obtain travel documents.[52]

Even newcomers to these cities who had arrived with no intention of emigrating to the United States sometimes found themselves reconsidering in the face of smugglers' salesmanship skills. In July 1926, officials at Ellis Island questioned thirty-four-year-old Leo Farber about his fraudulent visa. Speaking through a Yiddish interpreter, Farber told them that when he sold his restaurant in Bialystok, Poland, and moved to the port city of Danzig, he was looking for employment, not a visa to the United States. But a man Farber could identify only as "Zuckerman"—apparently one of the top members of the Weisstein-Rubinsky ring—struck up a conversation with Farber in his hotel and convinced him otherwise. "You must know," Farber reported the Yiddish-speaking stranger told him, "that it will be impossible for you to obtain employment in Danzig . . . I would advise you to go to the United States. For a matter of $300 I could fix you up with the necessary documents with which to proceed to America."[53] Farber agreed to the deal, only to get caught once he arrived in New York.

Smugglers also knew that people in transit were good business bets. They cultivated the art of listening to travelers talking about why and to where they were en route. In 1936, for instance, fifty-five-year-old Isaac Limonsky, a Jewish meat and produce dealer from Boston, recalled for a congressional committee what had seemed like a chance encounter on a train ride a decade earlier. He was traveling from his home in Lithuania, where his family was struggling to make ends meet, to Berlin. He planned eventually to go to Uruguay. But during Limonsky's rail journey, a young man sitting nearby struck up a conversation with him in Russian. Limonsky confessed that he had long dreamed of emigrating to the United States. At this, the young man offered his assistance: " 'Would you like to go to the United States? . . . I live in Berlin and I am a lawyer. Maybe I can do something for you.' " Limonsky replied, "If you can do something for me, all right. Why not?"[54]

Smugglers also converged in cities on the other side of the Atlantic. In 1925 an informant in Havana directed Inspector Weiss to "Sol, Acosta, Porvenir, San Isidro, Paula, and Havana Streets," thoroughfares near the waterfront known for their "alien boarding-houses which are chucked full with all sorts of foreigners," including Jews from all over eastern Europe.[55] Smugglers solicited openly in the neighborhoods where foreigners lived and gathered. "There is a Greek," the same informant explained to Weiss, "who comes nearly every evening to offer his services to us foreigners who live in the alien boarding houses, to take us across. There is another fellow who walks along the water-front and approaches aliens there and offers to ship them across for good money."[56] Indeed, this is precisely how the smuggler Samuel Weisstein made his sale in 1928 to the Polish Jew Chaim Listopad, whom the smuggler approached as Listopad sat on the Malecon, Havana's seaside promenade.[57]

Alien smuggling was embedded in a landscape of shady businesses. In Havana, Inspector Weiss and his partner Joseph Mitchell concentrated on observing the criminal underworld centered on San Isidro Street, which the inspector described in his characteristically colorful language. San Isidro, he informed his employers in Washington, was "one big mass of squirming sailors, firemen, dope-peddlers, barrooms, fast houses (white and black) and the worst hell-hole in creation for concocting schemes to cheat Uncle Sam."[58] Havana was Cuba's most important port, but it was not the only place on the island where the business of alien smuggling thrived in conjunction with other illicit commerce. In 1929 the *New York Times* reported, for example, on the alien smuggling underworld in Isabela de Sagua, which the paper called "one of the most notorious centers for clandestine embarkation of aliens to

the United States." The paper explained that the epicenter of alien smuggling there was a cabaret, which Cuban police described as "notorious for
scandals" and possibly also a "headquarters for smugglers of narcotics." The
cabaret was run by an American woman identified only as Mrs. Friedman (a
name that would have suggested to readers that its bearer might well be Jewish, though the paper does not specify). Mrs. Friedman's reputation suggested
that the illicit culture that flourished in her establishment was rough. "The
proprietress," the article reported, "was capable of holding her own in nightly
fights said to have occurred there. . . ."[59] On the North American continent, the
Mexican cities of Veracruz, Tampico, and Juarez, and the Canadian cities of
Montreal, Toronto, and Windsor, each had their particular geographies of foreigners' hangouts. Along the waterfront in Windsor, just across the river from
Detroit, was a "huddle [of] frowzy little hotels and boarding houses which act
as clearing houses for the smugglers," according to one journalist. "The two
streets containing them have been dubbed Alien Row."[60]

The smuggling routes into the United States had their distinctive geographies. The classic routes of European immigration history—major port to
major port—can be plotted on a simple map, but smugglers often worked in
a kind of alternate universe, with ports and routes outside the expected ones.
Weiss, for example, reported that the Jewish alien smuggler Jamieson often
chose the port of Jaimanitas, conveniently located not too far from Havana's
main harbor, to launch his operations:

It is an ideal spot for smuggling, for putting the aliens on board a schooner.
It is a nice little enclosed bay, not large but . . . large enough to take in small
schooners. There are practically no port officials there. . . . There is a dandy
road which goes right to Jaimanitas from Habana [Havana], . . . and in 35
minutes they [the smugglers] deliver the people right on the schooner. It is
absolutely secluded, you cannot see the boats from anywhere, there is low
land and bushes and trees allaround, and it is just a wonderful place for that
sort of thing.[61]

Alien smugglers carved out obscure routes from their points of departure to
their destinations in order to evade detection, hopscotching from one out-of-
the-way place to another. Daniel Lewis, the government informant, explained
the Miami-based alien smuggler Jacob Lauton's multipart transportation strategy. Lauton asked Lewis to take a boat loaded with bootlegged aliens and liquor from Havana to Nassau in the Bahamas, and arrange there for an official

journey to Nova Scotia. On the way to Canada, however, he was to make several clandestine stops, first at an island near Charleston; then on Cape Cod; and finally at Mt. Desert Island off the coast of Maine, to unload his cargo.[62] When Lewis demanded more money than Lauton would agree to pay for executing this plan, Lauton suggested an alternative though equally complex method to funnel the aliens slowly through the Bahamas:

> [I would] go in a boat from Miami to Havana, Cuba, and take on some Russian and Hungarian Jews, and then go to the Isle of Pines and get some more, and bring them to Nassau, and he was to hire a house at Nassau, up on the hill by the hospital, and keep them in there, and from time to time we were to deliver them to the German engineer on the S.S. "Yankten,"... and he was to bring them on the S.S. "Yankten" as assistants to him in converting the coal burning engine into an oil burning engine.... Some of the Jews and Greeks were to be taken from Nassau to Bimini, and they were to be housed in some negro huts at Bimini.[63]

Many routes that smugglers used to get their clients into the United States relied on a detailed knowledge of the messy contours of the nation's edges, places that immigration authorities—even where they were supplemented by customs and prohibition officials—could not begin to patrol effectively. Government officials realized that smugglers taking aliens from Cuba to the United States had coastal geography on their side. Joseph Wallis, assistant commissioner of immigration in New Orleans, warned his superiors in 1923 that "from all accounts Cuba is honey-combed with inadmissible European aliens who will take any risk and pay large sums to get into this country" via the Gulf coast. He elaborated on his apprehensions a year later:

> [A]ll possible means of communicating with the Barataria section of Louisiana were employed with very unsatisfactory results. That section is known as the marsh country and is inhabited mainly by fishermen engaged primarily in taking and drying shrimp and bedding and fishing oysters in season. There is no telephone, telegraph or wireless communication with that section and as there are many water routes from that section into New Orleans, it is well adapted for the smuggling of aliens, narcotics and liquor.[64]

Immigration officials working along the US-Canadian border reported similar difficulties to those experienced by their southern colleagues.[65] Those on the front lines of government, in short, were confronting a problem that has always been at the heart of immigration law: controlling borders is easier legislated than actually accomplished.

Some alien smuggling was simply a matter of transporting illegal immigrants from one side of the border to the other. Although many aliens were taken to the United States via convoluted routes through the Bahamas or elsewhere, many others were ferried clandestinely, under cover of darkness, more directly—by car from Canada to New York at night, or by boat from Cuba to Florida, or by foot over the Mexico–US border. The reports of journalists and government officials indicate that alien smugglers had access to considerable resources to aid their efforts, including state-of-the-art communications and transportation technology. They connected their far-flung networks by means of telephone and telegraph. Some alien smugglers transported their contraband on small, fast private boats or big commercial steamers. By the late 1920s, alien smugglers were also using airplanes to get across borders undetected.[66] Of course, US officials had reason to describe alien smugglers as well equipped. It helped create the impression of formidable-sounding adversaries, which was key not only to explaining the authorities' inability to catch up with alien smugglers but also to using the smuggling scene as leverage to secure better funding. J. L. O'Rourke, for example, chief border patrol inspector for the Buffalo district, pled for more money when he went before Congress, citing his agency's ill-equipped state. The *Buffalo Courier-Express* reported that the inspector told lawmakers that "the present border patrol is sadly lacking in equipment," and that he requested "that at least three moderately fast motor boats be supplied the border patrol and that several additional automobiles be furnished to halt the illegal entry of aliens."[67]

But transportation and communication were not the technologies most central to the smugglers' business. Migration had become a process in which people's official identities—certified by state authorities by means of documents—were as crucial to effecting the journey across space as ships or trains. National borders were real, geographically located places, but they existed equally on paper, in the quota laws and government regulations, and in the entire attendant system of documentation—applications, passports, and visas—that was supposed to let some people in and keep others out based on who they were and where they came from. Just as the history of smuggling sheds light on the complexities of geographic borders, so it helps illuminate the untidy terrain of documentary ones. The interconnected documents that immigrants might need or use to enter the country, from affidavits to birth records, certificates of naturalization, and tourist identity cards, reflected the complexities of immigration law, and smugglers knew their ins and outs just as they knew the intricacies of the coastlines.

In carrying out their work, alien smugglers relied on a performative sleight of hand that depended on the government's own apparatus of immigration: passing off illegal immigration as legal. Whether immigrants came in with counterfeit papers, someone else's papers, or in disguise as a member of a ship's crew, the strategy was essentially the same—making immigrants appear to be something they were not. Two theorists of contemporary alien smuggling have described this art of illicitly moving people posing as other people over state borders as "identity laundering," a term as useful for the quota era as it is for our own.[68]

The documentary system entailed certain contradictions that proved a boon to smugglers. The effectiveness of using identity documents for administrative control purposes depended on those documents' looking recognizably official. But the more the US government sought to standardize its documents to better manage their use, the easier they were to counterfeit. The new documentary requirements of US immigration law produced an immediate upsurge of counterfeiting, as the large-scale manufacturing of fake US passports and visas became lucrative.[69] Authorities were aware of this problem. Just as the government increased patrols and inspections along its borders to combat smuggling operations, so it also tried to make its documents secure. US documents had distinctive inks, stamps, signatures, and seals, but smugglers were ingenious in finding back doors to exploit. In 1923, the American consul general in Warsaw reported to the secretary of state that the local police had discovered a stash of blank affidavit forms for visa applicants in the possession of Joseph Rubinsky. Signed and sealed by a New York notary public named Jacob Marder, the forms could be used to make visa applications appear legitimate and thereby result in the issue of a fully valid visa. Rubinsky was also in possession of printed New York State certificates of naturalization.[70] Further investigation revealed that "Jacob Marder" was a fictitious name, though it remained unclear how Rubinsky came to possess the blank certificates of naturalization.[71] Another scheme the US government uncovered in Poland involved provisions of the immigration law that exempted children of US citizens from quota restrictions if they were under eighteen years and that gave those under twenty-one years preference within the quotas. The American consulate in Warsaw reported in 1933 on several recent cases in which "Szymon Blumenberg, Keeper of the Jewish Vital Statistics Records of Tyczyn, issued for a certain compensation fraudulent birth certificates" stating that people were young enough to be eligible for nonquota visas or preference within the quota.[72]

In the years between the 1921 and 1924 quota acts, the law's policy toward immigrants in the Western Hemisphere made for a particularly easy method of fraud. According to the law, immigrants who had resided in Western Hemisphere countries such as Mexico, Canada, Cuba, or Argentina for at least one year (later this length-of-residency requirement was extended to five years) were permitted to enter the United States outside the quota. Throughout the region, documentation to this effect could be bought and sold. In 1924, for example, the American consul general in Buenos Aires wrote to the secretary of state to warn him about a number of European Jews who had been trying to enter the United States by presenting proof, in the form of certificates issued by the local police chief, that they had resided for at least five years in La Plata, Argentina. "I am of the opinion," he wrote, "that none of these certificates should be accepted as bona fide evidence of the residence claimed. While it is impossible to get any tangible evidence that these certificates have been bought, it is an open secret that such is the case." Moreover, he added, this was not true merely of the certificates from La Plata, but also of "all other certificates issued by the Argentine officials."[73]

The 1924 immigration law abolished the residency loophole, decreeing that immigrants must apply for quotas from the country of their birth. Even under that stricter law, however, Western Hemisphere natives were permitted to enter the United States as nonquota immigrants—meaning they were not subject to numerical restriction as long as they met all other requirements for legal entry. European migrants who could purchase birth certificates on the black market in Latin America or Canada thus had a way into the United States.[74] In 1926, for example, officials in New Orleans questioned two Jewish immigrants arriving from Mexico with Cuban birth certificates. Neither of the travelers struck the officials as convincingly Cuban, and on further questioning the immigrants admitted that they had bought the documents while in Cuba.[75]

The alien racket extended beyond the moment of illegal entry as well. Successful illegal immigration schemes might get immigrants across the border, but ensured neither that immigrants would be allowed to stay nor that they would be able to gain full membership in the society. Unlawful entry was grounds for deportation; application for naturalized citizenship required proof of lawful arrival in the country. Immigrants who entered the country illicitly thus had strong reasons for seeking retroactively to render their entry "legal." Therein lay lucrative business opportunities. In 1931, authorities uncovered an intricate scheme in which a number of government officials, lawyers, and steamship company agents colluded to provide illegal immigrants with forged reentry permits (documents granted to legal immigrants who wished to leave and return to the country) and arrival records in exchange for hefty fees.[76] Four years later, the federal government launched an intensive investigation into fraudulent naturalizations and related offenses. During the course of the investigation, they discovered rampant corruption and illegality, including a complicated multiethnic ring in New York City in which a number of government employees worked together to alter ship manifests and to forge certificates of arrival so that hundreds of aliens who had entered illegally could be rendered "legal" in retrospect.[77] Both the 1931 and 1935 schemes involved Jewish and non-Jewish aliens and smugglers.

A number of individual operators also attracted government officials' attention for their unscrupulous dealings with aliens in the country illegally. In 1932, Louis Fried left his government job as a naturalization examiner and established a private law practice in Brooklyn, where he became well known for his expertise in immigration and naturalization issues. He helped many immigrants who had entered the country illegally to "legalize" their status by going to Bermuda, where the local US authorities were notoriously lax about granting visas. He also engaged in bribery, forgery, and other illegal means of procuring naturalizations, for which crimes he was convicted in a federal court in 1935.[78] Another such high-profile case was that of the New York– and Havana-based Jewish "immigration consultant" H. Ely Goldsmith. Goldsmith was convicted in 1929 for fraudulent attempts to secure a temporary visa for an immigrant in Argentina and served a two-year sentence in Atlanta's federal penitentiary.[79] A few years later, however, he restarted his business. He made especially good use of the "preexamination" policy the federal government instituted in 1935. Under this policy, immigrants who had entered the United States illegally could travel to nearby countries and apply for a visa to reenter legally as long as they could meet all visa requirements, including strict financial ones put into place during the Depression to insure that no one at risk of needing public assistance would be permitted to immigrate.[80] Goldsmith helped many such immigrants, Jews and other Europeans, game the visa process by providing them with fake affidavits attesting to high salaries as well as other forged documents. He had a number of associates and an extensive mailing list. He slipped up when he mistakenly mailed his business card to the federal judge who had sentenced him in 1929 and was convicted again of violating immigration law in 1939.[81]

Like all businesses that rely on counterfeiting, the alien smuggling underworld of the quota era illuminates the simultaneously antagonistic and symbiotic relationship between legality and criminality. The bureaucratic approaches to control and enforcement, a central principle of the modern state, always contained the seeds of their own partial undoing.

LEGITIMACY AND CRIMINALITY

Given how much immigrants, the press, and government officials knew about alien smuggling, it might seem surprising that smugglers managed to evade US and foreign authorities as often as they did. In part, the alien smuggling business succeeded because it relied on far more people than the small cohort of leaders the government generally chose to pursue. Weiss wanted his supervisors to understand the way this worked in Havana: "Smugglers range from . . . officials and men of wealth and position, to the lowest water-front scum, dive-keepers, murderers and pirates. There are rings of smugglers, and rings within rings, which are interlocked."[82] In other words, alien smuggling was an extensive underground economy that depended on complex networks along every part of the route, which included prominent community members and government officials. The network also included ordinary people working regular jobs, who were involved with smuggling on the side: boarding house, café, and hotel employees who might solicit business or serve as messengers; or train conductors and ship workers who would turn a blind eye to aliens illegally in transit.[83] Smuggling rings were elusive in part because they were intertwined with every element of the social spectrum. Even the trade's bigwigs often straddled the worlds of legitimate and criminal enterprise. As with the issue of ethnicity, the question of smugglers' legitimacy and criminality reveals the slipperiness of the very categories themselves.

Both government officials and newspapers had reason to be interested in painting smugglers as sinister gangster types—government officials because the smugglers were their antagonists, the press because they wanted to sell papers. The *Saturday Evening Post*, for example, portrayed "menacing" alien smugglers as the cruelest of the cruel in the slangy language of pulp fiction:

As a lot they are distinctly bad hombres. Recruited from water-front rats, cutthroats and racial outcasts, the criminal riffraff of all nations, attracted by the big money rewards, the ringleaders in this human traffic trim their unfortunate victims going and coming, relieve them of their wads without rendering the slightest quid pro quo, and when caught in a jam with the law, jettison them without mercy.[84]

Alien smugglers, like their better-known liquor bootlegging counterparts, did resort sometimes to violence and intimidation. In 1934, a Mrs. Schwartz, acting as a decoy and informant in Havana for US authorities investigating alien smuggling, wrote a panicked letter to the official working with her on the case of one smuggler known to traffic in Jewish aliens. When she told the smuggler's henchmen that she needed to delay her travel, they threatened her with violence. "Things are very hot, Mr. Melick," she wrote:

> The two men acted like murderers and told me to be very careful not to fool [the smuggler Castells] because he is ready and prepared to do anything to me if I should try and fool him. . . . All I can tell you, Mr. Melick, is that they are very dangerous men. Please do something because I am afraid that they may do something to me if I don't make the trip.[85]

Inspector Weiss also passed on to the Bureau of Immigration grim assessments of the smuggling scene. His local informant, Jose Garcia, told him that "immigration smuggling in Cuba is a small war. Plenty of people killed, nobody knows about it, but God and the water."[86]

Despite such testimony, many accounts suggest that alien smuggling could often seem a rather ordinary business. Indeed, some observers found it noteworthy that alien smugglers of the 1920s and 1930s conducted their business with more restraint than contemporaries expected from criminals. In 1927, for example, a journalist writing in the *Buffalo Courier-Express* contrasted them—somewhat wistfully—to Chinese alien smugglers of the past. He noted that "[t]he smugglers of today are not the devil-may-care villains of . . . the infamous '90s when Chinese human contraband died at the approach of danger, knocked on the head with a smuggler's oar and mercilessly dumped overboard."[87] Inspector Weiss noted that the alien smugglers in the Florida area tended to eschew violence, avoiding the gun battles for which their colleagues in the rum-running business were famous. "So far," he reported, "the alien smugglers have put up no fight, like the rum-smugglers have done outside of Sandy Hook. On the contrary, the alien smugglers around Tampa and Tarpon Springs prefer to run away from the official chasers." He reckoned that this was likely because they believed that shooting at government authorities would put them in the category of really serious criminals, "and the game is not worth the candle, apparently."[88]

Generally, alien smuggling seems to have been a relatively low-risk job that people engaged in because it offered decent, steady money. Like other industries during this era of corporatization, alien smuggling was becoming increasingly rational and efficient. As Weiss reported, the smuggling businesses that ran via large ships operated as clandestine versions of their legitimate counterparts, the shipping companies, with just as many middlemen performing the relatively mundane labor of moving people from place to place. "The larger combinations of smugglers have regular representatives in the States just like a legitimate steamship enterprise has offices in various cities," he wrote. "They also have responsible businessmen with post-office box addresses at their command, in whose care the smuggler fee is mailed by relatives of smuggled aliens."[89] Similarly, in a 1931 story on the government's ramping up of its anti-smuggling efforts, the *New York Times* quoted Assistant Secretary of Labor Murray W. Garsson as saying that the alien smugglers "have offices in the large American and European cities, retain able lawyers . . . and have considerable political influence."[90] At least one ring of smugglers, Weiss learned in Havana, "operated so brazenly that they handed cards out on the streets where aliens lived, guaranteeing to take them to the States for a set sum at regular scheduled time[s], bi-weekly sailings being advertised like in any legitimate enterprise."[91]

Some smugglers were involved in an overlapping mix of legitimate and illicit businesses.[92] Dr. Jamieson, the American Jewish optician in Havana whom Weiss called a "smuggler king" and who specialized in transporting eastern European Jews, operated a perfectly proper optical store and moved in respectable social and legitimate business circles.[93] In Miami, the informant Daniel Lewis explained to government officials that alien smuggler Jacob Lauton was part of a network of Jewish businessmen for whom smuggling was a sideline that supplemented their more legitimate enterprises. Lauton's colleague Aronovitz, for example, who "was furnishing money to bring [immigrants] from the old country to Havana, Cuba, and from Cuba over here," was also the owner of a local hotel. At least some of those who earned their living in the smuggling trade seemed proud of their identity as respectable businessmen. Daniel Lewis told officials that Lauton was indignant when Lewis expressed concern about the risks of working for the smuggling operation:

When Jacob Lauton was trying to get me to go into the business of smuggling immigrants into this country I asked him what assurance I would have that I would get any money, or that I would be cared for in case anything happened, and he said, "Mr. Aronovitz is good, Mr. Cline is good, Mr. Miller is good," and he told me that I could look them up in Bradstreet's or Dunn's, and that they were men of their words, and he told me that he was good, and he said, "See what I own. I own this house here, and I have a place in Bayonne, N.J.," and he said his sons were in business there … and he said there would be no trouble at all, and that I would get my money.[94]

Of course, many smugglers probably used legitimate businesses merely as fronts. Reports on Joseph Rubinsky make it seem doubtful, for example, that he ever really intended to make his money exporting furs from interwar Poland, as he claimed, or that his colleague Weisstein had prospered in the mushroom trade, which he asserted was his business.[95] Rubinsky also claimed to represent the Russian American Relief Package Forwarding Company, Inc., which, government investigators discovered, had indeed existed and even accepted packages in the United States for immigrants' friends and family in Russia. The company ceased operations in 1923, however, after people who had sent packages complained to the Kings County district attorney that the shipments never reached their destinations.[96]

Whether or not those who headed alien smuggling rings were engaged in legitimate business ventures, they were at ease in the role of international entrepreneurs, were experienced travelers, were comfortable in the realm of high-finance business transactions, and were able to speak several languages.[97] They often carried themselves, as descriptions of their demeanor and stylish clothing suggest, with a certain finesse. The Cuba-based optician Dr. Jamieson, for example, dealt not only in aliens and bootleg liquor but also in at least one Stradivarius violin, according to Inspector Weiss. In the course of his undercover work, Weiss called on the doctor at home on the pretense of wanting to buy the Strad. "He received me cordially," wrote Weiss, "though he was rather nervous because there happened to sit in his elegant parlor two rather shabby looking Jews," a contrast to the genteel figure of the doctor himself, who did, indeed, produce the fine instrument for Weiss' inspection, suggesting, naturally, that Weiss take it through US customs on the sly.[98]

In addition to business acumen, American citizenship also proved to be an important asset to alien smugglers in their professional dealings. Authorities insisted that smugglers were almost always aliens themselves, and the alien smuggling business did certainly employ people of a range of nationalities.[99] Being American, however, conferred some advantages. Both Rubinsky and Weisstein were naturalized citizens. Although they were apparently out of the country for years at a time, their status as citizens allowed them to come and go across US borders—and European borders as well—as they pleased. Citizenship also made it easier for some smugglers to bring in aliens illicitly as "paper relatives" who would be treated as exempt from the quotas.[100] In 1925, for example, two smugglers, one a native-born and one a naturalized US citizen "of the Spanish race," were apprehended in Laredo, Texas. They claimed that the six aliens (five Jews and one Spaniard) in their company were their children, a scheme that seems to have succeeded for one of the smugglers many times before.[101]

Like children of citizens, wives of citizens could also enter the United States outside quota restrictions. Morris Baskin of Brooklyn, a Jewish alien smuggler and naturalized US citizen whose criminal conviction made news headlines in 1930, was one of many smugglers who turned this principle into profit. Among the various visa scams he offered was one in which he acted as a proxy bride-groom at wedding ceremonies in Poland. After bribing a local rabbi, Baskin would "marry" a woman under the name of a naturalized US citizen. After the ceremony, Baskin obtained a nonquota visa for his quasi brides from Harry Hall, the American vice consul at Warsaw who was in on the game.[102] Being a citizen could also mean easier access to US government representa-tives. In 1923, Joseph Rubinsky got New York Congressman Albert Rossdale to intercede with the authorities in order to expedite the process of issuing a new copy of Rubinsky's naturalization papers, which Rubinsky claimed had been destroyed.[103]

Alien smugglers also had other forms of political capital. Foreign govern-ments did sometimes cooperate with American authorities in tracking down smugglers (e.g., Polish authorities joined in the hunt for Morris Baskin). But smugglers, as Garsson indicated in his comment to the *New York Times*, sometimes kept themselves beyond the reach of American law by dint of their political pull with governments abroad. Havana-based smuggler Castells, ac-tive in smuggling Polish Jews, proved frustratingly elusive to United States authorities precisely because his business expertise had won him powerful allies. "During [Gerardo] Machado's regime Castells, as a smuggler of aliens, assisted a large number of revolutionists in leaving Cuba, in most cases without charging them anything for the trouble," reported an American immigration official based in Havana to his superiors in 1934. "These revolutionists have now returned and many of them hold high offices and naturally are grateful to the man who in many instances saved their lives."[104]

Bribery was another good investment for alien smugglers, as well as an-other way that employees of legitimate enterprises and institutions who were otherwise not working in the smuggling trade could become involved in the business. Some rabbis and town officials in Poland could be persuaded—for a fee—to sign marriage certificates and fake birth certificates. Judges in Havana, Weiss learned, were similarly amenable.[105] In his final report, the inspector detailed the layers of bribes entailed in getting a shipment of smuggled aliens from Cuba to the United States via one of the major shipping lines, such as Munson or Ward, or on one of the ships of the United Fruit Company: "The way the trick is pulled," he wrote, "is this: . . . Generally the Boatswain, the Chief Steward, and especially the Engine crew and some of the sailors are in the pay of the smugglers." Payments could take the form of assets other than cash, he explained: "On the Ward liners there is always between 50 and 200 cases of booze taken to New York to be used as bribe of all the officials on the dock from the lowest to the highest (I mean officials of the Line) and sometimes customs and immigration officials also, so that they do not interfere with the landing of the clandestine passengers."[106] The businesses of liquor bootlegging and alien smuggling were thus further intertwined, as one valuable contraband commodity was offered in payment to smooth the entry of another, and both were often carried out through legitimate business channels.

Despite government officials' insistence in their correspondence and reports that smuggling was something done by operators out there in a shadow world of their own, the networks of those enforcing the laws and those evading them were often linked. American officials who wanted to take advantage of the power afforded by their positions to cash in on the demand for smuggling services sometimes went beyond the relatively passive step of accepting bribes, as demonstrated by the above-mentioned forgery and fraud schemes uncovered in New York City in 1931 and 1935, which involved both consular employees and employees of the naturalization and immigration services.[107] There were other instances as well. In 1933, a Havana correspondent for a New York Jewish paper told the American consul general there about Bernard Kohn, a Jewish clerk who worked at the consulate and sold fraudulent visas on the sly.[108] And Warsaw Vice Consul Harry Hall (though ultimately released on probation as a reward for serving as the State's witness at the 1930 trial of Morris Baskin) pleaded guilty to selling fraudulent visas to smugglers, albeit while insisting that he only agreed to the scheme because he was under the influence of the vodka with which the smugglers plied him.[109] Officials with the Bureau of Immigration itself were also on the take sometimes. Chief Immigration Inspector Schmucker at Key West, for example, was reportedly involved in 1922 with a mostly Jewish ring smuggling aliens from Cuba to Florida and New York.[110]

Smuggling and government were also interconnected in other ways. Jewish immigrant aid societies publicized cautionary tales of immigrants who were barred from entry when it was discovered they had arrived with false papers that they really believed were issued by American authorities. Some smugglers lured clients by mimicking government personnel. "Morris Baskin," the *New York Times* reported during the smuggler's trial, "posed in the country districts of Poland as a high American official, and in order to impress his supposed dignity on the credulous people he wore a high hat and silk knickerbockers."[111] One immigrant who entered with forged documents recalled that he got his papers at what he thought was the American consulate in Warsaw, but was in reality only an office that smugglers were using in the consulate building.[112]

However much of a con game, smugglers' impersonation of government officials rested on a certain truth about their similarity to each other. Just as smugglers' shipping operations offered similar services to those of the regular lines—albeit with much greater risk to immigrants—so alien smuggling rings also functioned in some ways like government bureaucracies, issuing the papers that made travel possible and accepting fees for these services. In ironic acknowledgement of this, Jamieson's colleagues, Weiss reported, referred to him as "the Jewish Consul."[113]

Samuel Weisstein provides at least one instance in which a Jewish smuggler tried to masquerade as a Jewish aid organization: he told government officials that he worked in Poland under the auspices of the Zbarazer Relief Society.[114] According to Inspector Weiss, meanwhile, the "Jewish Immigrant Society" in Havana appeared to be operating "openly above board, but secretly," he reported, was "helping immigrants over to the States."[115] Similarly, the "Jewish Aid Society" of Havana, Weiss had been assured by a local informant, though "officially . . . on record as favoring law enforcement," was "unofficially, however . . . aiding and abetting in the shipment clandestinely of Jewish aliens to the States. The facts prove it," the informant insisted, "for the Jews slowly but surely diminish in number in Havana, yet very few go back to Europe. And very few get visas. So they must be smuggled to America."[116] This may have all been pure fiction. Because government authorities had long suspected legitimate Jewish operations of illegal meddling in Jewish immigration, however, such evidence likely served to blur the boundaries between legal and criminal operations further. With the rise of alien smuggling rings, Jewish organizations now struck authorities as excellent fronts for smuggling. After all, smuggling rings in some ways served functions similar to the work of established, and beleaguered, Jewish organizations like the Hebrew Sheltering and Immigrant Aid Society—helping prospective immigrants obtain necessary documents, and managing the flow of money and communication between European Jews and their American relatives.

The strong association between Jews and alien smuggling in the years after the quotas passed was worrisome to American Jewish leaders. Just as they were concerned that news of Jewish illegal immigration made for bad publicity for American Jews, so they feared that their own work and reputations would be jeopardized by the association with organized smuggling operations. They knew about Jewish involvement with alien smuggling rings, but were reluctant to discuss it openly. Dr. Joseph Shohan of the Joint Distribution Committee expressed this anxiety in 1922, in a report on the large numbers of eastern European Jews arriving in Cuba and prevented by the new quotas from going legally to the United States. "I had not been in Havana very long before I learned that a considerable number of the refugees managed to find their way into the United States by all sorts of devious ways," he wrote, somewhat obliquely. "It became apparent to me that as a representative of the Joint Distribution Committee it devolved on me to do everything possible to keep the Joint Distribution Committee as far in the background as possible."[117] Throughout the 1920s and 1930s, the news of investigations, indictments, trials, and convictions of smugglers, "racketeers," and others involved in the alien smuggling business kept the issue in the public eye. The American Jews who worked on immigration issues during this era must often have had that very real world of illegal activity and the official consternation it caused at the forefront of their awareness. Their efforts to advocate for Jewish immigrants must be understood in the context of this ever-present notion of alien criminality, a notion from which American Jewish leaders tried hard to distance themselves and the communities they served.

SMUGGLING AND THE REALITY OF THE QUOTA LAWS

An understanding of how the quota laws actually functioned in practice requires taking the alien smuggling underworld into account. First, the criminal networks of Jewish alien smuggling helped shape the dynamics of migration during this era. The history of the smuggling rings that moved people from Europe to the United States highlights the extent to which the immigration of "undesirable" people did not stop with the quota laws. Second, alien smugglers shaped the realities of the immigration quota regime as much as the government officials charged with enforcing it. The quota laws produced the recipe for their own subversion, but the reverse was also true. Evasion of immigration law and enforcement of it developed together, in relation to each other. In other words, enforcement produced criminality and vice versa. Alien smuggling and illegal immigration provided a raison d'être for immigration authorities—the reason they needed more financial resources; more personnel to screen, investigate, report, and deport; more training; and more equipment.

Finally, the networks that alien smugglers created also helped shape the daily on-the-ground reality of immigration law for immigrants during the era of the quota laws. Established and trusted Jewish aid organizations, such as the Hebrew Sheltering and Immigrant Aid Society or the Joint Distribution Committee, were invested in helping would-be immigrants, but limited by their pressing need to remain law abiding. Smuggling rings had no such constraints. The possibility of profit meant that smugglers were willing to take risks in order to provide the means for people to immigrate to the United States. There were benefits and costs as well to those immigrants who availed themselves of smugglers' services. They improved their chances of being able to enter the United States, despite the quota laws that were designed to keep them out, but, in doing so, they exposed themselves to considerable danger along the way, and the possibility of deportation in the event that they were discovered by US authorities. In sum, smugglers and prospective immigrants together created a landscape of Jewish migration with which the authors of the US immigration restrictions had not reckoned.

CHAPTER 4

Illicit Journeys

What do Jewish illegal immigrants' experiences reveal about the workings of the quota laws? How did those laws—and the acts of violating them—shape Jewish migrants' experiences? Consider four tales of Jewish illegal immigration during the quota era. The first is that of Phil Lutzky (born Phishl Rutzki). In 1918, Lutzky fled his native Brainsk, Poland, after the Poles took it over from German occupiers. He went to Brest-Litovsk, then part of White Russia (it would later become part of Poland), using a cousin's passport. There he made a living on the thriving black market, smuggling saccharin across national borders, counterfeiting cigarettes, and trading in gold coins. Resolving to get a visa for the United States, he procured a fake Brest-Litovsk birth certificate—possible since all records had been burned with the city during the war—under the common local surname Lucki. He then used that birth certificate to procure a passport. He proceeded to Warsaw, where a well-timed bribe secured him the necessary additional official validation for that passport in the summer of 1922. As luck would have it, the new annual quota came open just as Lutzky was in Warsaw, and, to his surprise, he had no trouble obtaining an American visa. He sailed to New York on the Baltic America Line with his new name, new place of birth, new passport, and valid visa.[1] Authorities never discovered his fraud.

The second story is that of Max Weinriter, whom Rabbi Martin Zielonka of El Paso encountered in March 1923. A nineteen-year-old Polish Jew, Weinriter had been jailed in El Paso in September 1922 for having immigrated illegally over the Mexico–Texas border. His route had been circuitous. He had stowed away from Poland to London, received help, including some money, from a Jewish organization there, and bought passage to Cuba. Unable to make ends meet in Cuba, Weinriter stowed away again on a French vessel, unsure of where it was going. As it happened, the ship was bound for Veracruz. The penniless Weinriter explained his situation to the ship's Polish-speaking crew members; they chipped in to give him enough cash to get to Mexico City, where he worked and saved some money. Then he headed north, walking and hopping trains. In Juarez, he borrowed money from a fellow migrant for streetcar fare, grabbed an English newspaper, and crossed the border at night without being stopped. Broke and thirsty, he asked for water at a farmhouse, whose owners happened to be Polish Catholics. Weinriter told them that he, too, was Polish Catholic, at which his hosts gave him not only water but also food, a dollar for lodging, and help getting a job in El Paso, where he worked until his arrest a few months later.[2]

The third story is that of three members of the Limonsky family—father and two sons—originally from Lithuania. All entered the United States in 1926 with fake German papers. Isaac Limonsky, the father, unable to get a US visa, intended to go to Uruguay, but (as mentioned in the previous chapter) met a smuggler on the train to Berlin who suggested that he go to the United States instead. Son David Limonsky, separated from his family by the war, went legally to Cuba hoping to enter the United States. Finding that he could not, he returned to Europe. He then tried to emigrate to Palestine, but the English consul in Berlin refused to grant him a visa. He considered going to South America. At the Berlin office of the Argentine consul, however, he met a Yiddish-speaking man named Hymie who, for a fee, supplied David Limonsky with a US visa made out in the name of David Binder, described in the papers as German born. Finally, David's brother Lazer Limonsky also went to Berlin; he hoped to go to Canada in order to cross the border illegally into the United States. In the Berlin ticket office of the Cunard Line, however, he, like his father and brother, met a man—a Galician Jew—who helped him obtain German papers for the United States as Louis Meerowitz.[3]

The last story is that of Clara and Tola Zacharjasz. Early in the morning of May 27, 1926, the fourteen-year old twin girls, "natives and citizens of Poland, of the Hebrew race," were arrested in Bombay, New York, near the Canadian border. They had crossed into the United States illegally, packed in a smuggler's automobile with four Irish men, an Irish woman, and her three children. In a hearing on June 2, the girls explained that they had come to Montreal in January to live with an uncle, but had altered their plans after meeting a Yiddish-speaking man there who promised to transport them to their parents in New York City, for a fee to be paid on arrival. US officials recommended deporting the girls to Poland. But after the Hebrew Sheltering and Immigrant

Aid Society (HIAS) interceded, the government temporarily stayed the deportations. Over the next five years, on repeated appeals, the government continued to grant the sisters extensions on that stay of deportation; meanwhile, the girls lived with their parents in the Bronx and completed high school. In 1931, the original arrest warrants were voided, and the twins were permitted to depart the country voluntarily rather than by deportation. Their father's recent naturalization and the dropped deportation orders would make it possible for the sisters to return legally.[4]

Jewish would-be immigrants' relationships to the quota laws in the post–World War I era were, to say the least, complicated. The arena of illegal immigration was one in which geographical routes were circuitous; where legality was a conceptual gray area; and where identities were in hectic play, getting desperately exchanged like getaway cars. Attention to how the quota laws, which sought to classify people around the world and control their movements, affected people's lives on the ground yields a different sense of the laws' meanings than those that emerge from the other perspectives considered in this study. The Jews who wanted to come to the United States but could not do so legally under the new regime presented the US government with a new category of potential lawbreakers, alien smugglers with a new market, and Jewish aid organizations with a new kind of communal crisis. Their understanding of the quota laws, in other words, was necessarily focused (albeit from very different points of view) on the policy's large-scale implications. Would-be immigrants encountered the new US immigration restrictions on a personal and not an aggregate level, however, and for them the law presented different challenges. It was certainly obvious that the quota laws would make it much harder for many European Jews to come to the United States. However, it was often unclear what the laws would mean for any given person or family. As the stories above demonstrate, people scrambled to make the best decisions amidst great uncertainty. US law "closed the gates" to America in macroterms, but the stories of Jewish illegal immigrants point to the extensive landscape of people not acting according to the grand political and historical narrative.

The history of Jewish illegal immigration also demonstrates just how untidy the boundary between "legal" and "illegal" immigration remained after the quota laws, despite the best efforts of the US government. This untidiness is particularly evident from the perspectives of the individuals involved in illegal immigration. From migrants' standpoints, "illegal immigration" was actually a complicated bundle of different experiences. Immigrants' legal or illegal status is often perceived as something that reflects their actions on entering the nation: did they or didn't they enter according to the law? As the above stories demonstrate, however, it is also true that the acquisition of legal or illegal status could be a winding process with unexpected twists. An immigrant's status as illegal or legal once in the United States could be predicated on a long chain of events originating far from the point of entry: family members' earlier migration choices; relationships to the legal regimes or underworlds of different countries; and chance encounters along journeys with uncertain destinations. Indeed, the very boundaries between legal and illegal status function in a range of ways across the stories, and people were deemed "legal" or "illegal" immigrants in different ways at different times. The Zacherjasz twins were immediately apprehended but also quickly granted temporary release and later permanent amnesty, thanks to the intercession of HIAS and to their father's acquired citizenship. The Limonskys' illegal entries were not discovered for a decade, when the Department of Labor learned about a number of similar cases. Lutzky's illicit procurement of Polish documents with which he obtained a valid US visa was never discovered or declared illegal at all.

The history of Jewish illegal immigration draws our attention, too, to the shifting terrain of national borders, on the one hand, and of ethnic and national identities in the post–World War I era, on the other. Individual Jews' experiences show, somewhat paradoxically, both the efficacy and the failures of the conjoined state projects of controlling territory and defining individual identities. As all the above stories demonstrate, immigrants had to contend with a world in which national borders and personal identities were taking on new meanings in relation to each other. Individuals' identities, as evidenced by official state documents such as passports and visas, had become crucial for legitimate movement across borders and for immigration to the United States in particular. The policing of borders, meanwhile, both in Europe and in the United States, was intimately bound up with new forms of classifying, documenting, and tracking those people who sought to cross them.[5] Jewish illegal immigration was produced by the new regime of papers and borders, but also called its underlying logic into question. This was particularly so in cases in which, like the Limonskys and Lutsky, immigrants presented themselves to government officials with documents acquired fraudulently. Identity documents, by definition, assert that they are truthful reflections of the people who carry them. The documents that immigrants in this era were required to show purported to describe their bearers' nationality, race, and sex; visas reflected consuls' judgments, too, about health, financial, and familial status. All these categories were of vital importance to states in their pursuit of migration and border control. Their presence on official documents, indeed, announced that such categories were matters for the state to define and assign. In reality, however, the papers that migrants carried could sometimes say less about who they were than who they needed to appear to be in order to get somewhere else. The US government's efforts to limit immigration by the more stringent forms of counting, classifying, documenting, and policing entailed in the implementation of the quota laws were undeniably powerful. Together with the broader documentary enforcement regime to which these efforts contributed, the laws helped restructure the meanings of national borders and identities on the deepest level and to reshape the flow of people around the globe. Yet, even as the history of illegal immigration reflects just how powerful the extension of state control proved to be, it also reveals that this process was never complete. It is in the tensions between the personal tales of evading the quota laws and the mass effects of the laws, between state-imposed categories of identity and people's varied success at slipping in and out of these categories, and between the micro- and the macrohistorical, that we begin to see the power of legal regimes in defining experiences and identities and the limits of such power.

THE NONLINEAR ACQUISITION OF ILLEGALITY

From the point of view of Jewish migrants, illegal immigration to the United States was rarely an act that took place at just one moment or one place; rather, it was a process that emerged across many moments and many places. Much immigration, including legal immigration, to the United States, was a multistage venture, involving many legs of a journey and plenty of unexpected obstacles. But illegal immigration could prove especially circuitous and unpredictable, frequently entailing changes of plan, en route complications, and roundabout journeys. Similarly, the legal status or statuses associated with migration were not always acquired in a straightforward, linear fashion. Both the process of migration and the acquisition of legal or illegal status involved multiple kinds of circuitry spanning geographic distance—those channels through which information, money, and people passed.

Moreover, individual Jewish immigrants had to juggle, at every juncture, both personal and macropolitical considerations to maximize their options, taking into account family relationships and resources; financial and health issues; means of transportation, housing and employment; and the laws of various lands. Indeed, Jewish migrants' decisions to violate US law must be understood in an international context. Even Rabbi Martin Zielonka of El

Paso, whose own unforgiving frame of reference was that of American politics and laws, understood that. The Jewish immigrants who had crossed into Texas over the Mexican border, Zielonka reflected in 1926, "had crossed other borders and one more crossing meant little to them."[6] The rabbi thus acknowledged—albeit unsympathetically—an important truth about the Jewish illegal immigration he was trying so hard to stem. Jewish illegal immigrants had often crossed several national borders and thus had to confront the obstacles posed by laws in a range of places, not just the United States. At any given moment, then, an individual's migration might be legal, illegal, quasi legal, or some combination of these, depending on which state's laws he or she considered.

Other American Jews involved in immigration issues noted that European Jews had a hard-won expertise in dealing with antagonistic structures of authority and official barriers, and that this expertise shaped their ideas about migration. In his report about the Jews stranded in Europe by the Immigration Act of 1924,[7] the Joint Distribution Committee's Werner Senator described the pathological stubbornness that he felt European Jews' clashes with authorities had engendered:

[T]he employees of the United States Line threatened those persons, who, for years, had not paid for their food and lodging, with expulsion and return to Russia. The emigrants were not nonplussed. Neither the police of Bremen nor the employees of the United States Line could frighten them. They had experienced pogroms, bolshevism, wanderings for many years, and were able to stand what the Bremen police might possibly inflict upon them—only another proof of the indifference, obstinacy and demoralization prevailing among these emigrants.[8]

Senator's views reflected his frustration with the way individual Jewish migrants' insistence on waiting for US visas sometimes derailed his organization's efforts to "solve" their problems by procuring them visas for other places (e.g., South American nations). However, Senator's observation that Jewish migrants' decisions and behavior were born of experience with the "wanderings for many years" occasioned by war and political upheavals, and with government intimidation and legal constraints, is apt. Would-be Jewish immigrants to the United States of the post–World War I era had often become skilled at calculating how to move through a world in which national borders, the regulations of political regimes, and official identities made little consistent sense—often changing overnight—even as they were life and death issues that determined where and when one could move at all. European Jews drew upon this skill in assessing the new international migration situation created by the drastic change in US law.

A crucial element in shaping the choices people made about migration in the confusing postwar world was information. Ideas and decisions about migration were often forged communally, in both the public and private realms.[9] Jews hoping to get to the United States had to put in effort to obtain information about the workings of US law and to determine what, at any given moment, they might try to do, whether legally or illegally. Their families did the same. Circuits of information—formal and informal, public and private—crisscrossed the ocean. Information could be conflicting; thus, migrants constantly had to choose which information to take into account and whose advice to follow and whose to disregard.

Both the European and American Jewish press played an important role in the circuitry of news and rumor about what was legal and what was not vis-à-vis the new US laws. The New York–based Yiddish *Forverts* (Forward), for example, ran practical articles for its readers on the subject, such as a 1921 piece explaining to those who could no longer bring their relatives into the United States how to get them to Canada instead.[10] Beginning in 1925, the *Forverts*'s rival daily the *Tog* (Day) featured a regular column on immigration issues in which readers' queries about the quota laws' complexities were answered by the Jewish New York Congressman Samuel Dickstein, and later by HIAS. (The Jewish immigrants stranded in Bremen requested a subscription to the *Tog*, presumably in part so as to keep abreast of legislative developments that could determine their fate.)[11] In some large eastern European cities, meanwhile, prospective migrants could consult periodicals focused entirely on emigration.[12]

Jewish organizations on both sides of the Atlantic, as institutions directly involved with migration matters, were also crucial conduits of information and news, as they had been before World War I. These groups disseminated information about immigration to the United States both in person at their branch offices and by means of their own publications and statements to the press. Indeed, they often saw themselves as working to counter misinformation about legal issues widely published in the press. They noted, for example, that newspaper reports on the subject of legal loopholes or impending changes in American immigration legislation could lead migrants to make decisions that the organizations deemed ill considered. The Joint Distribution Committee's Werner Senator expressed the opinion that the media fostered false hopes that led migrants to reject organizations' advice to emigrate somewhere besides the

United States. "The Yiddish press of Europe and America," he wrote, "is full of news about motions for amendments to the American immigration bill. And influenced by these news, often spread unscrupulously, the emigrants prefer their misery to some decisive step."[13] Similarly, in October 1928, the newsletter of HIAS-ICA-Emigdirect (an umbrella group of American and European organizations formed in 1927 after the dissolution of the United Evacuation Committee) printed a statement forwarded from the New York headquarters of HIAS. Apparently, Jews in Poland, Romania, and the Baltics had been writing to their American kin about a rumor that eastern European Jews could emigrate to Honduras, acquire Honduran citizenship, and then come into the United States outside of the European quotas.[14] "This report," HIAS warned, "is absolutely false. It is known that entry into the United States depends not on the citizenship of the immigrant, but rather on his native land."[15]

The HIAS-ICA-Emigdirect newsletter item suggests the way that personal letters, long the most important way for families on opposite sides of the Atlantic to stay in touch, were now a forum for discussing options and plans in the face of the new laws. Family consultations could prove more important in European Jews' decision-making process than the warnings of aid organizations. The report of a social worker for the Boston section of the National Council of Jewish Women (NCJW) also shows this dynamic in action. In January 1926, she paid a visit to a Mr. Shuman, hoping to enlist his help in convincing his brother-in-law, among those migrants stranded in Europe by the Immigration Act of 1924, to accept a visa for a nation other than the United States. He listened politely, she wrote, but was "entirely opposed to [the] proposition." He had received a letter from his brother-in-law just two weeks earlier, stating that he and his family expected to obtain their US visas by the coming July. Furthermore, Mr. Shuman suggested, he and his relatives did not need the advice of the NCJW:

> Mr. Shuman told worker that his brother-in-law is an intelligent man, who understands the immigration situation thoroughly and is fully cognizant of his own position. His brother-in-law, he says, is a man who has been in business for himself and can fully realize his own problems and needs. Mr. Shuman, himself, is an intelligent person, is acquainted with the immigration laws of this country and keeps in touch with the various movements to assist immigrants.[16]

Both the above examples demonstrate how conduits of private and public information might function both in tension and in concert for those trying to make the best decisions about what to do and where to go. If the HIAS-ICA-Emigdirect newsletter took a cautious stance on the issue, warning would-be immigrants that Honduras was not a back door to the United States, individuals themselves were nevertheless grappling with a new list of unknown variables and doing so in conversation with family members abroad. The existence and circulation of the Honduras rumor illustrate how American immigration restrictions forced European Jews and their US-based relatives to reimagine the world in terms of a new relationship between US laws and European Jews' geographic trajectories.

Family members' opinions could play particularly important roles in people's migration decisions when would-be immigrants were being financially supported by relatives in the United States. Twenty-two-year-old Sima Malkin was one of the migrants stranded with a defunct US visa in Bremen after 1924. The Jewish organizations involved there were urging her to go to Canada. Her mother, however—who had been deported with Sima to Bremen but readmitted on a nonquota basis to the United States, without Sima, after marrying her brother-in-law, an American citizen—was adamant that Sima not emigrate to Canada. "She wishes the girl," wrote the NCJW to the United Evacuation Committee in 1925, "to remain in Bremen until she is granted a visa" and could come legally to the United States.[17] In 1926, Fruma Portnoy, in a situation similar to Sima's, acquiesced to the desire of her relatives in the United States that she should try to leave Bremen for Canada (it is not clear whether this was with the ultimate goal of coming to the United States).[18]

Although many European Jews chose to follow family members' advice in their decisions about migration, the issues involved in such decisions were so difficult that families could be divided over the right thing to do, particularly when lawbreaking was involved. In 1921, a young European Jewish man—one S. Goldberg—tried unsuccessfully to cross from Juarez into El Paso. He was stranded and in desperate need of money. A worker from a Brooklyn Jewish aid agency, presumably alerted by Rabbi Martin Zielonka to the situation, paid a call on the young man's father, Joseph Goldberg. The senior Goldberg, a cobbler who had come from Europe over a decade earlier, leaving his wife and son behind, was not sympathetic to his son's current predicament. He explained that his wife had died; the son had gotten in some kind of trouble and expressed to his father his desire to come to the United States. Joseph Goldberg warned strongly against this, fearing difficulties. The son, Goldberg told the social worker, went against the father's wishes and "listened to his cousin . . . who advised him to come to the United States through Mexico." Goldberg had already cabled his son nearly a thousand dollars and refused to send more. The social worker reported, "[Goldberg] is very unhappy about the state of affairs. States that his son has constantly deceived him. Also wrote him untruthful stories and he would prefer to have him deported rather than have him remain in Mexico."[19]

The fact that the son disobeyed his father and heeded his cousin's advice, and that the son's dishonesty and repeated requests for money so rankled with the father, speaks to the way decisions about migration could be shaped by the particular dynamics of family relationships. Indeed, sometimes Jewish migrants came to the United States illegally because they were bowing to the wishes of family members who desired them to do so. Chaim Wolf Reiter, for example, was happy in Argentina, where he had come from Soviet Russia around 1924 to join his brother Oscar. It was only because he felt a deep obligation to his family in the United States that he undertook to purchase the identity documents of a Uruguayan-born Italian man named Gaspar Giuseppi, which he used to enter the United States in 1926. Later, his family wanted Reiter to engage in yet another round of illegal immigration: to return to Europe to "marry" his own sister, presumably under a false name, so that she could join the family in the United States. (Ultimately, Reiter's family paid someone else to do this.[20]) In another instance of family pressure, the family of Harry and Tillie Friedman—originally from Russia, the couple met and married in Montreal—decided that Harry's gambling habit had gotten out of hand and that he would be better off working for his brothers' scrap metal business in Boston. They arranged to send him there illegally some time around 1926. Tillie followed soon thereafter, crossing the Canada–US border in a farmer's sled.[21]

For many European Jews, then, immigration to the United States remained, as it long had been—and despite the quota laws—a family affair. That is, many families approached migration as family units, even when families were increasingly of "mixed legality" in relation to the law.[22] The legal immigration status of some family members was often a factor in convincing others to come illegally. This seems to have been important for Shaya Petlin, the migrant described in chapter 2 who illegally crossed the Mexican border in an attempt to reach his sisters, legal immigrants living in Dayton, Ohio. The young Zacherjasz twins, for their part, probably would not have set out for the United States from Canada had they not had close relatives there to receive them.[23] Many European Jews, particularly young, single men, braved illegal immigration alone, but many more had family to come to, to put up capital for the trip, and to shelter them once they arrived. Often that family was in the United States legally. This fact could serve to make immigrants who came illegally feel that their choices were aboveboard. Isaac Limonsky, testifying in 1936 before a congressional committee considering amnesty for a number of immigrants whose fraudulent documents had been belatedly discovered, argued as much before the nation's lawmakers. "I think I cannot be blamed for that [decision to come to the United States illegally]," he testified, "because all of my family is here."[24]

The tale recounted above of Tilly and Harry Friedman, Russian Jews who had settled in Canada but then decided to cross the border illegally into the United States to help Harry get a fresh start, points to another theme that characterizes the stories of many Jewish illegal immigrants in the quota era. Some migrants who never intended to go to the United States, believing that the new US restrictions precluded this choice, reconsidered later in their journeys. Experiences after migrants left home, in other words, often propelled them into their decisions to try to enter the United States and then shaped the means they chose to do so. Many European Jews who entered the United States illegally did so because they were improvising. They left home without knowing where they would end up, or they changed their routes along the way and opted to try an illegal entry into the United States. Like Max Weinriter, many European Jews had to make their decisions en route. And like him, as well as Tillie and Harry Friedman, the Limonsky family, and the Zacherjasz twins, many individuals decided to go to the United States illegally only after spending time in another country or countries, such as Germany, Cuba, or Canada. By the same token, many of those people who went to Mexico, Cuba, Canada, or other countries in the hopes of entering the United States illegally from there ended up changing their minds and staying. All migration entailed encounters with new people and places, and complicated decision making along the way; it could be an even more unpredictable process when the final destination was unknown and when laws were in flux even as people were in motion.

The decision to enter the United States despite the quota laws often came to seem the best possible option when European Jews ran into economic trouble after migrating elsewhere. David Limonsky's and Max Weinriter's realizations that work was scarce in Cuba—especially the case in that country after the international sugar market crashed in the 1920s—led them onward.[25] Similarly, as Rabbi Martin Zielonka realized when he decided to organize the International Order of the B'nai B'rith's Mexican Bureau, the fact that many European Jews in Mexico had difficulty earning enough money to live, and that they had no organized or informal communal aid to fall back on, were crucial factors in their decisions to head for the United States.

Wherever European Jews tried to go, the very act of migration in the era of

the quota laws offered an education in the difficulties and possibilities of finding a route to the United States. Everywhere, this issue was a subject of discussion. We have seen, for example, how alien smugglers propositioned Jews on
European trains who admitted having uncertain travel plans, and how those
smugglers offered their services to Jews who were in consular offices pursuing legal US visas in vain. Many European Jews learned about their options
somewhere along their journey from fellow migrants to whom they might turn
for financial assistance or local advice. In port cities and transit hubs, there was
a lively culture of talk about the best means, both legal and illegal, of getting
to the United States. In early 1921, a HIAS worker described such a culture
already in operation in Havana's Parque Central, a well-known gathering place
for European Jewish migrants:

> The south-eastern corner being the most shady the immigrants selected that
> as their assembly ground. There one could find at all times groups of immi-
> grants discussing their problems, sharing their last pennies with those who
> had none, and some of them sleeping night after night and week after week
> on the stone benches. The principal topic for discussion at all times was the
> question of procuring visas and of going to the United States.[26]

The alien smuggling business, along with more informal modes of entering
the United States illegally, generated stories, gossip, and conversation that in
turn must have led many people to decide to enter the United States illegally.
Those congregating in Parque Central during the quota era, for example,
would have learned that smuggling to Florida or Louisiana by boat was possible and, perhaps, under the circumstances, the best choice.

As important as family considerations and experiences en route in shaping
European Jews' relationship to illegal immigration to the United States was
the legal context from which they came. For many eastern European Jews, in
particular, finding ways around restrictive and arbitrary-seeming laws was a
necessity, and the US quota laws presented just one more such barrier to be
surmounted by whatever means were possible. As noted earlier, the World
War I era witnessed the establishment of documentary border guarding not
only in the United States but also throughout the region from which European
Jews were coming, as well as those through which they passed en route to
the United States. The Austrian Jewish novelist and journalist Joseph Roth,
one of the period's keenest commentators on the difficulties of eastern European Jews who undertook to migrate westward, described the desperate
absurdities involved in what he dubbed "the Eastern Jew's bitter existential

struggle against papers."[27] In Poland, Russia, and Romania, for example, obtaining passports and visas was a costly, time-consuming struggle involving a string of bribes to officials and other parties on the take, including forgers of birth or marriage certificates. In the western nations such as Germany or Austria, meanwhile, eastern European Jews were expected to produce orderly proof of identity. In one article, Roth describes how eastern European Jews trying to register with the police in Vienna, as they were required to do upon arriving in the city, were met with the demand "to see papers. Exotic, improbable papers . . . The birthdates are inaccurate. The papers have generally been burned. (The registry offices in small towns in Galicia, Lithuania, and Ukraine were continually ablaze.) All the papers have been lost. Nationality is a moot point. Following the War and the Treaty of Versailles, it's become still more complicated."[28] Official demands for neatly packaged legal Jewish identities, Roth noted, in fact produced illegal Jewish identities. The demand for proper documentation refused to acknowledge the realities of Jewish lives:

> So he's sent packing, and again, and again, and again. Till it dawns on the Jew that he has no option but to give false information for the correct impression. . . . The police have given the Eastern Jew the idea of concealing a true but tangled set of circumstances behind bogus but tidy ones. Everyone professes astonishment at the capacity of Jews to give false information. No one professes astonishment at the naïve expectations of the police.[29]

As Roth's article indicates, Jewish migration in the European postwar context was often a shady business, however much it was characterized by the trappings of legal bureaucracy—indeed, it was precisely such trappings that allowed the underground market in forgeries and smuggling to flourish. As noted in the previous chapter, the Jewish migration experience in Europe had long been characterized by such illicit practices, to the extent that illegal border crossings had become the norm.[30] Indeed, the tradition of illegal emigration from the Russian Empire, where Jews' relationship to the state had been precarious—targeted as Jews were by special laws limiting their rights as residents and workers, as well as by state-sponsored violence—reflected the longstanding tenuousness of Jewish legal identity.

This was doubly true for that vast portion of the male population in violation of the dreaded military draft in the Russian Empire. Many Jews had regarded military service in the tsar's brutal and anti-Semitic army as essentially a death sentence. Like David Limonsky, who explained to Congress that he left Lithuania for Germany with false papers because he had avoided military service, eastern European Jewish men had long found the draft an important reason for emigrating by illicit means. So many individuals chose emigration in the late nineteenth and early twentieth century—illegally, as draft evasion precluded obtaining the necessary papers—as their means of escaping military service that the practice was firmly institutionalized. "There was an established system for aiding and abetting those who desired to run away," recalled Israel Davidson in his memoir of his emigration.[31] Evading military service remained an urgent issue for many eastern European Jewish men during the postwar era, as the new regimes persisted in hostility toward their Jewish populations. The urgency of avoiding military service was augmented by the fact that, in many places in the region, hostilities continued for several years.

The issue of draft evasion points to the way illegal migration—whether emigration or immigration—was often intertwined with Jewish migrants' fraught relationship to the law in other contexts. Emigration was only one of many arenas in which eastern European Jews relied on illegal methods. Buying and selling on the black market, smuggling, assuming fake identities, and obtaining forged papers were, particularly in the chaos that followed World War I, facts of life. Philip Lutzky made this point in his account of his own life, as narrated to his grandson. "You must remember," he said, after recounting his exploits selling counterfeit cigarettes in postwar Poland, "that at the time people were not completely legitimate." Starting from the time the Poles reconquered his home town of Brainsk, Poland, Lutzky's life was, in many ways, defined by illegality, from his flight with fake papers to Brest-Litovsk, to his jobs smuggling saccharin across the Russian border and selling gold coins on the black market, to his efforts to obtain the papers that were the prerequisites for a US visa. Those immigrants who entered the United States in violation of US law, then, were often doing so in the context of longer histories of necessary lawbreaking.

Indeed, Lutzky's story illustrates how hard it can be to determine just where the boundary between illegal and legal migration lies at all. His US visa, though obtained only by virtue of forged papers and documents procured via bribery, was itself authentic. Lutzky recalled that he took pride in what he understood to be his legal status: "I was proud that I was . . . legally allowed to emigrate to this country. All I cared for was that had my passport and visa with my picture attached, properly stamped and approved by the authorities." At the same time, he was aware of the illegal underpinnings of this legal status and the danger he might be in: "If anybody wanted to point a finger at me," he remembered realizing, "and say I am not the person I claim to be I would be in trouble."[32]

While the distinction between his forged European papers and his authentic US visa mattered to Lutzky, at least in his recollection, for other Jewish illegal immigrants this was not the case. Many of those individuals who entered by means of fake papers had reason to understand their legal status under US law ambiguously, given the situations from which they came. National identities themselves, which passports and visas were meant to represent conclusively, were not always clear to people from a region in which borders and sovereign control had long been violently contested. A great many eastern Europeans, indeed—Jews as well as others—had been rendered not only homeless but also stateless by the war.[33] A Jewish man tried to articulate some of the regional complexities around the concept of nationality for the congressional committee that convened in 1936 to consider the cases of the Limonskys and others. His wife's illegal entry into the United States on German papers might well have seemed legal to her, he explained. "During the war and right after the war there was such a mixture that the states themselves did not know," he told the lawmakers. "The Lithuanian Government claims a lot of territory today which Poland claims."[34] Lazar Limonsky testified, in a similar vein: "I don't know where I was born. When I was born Lithuania was under Russia, under the Tsar, so I do not know where I was born, whether in Lithuania or in Russia."[35] Smugglers who convinced Lithuanian Jews to enter the United States on German papers by reminding them that Lithuania had been under German control before and during World War I (and that residents had possessed German papers at the time) were, in a sense, invoking the logic of the quota laws themselves—the idea that the primary consideration for the US government was the country where one was born. As still another immigrant explained to the congressional committee, "In Lithuania there was all German citizens. I did not know it was a crime. If I knew, I would not have come and bring up my children here. . . . [I]n Lithuania we was German citizens. . . . I did not know it would be so bad. I thought it was all right. . . . I thought everything was perfect."[36]

Furthermore, the fact that the migration business in Europe, like many other sectors of the economy and government, was mired in corruption meant it could be hard to distinguish legitimate and illegitimate documents and dealings. As Lutzky's story suggests, such transactions were often all mixed together. Given that, as noted in the previous chapter, smugglers sometimes posed as US or other government authorities, and that the actual authorities were sometimes involved in smuggling, it is understandable that some people believed the channels through which they came were legitimate—or, at least, legitimate enough. "The very fact that I went to the consulate at Berlin and obtained them," one Mrs. Radin testified to Congress, "assured me everything was 100-percent right."[37] Indeed, several illegal immigrants testifying in those hearings and on other occasions made the rather convincing argument that had they known their status was illegal, they would never have had the gall to present themselves to the US authorities for naturalization—the moment, in many cases, that the authorities scrutinized their documents and identified them as law violators. As Mrs. Radin put it, referring to the naturalization process, "I would not have had the audacity to apply for second papers had I known anything was wrong."[38]

Even those Jewish illegal immigrants who admitted that they were fully aware that they had broken the law sometimes regarded their actions as violations of other nations' laws rather than those of the United States. That is, some migrants understood the illegal procurement of papers to enter the United States as a solely European matter—simply the way so much business there was transacted—that would have no bearing on their status in the United States. The "remote control" processes of immigration control implemented by the United States with the 1924 quota law, seemed, from the migrants' point of view, unconnected to the workings of US law.[39] "I really did not know it had to do with this country," Jacob Labovitz told Congress in 1936, by way of explaining why he had used false papers to enter the United States. "I figured it had something to do with Germany. . . . But in this country, I came here in order to become a citizen. I really did not know it was anything wrong." Another immigrant tried to explain to Congress that the legality of documents in Europe was a subjective, approximate concept: "The respect that they have for the birth certificates and for the correctness of these items is not as much there as it is developed and cultivated right here in the United States," he testified. "They will not trouble themselves about it. They do not consider it so serious."[40] From immigrants' perspectives, in other words, their illegal status in the United States could appear to be the product of a problem of translation from one legal regime to another. What struck US authorities as a serious breach of the new immigration law seemed, to many immigrants, a casual and necessary violation of the sort that they considered to be legitimate. Still other Jewish illegal immigrants argued that acquiring illegal status was an inevitable chain of causality, one fake paper making the next one illegitimate as well. "[W]hat could I do," one immigrant explained to Congress, making a point similar to the one the writer Joseph Roth made in his description of Jewish encounters with Viennese police, "when my entire line of papers was the same way. I considered it, but I could not help myself."[41]

Jews who had once lived in German-controlled Lithuania or who trusted the people who handed them papers in a consulate office might have believed it was aboveboard to enter the United States with German papers. Those who stowed away on ships or came over the border in cars during the night, however, would have been more likely to know they were breaking the law. Nevertheless, just as Rabbi Martin Zielonka made a distinction between illegal entry and other kinds of legal violations, arguing that illicit border crossing was not a "moral" crime, those migrants who recognized their acts as illegal did not necessarily see them as immoral, criminal, or worthy of punishment. In 1931, for example, the *Forverts* printed an impassioned account by Mordecai Freilich, an immigrant who was imprisoned after being apprehended trying to smuggle into Florida by boat. He was outraged by the prison experience. "They hold us," he wrote, "as if we were criminals, murderers, in dark stinking rooms with little to eat."[42]

The quota laws—and, more broadly, the international system of migration and identity control of which they were a part—created new categories of legal and illegal migration. How and when particular people became illegal immigrants, however, could be as complicated as people's migration routes themselves. Jews entering the United States illegally did so with diverse relationships to legality, as well as to the laws governing international migration. Jewish migrants' own understandings of law, forged in the contexts of family, community, and the places from and through which they were coming, shaped the actions they took in the face of the US immigration restrictions and thus the meanings the quota regime had for people at the time.

STRATEGIES OF ENTRY: MASQUERADE, FORGERY, DISGUISE

If Jewish immigrants' illegal status was forged gradually, in the course of a lengthy series of journeys and the acquisition of different documents, the moment in which they entered the United States was often laden with particular drama. Many of the immigrants who entered the country illegally did so with no recourse to disguise or forgeries. Like the Zacherjasz twins, some immigrants just crossed the border surreptitiously. Some came as temporary visitors and overstayed their visas, meaning that their status became illegal long after they actually crossed the border. For many others, however, the central question was how to get past the nation's gatekeepers, the inspectors who presided over the docking of ships and the traffic over land-crossing points, checked immigrants' papers, and decided whom to detain and whom to allow entry. One immigration official's pleased observation that, after passage of the quota laws, the immigrants at Ellis Island "looked exactly like Americans" provides a clue to one of the most important strategies illegal immigrants employed, namely, to *appear* right.[43] Either one had to look like the "right" kind of immigrant (either an immigrant of a nationality with a large quota, or an immigrant eligible to enter the country as "nonquota") or one must not appear to be an immigrant at all (for example, by carrying a naturalized American citizen's papers or slipping ashore as a sailor). The moments in which Jewish immigrants entered the country illegally thus often involved both performance and passing.

The restrictionist laws were predicated on the principle that there was a natural hierarchy of race and ethnicity. As we saw in the history of alien smugglers, however, the same laws that decreed some people unfit to immigrate provided the recipe for their own subversion. Record keepers were aware of the complexity of ethnic categories and shifting national borders, and they made extraordinary efforts to keep track of these variables. But however finely tuned the classificatory system, real people—real bodies—confounded discursive categorization.

Like tales of other kinds of passing, these brief episodes of masquerade speak to a highly charged contest over defining identities, as well as the difficulties in gauging "true" identities from people's outward performances. Scholars critiquing American constructions of race have long been interested in the phenomenon of racial passing, particularly black-to-white, and the ways such acts of passing have always expressed, as Gayle Wald puts it, "struggles for control over racial representation in a context of the radical unreliability of embodied appearances."[44] Other scholars have turned to the realm of "performance" to help reconceptualize the complex terrain of identities, including race, class, ethnicity, nationality, sexuality, and gender. Philosopher Judith Butler, for example, has argued that identities—especially gender and sexual identities—are performances embedded in everyday structures of action and meaning.[45] Other scholars have studied theater, film, burlesque, vaudeville, blackface minstrelsy, dance, radio, and television, to explore how people imagine and create who they are as they perform and spectate.[46] Scholars have read the stage and film performances of figures such as Al Jolson or Fanny Brice, for example, who put on and took off "Jewish" and other ethnic identities, as revealing allegories for the ways Jews navigated their relationship to American "racial formations," and rehearsed and staged their claims to Americanness.[47]

The moments in which Jews engaged in masquerade in order to "pass" into the country differ in some ways from other modes of performance and passing. Jewish illegal immigrants were involved in *multiple* strategies of impersonation at points of entry, and these strategies were interconnected and sometimes interchangeable. Although the effort to appear not to be an illegal immigrant sometimes entailed posing as a member of another ethnic or national group, there were many ways to accomplish entry into the United States beyond appearing "not Russian Jewish" or "not foreign." Passing as a temporary visitor to the country, a Jewish alien married to an American citizen, a naturalized foreigner returning from a tourist excursion, a Cuban citizen, or a stevedore could all serve the same function of getting immigrants into the country. Thus, illegal immigration via disguise or forgery highlighted not only the ways that US immigration law depended on efforts to define and perceive race and ethnicity but also the way the law relied on categorizing people by marital status and citizenship, as well as their reasons for traveling.

Furthermore, unlike racial passing, which generally reflected the nature of race as embedded in laws and social structures in operation throughout the nation or region (however much race has also been understood locally), the instances of Jewish illegal immigration via disguise were about laws that functioned primarily at politically charged points of entry. The quota laws made identity a vexed issue there because those were the points at which people were most carefully scrutinized to determine whether they were "legal" or "illegal" according to the new regime. For Jewish immigrants (as for other Europeans targeted by the quota laws), successful passing at the US border meant that the ordeal of passing was over, at least for the time being. The distinctions between legal and illegal Jewish immigrants would, by and large, disappear in the nation's interior. In other words, in a place like Brooklyn or Chicago, a Jewish immigrant who had entered the United States illegally in 1928 would be indistinguishable from one who had entered legally in the same year, at least outwardly. In this way, the experiences of Jews and other Europeans were different from the experiences of Chinese or other Asian immigrants who engaged in similar subterfuges to enter the country. Asians—even native-born citizens—were marked throughout the nation as racial and legal outsiders in ways that Europeans were not. Moreover, Asian immigrants were likely to be heading to marginalized communities whose members were often racially "ineligible to citizenship" and the objects of widespread prejudice—communities, in other words, whose presence in the nation was deemed barely legitimate. Europeans, by contrast, were coming to well-established communities rooted in a history of legal immigration and the privileges of citizenship.[48]

Nevertheless, even though entering the United States with a forged identity was, for Jewish immigrants, a temporary interaction distinct from longer-term processes of identity formation, such interactions still spoke to some of the same forces shaping these sociological processes. These moments at the gates of the United States, as extremely fraught encounters with both the physical and discursive borders of nation, race, ethnicity, and citizenship, embodied broader tensions between exclusion and inclusion in the national home that characterized American Jewish life during this period. The period after the quota laws' passage was a time of Jewish assimilation and upward mobility, but it was also, as discussed earlier, an era characterized by increasing anti-Semitism, racialized nativism, and social discrimination. Were Jews able, and should they be allowed, to blend in with the general populace? What distinguished them from other foreigners or from other Americans? When was a Jew too foreign for the nation to assimilate? These questions, part of the era's national debate over ethnicity, race, and immigration, and important to American Jews in both their formal organizational lives and in their everyday experiences, were in literal play at points of entry. Jewish immigrants entering the nation through fraudulent means were contesting American assumptions about the nature of Jewishness and alienness even as they were making use of them.

Consider the issue of language, obviously an important clue for immigration officials as to immigrants' "racial" or ethnic identities. Some immigrants were indeed identifiable as Jewish by their mother tongue, Yiddish. But many also spoke Polish, German, Hungarian, Russian, or other tongues as their first, second, or third languages. After spending time in Cuba or Mexico, some learned enough Spanish to pose as natives of those countries. Others studied English until they could pass as foreign-born or native US citizens, such as one Jewish immigrant who arrived in Miami from Havana in 1927, claiming that he had been born in Chester, Pennsylvania, had lived in the United States all his life, and had gone to Havana on only a short jaunt. His documents—a birth certificate and tourist identification card, which he purchased from one Yacob Nayman in Havana—did not hold up under scrutiny. However, unlike a fellow Greek traveler who also tried unsuccessfully to pass himself off as American, "the Jew spoke good English, having studied the English language in . . . a college in Kief, Russia," and thus was able to make a far more convincing case for himself. Like the Polish Jewish carpenter, Chaim Listopad, who would try a similar strategy a year later, this traveler had never been to the United States. This fact was, however, difficult to prove. Jacksonville inspector Isaac Smith and his colleagues had to spend all day questioning the man. "I finally got a confession from him as the sun was about to set, and I would have been working on him yet if he had not confessed," wrote Smith in his report.[49]

Like language, physical difference was also supposed to mark immigrants' alienness. Authorities in border towns and coastal areas were on the lookout for, as one New Orleans official put it, "strange-looking aliens."[50] The alien "can be spotted without difficulty even in a big . . . crowd," an immigration patrol inspector named Bonazzi told the *Saturday Evening Post*.[51] One undercover US immigration inspector, staking out the home of a Jewish Torontonian named Klein, who was suspected of smuggling aliens (mostly Czechs) over the border, provided a log of his efforts to identify aliens: "Four men, apparently aliens, were seen to be hanging around house. . . . A young fellow closely resembling an alien, which he was, left Klein's house, went to Sylverstein's Bakery on Baldwin St., disappeared inside."[52] After engaging the young man in conversation by asking him for a match, the inspector decided that his accent gave him away as alien.

Despite these investigators' confidence in their work, alien spotting was not necessarily easy. Undercover agents, informers, and immigrants themselves often described people as "looking alien," or "looking Jewish"—or not Jewish—but they could not always be sure. Appearances could speak volumes. However, they could also be misleading. Consider the image of smuggler Samuel Weisstein in his white tropical suit and straw hat—hardly the picture of an Old World Jew or a New York one. Accents were sometimes telling, but they, too, could be changed, and even authentic accents were not definitive proof of the speaker's current residence or citizenship.

Nevertheless, those on the front lines of the laws' implementation persevered, often relying on their gut feelings about the legal status of aliens. "The officers [of the border patrol]," explained the *New York Times* in 1927, "become students of human faces and sift out doubtful ones for examination."[53] As an American official in Montreal explained in a letter to the commissioner general of immigration about aliens who posed as tourists but intended to remain in the country, "It often happens that our officers have an instinctive feeling that an alien is seeking permanent admission in the guise of a visitor."[54] One magazine article explained how agents often had to resort to a kind of "sixth sense" to guess at who might be illegal.[55] Such guesswork was made more difficult because foreignness and alienness were not necessarily the same thing. Citizenship was hard to see, especially given the sophisticated market in forged documents.

The inspectors' task was further complicated by the fact that, as the previous chapter demonstrated, there were many kinds of documentation, besides passports or visas, which migrants could purchase abroad and use to appear to be someone else as they entered the country. Some immigrants crossing the Canadian and Mexican borders into the United States, for example, presented the special border-crossing identification that was issued to regular local commuters. Those immigrants coming from Cuba could show the identification cards issued to American tourists on exiting the United States. Others, like Chaim Listopad or the immigrant who had studied English in Kiev, could show American naturalization papers. Finally, like Phil Lutzky, many illegal immigrants had bona fide passports and visas—but had obtained those documents fraudulently. This sort of deception was difficult to detect at the moment of entry.

Moreover, immigrants often employed a bewildering range of disguises, whether or not they were entering with false papers. Even superficial disguises could sometimes allow immigrants to enter the country without their identities being questioned at all. "An American suit of clothes and a hair-cut to match," the *New York Times* reported in 1927, could be sufficient to allow Europeans to cross the Canadian border without detection.[56] In Havana an informant told the undercover immigration inspector Feri Weiss about a woman who was smuggled into the United States on a big steamer, disguised as a sailor. "Many women have gone that way, though it sounds almost like a fairy-tale; but it is true just the same."[57] The shipping business afforded disguise for men as well as women. "[M]any times the stowaways are marched off right under [the immigration officers'] very nose by being dressed like dock workers, stewards, baggage handlers, engine-room crew, sailors, donkeymen, stevedores, passengers and only God knows what," the same informant reported.[58] For some immigrants, the same physical characteristics that marked them as "Jewish" *were* their disguise: "The Jews and other oriental races can easily pass as Spaniards, i.e. Cubans, because of their oriental faces and dark skin," Weiss was told.[59]

This is not to say that the use of disguise or role playing was rooted in an understanding of identities as fluid and performative. Rather, the effectiveness of disguise—like all forms of passing—depended, paradoxically, on essentialist notions of alienness or Jewishness (or other ethnic identities). Government investigators' own willingness to use disguises in the course of their investigations, without any sense of irony, is a measure of how deep such notions ran. "Anxious to obtain first-hand information about the workings of the house, one of the officers [ex]changed clothes with one of the aliens," reported the *Massena Observer* of efforts on the part of border patrol officers in upstate New York.[60] And Weiss, for his part, wrote that he and his partner, as they tried to get in both with smugglers and immigrants, "change our outfit to suit the occasion, as well as our names and occupations," posing as a French deck hand, dressing the "part of a stranded alien, [in] khaki pants, shirt without collar, dirty shoes," or "shaving my moustache off and dressing a la Spaniard." Weiss even developed a daring plan "to change entirely later on to an old [J]ew to be smuggled across," though he never went through with it.[61]

For immigrants, of course, the stakes were higher than they were for Weiss, whose reports make it sound as if he were rather enjoying prowling around Havana in his various costumes. After all, the degree to which immigrants could adequately perform the role of American citizen, a sailor, or a Cuban, could determine their fate. Those discovered by the US authorities could be put in jail and deported back to Europe. Even Weiss knew he was playing with fire, writing that "if one of my newly made smuggler friends recognizes me later"—that is, disguised as an "alien to be smuggled"—"my goose is cooked."[62] One way of measuring the urgency of this role playing is to consider what happened when the performance went badly. Authorities could subject immigrants to grueling interrogations, as they did Chaim Listopad and "Yacob Nayman." Immigrants had to know a great deal about the people they were posing as, because they might be asked about those people's families, hometowns, occupations, or other personal details. Pincus Magid of Bialystok, claiming to be a German Jew by the name of Gustav Kiene, did not sound very convincing during his hearing at Ellis Island in 1927. He had answers to the first few questions the inspectors posed about Oppeln, the German town listed on his papers. When the inspectors asked what synagogue Magid's family attended there, however, Magid could only answer, "The Jewish synagogue," and could not say what street it was on. "You lived in that place for more than thirty years," he was asked, "and you do not know the name of the street that the synagogue is on?" The transcript reports that Magid had no reply beyond a shrug of his shoulders. He finally admitted his real identity and that he had obtained the papers in Danzig. He did not appeal the authorities' decision to exclude him from entry.[63]

For those immigrants attempting to enter the country posing as someone else, thorough preparation was key to a convincing performance. There were different ways that immigrants rehearsed their roles in advance. In Magid's case, the smugglers who sold him his papers also provided him with instructions, coaching him, Magid testified, "in the statements that [he was] to make when . . . examined in the US." He explained that the smugglers gave him "a paper with the questions and answers written thereon." When immigration officials asked Magid what he had done with these instructions, he explained, "After I had everything in my mind, I destroyed the paper."[64] Immigrants already in the United States, and thus experienced in the bureaucratic processes that immigration entailed, also provided crucial coaching for those hoping to enter illegally. One immigration official wrote to his supervisor that "we find aliens in possession of letters from friends and relatives in the United States giving complete instructions as to how to evade Immigration inspection."[65]

Immigrants also wrote letters to their friends and relatives in the United States in order to prepare them for roles *they* would have to play. Theodore Rosenberg, a twenty-six-year-old butcher arriving on a ship from Antwerp in late 1927, pinned his hopes on such letters. His documents consisted of a German police certificate of identity in lieu of a passport and a quota visa issued under the German quota by the American consul in Berlin. He admitted to the authorities at Ellis Island that he was from Russia but insisted that he had been born in German-controlled Breslau and thus entitled to a German quota slot. He said that he was headed for the home of an uncle in New York City. When the uncle came to claim him at Ellis Island, he too was closely questioned and asked to produce correspondence from his nephew to corroborate Rosenberg's story. The uncle did so. However, this letter turned out to be a rather damning piece of evidence. In it Rosenberg provided vital information about himself, clearly coaching the recipient: his father's and brother's names, as well as his parents' whereabouts, and that he was born in German territory. The letter was explicit that having such information would be crucial in any interaction the uncle might have with immigration authorities on the nephew's behalf. "It is possible," Rosenberg wrote, "that they may not ask any questions but in case they do ask you should know what to do because all that has to tally." The two men's statements did not tally. They do seem to have been uncle and nephew, but their contradictory testimony on a number of matters—how many letters had passed between them, for example—undermined Rosenberg's credibility. The already suspicious officials ruled to exclude Rosenberg from entry for having misrepresented his nationality and attempting entry by fraudulent means.[66] Preparation strategies such as Rosenberg's could backfire in many cases, especially when immigrants failed to destroy the evidence the way Pincus Magid did. They could also incriminate the writers, who sometimes gave instructions based on their own success at entering the country illegally. "These letters," the immigration official quoted above explained, "have resulted in several deportations of prior illegal entries."

Linguistic proficiency could help convince authorities of the authenticity of someone's papers, as in the case of the immigrant who learned such excellent English in Kiev that he almost convinced officials that he was a naturalized American. However, language could also work against an immigrant whose skills were not polished enough. Pincus Magid, posing as the German Gustav Kiene, told inspectors at Ellis Island that he was literate in German. When they challenged him to prove it, their suspicion only intensified. "Alien reads German test with difficulty and with a distinct Yiddish accent," they reported. Although Magid failed to act convincingly German enough, rather than American enough, for the inspectors, many such instances of botched illegal entry recall the classic trope of "greenhorn" stories, in which some aspect of behavior or dress gives an immigrant away as embarrassingly foreign. In the context of illegal immigration, however, immigrants risked more than a humiliating lesson in blending in. "Greenhorn" behavior—anything that marked immigrants as the wrong kind of "foreign" for the situation—was something immigrants could not afford. Fraudulent entry thus often required an effort at acting more commonly associated with the process of acculturation and remaking of self that happens only well after immigrants "get off the boat."[67]

Illegal immigrants' successful performances at points of entry often depended on concrete props: convincing documents (preferably real ones obtained illegally rather than counterfeit ones) and appropriate clothing. Looking the part physically and sounding it were also important. But more ineffable characteristics could also be critical to pulling off illegal immigration successfully. These very serious acts of masquerade also called for a certain willingness to and capacity for bluff. While some immigrants had evidence or extensive backstories to support their false claims, others relied on pure bravado. Polish Jewish immigrant Leo Stein, for example, came to New York in 1923 by way of Argentina, where he had bribed an official for a visa. The visa stated Stein's occupation as "violinist." Despite Stein's lack of a violin and a missing middle finger (lost in an accident in a Buenos Aires bed factory), authorities did not question his visa. The ease with which Stein entered the country does not necessarily suggest that officials were convinced by Stein's ability to impersonate a violinist—they may have simply overlooked the discrepancies between papers and person. The story does, however, speak to Stein's willingness to try such a strategy.[68]

The case of nineteen-year-old Max Weinriter, recounted earlier, similarly suggests the importance of bravado to some immigrants' attempts to enter the country illegally. Indeed, in Weinriter's story a combination of daring, linguistic ability, and personal charm were crucial not just at the point of entry but all along his travels. It seems that everyone the young man asked for help along his journey was more than happy to give it—not only those at the Jewish aid organization in London but also the Polish-speaking sailors aboard his ship, the fellow immigrants who loaned him money, and the Polish Catholic strangers in a Texas farmhouse who gave him a drink of water and a meal after he crossed the border, and then found him a job the next day. Even El Paso's Rabbi Martin

Zielonka himself, not generally a soft touch, thought Weinriter was charming. After meeting him, the rabbi wrote:

> I have just come from the county jail where I visited . . . Max Weinriter . . . He left a very fine impression upon me. He seems to be a boy of good parts and one that will doubtlessly make a success if only given half a chance. His features are clean-cut and he looks like a decent, honest chap, a splendid physique, and one willing to work for the work he did in El Paso was manual labor.[69]

Weinriter obviously struck others, as he did Zielonka, as unusually good-looking, pleasant, honest, and hardworking to boot. More than that, Zielonka's narrative suggests that Weinriter did not hesitate to approach people for help, that he was skilled at quickly figuring out how best to present himself to strangers in order to make a good impression and win their generosity, and that he used this skill to his best advantage. Zielonka's comment that "the story as told to me naturally differs from the story that he [Weinriter] told to the government officials" points to Weinriter's talent for tailoring his story so as to seem most sympathetic to his listener, as when he told the Polish Catholic couple that he, too, was Polish Catholic. Possibly, elements of the story he told Zielonka were added for the rabbi's benefit. Weinriter had been caught and jailed. Nevertheless, his story suggests the extent to which immigrants' skills at subtle kinds of social "role-playing"—knowing how to talk to and charm strangers—might make them more inclined to imagine they could succeed at fraudulent entry and could also serve as a kind of capital that helped them reach the United States, make their way over the border, and secure shelter and employment once they were in the country.

Different forms of fraudulent entry required varying degrees or kinds of performativity; some frauds drew more on immigrants' real selves than others. Some identities, in other words, had to be thoroughly faked, while some were rooted in elements of people's previous experience. Disguises as stevedores or sailors could be adopted with relative spontaneity and had little to do with migrants' experiences or identities as eastern European Jews. Something like speaking German, meanwhile, and being prepared to exhibit some familiarity with one's supposed German hometown, required a level of knowledge that reflected the cultural experience of many Jews in the region.

Just as "legal" and "illegal" immigration reflected Jewish experiences in a larger international and historical context, so, too, did such instances of evading authorities through strategies of identity switching and disguise. In places where official regimes were deeply hostile to Jews, there were many reasons to not appear Jewish. Phil Lutzky, for instance, describes his experiences on the train to Warsaw:

> [I]f the Polish soldiers found out that a passenger was Jewish they literally made a monkey out of him. I witnessed a soldier laugh and spit at a man, then rip his clothes, beard and hair with a knife. If I didn't laugh with the rest of the passengers I would have really had it from the soldiers. I felt like a disguised Jew because I didn't have a beard, though I was now old enough to shave.[70]

Although this scene took place in 1919, it reflected a longer history of official harassment of Jews that likely led many to hide their Jewish identity in public places.[71] And, as indicated earlier, another long-term strategy to evade hostile state authorities was to adopt a new identity to escape military conscription. Leo Stein's father, for example, did this by taking the name of a neighbor who died.[72]

The history of Jewish name changing, in particular, says a good deal about the conundrum of Jewish identities in eastern Europe, and the extent to which living as a Jew in that region by definition entailed enacting and naming multiple versions of oneself. The author Joseph Roth observed this vexed relationship of Jews to official forms of identity:

> Jews, Eastern Jews, have no names. They have compulsory aliases . . . Their family names . . . are pseudonyms foisted upon them. Governments have commanded Jews to have names. Does that make the names their own? If a man's name is Nachman, and he changes it to the European Norbert, what else is Norbert but camouflage?[73]

The increasing pressure to have papers in postwar Europe, combined with the documentary chaos of the era, seems to have made the act of acquiring new identities more common. Lutzky, for example, described how he obtained the birth certificate that gave him a new identity as a native of Brest-Litovsk, with which he ultimately acquired his American visa:

> At that time nobody had any identification because Brestlitovsk was burned to the ground during the war. People's names were never questioned (although they may have been fictitious) because no records could be verified. Within a short time I managed to get three witnesses to vouch for me. . . .

We met with a notary public and swore on an affidavit that my name is Lucki, and born in Brestlitovsk on such and such a date. I changed my name from Rutzki to Lucki because I didn't want the Pollacks to have a chance to trace it.[74]

Thus, many Jewish migrants—whether they intended to enter the United States legally or illegally—would have had some experience exchanging one identity for another.

Jewish migrants were especially untroubled about changing their names given that, in the context of immigration to America, name changing was already a classic trope. In the 1936 congressional hearings considering the cases of a number of immigrants whose fraudulent entry had been belatedly discovered, one Jewish man was asked why he saw nothing fishy when a smuggler in Berlin gave him a card addressed to "Abraham Levin"—not his real name—and told to present himself with it at the American consulate. The man replied that he had asked the smuggler about the name change, and the smuggler replied that the man's original name was too hard to pronounce. This made sense to the would-be immigrant. "Knowing of my relatives in the United States changing their names here," he explained to the congressional committee, "I did not see anything much about it."[75]

To be Jewish in eastern Europe, then, and, in particular, to be an eastern European and Jewish migrant, often meant having already engaged in a process of creating improvisational and shifting identities. The complex relationship European Jews had with official identities thus set the stage for their understanding of US law. It also meant that, when they embarked on the process of illegal immigration, they possessed a certain expertise in sliding around the demand for officially documented identities that, at least sometimes, helped them get past the nation's gatekeepers.

JEWISH ILLEGAL IMMIGRANTS IN AMERICAN JEWISH COMMUNITIES

The number of Jews who succeeded in entering the United States illegally during the decades the quotas were in force is impossible to know precisely. As mentioned earlier, it probably numbered in the tens of thousands, a relatively small number by our contemporary standards. Illegal immigration, however, shaped the choices and ideas of far more people than only those who undertook it themselves. Therefore, it must be understood as a phenomenon that extended well into the social consciousness of Jews both in the United

States and abroad, as well as that of members of other ethnic communities, alien smugglers, political commentators, and government officials. Jews in the post–World War I era had to confront new barriers to migration, including the US laws. Even the widely known possibility of illegal immigration to the United States forced prospective immigrants—whether or not they ultimately attempted to enter the United States illegally—to grapple with shifting ideas about borders, identities, and the law.

As the examples discussed in this chapter and elsewhere demonstrate, migrants' US-based friends and relatives, too—as well as both the organized American Jewish community and alien smugglers—had to engage with such issues. Family members in the United States, as the above examples demonstrate, were often intimately involved with their relatives' illegal immigration, even if they themselves had entered the country legally. They put up capital for the trip, corroborated fraudulent stories when necessary, and provided homes and other means of support for immigrants once they entered the United States. Evidence suggests that many family members saw illegal immigration as a perfectly legitimate choice. Sam Zuckerman was a Polish Jew who came to the United States illegally from Canada in the early 1920s (first as a liquor bootlegger making deliveries and later permanently). His two brothers, who had come legally, and his father-in-law, were supportive. "No one disapproved," Zuckerman's daughter recalled. "Everyone thought it was the right thing to do."[76]

Indeed, most people in immigrant neighborhoods probably knew someone who had a story of having come to the country illegally. Jews in such neighborhoods would have been acutely aware of the strong reasons those in Europe had to try illegal strategies for entering the United States. They may well have had occasion to witness firsthand government crackdowns in response to illegal immigration, since government officials pursued individuals when evidence of illegal entry was discovered retroactively. Those living in the vicinity of suspected illegal immigrants, for example, would have seen something was afoot any time immigration inspectors went to homes to investigate. In their searches, inspectors buttonholed neighbors, asking detailed questions and showing photographs of the wanted aliens. When Inspector M. A. Pitt called several times at 315 Snediker Avenue in Brooklyn looking for members of the Koren family in the course of an investigation into illegal immigration, for example, a woman on the top floor heard him banging on the downstairs door and calling out "Mr. Koren." She was the building's owner, and though initially uncooperative, ended up talking to the inspector about the case and conveying messages to and from the Koren family.[77] Workplaces, too, would have brought people into contact with the illegal immigration dramas of others in the community. When M. Kusnetz, who had smuggled over the US border by car from Montreal, was hauled out of her garment shop by immigration inspectors who took her to Ellis Island for questioning, her coworkers would naturally have noticed.[78] Even those without family, friends, or neighbors who were part of the new circuits of illegal immigration could hardly have escaped stories of strangers' experiences evading US immigration law. Readers of Yiddish- and English-language papers, for example, would have been familiar with the action-packed tales of migrants who tried to enter the United States illegally, such as the 1931 *Forverts* piece about Mordecai Freilich's ordeal.[79] Jewish illegal immigration was, then, a matter of both private and public knowledge during the years following the quota laws' passage.

European Jews, as we have seen, were confronted by those laws during an era when regimes, national borders, and documentary requirements in much of Europe were changing underneath people's feet. Jews' lives were often a constant jumble of lost papers, forged papers, expulsions, flight, and improvisation. Jewish migrants who skirted the quota laws to enter the United States brought with them, and deployed, their experience in getting through the cracks of official state regimes of control over population and identity. They did not, in other words, accept that the US laws had closed the gates to them. When they could, they took up their places amidst the Jewish immigrant communities that in earlier years they would most likely have been able to get to in accordance with US law.

CHAPTER 5

Battling Alien Registration

On May 18, 1931, the Michigan legislature passed a far-reaching law. The law required that all aliens—meaning all unnaturalized foreigners—living in Michigan had to register with the state government. They had to get fingerprinted and photographed, and acquire official "certificates of legal residence" verifying their lawful entry into the country. Any alien without such a certificate was henceforward barred from conducting business or obtaining employment in Michigan, and even from entering the state. Employers had to demand these certificates and report any alien who could not produce one. Police officers were required to arrest aliens lacking certificates and hand them over to the US Bureau of Immigration. Finally, the measure decreed that aliens who had entered the United States illegally or were "undesirable aliens as defined by the laws of the United States" were ineligible to register in Michigan and thus subject to deportation.[1]

The law, which had been quietly rushed through the legislature, unleashed a storm of controversy. Those in favor of the measure, including top lawmakers, labor organizers, government officials, and many powerful industrialists in the state, insisted that the law would protect everyone—citizens and aliens alike—by identifying immigrants who were in the United States unlawfully. They argued that these immigrants were taking jobs away from deserving citizens, fomenting political and labor unrest, and committing a disproportionate number of crimes. On the other side of the issue, Michigan's immigrant communities expressed their outrage. "Thousands of protests," reported the *Detroit Jewish Chronicle*, "flooded the desk of Governor Brucker, and Polish, Hungarian, German, Italian and other elements joined in opposition to the bill."[2] The American Civil Liberties Union (ACLU) and various ethnic organizations, including a broad range of national and local Jewish groups, joined together in vigorously decrying the bill as anti-foreigner, unnecessary, and decisively un-American. A group of prominent lawyers organized quickly to file a case against the state in the US District Court for the Eastern District of Michigan, arguing that the law was unconstitutional. In other states, legislators who were prepared to pass their own such laws waited to see what would happen.[3]

The issue of alien registration, largely passed over by historians, constitutes a crucial window onto the highly charged politics of foreignness in the 1920s and 1930s.[4] Throughout this period, "patriotic" organizations, anti-immigration lawmakers in Congress and state legislatures, the nativist press, and, at times, organized labor, pushed hard for legislation similar to the 1931 Michigan law. The government had previously demanded such documentation only from Chinese immigrants in the wake of the Chinese Exclusion Act of 1882 and from those classified as "enemy aliens" during World War I.[5] Thus, the stakes in the heated controversy over instituting a general alien registration were high. The idea of applying registration laws to the nation's general alien population generated heated debate. Focused as it was on what separated insiders from outsiders, the debate about alien registration was a referendum not only on the status of foreigners illegally in the country but also on the status of all foreign-born individuals—aliens and citizens—and on that of ethnic groups more broadly.

American Jews in the United States were at the forefront of the battle against alien registration throughout this era. The same editors, rabbis, lawyers, politicians, and activists who advocated on behalf of immigrants more generally also fought fiercely against registration legislation, denouncing such measures in Yiddish- and English-language newspapers, pamphlets, sermons, protest meetings, congressional hearings, and private correspondence. Though often divided by politics, culture, and language, Jews from across the social spectrum agreed that registration threatened to erode the liberties not only of immigrants and ethnic communities but also of the citizenry as a whole.[6]

In the vast historiographical literature exploring when and how the "second-wave" European immigrants and their children "became American," the interwar years are often depicted as the time when these ethnics identified increasingly with the linguistic, commercial, and political cultures of the nation in which they now lived. Scholars have rightly noted that this transformation did not proceed smoothly, linearly, or without contestation. In particular, much recent scholarship has focused on this era as one in which the nation was hashing out European ethnics' relationship to "whiteness," a crucial category of American racial belonging. A number of scholars have argued that this was a period of great racial uncertainty in which Jews and others who would later be unequivocally accepted as "white" still occupied a fraught "in-between" niche in the national racial hierarchy.[7] Others have regarded the interwar era as a more definitive turning point, a historical moment when these groups' whiteness became firmly established.[8] Still others have contended that, while southern and eastern European immigrants were certainly disparaged during this period in racialized terms, they were never in danger of being denied official "whiteness" or permanently grouped legally or socially with those long deemed "nonwhites," however much their biological or cultural fitness for civic membership might have been in doubt.[9] While the scholarship on whiteness thus disagrees on how and when precisely European immigrants and their children came to be defined unequivocally as "white," taken together it nevertheless serves to demonstrate that during the interwar period a number of important political, economic, and cultural developments were underway that would ensure that, by the postwar era, Europeans' whiteness was fully self-evident. During the interwar years, for example, "racial" or biological differences among European ethnics came to be seen as far less important than the color line that divided them and other "whites" from those regarded as "nonwhite," including African Americans, Asians, and, increasingly, Mexicans. The US government, in its court decisions regarding Asians' right to US citizenship and its policies regarding Filipino and Mexican immigrants, mobilized a taxonomy of race that helped consolidate and codify European identities as "white."[10] Simultaneously, with the mass migrations of African Americans from the South to the urban North, questions of economic and social power revolved increasingly around the color line and, in historian Matthew Frye Jacobson's words, "solidified whiteness as a monolith of privilege" in the northern communities where European American ethnics clustered.[11]

As the controversies over alien registration demonstrate, however, it is worth paying more attention to the variable of "alienness" in the study of those groups that would become known by the postwar years as "white ethnics" and of their connection to evolving definitions of national and racial identity in the interwar period. In its focus on "whiteness," much recent historical scholarship has neglected the extent to which foreignness—and its cousin concept, the negatively valenced "alienness"—continued to be a pressing political issue that complicated and challenged the stability of a white, American identity throughout these years. Indeed, the alien registration controversy was part of the era's larger legal and political struggle to define the line between Americans and aliens, insiders and outsiders. Court cases over the racial limitations on naturalization, reports of an upsurge in illegal immigration, and debates over the government's increasing use of deportation all made evident the gravity of the issue. Registration, American Jews feared, could radically redraw the line between Americans and aliens, not only rendering all foreigners suspect but also tainting broader ethnic communities by association. The history of American Jewish leaders' fight against alien registration thus illuminates a key episode in the longer political struggle that American Jews waged to uncouple themselves from the notion of illegal immigration and to make a case for the legitimacy of American Jewish communities.

In particular, what begins to come into focus through an examination of this history is a political strategy on the part of American Jewish leaders that can be easy to miss because it was, in part, one of selective activism and selective silence. During the 1920s and 1930s, many Jews decried alien registration and other discriminatory immigration policies in a general way, but did not usually express solidarity with groups such as the Chinese, Mexicans, or Filipinos, who were targeted as alien in extremely racialized ways. It is noteworthy, for example, that Jews speaking out against alien registration during the Depression years generally remained silent about what became the main focus of the government's efforts to get rid of aliens—and often citizens—by the early 1930s: the removal of Mexicans and Mexican Americans from the Southwest and other regions, including Michigan. In these cases, authorities did not even bother proposing registration—which implied at least some semblance of due process—but went straight to coercion and force.[12] Just as there were reasons to battle constructions of "alienness" that cast the loyalty and civic fitness of Jewish immigrants (and, by extension, of American Jews) into doubt, so were there clear incentives for keeping quiet about racialized constructions of illegal alienness that spared them.

Scholars' particular focus on excavating the foundations of whiteness has tended to obscure moments during this era when European ethnics' whiteness might not have been directly in question, but when the status of European ethnics as "belonging" to the national home was nevertheless profoundly threatened.[13] Such ongoing insecurity, in fact, is key to explaining the fierce investment that European ethnics had in both Americanness and whiteness. The trajectory to insider status for European Americans—to Americanness, to nativeness, and to unambiguous whiteness—is easier to discern in retrospect than it was then.[14] The history of alien registration proposals helps recapture the intense uneasiness European ethnics still had along the way. Jews expended so much energy on the antiregistration battle because there was a great deal at stake: the legal and social parameters of national belonging.

In addition to being a referendum on the status of the foreign born and ethnic communities, the alien registration issue also threw open questions about the proper scope and limits of government power. American Jews' involvement in the controversy was thus part of their ongoing struggle to play a role in defining both the symbolic and practical import of the quota laws. The quota laws reached far outside the nation to control immigration. They also served to redefine the nation's borders as gates to bar "undesirables" from entering. Now alien registration—like its corollary enforcement measures, such as imprisonment and deportation—brought the issue of immigration control into the nation's interior.[15] This "internal border control" raised a number of questions. How and where should the government go looking for illegally entered immigrants? What kinds of documentation could the government demand from aliens, and how did this compare to the government's right to collect data about its citizens? Could the government differentiate among illegal immigrants, legal aliens, naturalized citizens, and native-born citizens? Did state governments have the right to enforce federal immigration law? Indeed, opponents of alien registration argued that the true danger to the nation was not foreigners who entered the nation illegally, but rather the way that alien registration, with its authoritarian, "tsaristic" approach, threatened to transform the American legal system into something wholly foreign to the nation's liberal ideals: a police state.

THE NATIONAL DEBATE OVER ALIEN REGISTRATION

The passage of the Michigan law was a crucial episode in the era's broader national struggle over immigration and aliens. The quota laws did not resolve the question of the government's handling of immigration. Indeed, they produced an explosion of debate on the matter. A look at the legislative docket of the US Congress during the years after 1924 reveals the extent to which the laws created a host of new administrative and conceptual problems, as well as intensive disagreements over their implementation. Mae Ngai has written, for example, about the contentious debates provoked by the 1924 law's provision that, by 1927, the formula allotting each European nation an immigration quota based on 2 percent of the foreign born in the United States of that nationality would be replaced. The new formula called for capping immigration at one hundred fifty thousand and allotting quotas to each nation on the basis of "national origins," meaning the percentage of Americans who, in 1920, could trace their lineage to those nations. This proved so complicated to calculate that implementation of the national origins plan was delayed for two years in a quagmire of statistical and political debate and accompanied by a storm of controversy when it was finally introduced.[16]

During the same period, lawmakers proposed legislation with opposing purposes—some to further restrict immigration and others to loosen the existing restrictions. Legislators committed to a tougher approach to immigration, such as Congressmen John C. Box of Texas and James Aswell of Louisiana, introduced bills to apply quotas to Mexico and Canada, to facilitate deportations, to strengthen naturalization requirements, and to institute alien registration. Meanwhile, lawmakers such as New York Congressmen Samuel Dickstein and Nathan Perlman, with the backing of Jewish and other ethnic communities, proposed legislation to allow family members of citizens and "declarants" (those who had officially declared their intention to naturalize) to immigrate without regard to quota limits, or else to get preference within the quota.[17] A few of these efforts were successful. In 1928, for instance, the 1924 law was amended to give greater preference within each quota to husbands and parents of citizens.[18] The anti-immigration forces in Congress, for the most part, failed to get their postquota agenda adopted. They did, however, manage to keep their concerns on the legislative table and, with the help of sympathetic press and an array of voluntary organizations, in the public eye.

The fierce anti-immigrant sentiment that characterized the nation during this era presents, at first glance, something of a puzzle for the historian, for it flourished even as the country experienced a steep decline in immigration. The numbers of immigrants documented entering the country declined, even allowing for an increase in nonquota immigration from Europe and from countries not subject to quotas, such as Canada and Mexico. In the year before the 1921 law took effect, over eight hundred thousand immigrants were recorded entering the United States legally. In the year after the 1924 law came into force, fewer than three hundred thousand entered legally. The Depression helped spur additional restrictions. In 1930, President Hoover issued an executive order requiring that consulates abroad become far stricter in denying visas to anyone whom officials could deem "likely to become a public charge," a designation that constituted grounds for exclusion under US law. Given the abysmal state of the US economy during the Depression, this was a designation that consuls could place on nearly any immigrant who desired a visa. Consequently, immigration fell even more sharply. Fewer than one hundred thousand immigrants were legally admitted in the year ending in June 1931.[19]

As opponents of alien registration and other anti-immigrant measures were quick to point out, immigration was at its lowest point in over a century.[20] Neither the new policies nor the official statistics, however, quieted public fears about immigration. Indeed, the contrary was true. Although far fewer immigrants were arriving in the country, the foreign born still constituted an enormous, visible segment of the population, and the implications of this demographic fact were cause for heated debate. The 1920 and then the 1930 federal censuses were the first to tally the numbers of foreigners in the country who had not been naturalized, and the figures were large—roughly six million recorded in each census, a significant portion of the nation's largest-ever foreign-born population of approximately fourteen million.[21] In the minds of many nativists, these foreigners' failure to achieve citizenship was ominous proof that aliens were a pervasive, persistent presence in the nation that refused to blend into American society.[22]

Furthermore, as already discussed in the preceding chapters, the new laws of the early 1920s, though undeniably effective in reducing the numbers of immigrants, also fueled a growing business in illicit immigration at all points of entry into the nation. This, in turn, generated a new public debate about the dangers that "smuggled aliens" posed to American citizens and even legal residents. Throughout the decade after the quota laws' passage, journalists and government officials speculated that there could be large numbers of smuggled aliens at large in the United States. A 1925 headline in the *New York Times* proclaimed that "2,000,000 Aliens Are Here Without the Right to Stay."[23] Indeed, many were alarmed precisely because it was hard to know how many immigrants had entered illegally. The *Saturday Evening Post* opined that "this mortifying fact alone is ample excuse . . . for a thorough housecleaning."[24]

As noted earlier, the American public was aware that the phenomenon of illegal immigration was not wholly new. Chinese immigrants had long exercised strategies for evading the ban on their entry, and other immigrants had entered in defiance of the increasingly strict regulations implemented in the late nineteenth and early twentieth centuries.[25] The sweeping quota laws passed in the 1920s, however, produced illicit immigration on a correspondingly broad scale, transforming the problem from one of limited scope to one that served to make nearly all immigration suspect. By the end of the 1920s, then, the discourse about illegal immigration had intensified. This discourse both reflected and fueled the widespread sense that ethnic communities were fertile breeding grounds for criminal and subversive activities, both of which seemed to many observers to be constantly on the rise. The spectacular successes of organized crime during this decade, along with the high-profile trial and execution of

Italian anarchists Sacco and Vanzetti, seemed to bear this logic out. In turn, the surge in lawbreaking produced by the quota laws—alien smuggling and illegal entry—sharpened the suspicion with which the public and lawmakers regarded immigrants and the ethnic communities to which they came.

In other words, the association between unauthorized immigration and criminality grew during these years, along with a sense that a lack of effective enforcement of immigration law was allowing this criminality to flourish. An article in the *Saturday Evening Post* made this reasoning explicit:

In this country there are immense numbers of persons not lawfully here. Some of them entered without inspection, in violation of law. Some of them passed inspection, but passed it by means of misrepresentative statements, in violation of law. Some of them have committed serious offenses punishable by deportation and are nevertheless still resident here, in violation of law. All three classes are surely a daily affront to the self-respect of the Government of the United States. There is no other country in the world in which many hundreds of thousands, if not millions of aliens persistently abide on national territory in defiance of the national will.[26]

Such sentiments were widespread. President Hoover himself stated that the very act of a foreigner's unlawful entrance indicated "objectionable character."[27] By the decade's end, Congress passed a law officially making unlawful entry, previously punishable only by deportation, a misdemeanor for a first offense and a felony for a second offense, thereby solidifying the definition of illegal immigration as criminal activity.[28]

Other government policies at the national, state, and local levels lent legitimacy to these intensified and interlocking antialien views. The stringent new anti-immigration policy promulgated by Hoover in his 1930 executive order, for example, was described as a measure to diminish unemployment.[29] Meanwhile, Hoover's new secretary of labor, William N. Doak, promised to crack down on alien smuggling rings and illegal aliens in the United States with whatever tools he had at his disposal. Under the leadership of "Doak the Deportation Chief," as the *Nation* dubbed him, federal and local authorities went on raids aimed at catching and deporting illegally entered immigrants.[30] The New York City Police Department's alien squad, for example, made headlines for its sweeps of immigrant gathering places, such as a Finnish workers' dance at which the police demanded that more than a thousand attendees prove that they were legally in the United States.[31] Doak stated explicitly that a lack of alien registration laws left him no choice but to advocate and use such drastic tactics. "If people don't like our method they ought to adopt registration," he explained. "They ought to make all these people give us their thumb prints and hand prints when they come into the country and we'd keep records of them. Then we'd be sure where to find them and wouldn't have to raid dances."³²

Calls for general alien registration during these years were thus a response to growing anxieties about illegal immigrants and to the idea that the government had no way of finding them. An explicit hope of those in favor of registration was that mandatory identification would make it easier to ferret out those who had entered the country illegally and deport them. As the *Saturday Evening Post* put it, "We might as well face the fact that we have got to have a national housecleaning."³³ The practice of deportation, used only sparingly in the prequota years, had become one of the Bureau of Immigration's major concerns and functions.³⁴ The US government carried out 256 deportations in 1900 and 2,762 in 1920. In 1930, it deported 16,631 immigrants.

The controversy that emerged over the 1931 Michigan law also highlighted a fundamental tension in immigration policy, which continues to this day. The regulation of immigration and control of national borders was the business of the federal government, but states and localities felt pressure to act when the federal government was unable to control immigration effectively. Proregistration forces argued that the quota laws had created a new class of illegal immigrants who were disappearing into the enormous population of the foreign born. They claimed that registration would provide the government with better information that officials could use to take "border control" into the interior. Alien registration was meant to compensate for the federal government's enforcement failures; immigrants, after all, were slipping past federal officials at the nation's borders and making their ways to cities and towns far beyond those borders. Michigan's law represented a state government taking the matter into its own hands.

One of the stranger moments in the registration debates captures the urgently felt need for better documentation, as well as organized Jewish resistance to such measures. In 1930, Nathan Perlman, a former congressman from Manhattan, was testifying to Congress on behalf of the Independent Order of Brith Abraham, a large Jewish fraternal organization, against an alien registration bill. The law, Perlman insisted to Senator Coleman Blease of South Carolina, the bill's sponsor, would only serve to make the good alien, the future worthy citizen, feel like a criminal. "He cannot think that unless he wants to do devilment," the senator snapped back. "An honest man is never afraid of anyone knowing who he is; only the dishonest man who is afraid of being arrested." "There are many native-born Americans," countered Perlman, "who would not like to have it known who they are at times by having to have a reg-istration certificate." "I would not mind having one," Blease replied. Perlman asked, "Would you have it with you?" "Yes," said Blease, adding, "*I have got my name on everything on my body.*"[35]

While it is impossible to be sure what the senator literally meant by this cryptic statement—embroidered monograms come to mind—he was giving expression, however inadvertently, to the essence of the alien registration issue for the proregistration forces. The arguments for alien registration, after all, reflected the sense that the "body politic" needed a comprehensive system of labels to avoid dangerous confusion. Although the senator said that he would be willing to have a registration certificate as a citizen, the bill that bore his name was, in fact, targeted at aliens. It was necessary to attach identifying doc-umentation to aliens because it was impossible to distinguish legal immigrants from illegal immigrants from citizens. Alien registration was a way of making it clear that the border should not only be in Texas, or on Ellis Island, but also everywhere, all the time. Every body, or at least every potentially alien body, should be a border, a checkpoint.

An irony exists here. Even as alien registration proposals insisted on the power of data and documentation to regulate national borders, they also called this power into question. As the many pages of tables and charts that the com-missioner general of immigration produced each year in his report attest, the quota laws themselves generated, and were based on, a vast body of statistical information about immigration and about the nation at large. The laws' imple-mentation relied, too, as we have seen, on a complex system of documentation. But neither the data nor the new stamps, seals, and forms the State Depart-ment implemented to make visas counterfeit proof, nor the careful scrutiny of documents by consuls abroad and immigration inspectors at borders and seaports, could provide the kind of control for which they were intended. Comprehensive statistics and rigorous documentary requirements could not always stop real people from coming into the country with fake papers or no papers. Proponents for alien registration simultaneously acknowledged this and ignored it. Despite the fact that people skirted the quota laws by taking on false identities, proponents of registration never questioned the logic of the laws themselves, namely, the idea that it was imperative and possible to sort people neatly into categories of race and nationality. Rather, those in favor of registration wanted to employ more layers of the same information technology that was already failing, this time to sort legal from illegal immigrants.

American Jewish leaders, like those in other ethnic communities, feared that alien registration would endanger immigrants and native-born ethnics alike, putting them at the mercy of a police state. Throughout the quota years, Jews forcefully rejected the scapegoating of aliens for the nation's ills. Louis Marshall, prominent New York City attorney and president of the American Jewish Committee, told activists meeting to organize against alien registration laws that such measures were about as much a panacea as "sarsaparilla and . . . Hotstetter's Bitters."[36] Reform Rabbi Stephen Wise, activist and founder of the American Jewish Congress, thought alien registration "nothing more than another hysterical post-war psychosis measure."[37] Jewish labor activists charged that cracking down on immigrants would serve the interests of employers and not workers. For example, Sidney Hillman, president of the Amalgamated Clothing Workers, insisted that "[a] law of this kind will merely provide the anti-labor forces with a new weapon to be used in terrorizing the workers from joining organizations which protect their economic and social rights."[38] Together, groups such as the American Jewish Committee, the National Council for Jewish Women, the Hebrew Sheltering and Immigrant Aid Society, and International Organization of the B'nai B'rith, all well organized on immigrant and civil liberties issues and often with access to considerable financial and professional resources, worked effectively against alien registration proposals. Together with groups like the ACLU, Jewish leaders had managed to hold such measures at bay until the Michigan law was passed.

PASSING THE MICHIGAN ALIEN REGISTRATION LAW

By 1931, alien registration had been a national political issue for years, and the Michigan law both emerged from that national context and carried national policy implications. The US district court case brought against the Michigan law was a test case, both concretely and metaphorically. It put Michigan's right to pass such a law on trial, but it was also, more broadly, a case about the legitimacy of alien registration—and the immigrant communities at whom such registration was aimed.

The fight over the Michigan law, however, was also a profoundly local affair. There were strong reasons why the measure had succeeded in Michigan, a state whose economy, geography, and demography made the issue of immigration policy particularly relevant to its residents. The 1931 law had as much to do with Michigan's volatile labor and ethnic politics as it did with the politics of the nation at large.[39] Michigan was a heavily industrialized state where immigrants constituted a significant and highly visible proportion of the population: the 1930 census recorded 840,268 foreign-born residents, of whom 382,980 were not naturalized.[40] Detroit, in particular, had experienced a massive immigrant influx during the first three decades of the twentieth century, when its automobile industry was booming. Between 1920 and 1930, the city's population grew from 993,678 to 1,568,662 residents as European immigrants were drawn to work opportunities, along with an ever-increasing number of African American migrants from the South.[41] By 1930, the million or so foreign-born residents and their children made up nearly 60 percent of the city's population. Poles, Canadians, and Germans predominated, but Detroit, like other large industrial cities, was an ethnic and linguistic mélange, with Italians, Russians, Scots, Irish, Hungarians, Yugoslavs, and Mexicans living and working along native-born whites and blacks.[42] Jews constituted only a bit less than 4 percent of Detroit's population, but, at about seventy-five thousand, were still the sixth largest Jewish community in the country and visible in their neighborhood enclaves—Detroit's East Side around Hastings Street and, later, the Oakland area.[43]

Despite the state's need for labor, however, the city's newcomers were often regarded with suspicion, even during prosperous times. Southern black migrants faced the harshest forms of racism and discrimination in the arenas of housing, employment, politics, and social life, but foreigners and immigrant communities more broadly contended with prejudice, too. As mentioned in chapter 2, the notorious 1920s rants against the "international Jew" published in Henry Ford's newspaper, the *Dearborn Independent*, roused particular alarm among American Jews.[44] Such views, while extreme, were nevertheless in keeping with a diminished postwar faith in the notion that immigrants were capable of being "Americanized." This was reflected, too, in the upsurge of the virulent antiblack, anti-immigrant, anti-Semitic, and anti-Catholic views espoused by the newly ascendant Ku Klux Klan, which had a large following in Michigan during the 1920s.[45]

Detroit's position on an international border—separated from Canada by narrow waterways—also made immigration a charged issue in Michigan. When the quota laws spurred large numbers of foreigners to try their luck with illegal entry, many found their way to Canada's border with Michigan. Detroit and its surroundings were ideal for the interlocking businesses of alien and liquor smuggling, and the city, with its ready market for labor and alcohol, provided an ideal destination for both commodities.[46] Indeed, by 1929, liquor smuggling was a major industry in Detroit, largely run by the Purple Gang, a Jewish group that dominated the interlinked criminal enterprises of Detroit during the Prohibition era.[47] Government agents charged with enforcing federal laws on immigration, customs, and Prohibition swarmed the area but had little success in stifling smuggling.[48] Local immigration authorities, as well as union officials outraged at the flow of unwelcome competition for jobs, suggested early on that more stringent policies, including alien registration, were needed to address the situation. In early 1924, for example, an immigration official stationed in Port Huron, Michigan, wrote his colleague downriver in Detroit that "[t]he evil should be most strenuously combated. . . . [A] system of registration . . . if put into effect will prove most potent in checking smuggling of aliens.[49]

Not until 1931, however, with the passage of the Michigan state registration law, did those advocating such measures get their wish. The Great Depression heightened antiforeigner sentiment in Michigan as it did nationwide, giving nativists new rhetorical ammunition and making their warnings against aliens—and their advocacy of alien registration—resonate more strongly with the general public. Press and lawmakers suggested both that aliens were taking up jobs that citizens should rightfully have and that these same aliens were swelling relief rolls.[50] They also insisted that aliens, especially those who entered the country illegally, were often dangerous political subversives. Registration, proponents hoped, would be a step toward ridding the nation of burdensome and dangerous foreigners, thus easing unemployment and helping to preserve social stability in a time of great turmoil.

The notion that the foreign population was full of dangerous radicals, criminals, and illegal immigrants who were taking Americans' jobs had particular potency in Depression-era Michigan, which was drastically affected by the economic downturn. A staggering number of workers were laid off in a short time.[51] The sudden popularity and visibility of leftist activism, as well as the spike in anti-Communist rhetoric, were also noteworthy in Michigan. Communists, working hard to bridge gulfs between black and white and between foreign and native-born working-class people, mobilized to organize the unemployed, demanding relief and battling evictions.[52] Marches of the unemployed, some which turned into bloody clashes with police, brought thousands into the streets of Detroit and other cities in the state. On March 6, 1930, a day of unemployed workers' demonstrations around the nation and abroad, eighty thousand turned out to march in Detroit, along with thousands in smaller Michigan cities, such as Pontiac, Flint, Hamtramck, Muskegon, Grand Rapids, and Kalamazoo.[53] Many observers, including government officials and certain leading industrialists, feared the rebellious disorder embodied in these large public demonstrations of widespread anger. From this standpoint, Michigan seemed to be at risk of social and economic disintegration. When a congressional committee investigating Communism came to Detroit in summer 1930, the lawmakers expressed particular concern about the March 6 demonstrations.[54] Like many in Michigan and nationwide, the committee was eager to determine how much such unsavory radicalism was to blame directly on foreigners and African Americans. Jacob Spolansky, himself a Russian immigrant and long-time industrial spy on behalf of the government and top industrialists, confirmed these fears when he described the local Communist scene for the committee. He estimated that there were "about 10,000 bona fide communists" in the Detroit area, including newly mobilized African American groups and "about 19 racial groups" operating semi-independently, including Finns, Armenians, Mexicans, Hungarians, and Russians. The Russian group included Jews, Spolansky informed the committee, and there was, moreover, "a Jewish bureau . . . of the Communist Party."[55] Among other recommendations, the committee urged stricter immigration, deportation, and naturalization measures as a critical strategy in combating the dangers posed by radical activity.[56]

Thus, although the 1931 Michigan law emerged from a national campaign for alien registration that had been going on for some time, its passage also reflected a very specific, local fear of worker agitation. Indeed, the Union League Club of Michigan, a politically influential association of a number of the state's major industrial and financial elites, took the lead in lobbying for the registration law. Governor Wilbur Brucker sat on the organization's advisory board. In the months before the registration bill's passage, the Union League Club's Committee on Subversive Activities, devoted to addressing the threat of radical activity among Detroit's workers, held a series of meetings exploring the pressing danger of Communist influence. The "star speaker" at two of these meetings, the *Nation* noted, was none other than Jacob Spolansky, the industrial spy.[57] There was particular concern in this group about the role of foreign labor and political agitators. Ultimately, the committee recommended almost exactly the same measures that the congressional committee had, including deporting all alien Communists and canceling the citizenship of all naturalized citizens affiliated with the Communist Party.[58] The Union League Club also went farther than the congressional committee by proposing alien registration as a means to achieve its broader goals. This then became the very first project that the Union League Club pursued. One of the club's directors, an automobile industry lobbyist by the name of W. O. Edenburn, shepherded the bill through the legislature, where it passed with overwhelming support in both houses: the House of Representatives voted 84 to 7 in favor; the Senate, 25 to

3.[59] Despite an immediate public outcry and the Michigan attorney general's warning that the legislation was probably unconstitutional, Michigan's Governor Brucker signed the bill into law.[60]

THE LEGAL CHALLENGE TO
MICHIGAN'S ALIEN REGISTRATION LAW

A team of prominent lawyers—high-powered professionals with impressive legal and activist experience—joined together immediately after the law was passed in order to block it from going into effect. The team included four respected Jewish attorneys: Captain Isadore Levin, a lawyer who had served as legal advisor to the American Zionist Organization's delegation at the Paris Peace Conference; Theodore Levin, an immigration lawyer and Detroit Jewish communal leader; Fred Butzel, a lawyer and sociologist, active on the American Jewish Committee and Detroit's Jewish Welfare Federation; and Nathan Milstein, an experienced Detroit immigration attorney. It also included their non-Jewish ally Patrick O'Brien, a former judge and head of the Detroit branch of the ACLU. In their fight against the law, these men worked in close consultation with the New York–based Jewish lawyer Max Kohler, one of the nation's leading experts on immigration law and chairman of the American Jewish Committee's Standing Advisory Committee on Immigration.[61] They were supported locally by community leaders such as *Detroit Jewish Chronicle* editor Philip Slomovitz, whose paper provided extensive coverage of the issue, and Reform Temple Beth-El's Rabbi Leon Fram, who joined the fight against alien registration both from his pulpit and in other venues.[62] The legal team's mission also had the blessing of local authorities. Frank Murphy, Detroit's liberal Democrat mayor, "declared himself wholeheartedly opposed to the measure."[63] The city's police commissioner echoed Murphy's disapproval for the bill, opining that the Detroit police would bear the brunt of the new work engendered by the law.[64] From farther afield, Jewish organizations, congregations, and press around the country also lent support.

The lawyers succeeded in their first effort, which was to get a federal judge in Michigan's Eastern District to issue an injunction blocking the law's enforcement, pending further hearings. After that, they prepared extensive briefs and arguments for the hearings on the law's constitutionality.[65] These hearings took place in early July before a special three-judge panel, which—because the state's sovereign power was at issue—included one judge from the US Court of Appeals for the Sixth Circuit in Cincinnati in addition to two judges from Michigan's Eastern District.[66]

Like the Jewish American activists involved in the cases of Jewish illegal immigrants and stranded migrants in the first part of the decade, the lawyers who were crafting the case against the Michigan law were walking a fine line. They were trying to advocate for immigrants and ethnics in an anti-immigrant climate, while not calling into question the civic virtue and essential Americanness of their position or of the communities they represented. A careful reading of their strategies suggests two intertwined approaches, one explicit and one implicit. On an explicit level, they argued that alien registration was an illegitimate deployment of government power. They tried to do this by turning the antiforeigner discourse of the proregistration forces on its head. They consistently made the case that it was not foreigners who threatened America with their dangerously foreign ways and subversive ideas, but rather the law that threatened law-abiding people—whether citizens or future citizens—with dangerously un-American tactics. Despite the fact that the cadre of lawyers crafting the case, except for O'Brien, were Jews, none of the legal, social, or moral arguments were made in defense of any particular ethnic group. Rather, they argued much more generally that it was wrong to scapegoat foreigners—potential citizens—for the nation's economic and social problems. And they made their case in constitutional terms, arguing that registration was a fundamentally illegal construct that threatened to undermine civil liberties for all.

There was a second part of the leaders' approach to battling registration that was implicit rather than explicit—embedded in the implications of their legal strategy and public statements. Though the rhetoric of dissent they employed was sweepingly broad, one important if less obvious effect of their arguments was to distance themselves from nonwhite ethnics already targeted as "alien." This is by no means to suggest that their explicit arguments were somehow a cover for a racist agenda; the community leaders involved in the antiregistration effort were passionate advocates for civil liberties and, all the records suggest, deeply committed to this as a social justice issue. They never sought to scapegoat others and would likely have been dismayed at the accusation that their strategies had racial implications. Indeed, in other contexts, American Jewish leaders often pushed an explicitly antiracist agenda. The American Jewish Committee's Louis Marshall, for example, lent his efforts to the cause of African American civil rights, including serving as a director with the National Association for the Advancement of Colored People; on another occasion, he represented Japanese immigrants in their efforts to have California's racially biased land ownership laws overturned. Attorney Max Kohler spoke out consistently against race-based immigration law and policy, particularly those regarding Asians.[67]

In the case of alien registration, however, even as Jewish leaders made their arguments in the broadest of terms, they were also invoking ideas that, given the social and legal contexts, had necessarily to do with race. To portray foreigners as potential citizens, for example, was automatically to introduce the racialized notion of naturalization, which was an uncontested right for immigrants deemed white but not for those judged to be racially "other."[68] Furthermore, the leaders linked their claims about the innocence of foreigners only to European aliens. The initial legal action, for example, was brought in the names of non-Jewish Detroiters of European descent: the publisher of a Polish newspaper, an Italian barber, another presumably Polish man named John Petrowski, and a British contractor, George Arrowsmith.[69] More broadly, they did not connect their struggle for legitimacy to other struggles over the inclusion and exclusion of foreigners. They made no mention in public statements about the Michigan law, for example, of the extraordinary pressure being exerted on Mexicans to leave the nation during the same time period.[70] Nor, with the noteworthy exception of Max Kohler, did they link the registration issue to the longstanding curtailment of Asian immigrants' rights.

They cannot have avoided this approach simply because such parallels had not occurred to them. It was clear, for example, that alien registration would put millions of people in the same vulnerable position as the Chinese, long the object of antialien sentiments and policies that were couched in economic language. Chinese immigrants had for many years been required to register, and those Chinese who were US citizens were often challenged to prove their citizenship. Attorney Max Kohler had been in charge of Chinese registration cases as assistant US district attorney in New York City and later played a key role in defending Chinese clients who faced deportation. He had often warned, in the context of debates over alien legislation at the national level, that alien registration requirements would be an excuse for arbitrary roundups of all kinds of foreigners, just as they had been for the Chinese. In his willingness to be outspoken on the links between the government's Chinese policy and alien registration, he was an interesting exception that serves to highlight a general silence in American Jewish communal discourse on the matter. Other leaders were familiar with the highly respected Kohler's argument on this score—indeed, in the Michigan case, as on many other immigration issues, he was immediately enlisted for his expertise and authority.[71]

Similarly, it would have been difficult to miss the parallels between the agenda of proalien registration forces and the situation that Mexican communities were facing with the onset of the Great Depression. National headlines during 1931 made it clear that Mexicans were being particularly targeted for deportation raids by immigration authorities, especially in California and the southwest. Such government crackdowns, in combination with intense anti-Mexican discrimination and pressure from local and national officials to participate in nominally voluntary "repatriation" programs, were spurring tens of thousands to leave hurriedly for Mexico, often abandoning homes and businesses to do so.[72]

That Jewish leaders lobbying against alien registration—with the important exception of Kohler—refrained from drawing attention to connections between anti-Asian or anti-Mexican measures and the Michigan alien registration law makes sense, of course, when one considers the extent to which that might have struck them as bad strategy. Making common cause with those already defined as racial and ethnic outsiders, the people crafting the antiregistration case may well have thought, could only serve to strengthen unwanted associations. The fates of Chinese and Mexicans must have seemed, in the face of the intensely xenophobic campaign on behalf of alien registration, altogether too close to home and something to be strenuously avoided. Such fears were not unfounded. District immigration director and alien registration supporter John Zubrick, for example, was still hopeful in 1932 that a state-orchestrated removal of impoverished Mexicans from Michigan could serve as a model for similar programs across the Midwest, aimed at poor Europeans as well as Mexicans.[73]

This implicit effort not to be cast as racialized alien outsiders was entirely entangled, however, with the issues about which Jewish leaders spoke out vigorously. On an explicit level, those battling the Michigan registration law set out to contest the logical underpinnings outlined by the measure's supporters. The public statement that Brucker made on signing Michigan's alien registration bill into law expressed the thinking of those in favor of such legislation. He insisted that "[u]ndesirable aliens ... here illegally" were "prominent among those urging the overthrow of our government," were often guilty of "criminal and seditious conduct," and were taking jobs away from deserving Americans.[74] He asserted that alien registration would encourage people who had entered the nation without proper documentation to leave the state of their own accord and that it would help identify and remove those who did not. The antiregistration side argued strongly against each of these justifications for the legislation. They argued that the claim that aliens were taking away jobs from citizens in these tight times and thus that registration would ease unemployment made little sense. Immigrants were not responsible for the calamitous unemployment with which the nation was struggling. On June 19, an editorial in the *Detroit Jewish Chronicle* pointed out that even stopping all immigration would not help alleviate citizens' job woes: "by keeping out 50,000 immigrants a year, the problem will [not] be solved for more than 7,000,000 unemployed."[75]

Those fighting the law similarly attacked the notion that ethnic communities were especially likely to harbor criminals in their midst. Brucker's statement on signing the bill into law explicitly pitched the legislation as an anticrime measure; similarly, an assistant US attorney's brief on behalf of the law claimed that aliens in the region, though 20 percent of the population, committed 46 percent of the crime.[76] Those on the other side argued, however, that registration would mostly target and criminalize innocent, law-abiding foreigners who were upstanding community members and future citizens. The notion of fingerprinting seemed particularly offensive, associated as it was with police procedures and suspected criminals.[77] "[F]inger-prints have been used principally for the identification of criminals," said Fred Butzel. "Now the next extensive use is to be for identification of persons who are legally in the United States. This would appear to be an unnecessary humiliation."[78]

Furthermore, those making the case against alien registration argued that such a measure, rather than help *prevent* crime, would actually *generate* it. In other words, alien registration was not a crime-busting bill but a crime-building bill. For one thing, it would create new opportunities for criminals, much as Prohibition had done. "[The law's] potentialities for blackmail and graft are so apparent as to make it a dangerous act," argued Butzel.[79] People in the country illegally would be sitting ducks for any unscrupulous party who wanted to extort money in exchange for not turning them in; furthermore, Butzel asserted, "there should also be created a large market for forged credentials."[80] For another, alien registration would serve to push the government itself toward criminal activity because such a law would inevitably produce official corruption. Max Kohler made this argument in a letter to Governor Brucker on May 20, 1931: "Such measures . . . open the door to boundless corruption, extortion and oppression, as witnesses our experience under the federal Chinese Registration Law."[81] Elsewhere, Kohler had elaborated on what he meant by this, citing numerous examples in cases in which he had been personally involved: inspectors who coerced Chinese into buying bogus registration certificates from them; a New York inspector who tried to bribe a US marshal to issue illegal blanket deportation warrants for a large group of Chinese; and another who extorted money from Chinese to discharge their cases.[82]

At the same time, antiregistration forces contended that the policy represented a shift toward a dangerously powerful state. It was not foreigners—the white ethnics who were the plaintiffs in the case and, by implication, Jews or other white ethnics—who were carriers of dangerous, subversive ideas from abroad; rather, it was the notion of alien registration that was the subversive foreign encroachment threatening to de-Americanize the nation. Registration, which would intimidate a large portion of the population, was the kind of mechanism characteristic of oppressive, "tsarist" states whose systems were anathema to ideas of American liberty.[83] To make the point that the heavy-handed treatment of foreigners embodied in the registration law would be sliding dangerously close to the kind of tyranny the nation was founded in order to escape, the *Detroit Jewish Chronicle*'s editor imagined how appalled Thomas Jefferson, Ben Franklin, George Washington, and the Adamses would have been by the Michigan law: "What would they have said to legislators, and to the governor of the state, who sanction the fingerprinting of strangers in our midst as if they were criminals?"[84]

The fact that some of the news articles on the Michigan law appeared on pages with pieces detailing the alarming rise of fascism in Europe also made at least an implied link to the contemporary international scene.[85] Jewish opponents of the law also argued more explicitly that registration would pave the way for even more oppressive measures, predicting that a general registration of citizens was bound to follow.[86] They consistently linked their plight, as a group targeted for suspicion, to the concerns of *all* law-abiding Americans. They were not making a claim that they should be protected as a special group or as minorities, but rather that they should be protected because they were members of the American mainstream—again, an argument that served to distance them implicitly from those already (or increasingly) defined, legally and socially, as outside the circle of American belonging by virtue of their outsider racial status.

Opponents of registration also had to rebut the argument that it was necessary to gather data on potentially dangerous aliens, and that indeed American citizens deserved such protection as much as the citizens of the many other countries that had such laws.[87] Supporters of registration reasoned that there was nothing un-American about the government gathering information from people. After all, did not the United States keep data on its own citizens? Were not citizens required to register to vote? Were not their names on tax rolls, their vital information a part of the census?[88] Moreover, registration advocates argued that the law was merely an extension of existing practices. The government had long been increasing the amount of data it collected about immigrants at ports of entry and later during the process of naturalization. In 1928, for example, the government began issuing identification cards to all arriving immigrants, as it long had to Chinese immigrants.[89] Registration advocates believed that mandatory alien registration was merely a way to further systematize and centralize. And centralization of information was sorely needed because, as the *Saturday Evening Post* put it, authorities trying to find deportable aliens without a registration system had to "try to summon local needles from local haystacks without any genuine integration with the local magnets for dragging them out."[90]

Antiregistration forces countered that there was a logical flaw in the idea that registration would improve government data and hence help ensure the public good, a flaw that could hurt law-abiding foreigners and spare those who had violated immigration law. In order to register, immigrants would have to produce documentation proving they had entered the country legally, but the system of record keeping and documentation was widely recognized to be imperfect and not everyone would be able to provide proof of legal entry. This, of course, was a problem registration aimed to solve—the government's failure to adequately track all the foreigners coming over its borders—but the measure's opponents begged to differ. "It is only within recent years that any particular check has been maintained at the Canadian border," Fred Butzel pointed out. "I am reliably informed that the records of many steamship companies have been destroyed. Even the records at Ellis Island are far from being complete."[91] Indeed, Theodore Levin made this point dramatically in the courtroom, introducing an affidavit "showing that the Ellis Island records were burned in 1897."[92] Meanwhile, registration opponents argued, the measure was hardly likely to help the government identify people who were willing to resort to resort to illegal means to enter the country in the first place, for those who had entered the United States with fake identifications would likely be able to thwart the registration system in the same way. Thus, the law would render some legal immigrants "illegals" because of the failures of the US government—not of foreigners—to document the flow of people across the nation's borders. The measure would only perpetuate, not redress, the problems inherent in government data collection.

Indeed, those protesting registration argued that the law not only would be creating "illegal aliens" out of law-abiding immigrants but also would be, even more broadly, recasting all immigrant and ethnic communities as inherently suspect "aliens." By moving immigration enforcement inside the nation's borders, the law would make not only all the foreign born but also all those who *seemed* like they might be foreign born, and even those who lived in a neighborhood of foreign born, into potential suspects. Labor lawyer Maurice Sugar put this well in his article in the *Nation* about the registration law: "It is obvious," he wrote, "that the bill will apply not only to aliens but to all foreign-born men, women, and children, since the required certificate would furnish their only protection, and even then not protection from arrest."[93]

Though the stated goal of the bill was to draw a sharp distinction between aliens and citizens, then, in fact a line would be drawn between foreign-seeming and native-seeming. Police officers on ordinary city streets would be, in effect, deputized as immigration officials, trying to do what authorities were supposed to do—but were failing to do entirely effectively—at points of entry, namely, to distinguish those with the right to be in the United States from those without it. The *Detroit Times* reported that the Michigan attorney general's staff admitted as much:

> The practical effect of the law is to require all persons who are not obviously American-born to carry and be ready to produce at all times proof of their citizenship, birth, or right of entry into the United States. Any policeman may require this proof. The law says he may hold any alien who has not a certificate issued by the commissioner of public safety. The result will be that he will hold any one, citizen or alien, who cannot prove his right to be in the United States.[94]

And recognizing who was foreign born was not, of course, an easy task. After all, as one Yiddish-language newspaper noted, "It is not written on one's nose whether one is a citizen."[95] (When labor department officials argued in 1928 that the new identification cards issued to immigrants on entering would never be demanded unfairly from earlier arrivals "because an alien who has been in this country for some time is distinguishable from a more recent arrival," they were engaging in the same slippery logic that allowed aliens who spoke good enough English or who dressed in "American" clothing to slip by inspectors at points of entry.)[96] Moreover, as Butzel pointed out, there were plenty of people who themselves did not know whether they were born in the United States or abroad.[97] Thus, those opposed to alien registration argued that the law would get hopelessly tangled in its own problematic assumptions, serving merely as a blunt instrument of repression and not as an effective mode of enforcing immigration law. Furthermore, by arguing that the law would affect aliens and citizens alike, the antiregistration forces were essentially arguing that alien registration in effect was a betrayal of the very principle of naturalization. How could foreigners gain insider status when registration mandated that anyone who seemed to a passing police officer like an outsider *would be treated* as an outsider by the state, whatever his or her official citizenship status?

Here, again, it is worth highlighting that these arguments functioned in implicitly racial ways, even if they were not meant in racist fashion. In other words, alien registration was motivated by its proponents' interest in identifying illegal immigrants who might otherwise disappear into American society. Asian and Mexican immigrants, clearly, did not have this luxury, for, in the American context, their racial otherness had come to mean that they were always already suspect as alien, whether or not they were citizens. While Asians and Mexicans were marked by their race as, and broadly defined by legal and social practice as, "alien," however, European-descended Jews were not so obviously marked or defined. But nor did they necessarily always seem American, even when their official papers said they were. European immigrants might have uncontested access to naturalization, as whites, but they nevertheless had to defend their right to be treated as citizens rather than as aliens—their right, in other words, to blend into white Americanness.[98]

Finally, the group bringing the issue to court in Michigan argued that the alien registration law was not simply "un-American" but also illegal and unconstitutional. In other words, the problem was not whether some foreigners were violating the law, but that the Michigan state legislature most certainly was. They pointed out, for example, that the measure was meant to rid Michigan of anyone defined under federal law as "undesirable aliens," but such a term was in fact not part of existing immigration law.[99] Furthermore, as Isadore Levin pointed out in his brief for the first injunction hearings, the law functioned ex post facto: "It now applies as a punishment for prior entry, penalties and disabilities which did not exist at the time of the performance of the act."[100] The legal team also argued that the state of Michigan was overstepping its authority, citing Supreme Court rulings asserting that the federal government had the sole right to regulate the coming and going of aliens. To enforce the law, Michigan would have to become, they argued, in effect a sovereign state, with its own immigration department regulating its own borders. "It is no exaggeration to say that the country will take on the appearance of 48 armed camps with officials and inspectors at every state line," the opponents stated in their arguments before the court. "Citizens will become less and less citizens of the United States and to a greater degree citizens of Michigan or Ohio or whatever State they may happen to reside in."[101] Ultimately, they argued, this internal targeting of "aliens" that the Michigan law introduced, including foreign-born citizens, could prove the undoing of the very notion of the United States. It would undermine its national geographic and political cohesion and, in so doing, dismantle the essence of citizenship altogether. This idea, too, was inherently racialized, even as it was also broadly about national belonging. During this era, only white Americans could reasonably expect this level of citizenship and entitlement; these opponents of registration were implicitly claiming that it would be the downfall of the country if all white Americans could no longer sustain those expectations.

THE COMMUNIST RESPONSE TO ALIEN REGISTRATION

The legal challenge was not the only antiregistration activism in which Jewish activists engaged. Jewish leftists, especially those aligned with the Communist Party, joined other radicals in public protests against the measure. These efforts emerged out of a different interpretation of the registration law and the antialien sentiments behind it than did the efforts of the Jewish lawyers who opposed the law in court and the community members who supported that legal action. Communists saw the bill as an antiworker measure and called for mass protest, rather than a court case, in response.

While it was the court case that ultimately proved the most effective in combating the registration law, the actions of leftists are an important part of the history of antiregistration activism, since they provide an alternative perspective on the politics of foreignness during these years and help demonstrate the political strategies that mainstream American Jews quite consciously did *not* adopt. Indeed, the Jewish leaders leading the legal fight against the Michigan bill assiduously distanced themselves from the leftists. Jews had particular reason to worry about being branded universally as Communists, for the long association between Jews and Bolshevism still held. Indeed, in the course of the court hearings about the law, the assistant attorney general of Michigan stated outright that "All the Jewish organizations are Communistic."[102] Like Louis Marshall in his work with the immigrants stranded by the 1924 quota law, Jewish lawyers working on the Michigan court case expressly discouraged their supporters from engaging in demonstrations. They feared that mass protests would look too much like the "un-American" Communist political tactics that so alarmed many in the press, government, and business. They were eager to prove that the registration law, obviously motivated by anti-Communism, had targeted the wrong people altogether. "[I]t is of great importance," the *Detroit Jewish Chronicle* editorialized, ". . . that the courts should not be prejudiced and that the false impression should not be created that Communists are in any way involved in this issue."[103] The Jewish leaders behind the court case, whose arguments rested on making the state seem "un-American" rather than foreigners, were careful not to ally themselves with an element widely perceived as anti-American.

While the accusations that Michigan Jews and Communists were one and the same group were certainly overblown, of course, some Jews were involved with leftist politics in Detroit during the 1920s and 1930s as they were nation-wide. Coverage in the left-wing Yiddish press of the Michigan law suggests, for example, the extent to which Jews were part of the leftist response to the alien registration issue. Leftists agreed with the mainstream lawyers and their allies that the law was aimed at Communists and radicals.[104] Most violently disagreed, however, that there was an important distinction to be made be-tween targeting Communists and targeting "innocent aliens," or that alien reg-istration was at heart a civil liberties or constitutional issue.[105] Instead, they understood the bill as an assault on the working class, a move to blacklist and intimidate. In their view, the legislation was a canny strategy designed to divide native workers from foreign workers, and black workers from white workers. The Communist national paper, the *Daily Worker*, editorialized on May 22 that the alien registration law was "primarily a strike-breaking proposition, intended to throw such a scare into the foreign born in this country that they will not dare to show their solidarity with the American born workers in their struggles."[106]

Though it was an oversimplification to say that this was a bill expressly tailored to suit employers and weaken labor (the local Manufacturers Associa-tion, for example, fearing a drain on their workforce, came out against it, even as the Detroit Federation of Labor came out for it), it certainly was meant to put a damper on radical worker organizing. The point here is that leftists had a different sense of what mattered than the mainstream Jewish leaders. The cat-egory of belonging they looked to was not so much citizenship, Americanness, or whiteness, but class; and the attempt to divide foreigners from native wor-ried them insofar as it was a wedge in working-class solidarity—*not* because it would deny aliens' acceptance by the bourgeois state or American society at large.

The leftists also differed completely on ideas about battle strategy. The *Daily Worker* warned against the "voodoism" of "liberal" lawyers, saying that " 'Constitutional' and 'unconstitutional' are words that mean nothing more than 'what the bosses want' and 'what the bosses don't want.' "[107] In other words, for the leftists the alien registration legislation was not primarily a mat-ter of the state of Michigan breaking US law and thus not a problem to be addressed through the justice system. Rather, for them the law was enraging because it was about capitalists acting like capitalists. As such, its passage de-manded a show of mass solidarity by workers rather than a response crafted by elites for the courts. Only mass protest, the *Daily Worker* asserted, represented an authentic response by the people, and only mass protest had any chance of success. Such exhortations were not mere rhetoric. During the months after the bill was passed, the Communists mobilized around the alien registration issue with great energy, organizing mass meetings and demonstrations in Michigan and other states as well.[108]

Rather than fighting for the rights of European aliens to disappear into the mainstream category of white American citizenship and be ensured the privileges attendant with that identity, Communists fought to unite all workers across racial lines. Indeed, the major rally they staged in Detroit in June 1931 especially reflected the ways the leftists' understanding of the alien registration issue differed from that of the more mainstream lawyers. The demonstration was not only meant to be exactly the sort of large, public event that mainstream leaders deplored as a tactic sure to cause a backlash, but was also intended to highlight something the Communists viewed as a central component of the bill's strategy—the effort to segment Detroit's workers along ethnic and racial lines. For the rally was in fact a dual-purpose event. It was not only a protest against the alien registration bill but also a demonstration on behalf of the Scottsboro boys, the nine young African American men whose rape trial in Alabama had become national news and a particular cause célèbre among Communists, who were providing legal defense in the case.[109] The *Daily Worker* explained that the Scottsboro boys' ordeal and the alien registration bill were integrally connected—both were capitalist efforts to crush working-class resistance. "The workers of Detroit," it said, "realize that it is the same ruling class which condemned these innocent boys to burn in the electric chair that has passed the infamous bill in the Michigan legislature to photograph and fingerprint the foreign-born workers."[110]

Linking these two issues together represented a strikingly different analysis from the one represented by the legal team that fought the alien registration law in court. The suggestion that these events in Scottsboro and Detroit were connected addressed an element of local labor politics—the tensions between African American and white ethnic workers in Michigan—that apparently did not interest the activists involved in the court case. The Communists' radical inclusiveness and insistence that workers' interests crossed lines of language, ethnicity, and class were an effort to undermine the time-honored strategy of controlling a heterogeneous workforce by pitting different groups against each other.[111] The leftists' rally, in short, was an effort to turn the alien registration bill into an occasion to help bridge rather than exacerbate these divides.

This is not to say that the leftists were somehow more heroic than the Jewish lawyers and other community leaders who fought so hard against alien registration. Rather, their approach highlights a particular kind of public

cautiousness that mainstream Jewish leaders adopted regarding alien registration. These leaders were not critiquing the nation in which they felt Jews
should have full and uncontested membership, or the nation's racially exclu-
sive implementation of such membership, at least not publicly. They were not
willing to yoke the cause of alien registration to the broader ones of racial or
economic justice because they did not see those as related or useful to their
legal fight. The leftists were addressing what they saw as the underlying injustices of the American political and economic system, as manifested by alien
registration; the mainstream leaders sought, instead, to portray themselves and
the communities they represented as loyal, upstanding members of the nation,
and alien registration as an un-American, oppressive mechanism that threatened to harm deserving communities like theirs.

Approximately three thousand five hundred people, representing a broad
array of Detroit's white ethnic and African American workers, showed up to
the leftists' rally.[112] The Communist Yiddish press's enthusiastic endorsement
and detailed descriptions of protest logistics suggest that a good number of
Jews were among the attendees (though the Socialist *Forverts* came out against
any involvement with Communist-sponsored protests of alien registration).[113]
What impact the rally had on public or judicial opinion remains unclear. Ultimately, it was the actions of the legal team of Levin and his colleagues that
proved the most powerful force in the battle against the Michigan alien registration law, whose fate was decided in court, not on the streets. The judges
deciding the case declared the legislation unconstitutional in December, 1931,
ruling that the state of Michigan had overstepped its jurisdiction.[114] The court
noted that states had often attempted to "regulate . . . the status of aliens upon
the theory that such legislation is sanctioned by the police power of the state."
This legal theory, however, the court noted, had not been upheld in previous
cases, nor would it serve in this one to justify the state's actions. "[T]he act . . .
is unconstitutional and invalid," wrote the court in its brief decision, "because
it seeks to usurp the power of government, exclusively vested by the Constitution in Congress"—and not individual states—"over the control of aliens
and immigration."[115] On all the other arguments brought by Levin and his colleagues, the court declined to comment.

TOWARD AN ESCAPE FROM ILLEGAL ALIENNESS

Within the legal system, at least, the case against state-based alien registration
had been made strongly. For the time being, the coalition of American Jewish
leaders and other civil libertarians had prevailed again. There were other at-

tempts to pass state and local laws mandating alien registration: for instance, in New York City in 1936 and in Pennsylvania in 1939.[116] None of these efforts were successful.[117] The push for a federal law continued, too, but the antiregistration forces managed to keep such a law from being enacted. Taken together, the antiregistration victories of the 1920s and 1930s were a significant demonstration of the political power and resources that Jews, as a group, could wield. It was important to the cause, for example, that wealthy, established American Jewish lawyers like Max Kohler, Theodore Levin, and Louis Marshall took on the issue of alien registration. Just as powerfully, the battles over alien registration reveal the anxieties that even these established leaders had about the unstable position of Jews in the United States, as well as the need for vigilance in this regard.

Only in 1940 did legislation requiring alien registration finally pass on the national level.[118] But though Jewish groups did express some concern over the national registration law, they did not respond with the same urgency to this measure as they had to the Michigan law of 1931.[119] With the outbreak of war in Europe, the national equation's variables—alienness, national security, and civil liberties—had changed. Wartime fears of aliens trumped other concerns, as evidenced most egregiously during these years by the Roosevelt administration's decision in 1942 to intern Japanese and Japanese Americans.[120]

The muted Jewish response to the 1940 law also reflects, in part, the fact that the position of American Jews had changed. By 1940, as a group, they had progressed in their attainment of insider status. Despite their anxieties about the rising tide of anti-Semitism during the 1930s in both the United States and abroad, Jews became more firmly ensconced in the national home as citizens, English speakers, voters, and suburbanites than they had been at any time before. The 1940 registration law thus had somewhat less power to alarm them than earlier measures. Moreover, American Jews' relationship to immigration policy had, like that of other European ethnic groups, changed during the preceding decade. This reflected in part the extent to which Jews' activism on issues like alien registration had, in concert with the political and economic privileges accorded them as whites, achieved its goals.

To be sure, the quotas and administrative restrictions remained in force, making immigration difficult or impossible for many—an enormous tragedy for those caught in Europe during the war. Illegal immigration of European Jews continued, as did the deportations of some of those whose unlawful entry was detected. Nevertheless, as Mae Ngai has demonstrated, the law became more flexible for European immigrants who had already entered the United States illegally, especially for those whose family members were citizens. The

Roosevelt administration, brought to power by an electorate that included large numbers of the naturalized European foreign born and their children, was far more sympathetic toward these immigrants and their advocates than its predecessors, and took seriously critiques of immigration policy such as those made by Max Kohler and his colleagues. Officials in this administration, for example, exercised their powers to suspend deportation in cases of "hardship" with much greater frequency than their counterparts in previous administrations, and European immigrants who had entered illegally were increasingly allowed to legalize their status by administrative discretion. Such administrative amnesties were generally reserved for Europeans. Asians, since they were ineligible to immigrate in any case, did not qualify. Mexicans, though not theoretically excluded from such policies, were nevertheless consistently denied the benefit of them.[121]

The history of alien registration helps demonstrate that immigration and immigrants continued to be urgent issues for Jews and the nation more generally in the decades following the restrictive quota laws of the early 1920s. Those quota laws escalated rather than settled struggles over questions of national inclusion and exclusion and created new gray areas between alienness and belonging. Alien registration was a key battleground on which these struggles took place. Jews were largely successful in these struggles, to the point where Jews ultimately came to be seen as an unquestioned part of the native-born, white population, and the notion of Jewish illegal aliens became one that was incongruous in the minds of most Americans.

CHAPTER 6

Abolishing the Quotas

In December 1965, US officials in Genoa, Italy, issued an immigration visa to a young Turkish Jewish man named Moises Mutlu. He was bound for Worcester, Massachusetts, where his parents and brother had settled the previous year. His was the first visa to be issued in Genoa under the new Immigration Act of 1965. Without that law, observed the executive director of the Jewish immigrant aid organization HIAS, Mutlu would have had a long wait before he could have joined his family.[1]

Seated at a desk dramatically placed in front of the Statue of Liberty, President Lyndon Johnson had signed the Immigration Act of 1965 into law on a sunny October day two months earlier. In the speech he gave to mark the occasion, Johnson promised that the new law would "repair a very deep and painful flaw in the fabric of American justice."[2] In other words, the law would restore a democratic fairness that had been derailed by the 1921 and 1924 quota laws, thereby showing the world that the immigration policy of the United States was no longer grounded in racist determinism. Introduced in Congress by Democratic Senator Philip Hart of Michigan and Democratic Congressman Emanuel Celler of New York, the Immigration Act of 1965 scuttled the restrictive schema established by those earlier laws. There would no longer be nation-by-nation quotas. Instead, there would be an overall numerical limit on immigration. Immigrants would be given preference if they were coming to join family members with US citizenship, if they could provide professional or other needed work skills, or if they were political refugees.[3]

The Hart-Celler Act, as the new law was known, had substantial practical consequences. Different immigrant groups felt the law's impact unevenly. It opened the country to significant numbers of immigrants from Asia, but by including the Western Hemisphere under the overall limit on immigration, it made new difficulties for would-be immigrants from nearby nations such as Mexico and Canada.[4] For Jews abroad with relatives in the United States, such as Moises Mutlu, the law promised to make legal immigration much easier. The law's most powerful implications for American Jews, however, were less concrete. The devastation of European Jewish communities during the Holocaust and the establishment of the State of Israel made the question of Jewish immigration to the United States less salient in 1965 than it had been in the years before, during, or just after World War II. The drawing of the Iron Curtain around much of Eastern Europe also made it more difficult for Jews who might otherwise have immigrated to contemplate leaving. Nevertheless, to Jewish communal leaders, a number of whom were present at the law's signing ceremony by special invitation, as well as to American Jews more broadly, the moment was laden with significance. Since the war's end, American Jewish organizations and lawmakers had helped lead a coalition of ethnic, religious, and civic groups that aimed to reshape immigration law and especially to overturn the quotas. Like Johnson himself, Jewish activists saw abolishing the quotas as connected to a wider battle against prejudice and thus as striking a crucial blow for universal freedom. The new law "means that larger numbers of men, women and children yearning to breathe free can have their hopes realized," said William Rosenwald, former chairman of the United Jewish Appeal, an umbrella group established in 1939. After this nod to the poem mounted at the base of the Statue of Liberty, he continued, "For this, President Johnson and the Congress of the United States deserve the commendation of the entire world."[5]

Beyond manifesting a new relationship between the United States and the world's peoples, however, the new law also had great symbolic meaning for American Jews. By ending the national origins quota system instituted in the 1920s, the law also broke with an official precedent that treated southern and eastern Europeans as "undesirable." By so doing, it helped to draw Jews and other white ethnics—the immigrants of that earlier era and their children—more definitely into the national polity. The quota laws, and the upswell of illegal immigration that followed, had thrown Jewish immigrants and American Jewish communities under heightened suspicion. The Hart-Celler Act marked a turning point for those American Jews who had been involved in a long struggle since the laws' passage to "legalize" and legitimize Jewish immigration, along with European immigration more broadly.

Immigration policy thus proved one important arena in which American Jews were able to press for and achieve social and political inclusion. That long-term process must be understood within two intersecting frameworks. First, it was the result of sweeping social, economic, and political changes, both domestic and global. Second, it was the product of a political project on the part of American Jewish activists and their allies from a range of civic and ethnic groups. It may seem evident that these activists operated without knowing how history would turn out, but this point is worth counterposing with the seeming inexorability of the era's macroforces. Historians' narratives about immigration policy during the postwar period often leave the impression that the era's profound traumas and far-reaching developments—the rise of Nazi Germany, World War II, the Holocaust, the Cold War, the civil rights movement, and the Great Society—made political and legal outcomes, such as the 1965 Immigration Act, nearly inevitable.[6] All these forces indeed reshaped the realm of US immigration policy, and set the stage on which all the historical actors in this story functioned. But a focus on macroforces obscures the uncertainties that attended the process for people at the time, which often underlay and drove their actions. The 1965 law came only after more than two decades of wartime and postwar political struggles over the meaning of immigration policy, struggles in which American Jewish leaders, intellectuals, and lawmakers played a decisive role, just as they had in the years before the war. If in hindsight the growing acceptance of European ethnics and the demise of the national origins quotas seem obvious, it is important to acknowledge that, to the historical actors in the decades before 1965, this process seemed much more fitful and tenuous. This perspective helps us understand the strategies and attitudes American Jewish leaders adopted—or did not adopt—in their work on immigration along the way. Such strategies played a role in shaping political outcomes and thus need to be considered together with the large-scale societal currents of the time.

Those societal currents included major changes in the nation's social and political landscape, which helped create a climate favorable to more-liberal immigration policies. The United States emerged from World War II with a profoundly different place in the world order, and the country soon began defining itself as it would for the next half century—as the leading force for democracy and against the spread of Communism. American lawmakers and commentators came to regard immigration policy as a crucial aspect of foreign policy and as an important tool in achieving the nation's strategic international aims. Moreover, this was an era in which many lawmakers and government officials came to press for racial justice more broadly. Indeed, the Hart-Celler Act was one of that decade's civil rights triumphs, a repudiation of formal, legal American racism on par with the 1964 Civil Rights Act and the 1965 Voting Rights Act. An increasing commitment to abolishing racist laws developed in response to Nazi-perpetrated horrors, as well as to the burgeoning African American freedom movement, and was guided by the work of leading intellectuals who helped turn the tide against the racialist thinking that undergirded immigration policy, as well as Jim Crow laws and other discriminatory practices. Moreover, both racial injustices at home and discriminatory immigration policy were seen as undermining the US image abroad. From the mid-1940s through the mid-1960s, the new official support of racial justice was also linked to "Third World" decolonization and the US's Cold War–era interest in securing the loyalties of emerging nations in Africa and Asia.[7]

Advocates of liberalizing immigration law championed various methods for doing so: admitting significant numbers of refugees; allowing certain immigrants to avoid deportation; and abolishing the national origins quotas. Exercising a greater power than their predecessors, postwar presidents pressed Congress for new policies and implemented others on their own.[8] Meanwhile, white ethnic voters—naturalized immigrants and their children—gained new power in shaping politics on a national level. Their power was evident both in the realm of electoral politics, where they represented a critical constituency of the Democratic Party, and in the sway exerted by the Congress of Industrial Organizations (CIO), whose working-class ethnic roots made for a more immigration-friendly stance than the older, more elite and traditionally restrictionist national labor organization, the American Federation of Labor (AFL).[9]

Indeed, the repeal of the national origins quotas reflected the changing status of European ethnics—Jews included—in the United States. The Americanization process that had begun for many of the "new immigrants" during the interwar years proceeded even more rapidly during and after World War II. By 1965, the "new" European immigrants (legal or not) and their children or descendants were in many ways "strangers no longer" in America.[10] Thanks to a number of factors, including generous veterans' benefits, a rise in union membership, a general postwar upswing in American prosperity, and increased access to higher education, European ethnic communities had become more securely middle class. This economic mobility was dependent not only on shifting political and economic currents but also on social and geographic consolidation of whiteness itself. Like other ethnics judged to be white, Jews were able to participate in the postwar American dream of education and homeownership made possible by the tuition and mortgage benefits of the 1944 GI Bill, whereas nonwhite veterans found their benefits limited by segregated educational institutions and housing opportunities. The race-based calculus of the Federal Housing Administration and openly racist lending and real estate practices allowed white ethnics to leave urban centers and buy homes in the nation's rapidly growing suburbs, in an age in which home-ownership and suburbia came to be identified with American identity itself. The suburbs became, both by default and design, places defined by race and class. As these immigrants and their children made the suburbs their own, they became part of the white American mainstream.[11] This shift made the national origins quotas' distinctions among more and less desirable European groups seem anachronistic.

These political, economic, and social forces thus played key roles in producing immigration policies that both reflected and helped ensure European ethnics' place in the national polity. But such policies were also the product of intense effort on the part of those ethnics, especially American Jews. In many ways, Jews' activism on immigration was more confident than it had been in the prewar era, reflecting the insider status and political clout they had since gained. Like much of the other antiprejudice and civil rights activism American Jews engaged in during this period, Jews' engagement with immigration issues was often expressed in terms of a universal battle for justice rather than as a matter of particular Jewish interest.[12] At the same time, however, American Jews' immigration activism grew out of an ongoing sense of insecurity. For American Jews, the years during and after the war did not always seem to be heading inexorably toward increasingly liberal attitudes, practices, and policies that would benefit them. Despite a dramatic decline in anti-Semitism across realms as diverse as employment, housing, education, and social life, American Jews still worried about, and organized to combat, ongoing prejudice.[13]

Such uncertainties extended to the domain of immigration policy. Throughout wartime and the postwar period, a restrictionist bloc, committed to the ethnic "controls" imposed by the national origins quotas and to immigration restriction on principle, remained vocal and strong inside and outside Congress. Toward the end of World War II, several bills were proposed in Congress to suspend immigration entirely, so as to ensure that immigrants would not take jobs away from returning servicemen.[14] Debates over refugee policy before, during, and after the war were strongly colored by anti-immigrant sentiment and anti-Jewish attitudes. The fears that had crystallized in the previous decades—about Jewish immigrants as undesirable or illegal aliens, criminals, and political subversives—persisted during these debates. Indeed, during the Cold War era, battles over immigration policy often carried an extra charge because of fierce disagreements over the extent to which immigrants—and even naturalized citizens—represented a security threat. Consequently, American Jews' relationship to immigration policy reflected complicated crosscurrents. Even as powerful economic and political developments helped shift American perspectives on immigration and ethnicity, and helped move Jews into the security of the white American mainstream, the process of inclusion was never straightforward. The American Jewish activism that shaped that very process was thus propelled by both empowerment and anxiety.

Several related developments illustrate how these dynamics played out in the realm of immigration policy. The first concerns the issue of refugees, a question of urgent concern to American Jews during the 1930s and 1940s. The lack of sympathy displayed by the international community toward wartime refugees and particularly toward Jewish victims of the Holocaust is well documented.[15] Nevertheless, after the war, the identity of "refugee" gained official status in US immigration law. This change came about thanks in part to intensive advocacy by American Jews, who helped define the problem of refugees as one fundamentally separate from general immigration issues. The newly codified category of refugees became crucial to US immigration policy, particularly in the nation's Cold War era efforts to support those fleeing Communist regimes and to project a liberty-loving image abroad. Indeed, it helped serve, both in law and in public discourse, to erase from national consciousness the earlier association between Jews (and Europeans more generally) and illegal immigration. Though the American public remained suspicious of any influx of immigrants, the plight of refugees (or at least of some refugees), in the wake of the war's horrors, thus recast the meaning of immigration.[16]

The second development is the broader process by which, during the decades during and after the war, Jewish immigrants in the American context, along with other European immigrants, continued to escape the association with illegal immigration. As earlier chapters demonstrated, American Jewish organizations were alarmed by the sharp rise in Jewish illegal immigration and alien smuggling after the quota laws came into force in the 1920s, as well as by the growing discourse of criminality around immigration. Their efforts during the 1920s and 1930s to sever the connection in the public mind between Jews and unlawful immigration—from their attempts to stem Jewish illegal immigration to legal battles over alien registration—met with partial success. It was in the following decades, however, that such efforts gained significant traction. Two striking phenomena combined to drive this change. First, as Mae Ngai has shown, the official erasure of European illegal immigration proceeded during this era via federal administrative mechanisms such as "preexamination" and "adjustment of status," formal processes instituted in earlier years that continued to allow Jews and others to legalize their presence in the nation.[17] Second, the idea of illegal immigration came increasingly during this era to be strongly associated with Mexicans. Even as other foreigners continued to be regarded sometimes as suspect aliens, Mexicans became defined in the public imagination as nearly synonymous with the notion of illegal immigration.[18] American Jewish activists did not go out of their way to push this characterization of Mexicans as the ethnic group most in need of targeting, but neither did they battle it.

The final development is the abolition of the quotas in the 1965 law. The Hart-Celler Act was a major victory for Jews both as a group historically targeted by those laws and as a group fighting against prejudice in postwar American society. At the same time, however, it also represented certain restrictive tendencies—the limiting of Western Hemisphere immigration and, indeed, all immigration more generally—that, by this time, seemed acceptable to American Jewish activists.

NEW CLAIMS ON THE NATION: REFUGEES AND DISPLACED PERSONS

Historically, refugees were not accorded preferential treatment under US immigration law, despite the nation's self-concept as a haven for the oppressed. The notion of "refugee," of course, was not new. The term was used widely before and after World War I by the American Jewish organizations trying to help European Jews displaced by the era's upheavals. It was invoked, too, by supporters of legislation that would have allowed Armenian victims of Turkish violence into the United States.[19] Despite these efforts, there continued to be no official recognition of refugees in American immigration law. That is, immigration law did not put people fleeing war or persecution into a different category from other would-be immigrants, except for an exemption from the literacy test (enacted as part of the 1917 Immigration Act) for those escaping religious persecution, something American Jewish organizations had pushed hard for in the early twentieth century.[20]

The rise of Fascism and, later, of Communism, in combination with the international leadership role the United States took on after the war, altered the political calculus in favor of refugees. The general public and many lawmakers remained reluctant to admit immigrants and suspicious of aliens, and such attitudes constrained the nation's legal generosity. Ultimately, however, inscribing the category of "refugee" into the nation's legal code signaled a measure of validation for the claims that European immigrants—and later, others fleeing Communist regimes—had on the American nation. The official recognition of refugee status reflected a new kind of national moral mandate to aid certain immigrants, even if decisions to admit refugees stemmed more from US foreign policy concerns than from a newfound commitment to humanitarian good will.[21]

This shift, however, was long in coming. With Adolf Hitler's rise to power in 1933, Germany—home to upwards of a half million generally well-integrated and prosperous Jews—suddenly became the most urgent focus for questions about Jewish migration. In the United States, as elsewhere, however, German Jewish refugees were not widely regarded as meriting special treatment under the law. Over the course of the next decade, as the Nazis seized control of more and more of Europe, Jews in those countries had pressing new reasons to try to leave. Emigrating often proved difficult. (Germany, for example, refused to let Jews leave without confiscating significant amounts of their capital.) However, finding a place to go could be even harder, as the previous years had seen many nations in addition to the United States severely limit immigration.[22] The dire economic situation worldwide meant that governments were not inclined to relax these policies. As noted in chapter 5, the Hoover administration's 1930 order to deny a visa to any would-be immigrant who could be construed "likely to become a public charge" meant that even immigration from nations with relatively large quotas, like Germany, was at a historic low. The era's grim joke that the world consisted of two sorts of countries, those where Jews could not live and those that Jews could not enter, aptly summed up the bind in which Europe's Jews found themselves.[23] In the United States, the 1924 quota law—and the strict consular apparatus that accompanied it—and the 1930 "public charge" restriction continued to pose a daunting barrier to entry even as the situation for European Jews rapidly deteriorated.

In the prewar years of Hitler's regime, during the depths of the Great Depression, many American Jewish spokespeople were reluctant to advocate too vigorously for any major change in US immigration policy. Even with widespread sympathy within the Roosevelt administration, forces conspired against American Jewish advocacy for admitting German Jewish immigrants. Some scholars have pointed to the lack of unity among American Jews as preventing effective efforts to liberalize the law in favor of admitting refugees from Nazism.[24] Others have noted the extent to which any advocacy on behalf of those refugees was constrained by the political and economic realities of the time. Anti-Semitism was virulent and widespread during this era, as evidenced by the popularity of groups such as the Ku Klux Klan, the pro-Nazi German-

American Bund, and the Silver Shirts, which preached and published their anti-Jewish conspiracy theories in print and at live gatherings. The largest audience for extremely anti-Semitic messages was the devoted following of "radio priest" Father Charles Coughlin of Michigan, whose broadcast and weekly paper had a nationwide audience. All these voices warned against Jewish plans to control American and world government and finance, as well as more specifically against the economic and political dangers posed by Jewish refugees.[25]

In addition, the immigration regime established by the quota system was so firmly entrenched in US policy that it became unassailable to officials and to the public at large.[26] In 1934, Harry Laughlin, a eugenics expert whose testimony had helped garner support for the quota laws, testified that no special admission should be granted to Jewish refugees, in the interests of maintaining national "race standards."[27] The State Department was deeply committed both to maintaining its policies of strictly screening potential immigrants for visas and to avoiding actions that might offend the German government, such as acknowledging that German Jewish applicants for US visas were facing a special emergency. Some of the department's key officials in Washington and abroad were personally anti-Semitic and suspicious of immigration, which, while not the deciding factor, also played a role in maintaining obstacles to liberalizing immigration policy.[28] Moreover, the principle remained largely unquestioned that allowing refugees into the United States during a time of high unemployment would undermine opportunities for Americans.[29]

Many American Jews, particularly among the established organizations, thus feared that any strong advocacy on behalf of refugees or liberalizing immigration policy would produce a backlash. And, indeed, even minor gestures toward loosening restrictive immigration policies toward Jews met with resistance. For example, when Roosevelt, in 1934, instructed US consular officials to grant refugees' applications the most generous possible consideration, those officials resisted. Consuls persisted in maintaining high levels of scrutiny, particularly regarding whether potential immigrants had enough money to avoid becoming a "public charge." Jews, barred by the German government from taking capital out of the country, were hard-pressed to do this.[30] In 1939, a legislative proposal to admit twenty thousand German refugee children outside the usual quotas in the aftermath of *Kristallnacht* (the November 1938 pogroms against German Jews) foundered when opponents protested that it was wrong to extend aid to German children at a time when so many American children suffered at home.[31] Opinion polls indicated that the American public was deeply set against admitting refugees, no matter how dire the situation abroad.[32]

The prevalence of American anti-Semitism and antialien sentiment fueled the widespread reluctance to admit refugees from Hitler's Germany. Another strain running through public objections to Jewish immigrants, one intertwined with the idea of their undesirability, was the specter of the smuggled alien, familiar from media reports about alien smuggling and legislative debates over immigration, deportation, alien registration, and naturalization during the previous decade. Indeed, the threat of an illegal influx was sometimes used as a rationale to push for drastic reductions in immigration and harsher deportation policies, as in 1939, when two southern Democrats introduced legislation in both houses of Congress that would have halted nearly all immigration. In the course of the hearings, Senator Robert Reynolds of North Carolina, one of the bill's cosponsors, warned that shiploads of European refugees were arriving in Cuba and would ultimately embark for the United States, slipping past the authorities along with thousands of others. During the hearing, Reynolds and others also expressed dismay that there were refugees who were entering legally as visitors but violating the law by overstaying their visas.[33]

Private correspondence among government officials reflected the concern that large numbers of Jewish refugees were slipping into the nation illicitly. Late in 1938, Assistant Secretary of State George Messersmith wrote to Coert duBois, consul general in Havana, to say that "a representative of a well-known welfare organization" had come into his office to discuss his fear that hordes of German Jews were coming into the country on Cuban citizenship papers. This person had recently been on a Washington–New York City train and, encountering a group of passengers "who looked very much like German refugees," surmised that they had illegally entered the United States via Cuba.[34] The consul general assured Messersmith that this could not be the case. Nevertheless, the shared concerns of Senator Reynolds and Messersmith's visitor, while overstated, were not unfounded. Some immigrants did find their way to the United States illegally via Cuba, as they had been doing for years. In spring 1939, for example, a US Marine Corps colonel in Havana wrote to the consul general that his secretary had informed him that a local hotel manager was arranging fraudulent marriages for Jewish women who wanted to go to the United States.[35] Around the same time, an anonymous author wrote to Havana's consul general, claiming that, as a Jewish immigrant trying to get from Cuba to the United States, he had been fleeced by a representative of a local Jewish organization, who had extorted cash from him in exchange for "fixing" his visa. Other modes of illegal entry persisted as well, including stowing away on ships, entering with fraudulent papers, and, as Reynolds and others had charged, overstaying visitors' visas.[36] US officials themselves were sometimes on the take, trading such visas for cash. Abraham Ascher, for example, whose family were Polish Jews living in Breslau (then Germany) in 1938, recalled his mother's arrangement with the local United States consul to provide Ascher's father with a visitor visa in return for five hundred German marks.[37]

Some of the anxieties regarding Jewish immigrants were not as well grounded. After the start of the war, the American public's suspicion of foreigners mounted. The most outlandish fear was that admission of Jewish refugees would allow for the infiltration of the nation by a "fifth column." One argument made in congressional hearings and in media reports, for example, was that Nazis might use Jewish refugees as spies under threat of harm to family members remaining in Europe. Another theory held that some Jewish refugees were actually Nazi spies in disguise. In a twist on the masquerades that Jewish illegal immigrants had long had to perform to get by immigration authorities into the nation, these spies, reported one source, had even studied Hebrew and Yiddish to pass as Jews.[38]

As many scholars have lamented, there was no fundamental change in US immigration policy in response to the unfolding disaster in Europe.[39] The Roosevelt administration was not able or willing to propose radical revisions to the nation's immigration policy, especially given public and congressional resistance to the idea. Nevertheless, sympathy in high places did lead to some unprecedented government action on behalf of refugees. Although the 1939 bill to admit German refugee children in the wake of *Kristallnacht* had failed, the administration did arrange to extend the stay of about fifteen thousand refugees who were already in the United States on visitors' visas and to organize special visitors' visas for about three thousand refugees who were deemed especially distinguished.[40] Internal advocacy and the president's position on the issue also prodded the State Department to ease up on its harsh visa policies by the end of 1936.[41] At the Evian Conference, the international gathering the Roosevelt administration convened in 1938 in Evian, France, the United States pushed other nations to accept more refugees, though to little avail. The United States itself admitted approximately one hundred thirty-eight thousand Jewish refugees between 1933 and 1944—certainly not all who would have wanted to come but more than any other nation admitted.[42]

Most European Jews, of course, remained trapped after the start of hostilities. By the war's end, the Nazi death apparatus had decimated Europe's Jewish population from over nine and a half million to three and a half million.[43] For those who survived, the situation was dire. Indeed, much of Europe was in disastrous circumstances; in addition to Jews, millions of other people had been displaced: those brought from eastern Europe to Germany as slave labor during the war; Ukrainians and Balts who fled the advance of the Soviet Army as it swept westward; and ethnic Germans being forced out of eastern and central Europe. About eight million of the tens of millions of people displaced by the war were marooned in the Allied occupied zones of Germany, Austria, and Italy, and were impoverished and desperate.[44] Together with the newly formed United Nations Relief and Rehabilitation Agency (UNRRA), the Allied Command was charged with helping these "displaced persons," or "DPs." Authorities decided some could be repatriated safely but agreed that many, including Jewish death camp survivors and those Ukrainians, Balts, and Poles who were judged to face persecution in their original homes, could not. The UNRRA and the Allied Command set up a network of DP camps, meant to house refugees until they could be resettled somewhere. Conditions in the camps were grim. Earl Harrison, the former head of the US Immigration and Naturalization Service (INS), who was dispatched by President Truman to Europe to study the DP issue, issued a scathing report in 1946. Harrison asserted that the US Army, through its ill treatment of DPs, was essentially perpetuating the legacy of Nazi concentration camps rather than helping to eradicate it.[45]

American Jewish advocacy regarding the urgent postwar predicament of European Jews took more than one path. Many American Jews, increasingly united around the Zionist cause during the 1930s, had hoped for and worked toward eventual Jewish resettlement in Palestine, and many American Jewish organizations continued to press for this option. British intransigence on the matter in the years immediately after the war, however, presented serious obstacles to such a plan. Other groups, such as the American Jewish Committee, which was only a recent supporter of the idea of a Jewish Palestine, and the anti-Zionist American Council for Judaism, thus turned their attention to US immigration policy.[46] In the years following the war, these groups led a wide-ranging campaign for special legislation that would admit European refugees outside the quotas. This campaign ultimately met with a fair amount of success, but the process was fraught with obstacles and setbacks.

Those who hoped the United States would extend a welcome to displaced persons faced a disheartening situation in the years immediately following the war. In 1945, Truman signaled an important executive willingness to take up the issue by ordering the State Department to resume consular activities near DP camps and to grant visas from underused quotas to death camp survivors and other DPs. However, this measure proved relatively inconsequential.[47] Moreover, Americans' opposition to admitting refugees remained high, as opinion polls indicated.[48] Indeed, opposition to immigration in general persisted, as evidenced by several bills introduced in Congress in 1945 and 1946 to further restrict or even suspend immigration altogether.[49] When Republican Congressman William Stratton of Illinois introduced a bill in early 1947 to admit four hundred thousand displaced persons—both Jews and other refugees generated by the war and postwar upheavals—the proposal met resistance from immigration restrictionists inside and outside Congress.

Besides insisting that admitting refugees would be economically detrimental to the nation, those opposed to such a measure also couched their arguments in terms of undesirability and criminality, thus questioning DPs' fitness for American citizenship. The persistence of the DP camps, critics of refugee admission suggested, indicated that DPs were sitting around in these camps collecting rations, rather than helping to rebuild the war-torn nations that housed them or finding new lives elsewhere. This passivity, the critics claimed, showed that DPs did not exhibit the economic and personal independence that were defining characteristics of good citizens. Opponents to admitting refugees also asserted that the DP population was riddled with "subversives," dangerous political radicals who would stir up trouble in the United States.[50] Texas Congressman Ed Gossett, in particular, gave voice tirelessly to these sentiments on the floor of the House, contending that the DP camps were "filled with bums, criminals, black-marketeers, subversives, revolutionists, and crackpots."[51] Gossett singled out Jews, contending that they unfairly received the majority of US visas and that, as a consequence, gentile refugees were forced to "masquerade as Jews" in their desperation for fair treatment.[52] Opponents of the Stratton bill feared that there were just too many Jews in the DP population, and that these were often black marketeers and thus criminals unfit for admission to the United States. Although by this point many of the "original" Jewish DPs had been resettled in Palestine, the Jewish population of the camps increased rather than decreased. In spring and summer 1946, for example, thousands of Jews poured into the Allied camps, fleeing fresh anti-Semitic violence in Poland.[53] The Stratton bill ultimately failed, suggesting the persistent potency of old stereotypes linking Jews with radicalism, lawbreaking, and general undesirability.

Advocates for refugees, however, were well organized, and they did not give up after the Stratton bill's defeat. In 1946, American Jewish organizations had mobilized a broad coalition of advocacy groups and formed the Citizens Committee on Displaced Persons (CCDP), which drafted the original version of the Stratton bill. Jewish individuals and groups—particularly the American Jewish Committee and the American Council on Judaism—provided the bulk of the CCDP's funding and the organizational resources.[54] The CCDP, however, kept these facts under wraps. Mindful of the climate of suspicion around

Jewish immigrants and the skepticism toward any advocacy on their behalf, the organizers of the CCDP sought out ways to ensure that the group would not seem "too Jewish." Earl Harrison, the former head of the INS, agreed to serve as chairman, and a number of prominent Protestants and Catholics lent their name to the committee's cause. The CCDP also sought out ways to garner support for the DP cause by getting the story out to media and to lawmakers, and they undertook an extensive public relations campaign that emphasized the "non-Jewish" nature of the European refugee problem.[55] Congressman Emanuel Celler of Brooklyn, New York, a fierce opponent of the quota laws from the time of their passage, worked closely with Jewish advocacy groups and the CCDP, from his seat on the House committee (later subcommittee) dealing with immigration, in a ceaseless effort to raise support for legislation to admit DPs. He always made sure to stress the ecumenical scope of the DP problem. In a piece he wrote for the *Brooklyn Eagle* in 1947, for example, he noted that a great many DPs were Catholics and Protestants.[56] Like many Jews in the public eye during this era, Celler also refrained from mentioning his own Jewish background in the course of his advocacy efforts.

Celler, like other supporters of DP legislation, strove to counter the objections that opponents of the legislation raised. He argued that admitting refugees would not worsen the economy. Refugees were not, by any means, all Communists, he contended; indeed, many of them were natives of lands under direct Soviet control and in danger of persecution if they were to return. And black marketeering among DPs, far from being evidence of raw criminality, was often the means for simple exchange and survival in a region with a devastated economy and scarce regular work or currency.[57]

In 1948, advocates for the immigration of DPs met with some success when Congress passed a measure to admit two hundred thousand to the United States, "borrowing" against future quota limits.[58] The passage of this new law owed something to the CCDP's well-organized public relations campaign. Also crucial to producing this large-scale exception to the regular workings of the quota laws, however, were the emerging dynamics of the Cold War. That is, the DP situation came to be seen not only as a response to a humanitarian crisis but also as critical for stabilizing the Western European lands in which the refugees were residing. The passage of landmark legislation to admit refugees, then, must be understood as an act in keeping with the establishment of the Marshall Plan and NATO; all three were meant to help create a bulwark against Communism.[59] Indeed, Secretary of State George Marshall himself made the case that helping the European refugees was crucial in this regard.[60]

Even though the new law opened up immigration to some displaced persons, many of the specific provisions of the 1948 legislation proved a bitter disappointment to the Jewish groups that had worked toward it. It was clear that anti-Jewish sentiment had helped generate some of the stipulations that distinguished this law from the earlier Stratton bill or from similar bills the CCDP had supported during the legislative process. First, the new law specified that those with agricultural expertise be given preference in admission. This shut out many of the Jewish refugees, who were far less likely than other DPs to qualify in that category. Moreover, the law applied only to those who had entered the western zones of Austria, Germany, and Italy by December 22, 1945. This provision excluded all those Jews who had entered the Allied-controlled territory later: for example those who had fled the violence in Poland in 1946. (Other refugees from the Soviet Union or countries newly under Soviet sway were similarly excluded in this way.) Meanwhile, another section of the law specified that once it was enacted, half the regular Austrian and German quotas should be set aside for *Volksdeutsche*, or ethnic Germans, who had been expelled from eastern European lands at the war's end.[61] Congressman Emanuel Celler, outraged, declared that the legislation was akin to the Nuremburg laws.[62] The American Jewish Congress and the Anti-Defamation League of the B'nai B'rith urged President Truman to veto it.[63] Truman signed the bill, but he also noted that it reflected an un-American spirit of intolerance, that it discriminated "in callous fashion against displaced persons of the Jewish faith," and that indeed he was not sure it was any better than having no such law at all.[64]

Once the bill was signed into law, there was an organized outcry by the CCDP and other groups against its restrictive provisions.[65] In the fall election campaign, Truman spoke of the need to change the legislation. In the same election that put him back in the White House, meanwhile, both houses of Congress came under more liberal Democratic control and a number of restrictionist legislators were ousted, though the staunch restrictionist Pat McCarran, Democrat of Nevada, remained. Despite McCarran's best efforts, however, the DP law was amended in 1950 in ways favorable to Jewish refugees, as well as to others who had fled Communist regimes after the war's end. The new version of the legislation no longer contained the agricultural labor provision and extended eligibility for DP visas to those who had entered the western zone by January 1, 1949.[66]

Taken together, the DP laws were a complicated victory for the American Jewish activists who had thrown themselves into the issue. The laws, together with the 1945 Truman directive, made possible the immigration of four hundred thousand European refugees to the United States, including roughly one hundred thousand Jews.[67] Moreover, in its implementation the legislation proved far more flexible than immigration law as it had been administered by traditional gatekeepers, the Department of State and the INS and its predecessors.[68] The DP laws established a new agency, the Displaced Persons Commission (DPC), which worked in concert with advocacy groups—such as the Jewish (but deliberately not Jewish-sounding) United Service for New Americans—the US Army, and the United Nations International Refugee Organization (IRO) on the logistics of screening and resettling refugees. The presidentially appointed officials in charge of the DPC proved to be far more liberal in their policy vision than other government agencies, and they worked hard to get as many refugees through the process as possible.

However, the value of the DP legislation for American Jews was unclear. For one thing, the establishment of the State of Israel in 1948 changed the terms of the equation, making the admission of European Jewish refugees into the United States less urgent. Indeed, some of the more committed American Zionists feared that a flow of refugees to the United States would siphon needed settlement away from Israel.[69] And while American Jews, such as those with the American Jewish Committee, who fought for the legislation continued to regard the issue as of both symbolic and practical importance, many also feared that the DP measures had served to bring former Nazis and other anti-Semites into the country.[70]

Moreover, the very liberality with which the DPC administered the law made for clashes with those other US agencies involved in determining visa eligibility. Prospective immigrants often found themselves caught in a complicated web of documentary requirements that they could not easily meet, given their circumstances.[71] Additionally, despite high public approval of the DP legislation, accusations persisted in the media and in Congress that there were political subversives among the refugees, along with many lawbreakers, and that these unsavory characters were slipping through because of the laxity on the part of the DPC.[72] Officials of the DPC found themselves contesting charges, for example, that a high percentage of Jewish refugees were making their way through the process by means of faked German birth certificates or fraudulent documentation that misrepresented length of residence in the western zones. Indeed, US officials from different agencies battled over the very meanings of documentation, eligibility, and fraud. They skirmished, for example, over whether erasures of dates on clothing ration cards issued to displaced persons constituted a violation of immigration policy, or whether such documents, as nonimmigration-related papers, fell outside the purview of visa considerations.[73] For their part, DPC officials believed that Jewish DPs were often singled out for particularly harsh scrutiny by authorities in the army, State Department, and INS.[74]

While some of the suspicion accorded DPs (Jewish and non-Jewish) was ungrounded, some of it did have a basis in fact. Official American army paper and ink found its way into black market "document mills" that rose to meet the displaced persons' need for papers.[75] Forged documents, procured from local officials, could also be the basis of fraudulent claims for visa eligibility under the DP law. Solomon Wiesel, a Jewish man from Romania who had been a prisoner of both the Nazis and the Russians, represented one such case. After the war, he made his way westward to Germany, crossing several borders illegally en route. He arrived in the American zone in 1948. There, he managed to obtain a document from the police chief in the town of Mühldorf certifying that he had resided there since 1945, which rendered him eligible for a DP visa.[76]

Sympathetic officials in the IRO, which administered the DP camps and worked with voluntary organizations, including Jewish groups, to organize the resettlement of refugees, were not above bending the rules either. Unlike the US consular and immigration authorities, who were charged with upholding American law, the IRO—like the DPC and private aid groups—saw their mission as solving the refugee crisis by getting the DPs resettled elsewhere. The IRO was not overly concerned with the accuracy of applications they helped the refugees to prepare.[77] The outcry raised by lawmakers about the processing of displaced persons ultimately had a chilling effect on these practices; the DPC increased its scrutiny of visa applicants in its later years, and fewer Jews were admitted under the law than had been earlier.[78]

Another counterforce to the liberalizing tendencies of the new DP legislation was the McCarthy-era National Security Act of 1950, which was shepherded through Congress by the longtime restrictionist, chairman of the Senate Judiciary Committee Pat McCarran.[79] McCarran was a bitter opponent of admitting displaced persons, which he saw as a dangerous step toward "tear[ing] down our immigration barriers" and flooding the nation with undesirable aliens.[80] Coming on the heels of the 1950 amended DP legislation, the National Security Act represented a "get tough" immigration policy toward those deemed radicals, whether they were outside or inside American borders. The law now required Communists in the United States to register with the US attorney general. Nonnaturalized foreigners who were members of the Communist Party, or even those who were judged to be political subversives more generally, were to be deported with all possible haste. Foreigners who wanted to enter the United States, meanwhile, now faced stringent screening for any history with Communist organizations.[81] For those officials who were charged with screening displaced persons' applications for visas, these new requirements made for a whole new level of difficulty, as authorities dealt with long lists of "inimical organizations" and struggled with complicated questions raised by individuals' histories—coerced, voluntary, or something in between—with such organizations.[82]

Despite these limitations, the displaced persons legislation did represent important changes in the established structures of US immigration policy, as well as in the national discourse on immigration. Though initially constructed to address the particular situation in the postwar American zones of Germany, Austria, and Italy, the legislation had broader implications. Advocates for refugees were successful in getting DP legislation passed in part because of their decision to separate this project from more general immigration reform.[83] Refugee advocates made a strategic distinction between general immigration reform and refugee policy, and this distinction helped develop the latter into its own important political and legislative arena, seemingly separate from questions about other kinds of immigration. It gave refugees a new, special status in US law, recognizing them as a category distinct from other immigrants.[84] By so doing, the displaced persons law—however limited and controversial it proved to be—acknowledged in unprecedented fashion that immigrants fleeing political upheavals had valid claims to entering the nation. Meanwhile, just as restrictionists who opposed the law feared, the laws admitting displaced persons did indeed serve as a lever for those who advocated abolishing immigration quotas, which is discussed below.

The concerns of the activists and lawmakers who helped get the DP legislation passed shaped the meaning of "refugee" in various ways. As Leonard Dinnerstein observes, for example, Jewish advocates during these years were focused on European displaced persons; the millions of Africans and Asians displaced by the war were not of immediate interest to them.[85] Because they played such an important role in shaping the American debate over refugees, then, American Jewish activists inadvertently helped define refugees as primarily a white, European phenomenon. The idea that "refugees" were Europeans was integral to US policy through the 1960s, albeit with some important exceptions.[86] Meanwhile, reflecting the priorities of many of the government officials involved in pressing for DP legislation, the laws also tied the official acknowledgment of refugees to Cold War concerns. This link had a profound effect on later policies that recognized as bona fide refugees those from Communist regimes but that were less likely to welcome refugees from other situations. The Refugee Relief Act of 1953, the "paroling" in by the attorney general of tens of thousands Hungarian refugees in 1956, and the refugee provisions of the 1965 law were all implemented in this vein.[87]

With the emergence of the "refugee" as a legitimate figure in US immigration law, a powerful new character was added to the national narrative about immigrants. Although suspicions of European immigrants by no means disappeared, the figure of the "refugee" changed the terms of the debate. A refugee might have entered the nation illegally, but he or she presented a different, more tragic kind of figure than the "bootlegged alien" of earlier years.

It is an interesting twist to the story of US policy and sentiment that the great surge of Jewish illegal immigration internationally helped to create the public notion of the refugee and thus to legitimize the very idea of "Jewish illegal immigration." As noted earlier, in the years before, during, and after the war, Jews fleeing Germany and elsewhere in Europe increasingly looked to Palestine for refuge, with the active encouragement of Palestine- and Europe-based Zionists. The British, however, were leery of opening Palestine to increased Jewish immigration and thereby angering the Arab population. Between 1934 and 1948, when the State of Israel was formally established, about one hundred thousand Jews immigrated illegally from Europe to Palestine, some fifty thousand of them in the postwar years.[88] Thousands were able to make the journey only thanks to an organized network that helped them illegally cross borders—both of nations and of occupation zones—to get from eastern to western Europe in the first place, an effort initiated by Jewish survivors and then also by Palestinian Jews. This project of moving Jews illicitly through Europe entailed widespread forging of documents, counterfeiting of currency, theft of needed supplies, and bribery of officials. Leaving Europe and setting sail for Palestine in violation of the British immigration limits involved yet more daring lawbreaking.[89]

This complicated enterprise in evading the laws of multiple nations was regarded sympathetically from many quarters. In the postwar years, the efforts of European Jews to reach Palestine illegally was anything but secret; international headlines followed the harrowing tales of the *Exodus* and other ships as they attempted to ferry Jewish refugees past the British blockade. Indeed, activists developed a media and public relations campaign around these gripping dramas of illicit migration, stories that they hoped would bring worldwide support to Jewish migrants and the Zionist cause. In this aim, they met with notable successes. Thus, when the British returned the Jews on board the *Exodus* to a German port, public opinion was not on their side; journalists reported on the horrifying spectacle of some of the refugees being forcibly removed from the ships by British soldiers.[90] Many American Jews, meanwhile, rallied behind the illicit efforts to get European Jews to Palestine. The Joint Distribution Committee, in particular, played a crucial role by funneling millions of dollars to the effort.[91] The tacit and sometimes open help of US Army personnel and workers at the UNRRA and its successor organization the IRO makes evident the sympathy granted the movement on the ground in Europe.[92]

It is noteworthy that none of the public or private commentators in the US warning of the dangers of admitting refugees, or of the associations between DPs and lawbreaking, seems to have invoked the phenomenon of international Jewish illegal immigration to help build their case. This omission suggests that they understood that such an argument might make Jewish immigrants seem more sympathetic, not less. Popular culture of the era also helps chart this shift in sympathies. Films such as *A Lady Without Passport* (1950), in which Hedy Lamarr stars as a beautiful Jewish concentration camp survivor trying to make her way illegally from Havana to the United States, anticipated the attitudes represented by the better known *Exodus*, which appeared a decade later (based on Leon Uris's 1958 blockbuster bestseller of the same name). In the same years that Jewish refugees met with a new kind of welcome (however qualified and grudging) in US law, they also found international sympathy for their efforts to find a new home, even when—indeed, especially when—those efforts were illegal.

THE LEGITIMATION OF JEWISH IMMIGRATION DURING AND AFTER WORLD WAR II

The new status of and sympathy toward refugees that emerged after World War II worked in concert with other kinds of changes that helped to legitimate Jewish and European immigration. New government classificatory practices put into place during World War II point to a transformation in official thinking about European immigrants. In 1940, for example, the INS started to classify European immigrants' race simply as "white" on naturalization forms, eliminating the blanks where applicants were expected to define themselves according to the more specific "racial" categories of earlier years (e.g., "Hebrew" or "Magyar").[93] During that same year, the federal census was conducted without distinguishing—as it had done a decade earlier—between native-born whites with foreign-born parents and those with native parents, thus amalgamating ethnic whites into the general white population.[94] After 1943, moreover, immigration authorities ended the practice of categorizing Jewish immigrants as "Hebrews" on ship manifests, apparently both in response to Jewish organizations' advocacy of this change and a desire to end policies that bore any resemblance to those of the Nazi regime.[95]

Meanwhile, a number of immigration policies—beyond refugee policy— during and after World War II also helped to recast erstwhile illegal immigrants from Europe as deserving Americans and thus to establish Jews' ever more solid inclusion in the national polity both symbolically and concretely. The trend described in the previous chapter of government leniency regarding European illegal immigrants continued during the forties and fifties, benefiting Jews and others who had entered via illicit means. European immigrants subject to deportation met increasingly with a great deal of administrative flexibility. This flexibility was a response to a combination of forces, including the longstanding agitation of liberal immigration activists to humanize deportation procedures and the increased political clout of white ethnic communities. Postwar, the leniency toward European immigrants also reflected the newly heightened sympathy for refugees from Fascism and Communism, some of whom were in the country illegally, as well as the tendency during the Cold War to regard European immigration as an important foreign policy issue.

One important measure that effected the transformation from "illegal" to "legal" immigrant was the so-called preexamination procedure practiced between 1935 and 1958, whereby European immigrants whose deportation was officially deemed a "hardship" were allowed to legalize their status by traveling to Canada temporarily, obtaining a visa, and reentering legally.[96] Indeed, this option seems to have been widely known about by Jewish would-be immigrants abroad even by the late 1930s. Abraham Ascher, for example, writing of his family's efforts to leave Breslau in 1938, recalls that his parents planned for his father to enter the United States on a visitor visa, then leave the country to change his status via this method.[97] Significantly, although this policy was originally not limited to Europeans, it became so. Asians, because they were deemed racially ineligible to citizenship, could not qualify for visas under the program; Mexican and Caribbean immigrants were explicitly excluded from the program in 1945.[98]

In other cases, administrative flexibility allowed certain immigrants to legalize their status without leaving the country. The 1940 Alien Registration Act, for example, although it codified the surveillance of foreigners that had been battled by Jewish and other civil liberties activists, also gave the attorney general discretion to suspend deportations in cases where they would cause hardship to citizen or legally resident family members. This discretion was apparently included as a mollifying political gesture toward those ethnic communities, most notably Jews, who had expended such energy working against alien registration. Over the following decades, as Mae Ngai has shown, the great majority of the beneficiaries of the suspensions of deportation allowed for by the 1940 law were Europeans.[99] The 1948 Displaced Persons Act and later refugee admission laws also contained provisions for "adjustment of status," so that those refugees who had entered the country as temporary visitors could apply for admission as permanent residents.[100] These measures, aimed as they were at the European refugees encompassed by the laws, also helped to decriminalize the illegal immigration of those European foreigners and, by extension, to draw a distinction between their illegal immigration and that of non-Europeans.

Even if other avenues of appeal failed, those individual immigrants who had aid organizations, lawyers, or lawmakers willing to advocate for them could have private relief bills brought before Congress to waive deportation or otherwise regularize their status. The INS reported that these bills became a standard strategy in the postwar era, with nearly twenty-five thousand brought before Congress between 1945 and 1960. Though merely getting such a bill introduced did not guarantee its passage, a substantial number of such bids for leniency met with success; about 20 percent of the private immigration bills introduced during that period were approved.[101] Such private relief bills were, theoretically, available to immigrants from anywhere and were indeed granted to people from Asia and the Americas. Government data indicate, however, that the majority went to Europeans.[102] This likely reflected a number of realities, all of which came into play in the legal proceedings: access to well-established community resources; family members who were native-born and naturalized US citizens and thus had particular claims on legislators' benevolence; and a willingness on the part of lawmakers to see European immigrants as deserving, upstanding members of their communities and families.

One such case, for example, was that of Chaim Eidlisz, brought before Congress in 1960 with the help of the National Council of Jewish Women. Eidlisz, a furniture salesman in Brooklyn, had lost almost his entire Hungarian Jewish family to the Nazi concentration camps. In 1944, he, his parents and his four brothers were deported to Auschwitz, where his mother and two brothers were killed; his father and brother died after being taken to another camp. Only Eidlisz and one brother survived. After the war, Eidlisz made his way to France and then stowed away on a ship bound for New York. He was fifteen years old at the time. He applied a decade later to adjust his status to permanent resident under a 1957 measure allowing refugees who had entered as visitors to do this but was denied because of his illegal entry. (Eidlisz's one surviving brother, meanwhile, who had also made his way to the United States after the war, did succeed in adjusting his status this way.) Eidlisz's effort with Congress, however, was successful. The bill granting him legal permanent resident status was signed into law in June 1960.[103] Leniency in Eidlisz's individual case—the case of a survivor of Nazi persecution who faced deportation to a country behind the Iron Curtain—meshed well with the postwar vision of the United States as the enemy of totalitarianism and defender of freedom. It probably helped his case, moreover, that Eidlisz was rooted in a wide familial network of permanent residents and US citizens (besides his brother, he had a large circle of cousins in New York City), all constituents of New York's Senator Kenneth Keating, who officially authored the relief bill. The National Council for Jewish Women, the group assisting Eidlisz with his bid to Congress and one of the most experienced immigrant aid organizations, no doubt also provided invaluable help in assembling the necessary documents and crafting his case. Eidlisz and others who were able to "adjust their status" in some way thus benefitted from a combination of political and social factors that helped redefine them as essentially "legal" people caught up in a difficult system.

Nevertheless, it is worth noting that, as with all the other shifts in immigration policy discussed here, this trend toward inclusion remained partial and contested. For one thing, not all applications for leniency succeeded. For another, the measures granting leniency to immigrants were sometimes regarded with suspicion. Some officials apparently thought that the swell in private relief bills encouraged the alien smuggling business, presumably by helping to make illegal immigration seem a more viable option for getting into the country on a permanent basis.[104] In 1955, the Judiciary Committee of the House of Representatives resolved to revisit its handling of the private relief bills, noting that they had devolved into a "racket" for unscrupulous lawyers out to swindle desperate aliens.[105]

Leniency practices also increased in counterpoint to ongoing national concern about illegal immigration of Europeans. Some observers worried about the extent to which European immigrants—particularly if hailing from Eastern or Central Europe—were likely to be political subversives. Government authorities insisted that they were keeping close watch on borders and ports in order to catch any incoming "Reds" but acknowledged that the system was imperfect. During the 1950s, immigration officials continued to warn that Europeans were able to smuggle themselves easily across the Mexican border and that Communists certainly were among them; there were fears that a similar situation might exist along the Canadian border as well.[106]

It was not possible, therefore, for American Jewish activists to feel entirely secure in their successes in the immigration arena, despite the enormous strides American Jews made toward social, economic, and political inclusion in the postwar era. Even in this period of prosperity and national confidence, anti-immigration sentiment remained strong in some quarters. Meanwhile, older public anxieties about illegal and unsavory European immigration persisted, fed by newer ones about a possible clandestine influx of subversives. Moreover, administrative and legislative acts of leniency or flexibility toward immigrants—even laws as significant as the displaced persons legislation—did not represent a wholesale shift in the essential structure of US immigration law. Rather, they were exceptions to the ongoing rule: the national origins quota law of 1924 remained in force.

THE RISING THREAT OF THE MEXICAN "WETBACK"

This much improved but still ambiguous status vis-à-vis immigration policy helps explain occasions like the Columbus, Ohio, Council of Jewish Women's 1949 meeting to discuss how the "wetback invasion"—meaning Mexican illegal immigration—was "menacing the political, moral, and ethical status of this country."[107] The theme of this gathering, held far away from the nation's southern border, hints at American Jews' complicated consciousness regarding illegal immigration during the postwar era. While suspicion continued to be cast on the legality of some European immigration, the nation increasingly focused its attention on Mexican immigrants, whose association with illegality came to eclipse that of other groups. Thus, central to the story of the incorporation of Jews and other white ethnics into the national polity in the postwar era is the ongoing companion story of (re)defining "illegal alienness" as quintessentially a problem connected to Mexicans. American Jews were not promoters of this notion, exactly—the Columbus group's meeting seems to have been unusual in its outspoken disapproval of Mexican "wetbacks"—but they did not vigorously contest it. Sometimes they reminded the American public that Mexicans, not Europeans, were the problem group. Unquestionably they, like other white ethnics, benefited by the shift in national discourse around illegal immigration. American Jews' own insecurities about the suspicions directed toward Jewish immigrants helps illuminate their stance on the Mexican issue.

As Mae Ngai observes, the increasingly close association of "illegal alienness" with Mexicans is at first glance an odd historical development, for Mexicans—like Canadians and other inhabitants of independent Western Hemisphere nations—were not excluded by the restrictive quota legislation of 1921 and 1924. The argument for exempting immigrants from the Western

Hemisphere from quotas was couched partly in terms of foreign policy; government officials made the case that open borders were important to maintaining good relationships with neighboring countries.[108] Furthermore, Mexicans, though widely disparaged as racially inferior, were regarded as so crucial to the agricultural production of the Southwest that powerful business interests of that region lobbied forcefully to keep migration over the border legal. As discussed in chapter 2, during the 1920s there were many legislative proposals to limit Mexicans' entry and a rising identification of Mexicans with illegal immigration. Nevertheless, the interests in favor of keeping that border largely open to Mexicans held sway. Mexicans always seemed qualitatively different than other immigrants because of the proximity of their homeland and, as those invested in keeping the flow of labor coming pointed out, because of their long tradition of circular migration.[109]

Through the implementation of policy, however, Mexicans were increasingly rendered "illegal aliens," even as their labor continued to fuel the Southwest's economy (and that of other regions as well) and even as, during the same era, immigration policy was modified to legalize the status of European immigrants who had entered outside the law. The enforcement mechanisms applied at the border in the 1920s, described in chapter 2, were one stage in this process, as Mexicans chose more frequently to skirt the border checks and head tax and enter outside the scope of the law.[110] Indeed, the law itself created ambiguous, "irregular" categories of legal entry for Mexicans. Legal but "fuzzy" practices such as cross-border commuting and temporary entry as seasonal labor, which were difficult to enforce, were widely regarded as lax modes of immigration control that encouraged law breaking. This ambiguity contributed to the process of defining Mexican immigration as illegal or quasi legal at best.[111] The Depression-era deportation and repatriation drives, which targeted even Mexican American citizens and legal immigrants, helped cement the equation of Mexicans and illegal aliens in the national mind.[112]

During World War II, immigration policies vis-à-vis Mexicans continued to develop differently from those that applied to immigrants from other regions, especially in ways that ultimately served to create the figure of "the wetback"— a term that, invoking the illicit entry into the United States via wading the Rio Grande, expressed the fusion of the identities of "Mexican" and "illegal alien." The agricultural guest worker program known as the "Bracero Program," instituted in 1942 in the midst of wartime labor shortages, recruited Mexicans to serve as a temporary labor force. As labor activists and other immigrant advocates had long complained, the program, which continued until 1964, helped create a deeply marginalized population of workers with no access to the rights of citizenship.[113] And while it was touted as a way to stem illegal immigration from Mexico, the Bracero Program in fact accomplished the opposite. Many workers, for example, dismayed at the poor conditions under which they labored, "deserted" their employers for better opportunities, thus becoming violators of US immigration law.[114] Moreover, economic conditions in Mexico continued to propel workers north, whether or not they could land a contract under the Bracero Program, and US employers continued to employ Mexican illegal immigrants alongside workers who had come legally as braceros. Indeed, employers sometimes preferred the former because there were no complicated government guarantees about wages or working conditions to worry about. Workers who were not part of the Bracero Program did not need to be replaced when their contracts were up, and, as longer-term workers, they often acquired specialized and much-needed skills that braceros did not.[115] Meanwhile, employers in Texas, Arkansas, and Missouri, who were excluded from the Bracero Program altogether because Mexico refused to send braceros to states where Mexicans were segregated from whites, relied heavily on an illegal immigrant workforce instead.[116] As the two flows of migration continued and grew together, all Mexicans in the Southwest, whether in the country legally or not, were confronted with the stereotype of "wetback," defining them disparagingly in terms of racial, class, and immigration status.[117]

By the 1950s, then, the Mexican border had become the main focus of the national discourse on illegal immigration. " 'Wetback' Influx Near Record," the *New York Times* wrote in 1953, noting—not without sympathy for the immigrants themselves—that the mass entry of undocumented Mexican laborers was "severely aggravating long rankling labor and social problems in the agricultural Southwest."[118] Other media and government reports, too, warned that the flood of Mexicans over the US border made for heightened crime and health problems, as well as a drain on employment opportunities and public resources.[119]

Correspondingly, the Southwest became the epicenter of federal immigration enforcement—or at least the show of enforcement, as politically powerful southwestern growers were often bitterly opposed to government interference with their labor force. The INS reported in 1953, for example, that "the human tide of wetbacks continues to be the most serious enforcement problem of the service" and cited its new efforts in that area, such as the construction of new detention facilities in McAllen, Texas, and Chula Vista, California.[120] The Border Patrol deployed more officers and equipment in the region and, in the first three years of the decade, doubled its apprehensions of immigrants to nearly nine hundred thousand.[121] Meanwhile, the INS stepped up its sweeps of the area for illegal immigrant farmworkers.[122] By 1953, the vast majority of deportations from the United States were to Mexico.[123] In 1954, Operation Wetback, the INS's highly publicized militarized roundup and deportation of hundreds of thousands of Mexicans (some legally in the country) in California, the Southwest, and elsewhere in the nation confirmed the official approach the United States would take toward Mexicans (even while, behind the scenes, agricultural employers were quietly allowed to continue hiring whomever they pleased).[124] This crackdown helped even more firmly establish the association, both in the public imagination and in law enforcement, between Mexicans and illegal immigration.

The hardships braceros and other Mexican migrant workers endured drew sympathy from many liberal policymakers, labor organizers, activists, and commentators, both in the established Mexican American and broader national communities. Indeed, despite guarantees to the contrary, many braceros labored under terrible conditions—widely publicized by newspaper and television reports—and strenuous objections to these working conditions, as well as to braceros' permanently disempowered status, contributed to the program's demise in 1964.[125] Southwestern employers had fought against this outcome, seeing both braceros and "wetbacks" as vital to the regional economy. Indeed, some argued, deploying the language of refugee policy, that employing Mexicans as domestics and farmworkers was a way of saving them from terrible fates at home. At least one Texas newspaper editor also reminded his reading public that the focus on Mexicans obscured the fact that there were likely "hundreds of thousands of Europeans . . . in this country illegally," too.[126]

But many in the United States had come to see both groups of Mexican immigrants, legal and illegal, as the primary threat in the realm of immigration. Even Mexican American organizations and press often defined themselves in opposition to "wetbacks" and sometimes to braceros, whom they saw as creating a troublesome presence in their communities and as exerting downward pressure on wages. At times, they urged more stringent deportation and border patrol policy.[127] Unions, while sometimes reaching out to Mexican immigrant workers, also often regarded both braceros and Mexican illegal immigrant workers with suspicion, seeing them as an unorganizable, quasi-enslaved workforce that undermined the labor movement.[128] All these views—even the ones that expressed dismay at the conditions of Mexican immigrants' labor—served to define Mexicans increasingly as quintessential outsiders, a special irony given the fact that much of the region "overrun" by "wetbacks" had been taken over from Mexico scarcely a century earlier. These views also helped reinforce the understanding of Mexican immigration and Mexicans' immigration status as essentially separate and different from that of other immigrants.

The notion that Mexican immigration existed in a different arena from other immigration points to one reason why many activists who were working to liberalize other aspects of immigration law did not include in their purview policies aimed at Mexican immigration. Senator (and former New York Governor) Herbert Lehman, for example, deeply involved in a range of Jewish organizations and causes, was a fierce advocate for liberalizing immigration law by abolishing the quotas. He expressed little interest, however, in addressing policy connected with Mexicans. Indeed, the fact that Mexicans and other Western Hemisphere immigrants had never been excluded by the quota system established in the 1920s meant that liberal activists battling that system likely did not see much reason for addressing the issue of Mexicans in the course of their arguments.[129]

While advocates for admission of European refugees, for leniency toward European immigrants, or for liberalizing the quota laws likely never set out to benefit from the increasing association between Mexicans and illegal immigration, they ended up doing so. Indeed, some invoked the problem of Mexican illegal immigration as evidence that European illegal immigration should not be an urgent national concern. For example, in 1947, in the course of debates over DP legislation, Ugo Carusi, former INS commissioner and former chairman of the DPC, sought to counter the accusation that "millions of European refugees are crossing our borders illegally." He asserted that the problem was not Europeans, but rather "the fact that many Mexicans are illegally crossing the southern border of the United States in quest of work." He emphasized, moreover, that Mexican immigration was completely different from European immigration: "these people are neither Europeans nor refugees."[130] Senator Herbert Lehman and Julius Edelstein, Lehman's top aide, important voices in the national immigration debate, likewise emphasized in their public statements that floods of "undesirable" immigrants, mostly "wetbacks," were coming via the "back door" of US land borders while "legal immigration" was being barred at the nation's "front door."[131] Like Carusi, Lehman and Edelstein thus participated in redirecting anxieties about illegal immigration toward the Mexican border.

Attorney Irving Engel, chairman of the American Jewish Committee's Executive Committee and former director of the Citizens Committee on Displaced Persons, took a similar tack in a long letter to the *New York Times* in 1951. Engel was critical of the discourse around "wetbacks"—he put the term in quotation marks—and remarked acidly on the extent to which policy governing immigration from Mexico had been formed by moneyed agricultural interests. He nevertheless pointed out that the vast majority of deportations were of Mexicans rather than of Europeans and took issue with a recent article that suggested that European aliens might be taking advantage of the porousness of the Mexico–US border to get "smuggled in as Mexicans seeking migratory work." East Coast dwellers might think of aliens as "D.P's or immigrants generally from Europe," he wrote, but in fact the heart of the immigration problem consisted of Mexican immigration to the Southwest.[132] Thus, the increasing scrutiny and fear of Mexican immigrants served to deflect attention away from remaining suspicions of Europeans, including Jews. Engel's letter also suggests the ongoing concerns American Jewish activists had regarding public perceptions of European immigrants, as well as the distance Jews and other advocates for European immigrants were putting between themselves and Mexicans. In this way, American Jewish activists and other liberal immigration reformers, in defending European immigrants, both reflected the shift in the discourse of illegal immigration toward Mexicans and contributed to it.

THE END OF THE QUOTA ERA: THE IMMIGRATION ACT OF 1965

It was not obvious at the start of the postwar era that those in favor of scrapping the national origins quotas would prevail. Throughout the 1920s and 1930s, the quota system had seemed inviolable. Indeed, even after the war, this remained the case for a number of years. As we have seen, the groups battling for admission of refugees in the 1940s opted to separate that issue from that of quotas so as to ensure greater support for their immediate cause. Over the course of the postwar era, however, the national origins quota system was thrown into question as racial injustice and foreign policy took center political stage in new ways.

As early as 1950, proposals to overhaul or do away with the quota system were made in Congress by prominent liberals such as Democratic Senators Hubert Humphrey of Minnesota and Herbert Lehman of New York and then reintroduced in every legislative session thereafter until the 1965 law was finally passed. Those who advocated abolishing the system argued that the quotas undermined American claims to being a just and democratic society and thus badly damaged the nation's image abroad, a question of urgent concern in the Cold War struggle for international influence. However, staunch and powerful opponents to this idea, in and outside of Congress, continued to make the case for the national origins quotas, countering that they played an important role in maintaining national security. Quota loyalists of the postwar era relied less on racialist thinking than their predecessors, but they continued to argue that the nation had a vested security interest in maintaining the sociological and cultural balance that they believed the quotas helped to guarantee. More specifically, the new language of national security also helped justify intense suspicion of those trying to immigrate from behind the Iron Curtain.

Democratic Representatives Francis Walter of Pennsylvania and Senator Pat McCarran of Nevada were crucial players for the committed proquota team. In 1950, concerned about the reform sentiments brewing in Congress, McCarran took charge of an enormous report on immigration (the most extensive since the forty-two-volume Dillingham Report of 1911), which, not surprisingly, concluded that the quotas were vital in ensuring the stability of the nation. Though it avoided the openly racist language of its early twentieth-century predecessors, focusing instead on questions of national security and anti-Communism, the report did echo the concerns voiced by earlier nativists about the changing ethnic character of immigration. It noted, for example, that Jewish immigration in the first half of the twentieth century was ominously out of proportion to the percentage of Jews in the national population.[133]

In 1952, the two legislators cosponsored and were instrumental in passing the McCarran-Walter Act, an omnibus bill that overhauled certain aspects of immigration law but nevertheless maintained the nation-based quotas as its central structuring principle.[134] Its one important concession to the changing climate around race was its abolition of blanket Asian exclusion, though it essentially provided for no more than token quotas for nations previously excluded altogether and stipulated that Asians must be categorized for immigration purposes by racial heritage, rather than by country of birth like other immigrants. If the displaced persons legislation of 1948 and 1950 had been important steps toward liberalizing US immigration law, the McCarran-Walter Act, in concert with the 1950 National Security Act, represented strong currents in the opposite direction. In taking this position, legislators had the support of a wide swath of the American public. Veterans' organizations, patriotic groups, and the AFL, for example, all expressed strong support for the law.[135]

The McCarran-Walter Act's recodification of the quotas distressed Jewish groups, along with other ethnic groups and immigration reform activists. The law, raged the president of Hebrew Union College (Reform Judaism's rabbinical seminary), was "the apotheosis of everything ignoble that America was created to oppose . . . a grievous and spreading cancer in our body politic which must be arrested and removed."[136] The next several years saw a protracted battle over this issue; as on other immigration questions, Jewish organizations, including the American Jewish Congress and the American Jewish Commit-tee, provided organizational leadership and substantial resources to the politi-cal effort. They worked on a local and national level to attack the law, making their case by publishing pieces in the press, lobbying lawmakers publicly and privately, orchestrating letter-writing campaigns, and organizing large pub-lic events such as one held on June 9, 1955, in Carnegie Hall that drew over twenty-five hundred attendees from various ethnic and labor groups.[137]

Opponents of the McCarran-Walter Act and the reenactment of the quotas made their case on a number of fronts. They argued, as Senator Lehman had pointed out during the congressional debate over its passage, that the law rep-resented an unacceptable embrace of the racial principles of the Nazis, who had expressed admiration for the US quota system and its preference for "Nor-dics" over lowlier groups.[138] Not only that, but the McCarran-Walter Act, in af-firming the quotas, was reinscribing in US law an immigration system that had helped Hitler achieve his genocidal aims. "By raising discriminations against the Jewish, Italian and other nationalities," the *Jewish Forum* opined, the quo-tas "enabled Hitler to give expression to his program of annihilation of the Jews of the world, and enabled 'Christian' nations to help bottle up the Jews in the various countries under Hitler's domination."[139] The law's opponents also noted that the eugenicists' biological rationale for the quotas had long since been discredited by reputable scholars. "This business of the national origin theory which is imbedded in our immigration laws is nonsense," contended Congressman Emanuel Celler in a 1955 speech. "The underlying theory is that one race is better than another. Scientists the world over have disproved this."[140] The argument about racial prejudice had particular resonance in this era of civil rights activism, a parallel pushed by those battling the renewed quota system. "We cannot eliminate racism at home and continue to practice it . . . abroad," argued Rabbi Maurice Eisendrath, president of the Union of American Hebrew Congregations, the organizing body of Reform Jews.[141]

Moreover, those angered by the new law asserted that the quotas had been undermined already by the piecemeal immigration policies of the postwar years. Given the various refugee laws and the range of administrative practices to admit or adjust status of immigrants, "the national origins theory has lost all practical meaning," as Celler put it in a 1961 speech. "Why then retain it on the books?" he asked.[142] Finally, in what may have been their most potent argument, they contended that the McCarran-Walter Act, in reenacting the quotas, was putting a powerful ideological weapon into the hands of the Cold War enemy. "The Soviet Union," said Celler, "sells the idea that it alone stands for the equality, for the dignity, for the wealth, the health, of each individual man, regardless of race, color, creed, or national origin . . . It holds up for the world to see the picture of ourselves we have enacted into law by a restatement of immigration policy . . . conceived in fear and born in confusion." Indeed, he said, the law represented an "iron curtain of our own."[143]

Supporters countered that these liberal attacks on the McCarran-Walter Act and the quota system were misguided. Walter protested on the floor of the Congress, somewhat oxymoronically, that the quotas simply helped maintain a desirable "homogeneity in this melting pot of nations."[144] (A New Yorker writing to Celler in 1955 expressed a similar idea, but more bluntly: "Haven't we got enough foreign bums here, especially in N.Y., without you trying to let down the bars completely?"[145]) To the argument that the law worked against the nation's Cold War interests, the laws' backers contended that the McCarran-Walter Act, which included more stringent provisions regarding screening and deporting radicals or others deemed "security risks," "provided an important rampart against subversive forces which could destroy the America we have."[146] Relatedly, some argued that the opposition to the legislation was merely a left-wing plot: "The Communists and those who travel with Communists did not want the McCarran-Walter Act on the books," wrote one supporter of the legislation in the right-wing *National Republic*, "because it would bar their overseas comrades from entering our country."[147]

Unlike in the interwar period, however, the groups in favor of abolishing the national origins quotas now had some powerful allies, and the restrictionist camp was more isolated than it had been. Most notably, labor, traditionally restrictionist, was now in favor of abolishing the quotas; with the 1955 merger of the AFL and the CIO, the CIO's more ethnic-oriented politics came to define the organization's stance. This ideological shift also reflected the fact that European immigration was no longer as central to the nation's labor market as it had been.[148] Finally, the antiquota position was in keeping with organized labor's enthusiastic embrace of Cold War politics.[149]

Presidential administrations, too, no longer supported congressional efforts to retain the national origins quotas; all the postwar presidents saw the quotas as deeply in conflict with their foreign policy aims. Truman, for example, who vetoed the McCarran-Walter Act with a statement of strong condemnation, commissioned his own extensive study of immigration policy. In 1953, this presidential commission published the report *Whom We Shall Welcome*, a forceful response to the McCarran report of 1950. *Whom We Shall Welcome* criticized the national origins quotas as discriminatory and outmoded, and deeply damaging to the reputation of the United States around the world. The report recommended getting rid of the quotas once and for all and moving instead to a system of preferences—favoring family members, workers with needed skills, and political refugees—within an overall limit on immigration.

Over the next decade, other writings by prestigious authors argued the need to undo the national origins quota system, which thus helped shift the opinion of American lawmakers and the public at large. Jewish organizations (again working behind the scenes) funded the publication and distribution of some of these works. In 1954, for example, the American Jewish Congress helped publish Hubert Humphrey's *Stranger at Our Gate*, which criticized American immigration policy as "bigoted."[150] In 1959, John F. Kennedy published his *A Nation of Immigrants*, commissioned by the Anti-Defamation League of the B'nai B'rith. Politically minded scholars (Jewish as well as non-Jewish) also pushed the issue, both in their academic work and in writings for broader audiences. The Harvard history professor Oscar Handlin, for example, not only wrote groundbreaking scholarly studies of immigration but also weighed in on contemporary policy, advising Truman's immigration commission and publishing pieces on the issue in venues including the American Jewish Committee's *Commentary* and publications for B'nai B'rith.[151] Historian John Higham, in his brilliant 1955 *Strangers in the Land*, meanwhile, took a harsh look at the history of America's anti-immigrant sentiment and policies, with their culmination represented by the quotas.[152] As critical as these writings were of the discriminatory nature of US policy, however, their perspectives tended to be heavily Eurocentric, focusing on celebrating the achievements of European immigrants and on stressing the injustices the quota system represented to this group.[153]

In 1963, the Kennedy administration submitted its own proposal to overhaul immigration law, including abolishing the national origins quotas and opening up immigration from Asian nations on the same principle as applied to other countries. In this proposal, immigration from the Western Hemisphere would continue not to be subject to numerical limits. Delayed by ongoing congressional opposition and then derailed by Kennedy's assassination, the proposal was introduced in Congress again the following year by Senator Philip Hart and Representative Emanuel Celler. They did so with full presidential backing. As a senator from Texas, Lyndon Johnson had voted for the 1952 McCarran-Walter Act and helped block other immigration reforms, but early in his administration he came to embrace the need to fundamentally change immigration law. Both abolishing the quotas and opening the way for immigration from Asia were in keeping with Johnson's urgent domestic priorities of civil rights legislation and his foreign policy objectives of maintaining

America's positive image and influence abroad. The issue also mattered to the white ethnic voters, including Jews and Italians, who formed an important segment of the Democratic Party's northern urban base.[154] Stymied by key opponents in Congress, however, the bill went nowhere that year.

In November 1964, congressional liberals saw their biggest spate of electoral victories in decades. In 1965, Senator Hart and Congressman Celler reintroduced the immigration reform bill. There were still significant forces arrayed against it: public opinion polls, for example, demonstrated significant support for maintaining the national origins quotas and distinct alarm over the idea of increased immigration.[155] Within Congress, the strongest opposition came from the Southern representatives, led by the conservative Democrats who opposed much of Johnson's legislative program and were explicitly concerned about the law's potential to increase nonwhite immigration from Asia, Africa, Latin America, and the West Indies.[156] Nevertheless, the Hart-Celler bill passed both houses of Congress with strong majorities in early autumn 1965, and Johnson signed it into law.

The new law abolished the national origins quotas—a change that would be phased in officially by 1968, with any unused quota spots meanwhile being "pooled" and made available to anyone eligible under the 1965 act. In the place of nation-based quotas, the law instituted an overall limit on immigration—one hundred seventy thousand for the nations of the Eastern Hemisphere, and one hundred twenty thousand for the Western Hemisphere. Immediate family members of US citizens were to be allowed in outside of any quota. For the Eastern Hemisphere, there was a country-by-country cap of twenty thousand visas per year. Within that cap, there was a hierarchy of preferences that determined how visas for immigrants would be distributed, with highest priority given to those coming to family in the United States (about 65 percent of visas were reserved for this group) and then to those who could offer needed labor skills to the nation (about 20 percent of visas were for this group). Refugees, defined as those fleeing "Communist or Communist-dominated" countries or countries of the Middle East out of fear of persecution, were allocated 6 percent of the overall Eastern Hemisphere quota.[157] In the Western Hemisphere, there was not yet a numerical limit for any country; such a limit would be instituted nine years later. Nor were there preferences for family reunification. Instead, all Western Hemisphere immigrants would have to meet qualifications as needed labor.

The Immigration Act of 1965, celebrated by President Johnson in his signing speech as a straightforward triumph for justice was, in reality, complicated in its effects. In some ways, the act was a radical liberalization of immigration law and a profound departure from earlier legislation. In abolishing the national origins quotas and the severe restrictions on Asian immigration, it officially rejected a system that had structured immigration policy for decades. For Jews and other European groups, as well as for Asians, then, the act represented a resounding victory, in that it was a clear renunciation of a restrictive policy that was grounded in racial discrimination.

In other ways, however, the law spoke to the ongoing power of the more conservative, restrictionist side of US immigration politics. It did grant a permanent place in US immigration policy to refugees, reflecting the new ethos of according special importance to this group. That place, however, was small, a mere 6 percent of the total visas allotted to the Eastern Hemisphere. The wording of the law, moreover, emphasized the centrality of Cold War logic—established with the very first Displaced Persons Act—to the determination of refugee status. The privileging of refugees fleeing Communist regimes over others proved to be a sorting mechanism that shaped US policy for years to come.[158]

Moreover, due to the political endgame that produced the legislation's final form, the law also instituted numerical limits on Western Hemisphere immigration for the first time. Kennedy's 1963 proposal had preserved the traditional nonquota status for these nations, and those lobbying to overturn the national origins quotas generally supported this approach in order to maintain friendly relations with America' near neighbors. But legislators who favored restrictionist policy pushed hard in negotiations over the law for a cap on immigration to be applied to all nations, and this compromise was accepted. In the years to come, the new restriction particularly affected Mexico, the country with the greatest pool of potential immigrants to the United States. With economic pushes and pulls as great as ever, Mexicans continued to migrate north to the United States along well-established routes. The limitations contained in the 1965 law, and the nearly simultaneous ending of the Bracero Program, helped ensure that much of this migration would continue to happen illicitly, thus bringing together more the association between Mexicans and illegal immigration.[159]

Finally, the Immigration Act of 1965 demonstrated just how established another crucial aspect of the 1924 law had become in the discourse over immigration policy: the notion that immigration needed to be limited numerically. No one made the case for open borders or for returning to a mode of immigration control that relied on evaluating individual immigrants without regard to numbers. The various post-1952 proposals for immigration reform all included a ceiling on immigration. Indeed, they took the 1924 law as a guideline in determining the appropriate number for that ceiling, reckoning that any new measure should hew to a limit that represented about one immigrant per six hundred Americans per year.[160]

The historical record does not reflect any extensive concern by American Jewish lawmakers or activists about the way the 1965 law hardened the barriers that kept out Mexicans and others from the Western Hemisphere. Nor does it suggest that American Jews were particularly troubled by the law's function of limiting immigration overall. Like most Americans, they had accepted the fundamental notion that immigration into the United States ought to be and could be restricted and controlled. Thus, even at the moment that they marked a profound step toward their own formal inclusion in the nation, American Jews were making their peace with expanded mechanisms of restriction and exclusion.

Epilogue

This book is the product of an era in which the national mood about immigration has undergone massive shifts. During the very earliest phases of this project, for example, President George W. Bush came into office promising—with an eye toward both Mexico and Latino voters—that his administration would consider relaxing its policy toward immigrants illegally in the United States. In early 2001, Bush and Fox met in Mexico to discuss matters related to migration; by early September 2001, the US government was seriously considering a broad program of legalization for illegal immigrants.[1] After September 11, 2001, however, such a transformation in US policy became unimaginable for many years. The Bush administration abandoned any notion of extending legal status to illegal immigrants and instead oversaw a mounting effort to crack down on them. Even the Obama administration, which originally campaigned on a pledge of significant immigration policy reform, continued construction on the expensive, much contested, and arguably ineffectual Mexican border fence. Deportation—which affects both undocumented and legal immigrants—has expanded. To be sure, at the time of this writing, Congress, having recently witnessed the rapidly growing clout of Latino voters, is once again considering an overhaul of immigration policy so as to allow for many people in violation of the law to be able to start on a "path to citizenship."

What such a law will look like in practice, however, remains to be seen. The currents driving the formation of immigration policy still run, as they often have, in different directions at once. The new possibilities for those currently in the country illegally to acquire citizenship will likely come clipped together with plans for yet stricter border guarding. Moreover, the large-scale jailing of detained immigrants, often in private prisons run for profit, continues for the present as well.[2] Meanwhile, state and local governments, as well as civic groups from across the political spectrum, continue to battle over the future of immigration policy. Recently enacted state laws in Alabama and Arizona, for example, require local police to actively participate in immigration enforcement; now that these laws have been upheld in the courts, more states will follow their lead. It is as yet unclear what would happen to such initiatives in the face of a large-scale shift in the law.

What does seem clear is that the national conviction that immigration must be controlled will persist, as will the sense that immigrants always represent a potential threat to the nation's well-being. Much of the nation's official approach to immigration in recent years reflects the enormous changes in public debate and policy—in many aspects of national life—that took place after September 11, 2001. In the wake of the terrorist attacks that day, crackdowns on immigrants were immediate. The government resolved to pursue visa violators more aggressively, step up deportations, and tighten control over national borders. The Immigration and Naturalization Service (INS), criticized for what was widely regarded as its lax enforcement of immigration law and its ineptitude at tracking aliens within the United States, was reorganized in 2003 as United States Immigration and Customs Enforcement (ICE). Now part of the new Department of Homeland Security, ICE is intended to be an agency that can better coordinate the government's project of confronting the perceived dangers posed by foreigners.

The scale and tenor of the US government's project of immigration control, abroad through the "remote control" mechanism of prescreening visa applicants, at points of entry (e.g., airports and borders), and far beyond the border as well, dwarf the control measures practiced in that earlier era.[3] And yet, it is also clear that today's policy regime stands on the shoulders of the immigration control efforts of the past. Throughout the years that I have worked on the research and writing of this book, there have been many moments in which the parallels between the past I was writing about and the present I was living in were both striking and distressing, and unavoidably embedded in the texture of my city's daily affairs. In 2002, for example, as I was beginning to write about the 1931 Michigan alien registration law, I was also listening to radio reports about men from "Muslim and Arab nations" lining up outside INS offices in downtown Manhattan to undergo mandatory registration. During the same period, the Brooklyn detention center not far from my home filled with men from those same nations, many destined for deportation. A Yemeni friend who worked in downtown Brooklyn—the city's largest Arabic-speaking community—told me of FBI investigators' visits to area businesses and of his friends' worries about registration and deportation. More recently, I followed debates about the efficacy of a multibillion-dollar "border fence" as I was returning to my research on Jewish illegal immigration from Mexico to Texas. As I revised my chapter on the struggles over alien registration in the 1920s and 1930s, the Arizona and Alabama state laws—similar to the 1931 Michigan law, though more far-reaching—were winding their way through the courts.

As in the era about which I was writing, a host of difficult questions connected to immigration have made for bitter political and cultural struggles in recent years. What sort of dangers do immigrants present? Why are the nation's borders more permeable in practice than they are in law? Are illegal immigrants particularly threatening to the nation's well-being? Should illegal immigration really be considered to be criminal activity? How do you distinguish illegal immigrants from their legal counterparts once they are in the country? What information should the government keep on immigrants when they enter, or later on? Do new technologies of identification inevitably lead to government abuse and curtailment of liberties? Do they make innocent people feel like criminals? What effect do crackdowns intended to catch dangerous aliens have on the broader immigrant community and on the nation's attitude toward immigrants? How should immigrants, their families, and communities respond when they find themselves in conflict with the law and the targets of negative public perception?

I pose these questions not for the purposes of answering them—that goes beyond the scope of this present project. Rather, I wish to observe that these questions themselves have complicated histories, as the preceding pages illustrate. The formulation of and debates over these questions have helped shape the apparatus of immigration law and enforcement we live with today, as well as Americans' understandings of what immigration—legal and illegal—means for our country. The historical roots of these questions (and the competing answers offered to them by different parties), however, often get lost in the commotion of our present-day battles over immigration issues. Even since well before September 11, 2001, political debates in the United States came to proceed from the assumption that it is an essential mission of national policy to control immigration and borders; indeed, worldwide, as Aristide Zolberg has pointed out, the default policy of affluent nations has become essentially one of "closed" borders.[4] Such control has come to be seen as constitutive, in other words, of national sovereignty itself. What we begin to see when we study the history of illegal immigration is the extent to which such an understanding developed slowly, hardening into the nation's unquestioned stance less than a century ago, with the passage of the quota laws during the 1920s, the establishment of the Border Patrol, and the increased reliance on deportation as a means of enforcement. These state approaches to control both grew out of and furthered the idea that immigration was a phenomenon that always presented potential economic, political, cultural, and physical threats to the nation.

The history of Jewish illegal immigration during the quota era also demonstrates, at the same time, that this process did not unfold in a linear, straightforward fashion. In the years after the quota laws, immigration authorities, the nativist press, patriotic societies, and restrictionist lawmakers railed against the way that "bootlegged aliens" from Europe and their bootleggers were a danger and an affront to the United States. During World War II, Jewish refugees were feared as potential foreign spies and, afterward, as potential political subversives. But even by that time the nation's concern had already largely shifted away from European illegal immigration to focus on the immigration of others, particularly Mexicans (whose ability to move freely across the border had gone largely unquestioned until the 1920s). The Immigration Act of 1965 helped underscore the national change of heart about the threat posed by European immigration, as well as what would prove to be an even more dramatic turnaround regarding Asian immigration. In other words, who and what get defined as dangerous and worthy of control, for what reasons and by what means, has been profoundly subject to historical change. The fact that the history of Jewish "illegal aliens" ceased to be a matter of public concern reflects, as we have seen, shifting political, economic, and racial dynamics within the nation, as well as intensive work on the part of American Jews to unlink their communities from the association with illegal immigration. Recovering the history of how the reality of immigration law shifts over time helps demonstrate the extent to which it did not emerge from the egg, as it were, fully formed, but rather was the product of ongoing contestation.

More broadly, attending to the history of Jewish illegal immigration—and of illegal immigration generally—serves to remind us of some of the contradictions inherent in the configuration of our modern international system of nation-states. Indeed, illegal immigration and contemporary nationalisms have developed in tandem, as this study suggests. Illegal immigration points to the impossibility of defining citizens and borders, insiders and outsiders, as cleanly as states would like, even as it also highlights the extent to which such definitions remain central to the building and maintenance of state power. There is a profound clash between unilateral state efforts to control borders and the forces of global migration, for however much states seek to regulate the movement of people in and out of nations, there are always those who continue to move transnationally and who elude state control.

INTRODUCTION

1. File 55423-414, Entry 9, Records of the US Immigration and Naturalization Service, Record Group 85 (hereafter RG 85), National Archives Building, Washington, DC (hereafter NA).

2. A few scholars have noted in passing that the laws produced a spike in European illegal immigration; however, they have tended not to investigate the subject in any depth. See, e.g., Aristide Zolberg's brief mention of the issue in his otherwise comprehensive history, *A Nation by Design: Immigration Policy in the Fashioning of America* (New York: Russell Sage Foundation, 2006), 266. There is also a brief discussion of postquota illegal immigration toward the end of a longer study of border control from the late nineteenth century through 1930 in Patrick Ettinger, *Imaginary Lines: Border Enforcement and the Origins of Undocumented Immigration, 1882–1930* (Austin: University of Texas Press, 2009), 147–48, 159, and 162–63. See also Gary Gerstle's cursory reference to European illegal immigration in his excellent study *American Crucible: Race and Nation in the Twentieth Century* (Princeton: Princeton University Press, 2001), 391n.59. Important exceptions to the scholarly neglect of European illegal immigration include Mae M. Ngai, *Impossible Subjects: Illegal Aliens and the Making of Modern America* (Princeton: Princeton University Press, 2004), chap. 2, and "The Strange Career of the Illegal Alien: Immigration Restriction and Deportation in the United States, 1921–1965," *Law and History Review* 21, no. 1 (Spring 2003): 69–107; and Maddalena Marinari, "Liberty, Restriction, and the Remaking of Italians and Eastern European Jews (1882–1965)" (PhD diss., University of Kansas, 2009), 71–73, 121–29, 161–68, and 219–20.

3. Several scholars of immigration policy have, however, explored the history of the passage of the quota laws. For an in-depth look at the range of legislative proposals Congress debated in connection with restricting immigration, see, e.g., Edward Prince Hutchinson, *Legislative History of American Immigration Policy, 1798–1965* (Philadelphia: University of Pennsylvania Press, 1981), 171–96. John Higham's classic *Strangers in the Land: Patterns of American Nativism, 1865–1925* (New Brunswick: Rutgers University Press, 1955; 2d ed., New York: Atheneum, 1977) remains an important source on the political battles surrounding passage of the quota

laws. Citations refer to the Atheneum edition. See also Kitty Calavita, *US Immigration Law and the Control of Labor, 1820–1924* (London: Orlando Academic Press, 1984), chap. 7; Desmond King, *Making Americans: Immigration, Race, and the Origins of the Diverse Democracy* (Cambridge: Harvard University Press, 2000), chap. 7; Daniel Tichenor, *Dividing Lines: The Politics of Immigration Control in America* (Princeton: Princeton University Press, 2002), chap. 5; and Zolberg, *Nation by Design*, chap. 8. For a lucid examination of the complexities of calculating the final version of the 1924 law's quotas, which were to be based on the "national origins" of the nation's population and which were not finalized until 1929, see Mae Ngai, "The Architecture of Race in American Immigration Law: A Reexamination of the Immigration Act of 1924," *Journal of American History* 86 (June 1999): 67–92.

4. I use the term "illegal alien" here and occasionally elsewhere in this book to invoke the complex cluster of meanings the term has acquired, and because I see the history of Jewish illegal immigration as connected to the larger history of the idea of the "illegal alien." It should be noted, however, that the term was not in common use until the post–World War II period, and then generally in connection with Mexicans in particular. See chapter 6 for further discussion of this shift. More common in the pre–World War II era were terms such as "smuggled alien" or "bootlegged alien"; "illegal entry," "illegal immigration," and "unlawful entry" were also all common terms. For an interesting discussion on her decision to use the term "illegal alien" throughout her study, see Ngai, *Impossible Subjects*, xix. On the changing language around immigration generally, see Donna Gabaccia, "Great Migration Debates: Keywords in Historical Perspective," in *Border Battles: The US Immigration Debates*, Social Science Research Council, July 28, 2006, http://borderbattles.ssrc.org/Gabaccia/.

5. Whether historians make reference to 1924 as an end date for European mass immigration—and many studies of immigration do not address directly the shifts in law—the periodization of the vast literature on European "second-wave" immigration as a whole reflects this understanding. In part this follows patterns set in the work of some of those scholars whose pathbreaking studies in the 1950s and 1960s helped define the field. Probably most important in this regard is John Higham's pathbreaking *Strangers in the Land* (1955), whose final chapter, "Closing the Gates," details nativists' success in passing the immigration quota law of 1924.

The literature on the "Americanizing" of European immigrants following the 1924 law is voluminous. For a cogent case that European ethnics during the interwar years increasingly identified as "Americans" via their experiences as workers, voters, and consumers, see Lizabeth Cohen, *Making a New Deal: Industrial Workers in Chicago, 1919–1939* (Cambridge: Cambridge University Press, 1990). In the Jewish context, an influential view of the era as characterized by a shift from the immigrant culture of the early twentieth century to a more American model remains Deborah Dash Moore, *At Home in America: Second Generation New York Jews* (New York: Columbia University Press, 1981). On the "whitening" of Jews and other Europeans in the 1920s–1950s, see, e.g., Karen Brodkin, *How Jews Became White Folks and What that Says About Race in America* (New Brunswick: Rutgers University Press, 1998); Matthew Frye Jacobson, *Whiteness of a Different Color: European Immigrants and the Alchemy of Race* (Cambridge: Harvard University Press, 1998), especially chaps. 3 and 5–8; and David R. Roediger, *Working Toward Whiteness: How America's Immigrants Became White* (New York: Basic Books, 2005). For an in-depth analysis of American Jews' relationship to whiteness, see Eric L. Goldstein, *The*

Price of Whiteness: Jews, Race, and American Identity (Princeton: Princeton University Press, 2006).

6. See, e.g., Richard Breitman and Alan Kraut, *American Refugee Policy and European Jewry, 1933–1945* (Bloomington: Indiana University Press, 1987); Henry L. Feingold, *Bearing Witness: How America and Its Jews Responded to the Holocaust* (Syracuse: Syracuse University Press, 1995), and *The Politics of Rescue: The Roosevelt Administration and the Holocaust, 1938–1945* (New Brunswick: Rutgers University Press, 1970); Saul S. Friedman, *No Haven for the Oppressed: United States Policy Toward Jewish Refugees, 1938–1945* (Detroit: Wayne State University Press, 1973); and David S. Wyman, *The Abandonment of the Jews: America and the Holocaust* (New York: Pantheon Books, 1984), and *Paper Walls: America and the Refugee Crisis* (New York: Pantheon Books, 1985).

7. *American Jewish Year Book* 29 (1927–28), 253.

8. There are a number of scholars who do an excellent job of looking at the lived experience of law in relation to other aspects of immigration policy, and my own study is indebted to these authors' works. Scholars of US and international anti-Chinese legislation stand out in this regard. One notable example is Adam M. McKeown, *Melancholy Order: Asian Migration and the Globalization of Borders* (New York: Columbia University Press, 2008). McKeown writes aptly that the narrow focus on public and political discourse in most nation-based histories of migration policy obscures "the effects of those policies, begging the question of how politics and legislation matter" (14). Other insightful analyses of immigration policy that explore immigration policies' effects in depth include Kelly Lyle Hernández, *Migra! A History of the US Border Patrol* (Berkeley: University of California Press, 2010); Estelle Lau, *Paper Families: Identity, Immigration Administration, and Chinese Exclusion* (Durham: Duke University Press, 2006); Erika Lee, *At America's Gates: Chinese Immigration during the Exclusion Era, 1882–1943* (Chapel Hill: University of North Carolina Press, 2003); and Lucy E. Salyer, *Laws Harsh as Tigers: Chinese Immigrants and the Shaping of Modern Immigration Law* (Chapel Hill: University of North Carolina Press, 1995.

9. There are many instances in which this is so obvious as to not need articulating. The mention of "Prohibition," e.g., immediately evokes the regime of organized crime that helped define the Constitutional amendment's meaning; similarly, it is clear that today the meanings—the "happening"—of narcotics laws are defined as much by international drug cartels as by any other actors.

10. In this sense, this book is something of a departure from much of the literature on European immigrants during the early twentieth century (as distinct from the literature on immigration policy), which has tended to focus more on cultural or communal aspects of immigrant life than on the relationship between immigrants and the state.

11. One of the most thorough overviews of Jewish Europe in this period remains Ezra Mendelsohn, *The Jews of East Central Europe between the Wars* (Bloomington: Indiana University Press, 1983). See also Michael R. Marrus, *The Unwanted: European Refugees in the Twentieth Century* (New York: Oxford University Press, 1985), chap 2; Saskia Sassen, *Guests and Aliens* (New York: New Press, 1999), chap. 5; and Zolberg, *Nation by Design*, 246–47. For a detailed contemporary chronicle of the international situation of Jews during these years, see *American Jewish Year Book*, published annually by the American Jewish Committee.

12. Throughout the book, I generally use the term "migrants" to refer to people who might be en route to the United States or elsewhere, but who have not yet arrived or whose destination is unclear; sometimes I refer to them as "prospective immigrants" or "would-be immigrants," if their intention to go to the United States is clear. I generally use the word "immigrants" to refer to people at points of entry into the nation or who have already entered the nation.

13. B. R. Cisco, Assistant US Attorney, Miami, to the Attorney General, Washington, DC, June 20, 1930, file 55423-414, Entry 9, RG 85, NA. It may be that a Jewish organization posted bond, given that he had only sixty-seven dollars at the time of his entry and, he claimed, no relatives in the United States.

14. For an insightful critique of the generally celebratory nature of American Jewish history, see Tony Michels, *A Fire in Their Hearts: Yiddish Socialists in New York* (Cambridge: Harvard University Press, 2005), 16–19.

15. For an argument that the administration of immigration policy was the critical factor in "unmaking" European illegal aliens, see Ngai, *Impossible Subjects*, 75–89, and "The Strange Career of the Illegal Alien."

16. On the emergence of the notion that Mexicans (and Mexican Americans) were illegal aliens, see Francisco Balderrama and Raymond Rodriguez, *Decade of Betrayal: Mexican Repatriation in the 1930s* (Albuquerque: University of New Mexico Press, 1995); Hernández, *Migra! A History of the US Border Patrol*; Abraham Hoffman, *Unwanted Mexican Americans in the Great Depression: Repatriation Pressures, 1929–1939* (Tucson: University of Arizona Press, 1974); and George Sánchez, *Becoming Mexican American: Ethnicity, Culture and Identity in Chicano Los Angeles, 1900–1945* (New York: Oxford University Press, 1993), chap. 10. On the way both Asians and Mexicans came to be defined as unwelcome racial outsiders, see Ngai, *Impossible Subjects*.

CHAPTER ONE

1. Quota Act of May 19, 1921 (42 Stat. 5).

2. Immigration Act of May 26, 1924 (43 Stat. 153).

3. Asian nations received token quotas of one hundred each, to cover the immigration of people not defined as racially ineligible to citizenship. The expanded exclusion of Asians was one of the central issues in the congressional debates over the law, for many in Congress and the administrative branches of government worried that Japan would take diplomatic umbrage. See John Higham, *Strangers in the Land: Patterns of American Nativism, 1865–1925*, 2d ed. (New York: Atheneum, 1977 [1955]), 319; Edward Prince Hutchinson, *Legislative History of American Immigration Policy, 1798–1965* (Philadelphia: University of Pennsylvania Press, 1981), 188; and Mae M. Ngai, *Impossible Subjects: Aliens and the Making of Modern America* (Princeton: Princeton University Press, 2004), 48–50.

4. Commissioner General of Immigration to the Secretary of Labor, *Annual Report* (hereafter *CGI Annual Report*), 1924, 25–26 (under the 1921 law, the quotas for Russia, Poland, and Italy had been 24,405, 30,977, and 42,057, respectively). The actual number of legal immigrants from countries to which quotas applied would be higher than the quota, since certain categories of people, such as wives or children aged less than eighteen years of US citizens would be admit-

ted as "nonquota" immigrants. Within the quotas, certain groups—such as mothers, fathers, and husbands of citizens—received preference. Immigration Act of May 26, 1924 (43 Stat. 153).

5. *CGI Annual Report*, 1923, 2–3; and Immigration Act of February 5, 1917 (39 Stat. 874).

6. Immigration Act of February 5, 1917 (39 Stat. 874). The "barred zone" of Asia was given in specific geographic terms: "persons who are natives of islands not possessed by the United States adjacent to the Continent of Asia, situate [*sic*] south of the twentieth parallel of latitude north, west of the one hundred and sixtieth meridian of longitude east from Greenwich, and north of the tenth parallel of latituted south, or who are natives of any country, province, or dependency situate on the Continent of Asia west of the one hundred and tenth meridian of longitude east from Greenwich and east of the fiftieth meridian of longitude east from Greenwich and south of the fiftieth parallel of latitude north, except that portion of said territory situate between the fiftieth and the sixty-fourth meridians of longitude east from Greenwich and the twenty-fourth and thirty-eighth parallels of latitude north" were not eligible to enter the United States. This encompassed a large swath of Asia—including India, Burma, Siam, Arabia, and Afghanistan. China was already dealt with under the Chinese exclusion legislation, and the immigration of Japanese laborers was effectively barred under the 1907 "Gentlemen's Agreement." The Philippines was also exempt, as Filipinos were considered to be American nationals.

7. Benedict Anderson, *Imagined Communities: Reflections on the Origin and Spread of Nationalism*, rev. ed. (London: Verso, 1991), 163–85.

8. James C. Scott, *Seeing Like a State: How Certain Schemes to Improve the Human Condition Have Failed* (New Haven: Yale University Press, 1998). Significantly, Scott opens his book by explaining that his project grew out of an interest in the antagonistic relationship between states and nomadic people, and the issue of why people on the move seemed to pose a particular challenge to state control. In other words, while state control and challenges to that control happen across a wide variety of realms, migration presents the potential for disorder that seems particularly threatening to the very boundaries of the nation itself. For more on the production of knowledge in bureaucratic, administrative settings, see also Peter Becker and William Clark, eds., *Little Tools of Knowledge: Historical Essays on Academic and Bureaucratic Practices* (Ann Arbor: University of Michigan Press, 2001). For a detailed study of the bureaucratization of surveillance in the American context, see Pamela Sankar, "State Power and Record-Keeping: The History of Individualized Surveillance in the United States, 1790–1935" (PhD diss., University of Pennsylvania, 1992).

9. Adam McKeown, *Melancholy Order: Asian Migration and the Globalization of Borders* (New York: Columbia University Press, 2008), 13; and Aristide R. Zolberg, "Global Movements, Global Walls: Responses to Migration, 1885–1925," in *Global History and Migrations*, ed. Wang Gungwu (New York: Westview Press, 1997), 279–80, and *A Nation by Design: Immigration Policy in the Fashioning of America* (New York: Russell Sage Foundation, 2006), 6–7, and 205–6.

10. Christiane Reinecke, "Governing Aliens in Times of Upheaval: Immigration Control and Modern State Practice in Early Twentieth-Century Britain, Compared with Prussia," *International Review of Social History* 54 (2009): 39–65; and Zolberg, "Global Movements," 300–301.

11. Zolberg, "Global Movements," 300.

12. On making this argument, I draw especially on Zolberg, *Nation by Design*.

13. Naturalization Act of March 26, 1790 (1 Stat. 103.)

14. Patrick Ettinger, *Imaginary Lines: Border Enforcement and the Origins of Undocumented Immigration, 1882–1930* (Austin: University of Texas Press, 2009), 16; and Zolberg, *Nation by Design*, 87–98.

15. Ettinger, *Imaginary Lines*, 18; John Torpey, *The Invention of the Passport: Surveillance, Citizenship and the State* (Cambridge: Cambridge University Press, 2000), 94; and Zolberg, *Nation by Design*, 110–13.

16. Gerald L. Neuman, "Qualitative Migration Controls in the Antebellum United States," in *Migration Control in the North Atlantic World: The Evolution of State Practices in Europe and the United States from the French Revolution to the Inter-War Period*, ed. Andreas Fahrmeir, Olivier Faron, and Patrick Weil (New York: Berghahn Books, 2003), 112; and Zolberg, *Nation by Design*, 78.

17. Ettinger, *Imaginary Lines*, 16–17; Gerald L. Neuman, "The Lost Century of American Immigration Law (1776–1875)," *Columbia Law Review* 93, no. 8. (December 1993): 1833–1901, and "Qualitative Migration Controls," 106–15; Daniel J. Tichenor, *Dividing Lines: The Politics of Immigration Control in America* (Princeton: Princeton University Press, 2002), 46, 58–59, and 67; and Zolberg, *Nation by Design*, 72–78.

18. Eric Foner, *A Short History of Reconstruction, 1863–1877* (New York: Harper and Row, 1988), 37; James R. Grossman, *Land of Hope: Chicago, Black Southerners, and the Great Migration* (Chicago: University of Chicago Press, 1989), 20–23; and Neuman, "Qualitative Migration Controls," 115–17. On northern states' legislative efforts in the antebellum period to restrict African American immigration from other states, see Leon Litwack, *North of Slavery: The Negro in the Free States, 1790–1860* (Chicago: University of Chicago Press, 1961), 66–74.

19. Higham, *Strangers in the Land*, 97–8; and Aristide Zolberg, "The Archaeology of 'Remote Control,'" in Fahrmeir et al., eds., *Migration Control in the North Atlantic World*, 198–99.

20. Tyler Anbinder, *Nativism and Slavery: The Northern Know-Nothings and the Politics of the 1850s* (New York: Oxford University Press, 1992); Ettinger, *Imaginary Lines*, 17; Higham, *Strangers in the Land*, 6–7; and Zolberg, "Archaeology of 'Remote Control,'" 215–20.

21. Tichenor, *Dividing Lines*, 46–49, and 59; and Zolberg, "Archaeology of 'Remote Control,'" 200.

22. Ettinger, *Imaginary Lines*, 18; and Keith Fitzgerald, *The Face of the Nation: Immigration, the State, and the National Identity* (Palo Alto: Stanford University Press, 1996), 106.

23. Ettinger, *Imaginary Lines*, 18; Tichenor, *Dividing Lines*, 67–69; and Zolberg, *Nation by Design*, 189–90.

24. Act of March 3, 1875 (18 Stat. 477); and Zolberg, *Nation by Design*, 188. This act built on the 1862 federal law intended to outlaw the "coolie trade." Although it was not directed directly at immigrants, but rather at those who might be transporting contract workers from China, some scholars argue that this law properly marks the start of the era of federal immigration restriction. See, e.g., Kelly Lytle Hernández, *Migra! A History of the US Border Patrol* (Berkeley: University of California Press, 2010), 26; and Moon-Ho Jung, *Coolies and Cane: Race, Labor, and Sugar in the Age of Emancipation* (Baltimore: Johns Hopkins University Press, 2006), 5 and 38.

25. Torpey, *Invention of the Passport*, 95–96.

26. McKeown, *Melancholy Order*, 330–31.

27. Zolberg, "Global Movements, Global Walls," 289–90.

28. Torpey, *Invention of the Passport*, 96; and Zolberg, "Global Movements, Global Walls," 290.

29. Act of May 6, 1882 (22 Stat. 58); and Zolberg, *Nation by Design*, 191.

30. On the history of Asian exclusion in international context, see McKeown, *Melancholy Order*.

31. Alexander Saxton, *The Indispensable Enemy: Labor and the Anti-Chinese Movement in California* (Berkeley: University of California Press, 1971). Saxton is notable for his early interest in the role the forging of white identities played in these political battles. John Higham makes the point that the anti-Chinese agitation itself spurred a nativist backlash by those who saw the anti-Chinese activists as dangerous foreign radicals; see Higham, *Strangers in the Land*, 31. In his analysis of the Chinese Exclusion act, Andrew Gyory takes a different position from Saxton, arguing that national electoral politics, rather than specifically regional politics, were the most important factor leading to the codification of anti-Chinese sentiment; see Gyory, *Closing the Gate: Race, Politics and the Chinese Exclusion Act* (Chapel Hill: University of North Carolina Press, 1998).

32. Lucy E. Salyer, *Laws Harsh as Tigers: Chinese Immigrants and the Shaping of Modern Immigration Law* (Chapel Hill: University of North Carolina Press, 1995).

33. Ngai, *Impossible Subjects*, 18.

34. Ettinger, *Imaginary Lines*, 47-68; Hernández, *Migra!*, 35; and Erika Lee, "Enforcing the Borders: Chinese Exclusion Along the US Borders with Canada and Mexico, 1882-1924," *Journal of American History* 89, no. 1 (June 2002), 54-86.

35. Lee, "Enforcing the Borders," 74-84.

36. McKeown, *Melancholy Order*, esp. chap. 8; Salyer, *Laws Harsh as Tigers*, esp. 17-20, and 46-48; and Torpey, *Invention of the Passport*, 97-99.

37. Estelle Lau, *Paper Families: Identity, Immigration Administration, and Chinese Exclusion* (Durham: Duke University Press, 2006); Erika Lee, *At America's Gates: Chinese Immigration during the Exclusion Era, 1882-1943* (Chapel Hill: University of North Carolina Press, 2003), and "Enforcing the Borders," 54-86; McKeown, *Melancholy Order*, esp. chaps. 8 and 10; and Salyer, *Laws Harsh as Tigers*.

38. Immigration Act of August 3, 1882 (22 Stat. 214); Ettinger, *Imaginary Lines*, 20-21; and Tichenor, *Dividing Lines*, 69.

39. During the strike, which extended from coast to coast, federal troops were called in. See Higham, *Strangers in the Land*, 30-31; Nell Painter, *Standing at Armageddon: The United States, 1877-1919* (New York: W. W. Norton, 1987), 15-24; and Howard Zinn, *A People's History of the United States*, rev. ed. (New York: HarperCollins, 1995), 240-46.

40. Higham, *Strangers in the Land*, 54-56; Painter, *Standing at Armageddon*, 47-50; and Zinn, *People's History*, 264-66. Four were eventually hanged; one committed suicide, and three were pardoned. Higham writes that "the Haymarket Affair was to go down as the most important single incident in late nineteenth century nativism" (*Strangers in the Land*, 54). For an in-depth examination of the Haymarket affair, see Paul Avrich, *The Haymarket Tragedy* (Princeton: Princeton University Press, 1984).

41. Saxton, *Indispensable Enemy*, 273-78.

42. Ettinger, *Imaginary Lines*, 39.

43. Ibid., 48.

44. Ibid., esp. chaps. 3 and 4.

45. Immigration Act of March 3, 1891 (26 Stat. 1084); Frank L. Auerbach, *Immigration Laws of the United States*, 2d ed. (Indianapolis: Bobbs-Merrill, 1961), 37; Ettinger, *Imaginary Lines*, 69; Higham, and *Strangers in the Land*, 99; and Hutchinson, *Legislative History of American Immigration Policy*, 102–3.

46. Zolberg, *Nation by Design*, 224.

47. Desmond King, *Making Americans: Immigration, Race, and the Origins of the Diverse Democracy* (Cambridge: Harvard University Press, 2000), 52–53.

48. Roger Daniels, *Coming to America: A History of Immigration and Ethnicity in American Life* (New York: HarperCollins, 1990). Daniels calls the Immigration Restriction League the group that became "the most influential single pressure group arguing for a fundamental change in American immigration policy" (*Coming to America*, 276). See also Higham, *Strangers in the Land*, 101–3; Matthew Frye Jacobson, *Whiteness of a Different Color: European Immigrants and the Alchemy of Race* (Cambridge: Harvard University Press, 1998), 77–78; King, *Making Americans*, 52–54; and Zolberg, *Nation by Design*, chap. 7.

49. For an exploration of the relationship between the nation's attitudes toward foreign people within the United States and abroad, see Matthew Frye Jacobson, *Barbarian Virtues: The United States Encounters Foreign Peoples at Home and Abroad, 1876–1917* (New York: Hill and Wang, 2000).

50. Jacob Riis, *How the Other Half Lives* (New York: Charles Scribner's Sons, 1890).

51. Figures cited in Ira Katznelson, "Between Separation and Disappearance: Jews on the Margins of American Liberalism," in *Paths of Emancipation: Jews, States, and Citizenship*, ed. Pierre Birnbaum and Ira Katznelson (Princeton: Princeton University Press, 1995), 188. Indeed, these "new" immigrants were far more urban than their earlier counterparts. The census of 1920 showed a boom in urban population since 1910 and that urban centers were dense with immigrants; US Bureau of the Census, *Increase of Population in the United States, 1910–1920* (Washington, DC: Government Printing Office, 1922), 110–11. See also Margo J. Anderson, *The American Census: A Social History* (New Haven: Yale University Press, 1988), 134.

52. Higham, *Strangers in the Land*, 88–96, and 158–61. For the suspicion with which the nation regarded Italians in particular, see Thomas A. Guglielmo, *White on Arrival: Italians, Race, Color and Power in Chicago, 1890–1945* (New York: Oxford University Press, 2003), chap. 4.

53. Arthur A. Goren, *New York Jews and the Quest for Community: The Kehillah Experiment, 1908–1922* (New York: Columbia University Press, 1970), 25.

54. Michael Berkowitz, "Between Altruism and Self-Interest: Immigration Restriction and the Emergence of American-Jewish Politics in the United States," in Fahrmeir et al., eds., *Migration Control in the North Atlantic World*, 253–70.

55. Edwin Black, *War Against the Weak: Eugenics and America's Campaign to Create a Master Race* (New York: Four Walls Eight Windows, 2003), chap. 10; Higham, *Strangers in the Land*, chap. 6; and King, *Making Americans*, chap. 6. For a general exploration of the development of eugenic thought, see Daniel J. Kevles, *In the Name of Eugenics: Genetics and the Uses of Human Heredity* (New York: Knopf, 1985). For an international perspective on how Jewish scientists abroad grappled with the new science, see John M. Efron, *Defenders of the Race: Jewish Doctors in Fin de Siècle Europe* (New Haven: Yale University Press, 1994).

56. Higham, *Strangers in the Land*, 131–57; Jacobson, *Whiteness of a Different Color*, 56–90; King, *Making Americans*, 166–95; and Zolberg, *Nation by Design*, 207–17.

57. Tichenor, *Dividing Lines*, 123; and Zolberg, *Nation by Design*, 229.

58. Immigration Act of February 20, 1907 (34 Stat. 898); and Tichenor, *Dividing Lines*, 127–28.

59. On the rise of the administrative state, see Stephen Skowroneck, *Building a New American State: The Expansion of National Administrative Capacities, 1877–1920* (Cambridge: Cambridge University Press, 1982).

60. On the history of the US census, see Anderson, *The American Census: A Social History* (New Haven: Yale University Press, 1988).

61. In 1903, the Bureau of Immigration was transferred from the Treasury Department to the Department of Commerce and Labor; from 1913 to 1940 it was part of the Department of Labor.

62. Scholars discussing the extent and nature of Jews' social "in-betweenness" in twentieth-century US history have debated whether the history of Jews can illuminate the workings of whiteness in particular and race in general. Some scholars have seen Jews as one major example of racial in-betweens in early decades of the twentieth century. See, e.g., Eric L. Goldstein, *The Price of Whiteness: Jews, Race and American Identity* (Princeton: Princeton University Press, 2006); Jacobson, *Whiteness of a Different Color*, esp. chap. 5; David R. Roediger, *Working Toward Whiteness: How America's Immigrants Became White* (New York: Basic Books, 2005); and Michael Rogin, *Blackface, White Noise: Jewish Immigrants in the Hollywood Melting Pot* (Berkeley: University of California Press, 1996). Others, however, have argued that there was never significant doubt about the whiteness of any European immigrants, whether Jews, Slavs, or Italians. Scholars taking this view have noted that there was no serious consideration of barring such groups from naturalization or any understanding of them in the national census as other than "white" immigrants. For this view, see, e.g., Eric Arnesen, "Whiteness and the Historians' Imagination," *International Labor and Working-Class History* 60 (Fall 2001): 3–32, and Eric Foner, "Response to Eric Arnesen," in Arnesen, "Whiteness and the Historians' Imagination," 57–60; and Guglielmo, *White on Arrival*. See chapter 5 for further discussion of this issue.

63. I do sometimes use the terms "ethnic" and "ethnicity" in this book, since consistently using "race" in its early twentieth-century sense—in which that word connoted national, linguistic, and religious backgrounds as well as what were understood to be meaningful biological divisions among people—would at times be confusing for the contemporary reader. Of course, all these terms remain profoundly problematic and unstable, as I hope this study makes clear. For useful discussions of the historical meanings of "race" and "ethnicity," and the argument that the language of ethnicity emerged during this period, around the politics of immigration, as a discourse distinct from that of race, see Victoria Hattam, *In the Shadow of Race: Jews, Latinos, and Immigrant Politics in the United States* (Chicago: University of Chicago Press, 2007); and Roediger, *Working Toward Whiteness*. For a forceful argument that using the terms "ethnics" or "white ethnics" in relation to the national discourse about immigration during the pre–World War II era obscures important elements of the history of race and of how "new immigrants" ultimately came to be considered as "whites," see Roediger, *Working Toward Whiteness*, esp. 27–34.

64. On the links between debates over the black-white color line and the racial status of the "new immigrants," see Heidi Ardizzone, "Red-blooded Americans: Mulattoes and the Melting

Pot in US Racialist and Nationalist Discourse, 1890–1930" (PhD diss., University of Michigan, 1997), 258–62, and 273–309. On the parallels Americans drew between African Americans and Jews, see Goldstein, *Price of Whiteness*, esp. chap. 2.

65. On the salience of early twentieth-century definitions of race for American Jews, see Goldstein, *Price of Whiteness*, chaps. 2–4.

66. Eric L. Goldstein, "Contesting the Categories: Jews and Government Racial Classification in the United States," *Jewish History* 19, no. 1 (2005): 79–107, and *Price of Whiteness*.

67. Hattam, *In the Shadow of Race*, chap. 2.

68. Goldstein, *Price of Whiteness*, chap. 2.

69. Goldstein, "Contesting the Categories," 84–85.

70. In 1903, the director of the census observed that the 1902 report of the Commissioner General of Immigration listed Hebrew arrivals from the following places, in order of number of arrivals from greatest to least: "Russian Empire and Finland; Austria-Hungary; Roumania; German empire; Turkey in Asia; United Kingdom; Turkey in Europe; France, including Corsica; South America; Switzerland; Servia, Bulgaria, and Montenegro; Europe, not specified; West Indies; Netherlands." Director of the Census Office to George B. Cortelyou, Secretary of the Department of Commerce and Labor, July 14, 1903, file Immigrants and Immigration: Correspondence and Reports Regarding Classification of Hebrews in the Immigration Statistics, 1903–1916, Jacob Rader Marcus Center of the American Jewish Archives, Cincinnati Campus, Hebrew Union College Jewish Institute of Religion (hereafter AJA).

71. US Commission on Immigration, "Brief Statement of the Investigations of the Immigration Commission, with Conclusions and Recommendations and Views of the Minority," *Reports of the Immigration Commission: Abstracts of Reports of the Immigration Commission*, vol. 1 (Washington, DC: Government Printing Office, 1911), 5–49. The complete list of races and peoples which the Bureau of Immigration used was as follows: "African (black); Armenian; Bohemian and Moravian; Bulgarian, Servian, and Montenegrin; Chinese; Croatian and Slovenian; Cuban; Dalmatian, Bosnian, and Herzegovinian; Dutch and Flemish; East Indian; English; Finnish; French; German; Greek; Hebrew; Irish; Italian, North; Italian, South; Japanese; Korean; Lithuanian; Magyar; Mexican; Pacific Islander; Polish; Portugese; Roumanian; Russian; Ruthenian (Russniak); Scandinavian; Scotch; Slovak; Spanish; Spanish-American; Syrian; Turkish; Welsh; West Indian (except Cuban); all other peoples" ("Brief Statement of the Investigations," 17).

72. US Commission on Immigration, "Brief Statement of the Investigations," 17–18.

73. Jacobson, *Whiteness of a Different Color*, 79. Joel Perlmann notes that in the early years of the Bureau of Immigration's record keeping on "races and peoples," the bureau was inconsistent in its use of the term, sometimes, e.g., just listing "race." Perlmann also suggests that the use of "peoples" may have "softened the impact of using a racial scheme." Joel Perlmann, "Race or People: Federal Race Classifications for Europeans in America, 1898–1913," Jerome Levy Economics Institute Working Paper no. 320 (January 2001), http://dx.doi.org/10.2139/ssrn.257921, 7–8, and 13. See also Roediger, *Working Toward Whiteness*, 14–18.

74. Goldstein, *Price of Whiteness*, 104–5; and Perlmann, "Race or People," 9–11.

75. US Commission on Immigration, *Reports of the Immigration Commission*, 42 vols. (Washington, DC: Government Printing Office, 1911). See also King, *Making Americans*, 58–81; and Tichenor, *Dividing Lines*, 128–32.

76. King, *Making Americans*, 58–59.

77. US Immigration Commission, *Reports of the Immigration Commission: Abstract of the Reports of the Immigration Commission*, 1:43–44.

78. King, *Making Americans*, 59–81; Tichenor, *Dividing Lines*, 131; and Zolberg, *Nation by Design*, 233–34. On the *Dictionary of Races or Peoples*, see also Hattam, *In the Shadow of Race*, 82–93; and Jacobson, *Whiteness of a Different Color*, 78–80.

79. Goldstein, "Contesting the Categories," 86, and *Price of Whiteness*, 102; Hattam, *In the Shadow of Race*, 81–82, and 93–94; and Zolberg, *Nation by Design*, 231.

80. Goldstein, *Price of Whiteness*, 102–3, and "Contesting the Categories," 88; and Zolberg, *Nation by Design*, 231. For an in-depth study of the relationship between Syrians and American notions of race, see Sarah M. A. Gualtieri, *Between Arab and White: Race and Ethnicity in the Early Syrian American Diaspora* (Berkeley: University of California Press, 2009).

81. Goldstein, *Price of Whiteness*, 102–3, and "Contesting the Categories," 88.

82. Various memoranda from the Department of State, file "Immigrants and Immigration: Correspondence and Reports Regarding Classification of Hebrews in the Immigration Statistics, 1903–1916," AJA.

83. Goldstein, *Price of Whiteness*, 107.

84. Director of the Census Office to George B. Cortelyou, Secretary of the Department of Commerce and Labor, July 14, 1903, file "Immigrants and Immigration: Correspondence and Reports Regarding Classification of Hebrews in the Immigration Statistics, 1903–1916," AJA.

85. W. W. Husband to William Wheeler, December 15, 1908, file "Immigrants and Immigration: Correspondence and Reports Regarding Classification of Hebrews in the Immigration Statistics, 1903–1916," AJA.

86. Goldstein, *Price of Whiteness*, 107.

87. US Bureau of the Census, *Increase of Population in the United States, 1910–1920* (Washington, DC: Government Printing Office, 1922), 115.

88. Christopher Capozzola, *Uncle Sam Wants You: World War I and the Making of the Modern American Citizen* (New York: Oxford University Press, 2008), chap. 6; Higham, *Strangers in the Land*, 195–200; and David Kennedy, *Over Here: The First World War and American Society* (New York: Oxford University Press, 1980), chap. 1.

89. Immigration Act of Feb. 5, 1917 (39 Stat. 174).

90. Hutchinson, *Legislative History of American Immigration Policy*, 534–43. Indeed, the amount of information about passengers required on ship had grown greatly over the years.

91. John Torpey, "The Great War and the Birth of the Modern Passport System," in *Documenting Individual Identity: The Development of State Practices in the Modern World*, ed. Jane Caplan and John Torpey (Princeton: Princeton University Press, 2001), 256–70; and Zolberg, *Nation by Design*, 240.

92. Craig Robertson, *The Passport in America: The History of a Document* (New York: Oxford University Press, 2010), 187–88; Torpey, "The Great War and the Birth of the Passport," 264–66, and *Invention of the Passport*, 117; and Zolberg, *Nation by Design*, 240–41.

93. See Ngai, *Impossible Subjects*, chap. 2, for a discussion of this era as marking the beginning of the phenomenon of "undocumented" individuals.

94. On tensions around migration during this era, see Torpey, "The Great War and the Birth of the Passport." For the confusion around the attempt to redraw Europe's map, in particular,

according to ethnic groupings, see Eric Hobsbawm, *Nations and Nationalism* (Cambridge: Cambridge University Press, 1992), 132–33.

95. Carole Fink, *Defending the Rights of Others: The Great Powers, the Jews, and International Minority Protection, 1878–1938* (New York: Cambridge University Press, 2004); and Ezra Mendelsohn, *The Jews of East Central Europe between the Wars* (Bloomington: Indiana University Press, 1983).

96. Maddalena Marinari, "Liberty, Restriction, and the Remaking of Italians and Eastern European Jews, (1882–1965)" (PhD diss., University of Kansas, 2009), 44.

97. Higham, *Strangers in the Land*, 301.

98. Melvyn P. Leffler, *The Specter of Communism: The United States and the Origins of the Cold War, 1917–1953* (New York: Hill and Wang, 1994), 6–18.

99. Higham, *Strangers in the Land*, 229–32; and William Preston, *Aliens and Dissenters: Federal Suppression of Radicals, 1903–1933* (Cambridge: Harvard University Press, 1963).

100. Whereas approximately fourteen thousand Jews arrived in the United States in the year between June 30, 1919, and June 30, 1920, one hundred nineteen thousand Jews arrived in the following year. See *American Jewish Year Book* 29 (1927–28), 252.

101. "Temporary Suspension of Immigration," 66th Cong., 3d Sess., H.R. Rep. No. 1109 (December 6, 1920), excerpted in Paul Mendes-Flohr and Jehuda Reinharz, eds., *The Jew in the Modern World: A Documentary History*, 2d ed. (New York: Oxford University Press, 1995), 510.

102. Ibid., 511.

103. Marinari, "Liberty, Restriction, and the Remaking of Italians and Eastern European Jews," 44. See chapter 2 for a detailed discussion of American Jewish organizations.

104. For details on the various legislative proposals circulating in Congress to restrict or halt immigration, see Daniels, *Coming to America*, 279–81; Higham, *Strangers in the Land*, 308–22; and Hutchinson, *Legislative History of American Immigration Policy*, 171–96.

105. "America on Eve of Closing Gates to Jewish Immigrants," *Jewish Telegraphic Agency*, January 1, 1924. Similarly, in 1923, an official of the Red Cross forwarded to the US Secretary of State a detailed memo from an American colleague in Constantinople who worked with refugees there. He strongly felt that Jews were taking up too much of the quotas from Russia and Poland, and suggested that the principles of the quota system—i.e., the ratio of group to entire population—should be applied to the granting of quota visas within a given country, so that the percentage of Jewish immigrants from Poland would be no greater than that of the Jewish population of that country. Arthur C. Ringland, Memo for Rear Admiral Mark L. Bristol, October 12, 1923; enclosed in Mark Bristol to Secretary of State, November 13, 1923, file 55166–45, Entry 9, Records of the US Immigration and Naturalization Service, Record Group 85, National Archives Building, Washington, DC.

106. McKeown, *Melancholy Order*, 332.

107. King, *Making Americans*, chap. 7; and Mae Ngai, "The Architecture of Race in American Immigration Law: A Reexamination of the Immigration Act of 1924," *Journal of American History* 86 (June 1999): 67–92.

108. Immigration Act of May 26, 1924 (43 Stat. 153).

109. Ibid.

110. Zolberg, "Archaeology of 'Remote Control,'" "Global Movements, Global Walls," 99, and *Nation by Design*, 264–67. Other scholars have observed that "remote control," as with many other mechanisms of the quota laws, was pioneered by the United States in its implementation of Chinese exclusion. McKeown, *Melancholy Order*, 16; and Torpey, *Invention of the Passport*, 99.

111. McKeown, *Melancholy Order*, 331 and 334.

CHAPTER TWO

1. Martin Zielonka, "The Jew in Mexico," *Central Conference of American Rabbis Yearbook* 33 (1923), 432. The story is also recounted by mining engineer Morris C. Scherer, who heard Zielonka speak at the University of Austin Menorah Society in 1923. Morris C. Scherer, "My Jewish Contacts in Mexico," *Jewish Monitor* (Fort Worth, Texas), May 10, 1929. Hollace Ava Weiner also begins her biographical sketch of Zielonka with this tale in *Jewish Stars in Texas: Rabbis and Their Work* (College Station: Texas A&M University Press, 1999), chap. 6.

2. *American Jewish Year Book* 27 (1925–26), 439–45; Mark Wischnitzer, *Visas to Freedom: The History of HIAS* (Cleveland: World Publishing, 1956), 111–15; "To Aid Alien Law Victims," *New York Times*, June 23, 1924; and "Imigratsye konferents beshlist shafn milyon dolar tsu helfn di flikhtlinge in eyropeyishe hafn shtet" [Immigration conference decides to raise a million dollars to help the refugees in European port cities], *Forverts*, June 23, 1924. The *Forverts* appears to have overstated the amount to be raised.

3. Marian Smith makes a similar point, invoking the term "middle ground" policy to describe the object of the lobbying efforts of one Jewish organization on behalf of migrants who entered the country illegally. Marian L. Smith, "Jewish Immigration to the US via Mexico and the Caribbean, 1920–1922," *Generations* [Jewish Genealogical Society of Michigan] (Spring 1999): 12.

4. Gulie Ne'eman Arad, *America, Its Jews, and the Rise of Nazism* (Bloomington: Indiana University Press, 2000), 65; and Sheldon Morris Neuringer, *American Jewry and United States Immigration Policy, 1881–1953* (New York: Arno Press, [1969] 1980), chaps. 4–5. For the perspective that American Jews actively contested the law, see Maddalena Marinari, "Liberty, Restriction, and the Remaking of Italians and Eastern European Jews, (1882–1965)" (PhD diss., University of Kansas, 2009).

5. The literature on the "Jewish question" is enormous, but for an examination of widespread anti-Semitism across Europe in this era, see William I. Brustein, *Roots of Hate: Anti-Semitism in Europe before the Holocaust* (Cambridge: Cambridge University Press, 2003). A collection of insightful studies of the relationship between Jews and states is Pierre Birnbaum and Ira Katznelson, eds., *Paths of Emancipation: Jews, States, and Citizenship* (Princeton: Princeton University Press, 1995). For an extensive look at the issue of Jewish national membership in the context of the Paris Peace Conference and the interwar era, see Carole Fink, *Defending the Rights of Others: The Great Powers, the Jews, and International Minority Protection, 1878–1938* (New York: Cambridge University Press, 2004). Regarding the impact of World War I and the Russian Revolution on Jewish ideas and communities, see Jonathan Frankel, Peter Y. Medding, and Ezra Mendelsohn, eds., *Studies in Contemporary Jewry IV: The Jews and the European Crisis, 1914–1921* (New York: Oxford University Press, 1988). On Zionism in western Europe,

see Michael Berkowitz, *Zionist Culture and West European Jewry before the First World War* (New York: Cambridge University Press, 1993); and a useful collection exploring east European Zionism in relation to the Jewish labor movement of the era is Zvi Gittelman, ed., *The Emergence of Modern Jewish Politics: Bundism and Zionism in Eastern Europe* (Pittsburgh: University of Pittsburgh Press, 2003).

6. Tobias Brinkmann, " 'Travelling with Ballin': The Impact of American Immigration Policies on Jewish Transmigration within Central Europe, 1880–1914," *International Review of Social History* 53 (2008): 481; Michael R. Marrus, *The Unwanted: European Refugees in the Twentieth Century* (New York: Oxford University Press, 1985), chap. 2; Ezra Mendelsohn, *Jews of East Central Europe Between the World Wars* (Bloomington: Indiana University Press, 1983); Saskia Sassen, *Guests and Aliens* (New York: New Press, 1999), chap. 5; and Aristide R. Zolberg, *A Nation by Design: Immigration Policy in the Fashioning of America* (New York: Russell Sage Foundation, 2006), 246–47.

7. Though many Jewish immigrants in the mid-nineteenth century came from the German-speaking regions of Europe, it should be noted that they were more diverse than the term "German Jewish" might imply to the contemporary reader. For one thing, Germany did not exist as such until 1871. For another, a significant number of Jews in the nineteenth-century United States were from non–German-speaking lands. And Jews from eastern or central European regions that later became incorporated into Germany had differing relationships to German language and culture. For an excellent exploration of this diversity, see Hasia Diner, *The Jews of The United States, 1654–2000* (Berkeley: University of California Press, 2004), chap. 3.

8. Deborah Dash Moore, *B'nai B'rith and the Challenge of Ethnic Leadership* (Albany: State University of New York Press, 1981).

9. Naomi W. Cohen, *Not Free to Desist: The American Jewish Committee, 1906–1966* (Philadelphia: Jewish Publication Society of America, 1972).

10. On the history of HIAS, see Wischnitzer, *Visas to Freedom.*

11. Faith Rogow, *Gone to Another Meeting: The National Council of Jewish Women, 1893–1993* (Tuscaloosa: University of Alabama Press, 1993).

12. For examinations of *landsmanshaftn*, or hometown-based Jewish organizations, see Rebecca Kobrin, *Jewish Bialystok and Its Diaspora* (Bloomington: Indiana University Press, 2010), chap. 2; and Daniel Soyer, *Jewish Immigrant Associations and American Identity in New York, 1880–1939* (Cambridge: Harvard University Press, 1997).

13. In 1880 there were approximately two hundred fifty thousand Jews in the United States. By 1924, that figure had increased to about four million, and over three-quarters of these Jews were eastern Europeans, their children or grandchildren. The census of 1910 recorded 1,051,767 foreign-born people who claimed their mother tongue as "Yiddish or Hebrew" (this almost always meant Yiddish) and 1,676,762 of "foreign stock" (second generation) who said the same. Figures cited in Roger Daniels, *Coming to America: A History of Immigration and Ethnicity in American Life* (New York: HarperCollins, 1990), 223–24.

14. For a broad look at the dilemmas of organized Jewish efforts to advocate for Jews with governments and the relationship between Jews and power, see, e.g., Benjamin Ginsburg, *The Fatal Embrace: Jews and the State* (Chicago: University of Chicago Press, 1993); and David Biale, *Power and Powerlessness in Jewish History* (New York: Schocken Books, 1986).

15. Historians have also made opposing arguments about whether American Jews were more or less unified during the interwar years. For the argument that the era was one of extreme fragmentation in American Jewish life, see, e.g., Henry L. Feingold, *A Time for Searching: Entering the Mainstream, 1920–1945* (Baltimore: Johns Hopkins University Press, 1992). For the opposite view—that as eastern European Jews moved increasingly into Jewish civic life, old divisions were muted—see, e.g., Mark Raider, *The Emergence of American Zionism* (New York: New York University Press, 1998), 43.

16. The most important examination of an attempt to create a coherent Jewish organizational structure in New York remains Arthur A. Goren, *New York Jews and the Quest for Community: The Kehillah Experiment, 1908–1922* (New York: Columbia University Press, 1970). The World War I–era establishment of the Zionist-oriented American Jewish Congress was an unprecedented effort to create a democratic body representative of American Jews. See Jonathan Frankel, *Prophecy and Politics: Socialism, Nationalism and the Russian Jews, 1862–1917* (Cambridge: Cambridge University Press, 1981), chap. 9; and Arad, *America, Its Jews, and the Rise of Nazism*, 54–58.

17. For histories of organized American Jewish aid, see Yehuda Bauer, *My Brother's Keeper: A History of the American Jewish Joint Distribution Committee, 1929–1939* (Philadelphia: Jewish Publication Society of America, 1974); Cohen, *Not Free to Desist*; Oscar Handlin, *A Continuing Task: The American Jewish Joint Distribution Committee, 1914–1964* (New York: Random House, 1964); Ronald Sanders, *Shores of Refuge: A Hundred Years of Jewish Emigration* (New York: Henry Holt, 1988); Zosa Szajkowski, "Private and Organized American Jewish Overseas Relief (1914–1938)," *American Jewish Historical Quarterly* 57, no. 1 (September 1967): 52–106, "Private and Organized American Jewish Relief and Immigration (1914–1938)," *American Jewish Historical Quarterly* 57, no. 2 (December 1967): 191–253, and "Private American Jewish Overseas Relief (1919–1938): Problems and Attempted Solutions," *American Jewish Historical Quarterly* 57, no. 3 (March 1968): 285–352; Selwyn Ilan Troen and Benjamin Pinkus, eds., *Organizing Rescue: National Jewish Solidarity in the Modern Period* (London: Frank Cass and Company, 1992); and Mark Wischnitzer, *To Dwell in Safety: The Story of Jewish Migration since 1800* (Philadelphia: Jewish Publication Society of America, 1948), and *Visas to Freedom*. The amounts of money raised by Jews in the United States during World War I were unprecedented. The JDC, e.g., disbursed about fifteen million dollars during the war. Handlin, *A Continuing Task*, 31.

18. Arad, *America, Its Jews, and the Rise of Nazism*, 60–62; Fink, *Defending the Rights of Others*, esp. chaps 5–8; Carole Fink, "The Jews and Minority Rights During and After World War I," Occasional Paper No. 3, Kaplan Centre for Jewish Studies and Research (Cape Town: University of Cape Town, 2001), and "Louis Marshall: An American Jewish Diplomat in Paris, 1919," *American Jewish History* 94, no. 1–2 (March–June 2008): 21–40.

19. An interesting example of the public debate among American Jews about the future of Judaism in the United States after the quota laws is a forum in the September 1924 New Year's issue of the *American Hebrew*. Titled "Facing the Future: Our Children's Children," it featured speculation by prominent Jews (including Boris Bogen, head of the JDC's European operations; Julian Morgenstern, President of Hebrew Union College, the Reform rabbinical seminary; and Stephen Wise, activist rabbi and president of the Jewish Institute of Religion); as well as non-Jews (including Helen Keller and W. E. B. Du Bois) on what the nation would look like

in the year 2000. The recently passed quota laws were explicitly part of the impetus for the project.

20. Records of various Jewish organizations emphasize that immigrant aid work was as demanding in the wake of the quota laws. The Philadelphia branch of HIAS, e.g., observed in its 1924 report that "it must . . . be kept in mind that the more difficult admission to the United States is made, the more arduous labor, the more effort is involved in appealing, through the case of detained immigrants, not to mention the work which is entailed in preparing the affidavits, certificates and other papers to be sent by relatives to prospective immigrants abroad for presentation to the United States consulates"; see HIAS, *Annual Report* (1924), 37, microfilm reel MKM 15.2, HIAS Papers, Record Group 245 (citations to this record group hereafter as HP), Archives of the YIVO Institute for Jewish Research, New York (hereafter YIVO). The Immigrant Aid department of the New York section of the NCJW noted in its annual report for 1927–28 that "[i]n view of the general impression that the restriction of immigration since the passage of the amendment act in 1924 has radically reduced the volume of our work, it is interesting to note that this past year was the busiest one we have had since that law became effective"; see National Council of Jewish Women, New York Section, *Yearbook* (1928–29), 48.

21. Arad, *America, Its Jews, and the Rise of Nazism*, 65–67; Neil Baldwin, *Henry Ford and the Jews: The Mass Production of Hate* (New York: PublicAffairs, 2002), esp. chaps. 8–10; Sidney Bolkowsky, *Harmony and Dissonance: Voices of Jewish Identity in Detroit, 1914–1967* (Detroit: Wayne State University Press, 1991), 80, 97–102; and Leo Ribuffo, "Henry Ford and *The International Jew*," *American Jewish History* 69 (June 1980): 437–77. The rise of the Klan was a more immediate threat for Jews in some places than in others. In Texas, e.g., the Klan had a good deal of success during the early twenties. This was obviously a powerful disincentive to "look bad" in this region in particular, given the anti-Semitic tenor of the group—secondary to some of its more pressing priorities but a salient feature of their philosophy nonetheless. On the Klan's success in Texas politics, see Neil Foley, *The White Scourge: Mexicans, Blacks, and Poor Whites in Texas Cotton Culture* (Berkeley: University of California Press, 1997), 87; and W. H. Timmons, *El Paso: A Borderlands History* (El Paso: Texas Western Press, 1990), 231–35. On the rise of the Klan nationwide, see Kenneth T. Jackson, *The Ku Klux Klan in the City, 1915–1930* (New York: Oxford University Press, 1967).

22. See Marcia Graham Synott, *The Half-Opened Door: Discrimination in Admissions at Harvard, Yale, and Princeton, 1900–1970* (Westport: Greenwood Press, 1979).

23. On American anti-Semitism in this era, see Arad, *America, Its Jews, and the Rise of Nazism*, 63–68; Leonard Dinnerstein, *Antisemitism in America* (New York: Oxford University Press, 1994); chap. 5; Henry L. Feingold, *A Midrash on American Jewish History* (Albany: State University of New York Press, 1982), 171–91; and John Higham, "The Rise of Social Discrimination," in John Higham, *Send These to Me: Immigrants in Urban America* (Baltimore: Johns Hopkins University Press, 1985), 117–52.

24. Szajkowski, "Private and Organized American Jewish Relief and Immigration (1914–1938)," 230. In 1920, the US Consul even borrowed money from HIAS so as to be able to rent a larger office. Ibid.

25. Szajkowski, "Private and Organized American Jewish Relief and Immigration (1914–1938)"; and Wischnitzer, *Visas to Freedom*, 107–9.

26. Wischnitzer, *Visas to Freedom*, 107–9. In April 1923, HIAS formed the HIAS Immigrant Bank, licensed by New York State, to perform its remittance work.

27. Report of Emil Sauer, American Consul, Cologne, enclosed with William Coffin, American Consul General, Berlin, to Secretary of State, January 12, 1921, file 54933–370, Entry 9, Records of the US Immigration and Naturalization Service, Record Group 85, National Archives Building, Washington, DC (citations to this record group hereafter as RG 85, NA).

28. Louis Marshall to James Davis, Secretary of Labor, December 9, 1921, file 55166–451, Entry 9, RG 85, NA.

29. Louis Marshall to James Davis, Secretary of Labor, April 27, 1921, folder Immigration 1920–23, General Correspondence 1906–32 (hereafter GC), American Jewish Committee Archives, New York City (hereafter AJCA). The JDC was so worried about government and public perception that it was crossing lines of legal work that even before the 1921 law it decided not to get involved with emigration activities, which was why HIAS was alone in its transmittance work.

30. Louis Marshall to John Bernstein, December 13, 1921, Louis Marshall Correspondence, microfilm reel MKM 16, HP, YIVO.

31. Reuben Fink, "Visas, Immigration, and Official Anti-Semitism," *Nation*, June 22, 1921.

32. Adolph Held to HIAS, New York, April 30, 1922, quoted in Szajkowski, "Private and Organized American Jewish Relief and Immigration (1914–1938)," 204–5.

33. Zielonka, "The Jew in Mexico," 432.

34. Martin Zielonka to Henry Cohen, February 17, 1921, microfilm reel 600, Zielonka, Martin, Correspondence and Reports while in Mexico, 1921–33 (hereafter Zielonka Correspondence), Jacob Rader Marcus Center of the American Jewish Archives, Cincinnati Campus, Hebrew Union College Jewish Institute of Religion (hereafter AJA).

35. Weiner, *Jewish Stars in Texas*, 70–73. For a history of the Galveston movement, see Bernard Marinbach, *Galveston: Ellis Island of the West* (Albany: State University of New York Press, 1983).

36. Henry Cohen to Martin Zielonka, February 24, 1921, microfilm reel 600, Zielonka Correspondence, AJA. Henry Cohen was quite an interesting figure in his own right. The London-born rabbi was nationally known for his political and humanitarian efforts, fighting anti-Semitism, working for prison reform, and organizing much of Galveston's immigration operation. See a biographical sketch of Cohen in Weiner, *Jewish Stars in Texas*, chap. 4.

37. Weiner, *Jewish Stars in Texas*, 112.

38. Ann R. Gabbert, "Prostitution and Moral Reform in the Borderlands: El Paso, 1890–1920," *Journal of the History of Sexuality* 12, no. 4 (October 2003): 575–604.

39. Weiner, *Jewish Stars in Texas*, 112.

40. Ibid., 112–13.

41. Martin Zielonka to Sidney Kusworm, August 25, 1921, microfilm reel 600, Zielonka Correspondence, AJA.

42. The National Council of Jewish Women's Miami section reported in 1929, e.g., on its approach to a dilemma similar to the one Zielonka faced in El Paso, namely the detentions of Jewish migrants who had tried to enter illegally via Cuba. "This past winter," they reported, "twelve such unfortunates were kept in jail for six weeks. Much as we decry the action of these

aliens in attempting to break our laws, our committee feels it incumbent upon them, neverthe-less, to render service to these people while they are incarcerated." *The Immigrant* [National Council of Jewish Women], June–September 1929, 8.

43. El Paso population figure cited in Timmons, *El Paso*, 235. Jewish population statistics drawn from *American Jewish Year Book* 28 (1926–27), 401.

44. Patrick Ettinger, *Imaginary Lines: Border Enforcement and the Origins of Undocumented Immigration, 1882–1930* (Austin: University of Texas Press, 2009), 13; and David Montejano, *Anglos and Mexicans in the Making of Texas, 1836–1986* (Austin: University of Texas Press, 1987), 94.

45. Ettinger, *Imaginary Lines*, esp. 93–98 and 105–22; and Erika Lee, "Enforcing the Bor-ders: Chinese Exclusion along the US Borders with Canada and Mexico, 1882–1924," *The Jour-nal of American History* 89, no. 1 (June 2002): 68–70.

46. Lee, "Enforcing the Borders," 60. For more on Chinese illegal immigration during the exclusion era, see, in addition to Lee's excellent article, Grace Delgado, *Making the Chinese Mexican: Global Migration, Localism, and Exclusion in the U.S.-Mexico Borderlands* (Palo Alto: Stanford University Press, 2012), chap. 3; Ettinger, *Imaginary Lines*, esp. 37–66, 98–100, and 149–50; Estelle T. Lau, *Paper Families: Identity, Immigration Administration, and Chi-nese Exclusion* (Durham: Duke University Press, 2006); Erika Lee, *At America's Gates: Chinese Immigration during the Exclusion Era, 1882–1943* (Chapel Hill: University of North Carolina Press, 2003); and Lucy E. Salyer, *Laws Harsh as Tigers: Chinese Immigrants and the Shaping of Modern Immigration Law* (Chapel Hill: University of North Carolina Press, 1995), 44–45, 61–62, and 150. For a global perspective on Asian migration and the law during the era, including the issue of Chinese illegal immigration to the United States, see Adam M. McKeown, *Melan-choly Order: Asian Migration and the Globalization of Borders* (New York: Columbia University Press, 2008).

47. Ettinger, *Imaginary Lines*, 76–80, 91–92, and 99; and Lee, "Enforcing the Borders," 73–80.

48. Lee, "Enforcing the Borders"; and Salyer, *Laws Harsh as Tigers*.

49. For a description of El Paso's role in the Mexican revolution, see Timmons, *El Paso*, 209–23. For a study of the Texas border region more generally during this era, see Don M. Coerver and Linda B. Hall, *Texas and the Mexican Revolution: A Study in State and National Border Policy, 1910–1920* (San Antonio: Trinity University Press, 1984).

50. Coerver and Hall, *Texas and the Mexican Revolution*, 123; and Gabbert, "Prostitution and Moral Reform in the Borderlands," 597.

51. Timmons, *El Paso*, 223; and John Torpey, *The Invention of the Passport: Surveillance, Citizenship and the State* (Cambridge: Cambridge University Press, 2000), 118.

52. Act of May 22, 1918 (40 Stat. 559); Torpey, *Invention of the Passport*, 117.

53. Timmons (*El Paso*, 227) writes that from July 1919 through July 1920, four hundred thousand American tourists came over the border to Ciudad Juarez. In addition to its saloons, Ciudad Juarez had other entertainment: "gambling tables, race track, bullring, cockfights, dance halls, brothels, honky-tonks, lewd shops, dope parlors, and the like."

54. Government officials never stopped worrying about Chinese immigrants, but in these interim years, at least some expressed the opinion that, as the official in charge of the El Paso district put it, "The problem of stopping the inflow of European aliens subject to the quota

law has almost entirely displaced the Chinese smuggling with which the border service had to contend for so many years." Commissioner General of Immigration to the Secretary of Labor, *Annual Report* (hereafter *CGI Annual Report*) (1923), 18.

55. Martin Zielonka, Report of Rabbi Zielonka's Trip to New York, March 23, 1921, Information on Jewish Immigrants to Juarez and Vera Cruz, Mexico: Small Collections, AJA (hereafter Report of Rabbi Zielonka's Trip to New York).

56. Zielonka, "The Jew in Mexico," 426. For an overview of the various debates Jewish organizations engaged in regarding Mexican colonization, see Corinne A. Krause, "Mexico— Another Promised Land? A Review of Projects for Jewish Colonization in Mexico, 1881–1925," *American Jewish Historical Quarterly* 61 (June 1972): 325–41. On Zielonka's own exploratory trip to Mexico under the auspices of the Central Conference of American Rabbis, the association of Reform Jewish clergy, see Weiner, *Jewish Stars in Texas*, 105–7. Zielonka felt that Jews in Mexico, riven by discord and without an infrastructure of Jewish communal institutions, were incapable of organizing on their own or Jewish immigrants' behalf; thus, American Jews had to do this for them.

57. Report of Rabbi Zielonka's Trip to New York.

58. Marx was inclined to be sympathetic in part, Zielonka suggested in his notes, because as a resident of the port city of New Orleans he was familiar with "the stowaway problem." Report of Rabbi Zielonka's Trip to New York.

59. Martin Zielonka to J. L. Weinberger, November 17, 1925, Zielonka Correspondence, microfilm reel 600a, AJA.

60. Archibald Marx to Judge Sanders, HIAS, September 2, 1921, Zielonka Correspondence, microfilm reel 600b, AJA. For their part, HIAS was angry at rumors that they encountered in Mexico that the IOBB people had told Mexico City's Jews to keep their distance from HIAS because HIAS was merely a "local organization." "I must take exception to your reference to our organization as a local body," Sanders wrote Marx: "For your information, I want to tell you that the Hebrew Sheltering and Immigrant Aid Society is the only Jewish organization in the United States which has looked after the interests of Jewish immigrants throughout the entire country." The IOBB's interference, Sanders suggested, was unprecedented. See Leon Sanders to Archibald Marx, August 22, 1921, Zielonka Correspondence, microfilm reel 600b, AJA. Marx wrote Sanders back just as hotly in late September that the judge misunderstood the fraternal organization's own mission, saying, "You should learn something of the B'nai B'rith and its activities and then you might understand that organizing Lodges is only incidental to its work. We have no axe to grind. Our motto might rightly be, 'We serve all who are oppressed and persecuted.'" Archibald Marx to Judge Sanders, September 29, 1921, Zielonka Correspondence, microfilm reel 600b, AJA.

61. In the cases of immigrants who came from the lands that became the Soviet Union, the US government would not necessarily have been able to carry out deportations. The United States had no diplomatic relations with Russia (later the Soviet Union) from the time of the Russian revolution up until 1933, which made for difficulties in securing permission to deport Russian immigrants back to their homes.

62. Martin Zielonka to Archibald Marx, September 19, 1921, Zielonka Correspondence, microfilm reel 600b, AJA.

63. Report, 1926, B'nai B'rith Mexican Bureau Reports, Small Collections, AJA; Minutes of

the Campaign Committee Meeting of the Emergency Committee on Jewish Refugees, February 12, 1926, file "Refugees: Emergency Committee on Jewish Refugees," GC, AJCA.

64. Report of Maurice B. Hexter, [October] 1925, enclosed with A. H. Fromenson, Emergency Committee on Jewish Refugees, to [?], October 28, 1925, file "Refugees: Emergency Committee on Jewish Refugees," GC, AJCA. See also Krause, "Mexico—Another Promised Land?," regarding other negative reports about the possibilities for Jewish colonization in Mexico.

65. *CGI Annual Report* (1923), 18.

66. Quoted in Smith, "Jewish Immigration to the US," 11.

67. Ibid, 9.

68. Information on Jewish Immigrants to Juarez and Vera Cruz, Mexico, Small Collections, AJA.

69. Smith, "Jewish Immigration to the US," 10–11.

70. Report of Rabbi Zielonka's Trip to New York.

71. Martin Zielonka to Sidney Kusworm, September 9, 1921, Zielonka Correspondence, microfilm reel 600, AJA.

72. Sidney Kusworm to Martin Zielonka, August 22, 1921, Zielonka Correspondence, microfilm reel 600, AJA.

73. Ibid.

74. Martin Zielonka to Sidney Kusworm, August 25, 1921, Zielonka Correspondence, microfilm reel 600, AJA.

75. R. B. Shaman to Martin Zielonka, August 28, 1921, Zielonka Correspondence, microfilm reel 600, AJA.

76. Sidney Kusworm to Martin Zielonka, September 6, 1921, Zielonka Correspondence, microfilm reel 600, AJA.

77. Martin Zielonka to Sidney Kusworm, September 9, 1921, Zielonka Correspondence, microfilm reel 600, AJA. "I am sorry that I cannot give you a more sympathetic reply, but I am trying to state facts," Zielonka wrote in the same letter.

78. Correspondence between Louis Marshall and both HIAS and the State Department on the matter can be found in folder Immigration 1920–23, GC, AJCA.

79. Martin Zielonka to Sidney Kusworm, September 9, 1921, Zielonka Correspondence, microfilm reel 600, AJA

80. Martin Zielonka to R. B. Shaman, September 1, 1921, Zielonka Correspondence, microfilm reel 600, AJA.

81. Martin Zielonka to Secretary of Labor, August 8, 1925, Zielonka Correspondence, microfilm reel 600, AJA.

82. Zielonka wrote his Dallas colleague: "It seems to me that Rev. Dr. Menkin is foolishly writing everywhere on behalf of his relative. He wrote to me and his letter has been answered long ago. He wrote to the HIAS and they forwarded the letter to me. Now I receive a letter from you, and since receiving the same I would not be surprised to receive letters from the various rabbis in Texas." Martin Zielonka to Rabbi Morris Taxon, March 13, 1925, Zielonka Correspondence, microfilm reel 600, AJA.

83. Martin Zielonka to Reverend J. B. Menkin, May 12, 1925, Zielonka Correspondence, microfilm reel 600, AJA.

84. Martin Zielonka to Rabbi Morris Taxon, March 13, 1925, Zielonka Correspondence, microfilm reel 600, AJA.

85. Martin Zielonka to Reverend J. B. Menkin, May 12, 1925, Zielonka Correspondence, microfilm reel 600, AJA.

86. Mrs Miriam S Van [Baclen?], Jewish Federation for Social Service, Dayton to Martin Zielonka, August 13, 1923, 1925, Zielonka Correspondence, microfilm reel 600, AJA.

87. Kelly Lyle Hernández, *Migra! A History of the US Border Patrol* (Berkeley: University of California Press, 2010), 89; Mae M. Ngai, *Impossible Subjects: Aliens and the Making of Modern America* (Princeton: Princeton University Press, 2004), 64; and George Sánchez, *Becoming Mexican American: Ethnicity, Culture and Identity in Chicano Los Angeles, 1900–1945* (New York: Oxford University Press, 1993), 55.

88. Daniel Kanstroom, *Deportation Nation: Outsiders in American History* (Cambridge: Harvard University Press, 2007), 158–59; Ngai, *Impossible Subjects*, 68; and Sánchez, *Becoming Mexican American*, 55–57.

89. Ettinger, *Imaginary Lines*, 150–52; Hernández, *Migra!*, 89; and Sánchez, *Becoming Mexican American*, 58–59.

90. Edward Prince Hutchinson, *Legislative History of American Immigration Policy, 1798–1965* (Philadelphia: University of Pennsylvania Press, 1981), 200, 204, 207, and 486–88.

91. Ngai, *Impossible Subjects*, 52; and Zolberg, *Nation by Design*, 256.

92. Ettinger, *Imaginary Lines*, 160–66; and Ngai, *Impossible Subjects*, 67.

93. On the politicization of Mexican immigration and the increasing association between Mexicans and illegal immigration during this era, see Francisco Balderrama and Raymond Rodriguez, *Decade of Betrayal: Mexican Repatriation in the 1930s* (Albuquerque: University of New Mexico Press, 1995), 17–19; Hernández, *Migra!*; Abraham Hoffman, *Unwanted Mexican Americans in the Great Depression: Repatriation Pressures, 1929–1939* (Tucson: University of Arizona Press, 1974), 26–30; Ngai, *Impossible Subjects*, chap. 2; Mark Reisler, *By the Sweat of Their Brow: Mexican Immigrant Labor in the United States, 1900–1940* (Westport: Greenwood Press, 1976); and Sánchez, *Becoming Mexican American*, 55–62.

94. "Imigratsye konferents beshlist shafn milyon dolar tsu helfn di flikhtlinge in eyropeyishe hafn shtet" [Immigration conference decides to raise a million dollars to help the refugees in European port cities], *Forverts*, June 23, 1924.

95. The full list of organizations officially involved in the ECJR, as indicated on the committee's letterhead, was as follows: Amalgamated Clothing Workers' Union, American Jewish Committee, American Jewish Congress, Bakery and Confectionary Workers' Union, Central Conference of American Rabbis, Central Relief Committee, Council of Jewish Women, Federation of Galician Jews in America, Federation of Hungarian Jews in America, Federation of Polish Hebrews in America, Hadassah, Hebrew Sheltering and Immigrant Aid Society, Independent Order B'nai B'rith, Independent Order Brith Abraham, Independent Order Brith Sholom, Independent Order Free Sons of Israel, International Pocketbook Workers' Union, Jewish Council of Greater New York, Jewish National Workers' Alliance, Joint Board Furriers' Union, National Federation of Temple Sisterhoods, National Federation of Ukrainian Jews, Order Brith Abraham, Poale Zion Organization, Union of American Hebrew Congregations, Union of Orthodox Rabbis of United States, United Cloth Hat and Capmakers' Union, United Hebrew

Trades, United Order True Sisters, United Roumanian Jews of America, United Synagogue of America, and Zionist Organization of America. A brief discussion of the ECJR's activities can be found in Marinari, "Liberty, Restriction, and the Remaking of Italians and Eastern European Jews (1882–1965)," 105–8.

96. *The Immigrant*, February 1925, 6.

97. *American Jewish Year Book* 28 (1926–27), 252.

98. Torpey, *Invention of the Passport*, 119–120. See various reports of "excess quota" immigrants in file 55166-451, Entry 9, RG 85, NA. Newspapers carried headlines such as "Liners with 4,000 Aliens in Harbor," *New York Times*, July 1, 1922.

99. File 55166-451, Entry 9, RG 85, NA; "Decision Compels Return of Aliens," *New York Times*, May 12, 1921; and "Upholds Exclusion of Surplus Aliens," *New York Times*, September 9, 1921.

100. Louis Marshall to Secretary of Labor James Davis, December 9, 1921, file 55166-451, Entry 9, RG 85, NA.

101. Ibid. There were also letter-writing campaigns sponsored by several Yiddish newspapers in 1923 on these migrants' behalf. The papers printed sample letters many people simply tore out, signed, and sent in; some people penned their own. Letters poured in from across the country. The message suggested by the papers was as follows: "On behalf of the immigrants, blood relatives of citizens and declarants, facing deportation because of the exhaustion of quotas, I appeal to your well-known exemplification of American sense of justice to admit them to this country. These unfortunates who have given up their all to be reborn to the ideals of liberty and freedom are the innocent victims of circumstances over which they had no control. Humanitarianism prompts the plea for admission" (files 55374-282a-b, Entry 9, RG 85, NA).

102. "Upholds Exclusion of Surplus Aliens," *New York Times*, September 9, 1921.

103. "Court Ruling Lifts Russian Quota Ban," *New York Times*, December 12, 1923.

104. "Excess Quota Immigrants to Land," *Wall Street Journal*, December 24, 1921; and "Free for Holiday, Aliens all Scatter," *New York Times*, December 25, 1921.

105. E. J. Henning, Assistant Secretary of Labor, to Emmanuel Celler, March 28, 1923, file 55166-451, Entry 9, RG 85, NA.

106. Aristide R. Zolberg, "The Archaeology of 'Remote Control,'" in *Migration Control in the North Atlantic World: The Evolution of State Practices in Europe and the United States from the French Revolution to the Inter-War Period*, ed. Andreas Fahrmeir, Olivier Faron, and Patrick Weil (New York and Oxford: Berghahn Books, 2003), 195–222, "The Great Wall Against China: Responses to the First Immigration Crisis, 1885-1925," in *Migration, Migration History, History: Old Paradigms and New Perspectives*, ed. Jan Lucassen and Leo Lucassen (New York: Peter Lang, 1997), 308, and *Nation by Design*, 264–67.

107. Wischnitzer, *Visas to Freedom*, 112; and *The Immigrant*, December 1925, 7.

108. See, e.g., "Immigrants Storm Consulate in Paris," *New York Times*, July 2, 1924. The article reported that eastern and southern European migrants in Havana as well as in the French capital were turned away from consulates. The NCJW reported in its newsletter that "appeals in increasing numbers reached the [NCJW] Department [of Immigrant Aid] from foreign organizations in behalf of Jewish refugees stranded in ports of entry in Danzig, France, Germany, Holland, Latvia, Roumania, Poland, etc": *The Immigrant*, December 1925, 7.

109. *American Jewish Year Book* 27 (1925–26), 444.

110. ECJR appeal letter, November 1924, folder Immigration 1924, GC, AJCA.

111. Typescript of hearings on admission of stranded migrants, before the US House Committee on Immigration and Naturalization, January 6, 1925, 26, folder I, box 122, Louis Marshall Papers, AJA (hereafter Hearings on Admission of Stranded Migrants). For a report of these hearings, see also "Would Admit 10,000 Aliens—Rabbi Wise and Louis Marshall Appeal for a Special Law," *New York Times*, January 7, 1925.

112. Louis Marshall to Senator James Wadsworth, February 28, 1925, folder 2, box 2, Louis Marshall Selected Papers, AJCA.

113. Louis Marshall to Congressman Johnson, February 25, 1925, folder Immigration 1924, GC, AJCA; Louis Marshall to Congressman Johnson, December 13, 1924, in Charles Reznikoff, *Louis Marshall: Champion of Liberty—Selected Papers and Addresses*, 2 vols. (Philadelphia: Jewish Publication Society of America, 1957), 1:220.

114. Hearings on Admission of Stranded Migrants, 38.

115. ECJR appeal letter, November 1924, folder Immigration 1924, GC, AJCA.

116. Although American Jews publicly decried the racist principles of the new law (including its almost total bar on Asian immigration), they had long expressed anxieties at other moments about being defined as "Orientals," fears that seem to resonate in Marshall's protestations that former and potential Jewish immigrants were super fit to be American citizens. On Jewish concern over being deemed "Oriental" in the context of court cases about the whiteness of Syrians, see Eric L. Goldstein, *The Price of Whiteness: Jews, Race and American Identity* (Princeton: Princeton University Press, 2006), 102–3. Regarding earlier fears of Jews that they would be associated with the anti-Chinese sentiments that led to the Chinese Exclusion Act of 1882, see Rudolf Glanz, "Jews and Chinese in America," *Jewish Social Studies* 16, no. 3 (July 1954): 219–34. This anxiety about being connected with "Orientals" may account in part for why the ECJR consistently focused on the Jewish migrants stranded in Europe and rarely mentioned publicly those Jews whose routes had left them similarly stranded in Shanghai or Yokohoma at the same time. The American Jewish organizations also did mobilize on behalf of these refugees but more quietly. The papers of Meir Birman, HIAS's director in Harbin, China, contains information on these activities; these papers are housed at YIVO, Record Group 352.

117. Louis Marshall to B. C. Vladeck, January 7, 1925, folder Immigration 1924, GC, AJCA.

118. This was especially the case with the National Council of Jewish Women, whose efforts, like that of its Christian and secular counterparts in the world of women's social work, were profoundly shaped by these two concerns. At least some of the immigrants presented themselves to the committee, moreover, in similar terms, as did the young woman who wrote HIAS from Rotterdam, " . . . especially we, the girls, what shall we do? . . . Maybe you are fathers of children, you will then be able to sympathize." Immigrants of Rotterdam to HIAS (translation from Yiddish, presumably by someone at HIAS), November 10, 1924, folder Immigration 1924, GC, AJCA.

119. Report of Maurice B. Hexter, [October] 1925, 5; enclosed in A. H. Fromenson, Emergency Committee on Jewish Refugees, to [?], October 28, 1925, file "Refugees: Emergency Committee on Jewish Refugees," GC, AJCA.

120. Cecelia Razovsky, "Survey of Conditions among Jewish Immigrants in Cuba," May 31, 1924, 6, microfilm reel 36, AR 21–32, Archives of the Joint Distribution Committee, New York

City (hereafter JDC). Echoing this, the ECJR noted in one of its appeal letters that European Jews did not have the proper constitution for the tropical climate in Cuba. See Louis Marshall to Cyrus Adler, October 2, 1924, microfilm reel 26, AR 21–32, JDC.

121. E. J. Henning, Assistant Secretary of Labor, Memorandum for the Secretary [of Labor], January 17, 1925, folder Immigration 1925–29, GC, AJCA. "While in Europe last Summer," Henning wrote in this memorandum, "I made a study of this situation, and made very extensive enquiries in a large number of countries. The representative of the International Hebrew Organization, organized years ago by the Baron de Hirsch, with Headquarters in London, called upon me at Rome, where I was attending the International Hebrew Conference on Emigration and Immigration at the time." The Jewish representative in question was prominent British Jew Lucien Wolf, who indeed brought up the issue of the migrants—shortly before the 1924 law was passed, in fact—with Henning. In a letter about Henning's memorandum, Wolf wrote, "Mr. Henning's reference to it [the conference] as a Hebrew enterprise, taken together with his invidious reference to the 'international Hebrew organisation organised years ago by the Baron Hirsch,' and other very distasteful digressions, lead me very reluctantly to the conclusion that his main object is to create prejudice in the United States against Jewish emigrants and the work of the Jewish Emigration Societies." Lucien Wolf to Otto Schiff, February 23, 1925, folder Immigration 1925–29, GC, AJCA.

122. E. J. Henning, Assistant Secretary of Labor, Memorandum for the Secretary [of Labor], January 17, 1925, folder Immigration 1925–29, GC, AJCA.

123. Ibid.

124. Louis Marshall to Ernest H. Schiff, March 4, 1925, folder 2, Box 2-Immigration, Naturalization, Right to Vote, Louis Marshall Selected Papers, AJCA.

125. Minutes of Meeting of Representatives of Various Jewish Organizations, Berlin, February 5, 1925, folder Immigration 1925–29, GC, AJCA.

126. Occasionally a smaller number was mentioned. In his testimony before Congress in January 1925, Marshall said "five or six thousand" (Hearings on Admission of Stranded Migrants, 29). In general, however, eight or ten thousand must have seemed a good round number, a group large enough to matter but not large enough to be a threatening influx.

127. Bernhard Kahn to Louis Marshall and David Bressler, Report on emigrants and refugees in ports and European countries, February 24, 1925, folder Immigration 1925–29, GC, AJCA. Kahn also estimated there to be about a thousand Jewish would-be immigrants in Harbin, China, two hundred with American visas, but here as elsewhere the migrants stuck in China (there were more in Shanghai) were considered separately. It is not clear how the ECJR distinguished between those refugees without visas whom they were willing to help and other Jewish refugees, though it may have been that these migrants were people accompanying family members with visas. Indeed, this very question arose in the course of congressional hearings. "You said your organization represented the refugees of the whole world," said one legislator to Marshall. "We do not represent any refugees," answered Marshall. "We represent American public opinion." "Does not your organization cover all the refugees in Europe?" insisted the congressman. "This," said Marshall, "is an organization especially organized about five months ago for the purpose of dealing with these stranded immigrants, the marooned immigrants." Hearings on Admission of Stranded Migrants, 34–35.

128. See, e.g., list of one hundred twenty-one migrants in Bremen enclosed in correspondence from the Hilfsverein der Deutschen Juden to the United Evacuation Committee, December 1, 1925, microfilm reel MKM 15.174, HP, YIVO.

129. Werner Senator, "Report on the Work of the United Evacuation Committee," May 25, 1926, 31, microfilm reel 26, AR 21/32, JDC.

130. Ibid., 32.

131. Similar negotiations had gone on with the Lithuanian government. See Wischnitzer, *Visas to Freedom*, 97.

132. Senator, "Report on the Work of the United Evacuation Committee," 7.

133. Ibid., 11.

134. Ibid., 13. An example of this conundrum was the Goodman family, who got stranded in Germany and refused a visa to Canada. The *Hilfsverein* observed in its letter to the ECJR, "Es handelt sich hier um eine ganz legale Sache" [What is involved here is something entirely legal]. Hamburg Committee of Hilfsverein der Deutschen Juden to Central Office of Hilfsverein der Deutschen Juden, Berlin, January 6, 1926, microfilm reel MKM 15.174, HP, YIVO.

135. Louis Marshall to ICA, September 26, 1924, folder Immigration 1924, GC, AJCA.

136. Bernhard Kahn to Louis Marshall and David Bressler, February 23, 1925, folder Immigration 1925–29, GC, AJCA.

137. Louis Marshall to ICA, September 26, 1924, folder Immigration 1924, GC, AJCA.

138. Louis Marshall to ICA, October 25, 1924, folder Immigration 1924, GC, AJCA.

139. Senator, "Report on the Work of the United Evacuation Committee," 8.

140. Ibid., 9. Moreover, despite the far-flung nature of the problem, the UEC opted for a certain amount of centralization, in part because all the migrants' cases involved the same group of shipping companies and thus negotiations for migrants in several places might be carried out at one time, but also, as Senator explained, for the "purely business side of it," and also "to direct the work of the local committees from a central office." Senator, "Report on the Work of the United Evacuation Committee," 15.

141. Bernhard Kahn to Louis Marshall and David Bressler, July 6, 1926, microfilm reel 26, AR 21/32, JDC.

142. Louis Marshall to Senator Wadsworth, February 25, 1925, folder 2, Box 2–Immigration, Naturalization, Right to Vote, Louis Marshall Selected Papers, AJCA.

143. Louis Marshall to Stephen Wise, October 24, 1924, folder Immigration 1924, GC, AJCA.

144. Arthur Lehmann to ECJR, December 1, 1924, folder Immigration 1924, GC, AJCA.

145. Louis Marshall to Adolph Stern, December 24, 1924, folder 2, Box 2–Immigration, Naturalization, Right to Vote, Louis Marshall Selected Papers, AJCA.

146. Reznikoff, *Louis Marshall: Champion of* Liberty, 1:221–25.

147. Louis Marshall to Dr. Percy Fridenberg, April 23, 1925, folder April 1925, Box 1597, Louis Marshall Papers, AJA.

148. Harry Schneiderman, November 3, 1924, microfilm reel 26, AR 21/32, JDC. For a report about the address, see "Marshall Depicts Suffering of Jews," *New York Times*, November 19, 1924.

149. Senator, "Report on the Work of the United Evacuation Committee," 5.

150. Ibid., 18.

151. Ibid., 19.

152. Ibid., 3.

153. Bernhard Kahn to Louis Marshall, February 24, 1925, folder Immigration 1925–29, GC, AJCA.

154. Senator, "Report on the Work of the United Evacuation Committee."

155. HIAS was the one organization that continued to be involved through its partnership with European groups, but there was no concerted American effort on these migrants' behalf after the dissolution of the UEC.

156. See chapters 4–6. See also Max Kohler, "Ameliorating the Quota Laws," in Max Kohler, *Immigration and Aliens in the United States* (New York: Bloch Publishing, Company, 1936), 32–45; and Marinari, "Liberty, Restriction, and the Remaking of Italians and Eastern European Jews (1882–1965)," 108–16, and 128–29.

157. Throughout these postquota years, e.g., the American Jewish Committee's *American Jewish Year Book* reported on court cases and other advocacy efforts.

158. Lucy Salyer, *Laws Harsh as Tigers: Chinese Immigrants and the Shaping of Modern Immigration Law* (Chapel Hill: University of North Carolina Press, 1995), 158–59.

159. On the JDC, see Bauer, *My Brother's Keeper*; and Handlin, *A Continuing Task*.

CHAPTER THREE

1. Inspector Feri Weiss, Reports, to W. W. Husband, Commissioner General of Immigration, January–March, 1925, file 55166–31ex, Accession 58A734, Records of the US Immigration and Naturalization Service, Record Group 85, National Archives Building, Washington, DC. Citations to all documents in this specific file hereafter as Weiss Reports.

2. Quota Act of May 19, 1921 (42 Stat. 5) and Immigration Act of May 26, 1924 (43 Stat. 153).

3. Rosalie Schwartz, *Pleasure Island: Tourism and Temptation in Cuba* (Lincoln: University of Nebraska Press, 1997), 3.

4. Feri Felix Weiss, *The Sieve, Or, Revelations of the Man Mill, Being the Truth about American Immigration* (Boston: Page, 1921).

5. Arrival date at http://www.ellisisland.org and in Bureau of the Census, *Fourteenth Census of the United States* (1920), Town of Winthrop, Suffolk County, Massachusetts, Roll T 625–742, ED 678, 32A, accessed at http://www.ancestry.com. It is hard to determine whether Weiss himself was Jewish, though it seems very likely that he was—his name suggests that he could well have been; his reports indicate that he was able to mingle with Jewish migrants and, it seems, to speak Yiddish. But available census data, which did not ask people about religion, indicates only that he and his parents spoke Magyar or Hungarian as their mother tongue, which is inconclusive. This historical ambiguity strikes me as exceptionally fitting in a story about an immigration inspector who fervently believed in the quota system and in the wisdom of ethnic and national sorting, as well as in his own powers to discern the truth about people's identities.

6. Weiss, *The Sieve*, dedication. Between writing his book and his assignment in Havana, Weiss worked in Boston as an agent for the Department of Justice. His particular focus was "Red" cases; indeed, he was involved in investigating Boston's most renowned such case—that of Italian anarchists Sacco and Vanzetti. For details on his role in that affair, see John Dos Pas-

sos, *Facing the Chair: Story of the Americanization of Two Foreignborn Workmen* (New York: Da Capo Press, 1970), 35–44.

7. Gur Alroey, "Bureaucracy, Agents and Swindlers: Hardships Faced by Russian Jewish Emigrants in the Early Twentieth Century," *Studies in Contemporary Jewry* 19 (2003): 217–18, and 222, and "'And I Remained Alone in a Vast Land': Women in the Great Jewish Migration from Eastern Europe," *Jewish Social Studies* 12, no. 3 (Spring–Summer 2006): 54–55; Pamela S. Nadell, "En Route to the Promised Land," in *We Are Leaving Mother Russia*, ed. Kerry M. Olitzky (Cincinnati: American Jewish Archives, 1990), 14–15, and "From Shtetl to Border: East European Jewish Emigrants and the 'Agents' System, 1868–1914," in *Studies in the American Jewish Experience*, vol. 2., ed. Jacob R. Marcus and Abraham J. Peck (Lanham: University Press of America, 1984), 49–77; and Jack Wertheimer, *Unwelcome Strangers: East European Jews in Imperial Germany* (New York: Oxford University Press, 1987), 14–15. Several works of memoir and fiction also invoke illicit intra-European Jewish border crossing in the late nineteenth and early twentieth centuries. A brilliant example is Sholem Aleichem, "Running the Border," in *The Letters of Menakhem-Mendl and Sheyne-Sheyndl and Motl, the Cantor's Son*, trans. Hillel Halkin (New Haven: Yale University Press, 2002), 179–85. See also Selig Brodetsky, *Memoirs: From Ghetto to Israel* (London: Weidenfeld and Nicolson, 1960), 15; and Alexander Granach, *There Goes an Actor* (New York: Doubleday, 1945), 136. Brodetsky recalls in his memoir that the passport could cost as much as a fifth to half of the cost of transatlantic passage (*Memoirs*, 15).

8. Brodetsky, *Memoirs*, 15.

9. Patrick Ettinger, *Imaginary Lines: Border Enforcement and the Origins of Undocumented Immigration, 1882–1930* (Austin: University of Texas Press, 2009).

10. On the establishment of this "remote control" system, see chapter 2, note 106.

11. Joseph H. Wallis, Assistant Commissioner of Immigration, New Orleans, to Commissioner of Immigration, New Orleans, March 14, 1923, file 55166 31-A, Entry 9, Records of the US Immigration and Naturalization Service, Record Group 85 (citations to this record group hereafter as RG 85), National Archives Building, Washington, DC (hereafter NA).

12. Commissioner General of Immigration to the Secretary of Labor, *Annual Report* (hereafter *CGI Annual Report*) (1923), 1.

13. Extensive information on Rubinsky is contained in file 55423–414, Entry 9, RG 85, NA.

14. [Unsigned] to "Gentelman [*sic*] of Ellis Island," August 4, 1924, file 55423–414, Entry 9, RG 85, NA.

15. Act of May 22, 1918 (40 Stat. 559).

16. For an insightful history of the Border Patrol, see Kelly Lytle Hernández, *Migra! A History of the US Border Patrol* (Berkeley: University of California Press, 2010).

17. Act of Feb. 27, 1925 (43 Stat. 1049); Hernández, *Migra!*, 35; and Aristide R. Zolberg, *A Nation by Design: Immigration Policy in the Fashioning of America* (New York: Russell Sage Foundation, 2006), 266.

18. "Bootlegged Immigrants," *New York Times*, May 5, 1924. Aristide Zolberg quotes another "conservative estimate" of annual illegal immigration following the quota laws as one hundred seventy-five thousand. Zolberg, *Nation by Design*, 266.

19. F. T. F. Dumont, American Consul General, Havana, to Secretary of State, September 14, 1932, file 55166–31-A, Entry 9, RG 85, NA. His count is by nationalities, thus the number of Jews I suggest is my estimate, based on the reports in both primary and secondary sources

that a large proportion of the eastern and central Europeans in Havana were Jews. Historian Robert M. Levine cites a somewhat lower estimate by a US consul around the same time: "One vice-consul claimed early in March 1930 that 14,000 immigrants had entered the United States through Cuba during the 1920s and that many had done so illegally." Levine, *Tropical Diaspora: The Jewish Experience in Cuba* (Gainesville: University Press of Florida, 1993), 33. One of Feri Weiss's informants, however, estimated in 1925 that in Havana alone there were fifteen thousand or more eastern Europeans "waiting to be shipped across to the states" (Weiss Reports, February 4, 1925). Weiss himself estimated that ten thousand immigrants per year were coming illegally to the United States from Cuba; although he did not hazard a guess at the ethnic breakdown of this illegal traffic, his reports as a whole observe that a large proportion of these were central and eastern Europeans, including Jews (Weiss Reports, April 4, 1925). In 1933, Congressman Samuel Dickstein, chairman of the Immigration Committee of the US House of Representatives, mentioned reports of forty thousand aliens having been smuggled to the United States from Cuba during an unspecified period: [Samuel Dickstein] to Frances Perkins, April 3, 1933, HR 73A-F13.1, Records of the House of Representatives, Record Group 233, NA. More generally, Zolberg cites a contemporary "conservative" estimate that one hundred seventy-five thousand aliens were being smuggled in annually in the years after the quotas passed, although he suggests no specific ethnic breakdown. See Zolberg, *Nation by Design*, 266.

 20. On the price of alien smuggling over the Canada-US border, see "Smuggling Aliens Across Our Borders," *Saturday Evening Post*, August 1, 1925; "$20 to Smuggle in Alien," *New York Times*, December 21, 1923; and "Alien 'Gate Crashers' Still Pour in Over Our Frontiers," *New York Times*, June 19, 1927. On the price for forged visas from Poland, see, e.g., Felix Cole, American Consul General, Warsaw, to Secretary of State, May 20, 1930, file 55423-414, Entry 9, RG 85, NA.

 21. In a letter to a friend at the Department of State, who seemed to be arranging to help finance the inspector's undercover work in Cuba, Weiss complained that Havana's booming illegal economy was in part responsible for driving prices there up: "Living is awful down here," he wrote, "very expensive. People make lots of money, gambling, cheating, raising sugar and tobacco, and so everything is very high. A suit I can buy in the States for $25 is $60 here. A meal in Washington 50 cents is at least a dollar here." Feri Weiss to "Brother Tolman," February 21, 1925, enclosed in Weiss Reports.

 22. Weiss Reports, February 25, 1925.

 23. Excerpt of testimony of Jose Bernardo Fernandez Valdes, Laredo, Texas Board of Special Inquiry No. 616, July 24, 1925, file 811.4, Havana vol. 532, Entry 417, Department of State Records–Foreign Service Posts, Record Group 84, National Archives at College Park, College Park, Maryland (hereafter NA-MD).

 24. On the centrality of gangsters and organized crime to American culture during this era, see Sean McCann, *Gumshoe America: Hard-Boiled Crime Fiction and the Rise and Fall of New Deal Liberalism* (Durham: Duke University Press, 2000); and David E. Ruth, *Inventing the Public Enemy: The Gangster in American Culture, 1918–1934* (Chicago: University of Chicago Press, 1996).

 25. The scholarly literature on Jews and criminality is small but growing. On Jews and early twentieth-century racketeering, see Michael Alexander, *Jazz-Age Jews* (Princeton: Princeton University Press, 2001), part I. On Jewish involvement with trafficking in women, see Edward J.

Bristow, *Prostitution and Prejudice: The Jewish Fight Against White Slavery, 1870–1939* (New York: Schocken, 1983). On Jews and liquor bootlegging, in particular, see Marni Davis, *Jews and Booze: Becoming American in the Age of Prohibition*, (New York: New York University Press, 2012). On Jewish gangsters, see Albert Fried, *The Rise and Fall of the Jewish Gangster in America*, rev. ed. (New York: Columbia University Press, 1993); Arthur A. Goren, *Saints and Sinners: The Underside of American Jewish History* (Cincinnati: American Jewish Archives, 1988); Jenna Weissman Joselit, *Our Gang: Jewish Crime and the New York Community, 1900–1940* (Bloomington: Indiana University Press, 1983); and Robert A. Rockaway, *But He Was Good to His Mother: The Lives and Crimes of Jewish Gangsters* (Jerusalem: Gefen Publishing House, 1993), and "The Notorious Purple Gang: Detroit's All-Jewish Prohibition-Era Mob," *Shofar* 20, no. 1 (Fall 2001): 113–30. For a discussion of Jewish criminals in literature, see Rachel Rubin, *Jewish Gangsters of Modern Literature* (Urbana: University of Illinois Press, 2000). On Jewish commercial smuggling in tsarist Russia and tsarist policies in response, see Salo W. Baron, *The Russian Jew under Tsars and Soviets*, 2d ed. (New York: Macmillan, 1976), 33, 85. For the European context in an earlier era, see Otto Ulbricht, "Criminality and Punishment of the Jews in the Early Modern Period," in *In and Out of the Ghetto: Jewish-Gentile Relations in Late Medieval and Early Modern Germany*, ed. R. Po-Chia Hsai and Hartmut Lehmann (Washington, DC, and Cambridge: German Historical Institute and Cambridge University Press, 1995), 49–70.

26. "Alien 'Racket' Source Traced by Garsson," *New York Times*, September 28, 1931. The Havana newspaper *El Pais* also made mention of Capone in symbolic connection with alien running, commenting that despite the fact that the "king" of vice was in jail, "others of his lieutenants work with the same effectiveness and with even greater boldness with the evil trio, whose names are drugs, liquor and undesirable immigration." "Reeditando los ancestrales fueros del Tratado de Utrech, se trafica entre Cuba y los Estados Unidos con cuerpos de esclavos blancos" [Reissuing the old clauses of the Treaty of Utrecht, they traffic in the bodies of white slaves between Cuba and the United States], *El Pais*, June 26, 1932.

27. *CGI Annual Report* (1927), 15.

28. "Smuggling Aliens Across Our Borders," *Saturday Evening Post*, August 1, 1925. Headlines such as "Plan to Watch Border More Closely—Liquor, Alien Problem Gets Investigation" in the *Buffalo Courier Express*, July 13, 1927, made the link explicit. On the connections between the discourse of Prohibition and that of alien smuggling, see also Mae M. Ngai, *Impossible Subjects: Aliens and the Making of Modern America* (Princeton: Princeton University Press, 2004), 62.

29. Inspector in Charge, Port Huron, Michigan, to Inspector in Charge, Detroit, January 2, 1924, file 53990–160A, Accession 60A600, RG 85, NA.

30. "Just now for one or two reasons the smuggling of rum is falling off and vessels are being held in Havana," Weiss explained, and "[c]onsequently the captains are looking around in an endeavor to find aliens or other cargo so as to make expenses." Weiss Reports, February 6, 1925, and April 4, 1925.

31. Weiss Reports, January 24, February 25, and April 4, 1925; and *CGI Annual Report* (1927), 15. The commissioner general of immigration added that it tended to be the cheaper and more disreputable "freebooters" among smugglers who were likely to "abandon his cargo at some isolated spot" or "hold up his charges at the point of a gun and strip him of his last penny."

32. *CGI Annual Report* (1923), 23–24. Fletcher Warren, American vice consul in Havana,

explained to Inspector Feri Weiss the status and function that the various kinds of contraband had in Havana: "I might say that there is 3 things these smugglers work on: rum, aliens and dope. They like to take liquor if they can get it. If not, they take aliens. I don't believe there is scarcely a vessel going out of Havana harbor, that does not take some dope, however. I understand they don't take much each time, just a little bundle, which a sailor can easily hide in his bunk without being caught." Weiss Reports, February 6, 1925.

33. Weiss Reports, February 16, 1925. The inspector's explanation of where he got this and related information is suggestive of the complexities of Havana's international, multiracial underworld, and also of the ways assigning ethnic/linguistic markers could seem both obvious and tangled: "All the above information," he writes, "we got within the last 48 hours from the following sources: Horvath, the Hungarian informant; Mr. Bratzel, the Y.M.C.A. manager of Merchant Marine branch; and particularly from a Mestizzo, half Jap and half Cuban negro, whom we picked up in a barroom on Teniente Ray, corner almost of Belgica Avenida; the place is an import house—such as it is—for Spanish products, especially certain liquors, wines, and also sells small fish, etc. We got acquainted with this Jap, who turned out to be one of the most active bootleggers in Havana, through the intermediary of two prostitutes, one a Swede and the other a Cuban negress, speaking German."

34. "Plan to Watch Border More Closely—Liquor, Alien Problem Gets Investigation," *Buffalo Courier-Express*, July 15, 1927.

35. See Bristow, *Prostitution and Prejudice*; and Egal Feldman, "Prostitution, the Alien Woman, and the Progressive Imagination, 1910–1915," *American Quarterly* 19, no. 2 (1967): 192–206.

36. On the late nineteenth- and early twentieth-century international traffic in women, as well as the widespread public concern about the issue, see Bristow, *Prostitution and Prejudice*; Feldman, "Prostitution, the Alien Woman, and the Progressive Imagination, 1910–1914"; and Eileen Scully, "Pre-Cold War Traffic in Sexual Labor and Its Foes: Some Contemporary Lessons," in *Global Human Smuggling: Comparative Perspectives*, eds. David Kyle and Rey Koslowski (Baltimore: Johns Hopkins University Press, 2001), 74–106. For a look at international feminist efforts to combat sex trafficking in the interwar years, see Jessica R. Pliley, "Claims to Protection: The Rise and Fall of Feminist Abolitionism in the League of Nations' Committee on the Traffic in Women and Children, 1919–1936," *Journal of Women's History* 22, no. 4 (Winter 2010): 90–113.

37. W. A. Leonard, American Consul, Warsaw, to Secretary of State, May 6, 1926, file 55423-414, Entry 9, RG 85, NA.

38. Sworn statement of Daniel Lewis to Immigrant Inspector Isaac L. Smith, Miami, Florida, November 14, 1922, file 55166-31A, Entry 9, RG 85, NA.

39. Weiss Reports, March 16, 1925.

40. *CGI Annual Report* (1923), 18–19, 26; Ettinger, *Imaginary Lines*, 98–99; and Grace Peña Delgado, *Making the Chinese Mexican: Global Migration, Localism and Exclusion in the US-Mexico Borderlands* (Palo Alto: Stanford University Press, 2012), chap. 3. On the way legal clashes between Chinese immigrants and US immigration authorities shaped US law and policy more broadly, see Lucy E. Salyer, *Laws Harsh as Tigers: Chinese Immigrants and the Shaping of Modern Immigration Law* (Chapel Hill: University of North Carolina Press, 1995); and Erika Lee, *At America's Gates: Chinese Immigration during the Exclusion Era, 1882–1943* (Chapel

Hill: University of North Carolina Press, 2003), and "Enforcing the Borders: Chinese Exclusion Along the US Borders with Canada and Mexico, 1882–1924," *Journal of Amerian History* 89, no. 1 (June 2002): 54–86.

41. Joseph H. Wallis, Assistant Commissioner of Immigration, New Orleans, to Commissioner of Immigration, New Orleans, March 14, 1923, file 55166 31-A, Entry 9, RG 85, NA.

42. Some of the sources about immigrants smuggling in over the Canadian border also drew comparisons to the networks that helped African American slaves escape in the other direction: "Had it not been for the Underground Railroad of Civil war days, many a slave would never have reached his destination in the north. Were it not for a similar system in use today, many an alien would never successfully elude the immigration officers and cross the border from Canada into the United States." "Tales of Border Patrol Rival Those of Fiction," *Massena Observer*, February [n.d.], 1927, located in file of newspaper clippings on activities of Border Patrol from late 1920s and early 1930s, file 55598-452, Entry 9, RG 85, NA. Whether this parallel indicates sympathy for the migrants of the present, or contempt for the runaway slaves of the past, remains unclear.

43. In their exploration of contemporary human smuggling, sociologists David Kyle and John Dale observe that "[s]tate boundaries add to the value of any commodity needed across borders": see Kyle and Dale, "Smuggling the State Back In: Agents of Human Smuggling Reconsidered," in Kyle and Koslowski, eds., *Global Human Smuggling*, 49. The quota laws, by making national boundaries far less permeable to human traffic, thus greatly contributed to what Kyle and Dale call the "commodification of migration" ("Smuggling the State Back In," 49).

44. W. G. Watson, Jr., Deputy Special Collector to Secretary of Treasury, April 28, 1922, file 55166-31, Entry 9, RG 85, NA.

45. Weiss Reports, February 25, 1925. Similarly, when American Vice Consul Fletcher Warren told Weiss about Kessler, another Jewish smuggler of aliens and opium based in Havana, he gave the inspector a description he thought would allow him to pick out the smuggler in the saloon where he hung out: "He is 5'4," squatty, florid complexion, Jewish features, no beard, clean shaved, no glasses" (Weiss Reports, February 6, 1925).

46. For example, one document in the files of the US Department of State describes an alleged smuggler named Sam Stone, who was taken into custody by the New York City Police in 1932: "Stone refuses to say a word, being a shrewd, little Hebrew." [?] to Mrs Shipley, October 29, 1932, file 150.069 (Stone, Sam), Entry 702, Visa Division, Correspondence Regarding Immigration, 1910–39 (citations to this record subgroup hereafter as VD), General Records of the Department of State, Record Group 59 (citations to this record group hereafter as RG 59), NA.

47. *St. Lawrence Courier* (New York, n.d.), located in file of newspaper clippings on activities of Border Patrol from late 1920s and early 1930s, file 55598-452, Entry 9, RG 85, NA. An article in the aggressively nativist *Saturday Evening Post* ("Smuggling Aliens Across Our Borders," August 1, 1925) wrote in similar terms of the smuggling industry in Montreal: "Here smuggling has been organized and standardized. There exists ring upon ring—Greeks for the Greeks, Poles for the Poles, and so on. Each ring with its own system of signals, second and third line communications, friendly stations and secret runways."

48. Weiss Reports, February 4, 1925.

49. Report enclosed with letter from J. Vining Harris, Attorney at Law, Key West, Florida to Attorney General of the United States, August 10, 1922, file 55166-31, Entry 9, RG 85, NA.

50. There are some important exceptions to this. For details about Jewish journeys in

particular, e.g., see the following by Gur Alroey: "Bureaucracy, Agents and Swindlers," "And I Remained Alone in a Vast Land"; "Information, Decision, and Migration: Jewish Emigration from Europe in the Early Twentieth Century," *Immigrants and Minorities* 29, no. 1 (March 2011): 33–63; and "Out of the Shtetl: In the Footsteps of Eastern European Jewish Emigrants to America, 1900–1914," *Leidschrift*, Jaargang 21, no. 1 (2007), 92–122. See also Tobias Brinkmann, "Ort des Übergangs: Berlin als Schnittstelle der jüdischen Migration aus Osteuropa nach 1918," in *Transit und Transformation: Osteuropäisch-jüdische Migranten in Berlin, 1918–1939,* ed. Verena Dohrn and Gertrud Pickhan (Göttingen: Wallstein Verlag, 2010), 25–44, and " 'Travelling with Ballin': The Impact of American Immigration Policies on Jewish Transmigration within Central Europe, 1880–1914," *International Review of Social History* 53 (2008): 459–84; and Nadell, "En Route to the Promised Land," and "From Shtetl to Border: East European Jewish Emigrants and the 'Agents' System, 1868–1914"; as well as Zosa Szajkowski, "Sufferings of Jewish Emigrants to America in Transit through Germany," *Jewish Social Studies* 39 (1977): 105–16.

51. "A Life on the Run," Oral history of Phil Lutzky (hereafter Lutzky), 19, Small Collections, Jacob Rader Marcus Center of the American Jewish Archives, Hebrew Union College–Jewish Institute of Religion, Cincinnati (hereafter AJA).

52. For reports about how smugglers approached immigrants with offers of papers in Berlin and Warsaw, see the testimony of immigrants to Congress in US House Committee on Immigration and Naturalization, Hearings, *Private Relief Bills Regarding Irregular Admission Documents at Time of Entry,* 74th Cong., 2d Sess., May 26–28, 1936, 6–10, 21, 93, 102, 104, and 194. On such interactions in Warsaw, see also Lutzky, AJA.

53. Testimony of Leo Farber, July 13, 1926, file 150.069 (Zuckermann), VD, RG 59, NA. This document is enclosed together with a 1932 memo from the Department of State's Visa Office, which suggests that Zuckermann might still be "engaged in the manufacture of fraudulent travel documents."

54. House Committee on Immigration and Naturalization, Hearings, *Private Relief Bills Regarding Irregular Admission Documents,* 83.

55. Weiss Reports, February 4, 1925. Weiss is quoting Geza Horvath, a Hungarian informant.

56. Ibid.

57. File 55423–414, Entry 9, RG 85, NA.

58. Weiss Reports, February 2 and March 5, 1925.

59. "Cubans Arrest Americans; Woman Cabaret Operator Accused of Aiding Alien Smuggling," *New York Times,* September 13, 1929.

60. "Smuggling Aliens Across Our Borders," *Saturday Evening Post,* August 1, 1925.

61. Weiss Reports, February 6, 1925.

62. Sworn statement of Daniel Lewis to Immigrant Inspector Isaac L. Smith, Miami, Florida, November 14, 1922, file 55166–31A, Entry 9, RG 85, NA.

63. Ibid.

64. Joseph H. Wallis, Assistant Commissioner of Immigration, New Orleans, to Commissioner of Immigration, New Orleans, March 14, 1923 and June 11, 1924, files 55166–31A and B, Entry 9, RG 85, NA.

65. For officials' reports describing the porousness of the Canadian border, see, e.g., *CGI Annual Report* (1923), 25, and (1924), 14–16.

66. *CGI Annual Report* (1927), 16. And in 1928, e.g., Samuel Weisstein was apprehended in connection with an alien smuggling scheme that involved air travel. An immigration official in San Antonio writing his superior about the case explained that his office had received several reports about this mode of smuggling in recent months. Erskine P. Ezzell, Senior Patrol Inspector Acting in Charge, San Antonio, to District Director, Immigration Service, San Antonio, August 15, 1928, file 55423–414, Entry 9, RG 85, NA.

67. "Plan to Watch Border More Closely—Liquor, Alien Problem Gets Investigation," *Buffalo Courier-Express*, July 15, 1927.

68. Kyle and Dale, "Smuggling the State Back In," 33. Patrick Ettinger (*Imaginary Lines*, 108–14) observes that this was true in earlier eras as well, when many of those entering illegally were simply trying to avoid drawing attention to themselves as they crossed loosely guarded borders, hoping to be seen as locals whom officials still had little interest in screening.

69. Craig Robertson, *The Passport in America: The History of a Document* (New York: Oxford University Press, 2010), 39.

70. L. J. Keena, American Consul General, to Secretary of State, January 16, 1923, file 55423–414, Entry 9, RG 85, NA.

71. H. A. Mintzer, Immigrant Inspector, Report to Commissioner of Ellis Island, January 24, 1924, file 55423–414, Entry 9, RG 85, NA.

72. Accusation Act, Prosecuting Office of the Circuit Court at Rzeszow, July 18, 1932, enclosed with J. Klahr Huddle, American Consul General, Warsaw, to Secretary of State, April 10, 1933, file 55423–414, Entry 9, RG 85, NA.

73. Henry H. Morgan, American Consul General, Buenos Aires, to Secretary of State, July 14, 1924, file 55398–2A, Entry 9, RG 85, NA. Feri Weiss reported on similar schemes in Cuba. Weiss Reports, February 10, 1925.

74. Levine, *Tropical Diaspora*, 60.

75. Case of Gregorio Deitz Cajan and Salla Feigel Lapides, 811.11, Volume 545, Consular Posts, Havana, Cuba, Entry 417, Department of State Records–Foreign Service Posts, Record Group 84, NA-MD.

76. "Federal Aides Held in Immigrant Fraud," *New York Times*, August 2, 1931; and "Indicts 17 in Plot to Smuggle Aliens, *New York Times*, November 28, 1931.

77. *Annual Report of the Attorney General of the United States* (1935), 65; (1936), 70; and (1937), 88; "1,000,000 Mulcted from Aliens Here," *New York Times*, April 10, 1935; and "Alien Frauds Laid to Ex-Official," *New York Times*, June 26, 1935. One of the scheme's leaders, Benjamin Bergman of Brooklyn, turned up dead of poison after he provided authorities with information about the ring. "Exposer of Racket Dies in a Mystery," *New York Times*, June 6, 1935.

78. "Alien Frauds Laid to Ex-Federal Aide," *New York Times*, Oct. 9, 1935; "Jailed in Alien Fraud," *New York Times*, July 29, 1936; and file 150.069-Fried, Louis, and file 150.069-Rossdale, Albert, VD, RG 59, NA.

79. "Convicted in Alien Case," *New York Times*, June 15, 1929.

80. W. F. Watkins to John Barber, Feb. 11, 1938, file 55560/559-C, entry 9, RG 85, NA. On the preexamination policy, see Edward Prince Hutchinson, *Legislative History of American Policy,*

1798–1965 (Philadelphia: University of Pennsylvania Press, 1981), 564–65; and Ngai, *Impossible Subjects*, 84–87.

81. "'Advisor' to Aliens Indicted by US Jury," *New York Times*, May 6, 1939; and "'Agent' Convicted in an Alien Fraud," *New York Times*, June 14, 1939.

82. Weiss Reports, April 4, 1925.

83. Weiss Reports, February 13, 1925, and April 4, 1925.

84. "Smuggling Aliens Across Our Borders," *Saturday Evening Post*, August 1, 1925.

85. Mrs. Schwartz to Immigrant Inspector Carlos Melick, July 17, 1934, enclosed in Carlos Melick, Immigrant Inspector, Havana, to Commissioner of Immigration and Naturalization Service, Washington DC, July 18, 1934, file 55875–827, Accession 58A734, RG 85, NA. Melick, in his own letter to his superiors, vouched for Mrs. Schwartz's impression: "It might appear from reading the report that Mrs. Schwartz is slightly hysterical," he wrote, "but I can assure you that she is not. The report will give you some indication of Castells' method of intimidating such 'clients' as he may have."

86. Weiss Reports, February 2, 1925.

87. "Border Patrol Wages Grim War on Alien Running," *Buffalo Courier-Express*, November 6, 1927.

88. Weiss Reports, January 11, 1925.

89. Weiss Reports, April 4, 1925.

90. "Alien 'Racket' Source Traced by Garsson," *New York Times*, September 28, 1931.

91. Weiss Reports, February 13, 1925.

92. For an insightful exploration of the blurred boundaries between organized crime and legitimate business during this era more generally, see Ruth, *Inventing the Public Enemy*, chap. 2.

93. Weiss Reports, February 10, 1925.

94. Sworn statement of Daniel Lewis to Immigrant Inspector Isaac L. Smith, Miami, Florida, November 14, 1922, file 55166–31A, Entry 9, RG 85, NA.

95. "Joseph Rabinsky (Rubinski)," Report (n.d.), file 55423–414, Entry 9, RG 85, NA.

96. Report of Immigrant Inspector Mintzer to Commissioner of Ellis Island, January 14, 1924, file 55423–414, Entry 9, RG 85, NA. Assistant District Attorney Isidor Neuwirth told Mintzer that about four thousand packages were being held in Russia because there were no funds to pay duty on them; Harry L. Epstein, Secretary of the Russian American Relief Package Forwarding Company, Inc., had apparently pocketed money from shippers "for his own needs and comforts." There was a warrant out for Epstein's arrest, but Epstein, Neuwirth explained, "had fled and is now believed to be residing at an unknown address in Pittsburgh, PA."

97. Weiss, e.g., wrote of one of the smugglers (whom he identified as "Paulas," a "Yugo-Slav type") he contacted during his undercover work in Havana: "He asked me if I was married, and when I said yes, he wanted to now [*sic*] where my wife is, and I told him I left her in Vienna, Austria. He wanted to know in what street she lived, and showed a remarkable knowledge of all of European capitals, and a fluency in German and French that was remarkable for a cut-throat which he really is. He told me he speaks Slav and Italian as well, or better even." Weiss Reports, February 13, 1925.

98. Weiss Reports, March 16, 1925. Weiss also notes that Jamieson was referred to as the "Judeo Errante," or "Wandering Jew"—an ironic appellation that highlighted the fact that

Jamieson, who stayed put and profited nicely by his alien smuggling business, was anything but a "wandering Jew" of the desperate sort whose desire to get to the United States financed his Havana lifestyle, even while it suggested that Jamieson's business was a new twist on a familiar Jewish history of migration, exile, and diaspora.

99. *CGI Annual Report* (1927), 15 and 18.

100. The creation of "paper relatives" was, as with many of the smuggling and fraud techniques used by Europeans, an established strategy of Chinese immigrants. See Estelle Lau, *Paper Families: Identity, Immigration Administration, and Chinese Exclusion* (Durham: Duke University Press, 2006); and Adam McKeown, *Melancholy Order: Asian Migration and the Globalization of Borders* (New York: Columbia University Press, 2008), and, "Ritualization of Regulation: The Enforcement of Chinese Exclusion in the United States and China," *American Historical Review* 108, no. 2 (April 2003): 377–403.

101. Correspondence related to the case of John Gelabert and Jose Bernardo Fernandez-Valdes, file 811.4, Havana vol. 532, Entry 417, Department of State Records–Foreign Service Posts, Record Group 84, NA-MD.

102. "Six Indicted in Plot to Smuggle Aliens," *New York Times*, February 24, 1930; "25 Held in Poland for Visa Forgeries," *New York Times*, February 28, 1930; "Alien Smuggler Gets 2-Year Term," *New York Times*, May 30, 1930; Bristow, *Prostitution and Prejudice*, 294–95; and file 150.069 (Baskin, Morris), VD, RG 59, NA. During 1929 apparently in Warsaw alone fifteen such marriages were performed. Bristow says that in at least some of these cases, the women disappeared, trafficked by Baskin into the US prostitution market. Some of those who married Baskin really thought, it appears, that they were marrying him as a "proxy" for a specific young man in the United States; others clearly realized they were committing fraud. The authorities themselves seemed often baffled by what to do about the widespread phenomenon of immigration marriages. In the 1930s, for instance, reports from US consulates in Canada expressed suspicion—particularly of Jews—of many of those applying for visas on the basis of marriage to a US citizen, but ultimately dropped the matter. See file 150.069 (Marriages), VD, RG 59, NA. For records of Baskin's trial, see also case file 26606, Records of the US District Court for the Eastern District, National Archives and Records Administration–Northeast Region (New York City).

103. "History and Status of Joseph Rabinsky (Joseph Rubinski)," Report (n.d.), file 55423-414, Entry 9, RG 85, NA.

104. Carlos Melick, Immigrant Inspector, Havana, to Commissioner of Immigration and Naturalization Service, Washington DC, July 18, 1934, file 55875-827, Accession 58A734, RG 85, NA. Weiss also reported that smuggling rings in Cuba involved "not only the low-down water-rats but also big financial backers . . . important politicians . . . customs officials . . . the Captain of the port . . . and only God knows what not and who not." Weiss Reports, March 4, 1925.

105. Weiss Reports, February 10, 1925.

106. Weiss Reports, February 19, 1925.

107. "Indicts 17 in Plot to Smuggle Aliens, *New York Times*, November 28, 1931. Like alien smuggling more generally, such corruption had historical roots in earlier eras. For the involvement of US officials in late nineteenth- and early twentieth-century trafficking of Chinese immigrants to the US from Mexico, see Delgado, *Making the Chinese Mexican*, 90–93; and Ettinger, *Imaginary Lines*, 115–16.

108. F. T. F. Dumont, American Consul General, Havana, to Secretary of State, February 14, 1933, file 150.069 (Kohn, Bernard), VD, RG 59, NA.

109. "Vodka Plays Part in Visa Fraud Case," *New York Times*, May 28, 1930. Hall received probation, living in Washington, DC, and working, his probation officer reported, at a laundry. This was a far cry from his original ambition to leave the foreign service and set up in business, which was the financial reason, he explained to the court, he had been attracted to the smuggling kickbacks in the first place. Order for Discharge of Probationer/Consent of the United States Attorney/Report of the Probation Officer, November 29, 1933, case no. 26606, Eastern District Court, New York, National Archives and Records Administration–Northeast Region (New York City). Extensive documentation on the Baskin case was also kept on file by the State Department in Washington, DC. See file 150.069 (Baskin, Morris), VD, RG 59, NA.

110. Report enclosed with letter from J. Vining Harris, Attorney at Law, Key West, Florida, to Attorney General of the United States, August 10, 1922, file 55166–31, Entry 9, RG 85, NA.

111. "Nine Indicted Here as Fake Visa Ring," *New York Times*, March 5, 1930.

112. House Committee on Immigration and Naturalization, Hearings, *Private Relief Bills Regarding Irregular Admission Documents*, 105.

113. Weiss Reports, January 31, 1925. Of course, this appellation is also interesting for the way it gets at the fact that Jews, as a nonnational group—one of the main reasons they were endangered in eastern Europe and looking to leave—had no consul.

114. L. J. Keena, American Consul General, Warsaw, to Secretary of State, April 11, 1923, and "Joseph Rabinsky (Rubinski)," Report (n.d.), file 55423–414, Entry 9, RG 85, NA.

115. Weiss Reports, February 12, 1925.

116. Weiss Reports, February 13, 1925.

117. Joseph Shahan, Final Report on Refugees Work in Habana, June 6, 1922, 7–8, microfilm reel 36, AR 21/32, Archives of the Joint Distribution Committee, New York City.

CHAPTER FOUR

1. "A Life on the Run," Oral History of Phil Lutzky (hereafter Lutzky), Small Collections, Jacob Rader Marcus Center of the American Jewish Archives, Cincinnati Campus, Hebrew Union College Jewish Institute of Religion (hereafter AJA).

2. Martin Zielonka to Archibald Marx, March 21, 1923, microfilm reel 600b, Zielonka, Martin, Correspondence and Reports while in Mexico, 1921–33 (hereafter Zielonka Correspondence), AJA.

3. US House Committee on Immigration and Naturalization, Hearings, *Private Relief Bills Regarding Irregular Admission Documents at Time of Entry*, 74th Cong., 2d Sess., May 26–28, 1936, 81–95.

4. Files 55559–237 and 55559–238, Accession 60A600, Records of the US Immigration and Naturalization Service (citations to this record group hereafter as RG 85), National Archives Building, Washington, DC (hereafter NA).

5. For this shift toward policing borders by means of documents during and after World War I, see John Torpey, "The Great War and the Birth of the Modern Passport System," in *Documenting Individual Identity: The Development of State Practices in the Modern World*,

ed. Jane Caplan and John Torpey (Princeton: Princeton University Press, 2001), 256–70, and *The Invention of the Passport: Surveillance, Citizenship and the State* (Cambridge: Cambridge University Press, 2000), 111–21.

6. Martin Zielonka, "The B'nai B'rith in Mexico: A Summary of Results," February 1927, Zielonka Correspondence, microfilm reel 600b, AJA.

7. Immigration Act of May 26, 1924 (43 Stat. 153)

8. Werner Senator, "Report on the Work of the United Evacuation Committee," May 25, 1926, 31, microfilm reel 26, AR 21/32, Archives of the Joint Distribution Committee, New York City (hereafter JDC).

9. For an insightful analysis of the role of information in Jews' decisions to migrate in an earlier period, see Gur Alroey, "Information, Decision, and Migration: Jewish Emigration from Europe in the Early Twentieth Century," *Immigrants and Minorities* 29, no. 1 (March 2011): 33–63.

10. "A vikhtige bekantmakhung fun 'HIAS' vegn keneder imigreyshn gezets" [An important bulletin from HIAS about the Canadian immigration law], *Forverts*, October 4, 1921.

11. Isaac Asofsky to S. Dingold, July 8, 1926, *Day-Morning Journal* Records, Record Group 639, folder 240, Archives of the YIVO Institute for Jewish Research, New York (hereafter YIVO).

12. For example, there was a Yiddish paper in Warsaw called *Der Yudisher Emigrant* [The Jewish Emigrant]. On the paper's influence before World War I, see Alroey, "Information, Decision, and Migration," 40–41.

13. Werner Senator, "Report on the Work of the United Evacuation Committee," 19, JDC.

14. Mark Wischnitzer, *Visas to Freedom: The History of HIAS* (Cleveland: World Publishing Company, 1956), 123.

15. "Zu den Gerüchten über Einwanderungsmöglichkeiten in Honduras" [Regarding the rumors about immigration possibilities in Honduras], *Di Yidishe Emigratsiye/Die Jüdische Emigration* [The Jewish Emigration], October 1928.

16. Frances F. Lipman to Vera Shimberg, January 14, 1926, microfilm reel MKM 15.174, HIAS papers, Record Group 245 (citations to this record group hereafter as HP), YIVO.

17. Cecelia Razovsky to United Evacuation Committee, December 28, 1925, microfilm reel MKM 15.174, HP, YIVO.

18. Cecelia Razovsky to United Evacuation Committee, January 21, 1926, microfilm reel MKM 15.174, HP, YIVO.

19. District Supervisor, United Jewish Aid Societies of Brooklyn, to Martin Zielonka, September 2, 1921, Zielonka Correspondence, microfilm reel 600, AJA.

20. Author's interview with Ester Reiter, January 23, 2002.

21. Author's interview with Joan Friedman, January 22, 2002.

22. Thinking of migration, legal or illegal, in family terms may have been particularly the case for Jews, whose migration had always been an overwhelmingly family one.

23. In a similar vein, Inspector Feri Weiss, reporting on a scene he witnessed at the dock in Havana, explained that legal Jewish immigrants expected their children to follow illegally later on: "Early this morning . . . we were on the Ward Line Dock to watch the SS 'Orizaba.' I mixed with the Jews and Hungarians, and Mitchell was watching the gangways and baggage shoots. . . .

I learned from their conversation that they had obtained visas through the efforts of their family and friends in America. Most of these aliens were broken down, old Jews, apparently fathers and mothers of Americanized children. At the Consulate we learned afterward that visaes had been issued to them. . . . Their children were all crying on the dock, and they were being encouraged by the elders not to cry as soon they will get a chance to follow them—apparently under the impression that they will be smuggled in as they are young and can stand the ordeal of a disagreeable ocean trip." Inspector Feri Weiss, Report to W. W. Husband, Commissioner General of Immigration, February 7, 1925, file 55166-31ex, Accession 58A734, RG 85, NA. Citations to all documents in this file hereafter as Weiss Reports.

24. US House, *Private Relief Bills Regarding Irregular Admission Documents*, 84. It is worth noting that family concerns about migration likely trumped not only secular law in immigration matters, but perhaps Jewish law as well, if the example of the Reiter family's desire for Chaim to "marry" his own sister is any indication.

25. Robert M. Levine, *Tropical Diaspora: The Jewish Experience in Cuba* (Gainesville: University Press of Florida, 1993), 36.

26. Report of Joseph Marcus, January 21, 1921, 18, microfilm reel 36, AR 21/32, JDC.

27. Joseph Roth, *The Wandering Jews: The Classic Portrait of a Vanished People*, trans. Michael Hofmann (New York: W. W. Norton, 2001), 82.

28. Ibid., 57–58.

29. Ibid., 58–59.

30. For a detailed description of Jewish migrants' journeys from eastern Europe to western Europe, including migrants' use of illegal means to cross borders, see the following articles by Gur Alroey: "Bureaucracy, Agents and Swindlers: Hardships Faced by Russian Jewish Emigrants in the Early Twentieth Century," *Studies in Contemporary Jewry* 19 (2003): 214–31; "And I Remained Alone in a Vast Land: Women in the Great Jewish Migration from Eastern Europe," *Jewish Social Studies* 12, no. 3 (Spring/Summer 2006): 39–72; "Information, Decision, and Migration"; and "Out of the Shtetl: In the Footsteps of Eastern European Jewish Emigrants to America, 1900–1914," *Leidschrift*, Jaargang 21, no. 1 (2007): 92–122. See also Tobias Brinkmann, "Ort des Übergangs: Berlin als Schnittstelle der jüdischen Migration aus Osteuropa nach 1918," in *Transit und Transformation: Osteuropäisch-jüdische Migranten in Berlin, 1918–1939*, ed. Verena Dohrn and Gertrud Pickhan (Göttingen: Wallstein Verlag, 2010), 25–44, and " 'Travelling with Ballin': The Impact of American Immigration Policies on Jewish Transmigration within Central Europe, 1880–1914, *International Review of Social History* 53 (2008): 459–84; Pamela S. Nadell, "From Shtetl to Border: East European Jewish Emigrants and the 'Agents' System, 1868–1914," in *Studies in the American Jewish Experience*, vol. 2, ed. Jacob R. Marcus and Abraham J. Peck (Lanham: University Press of America, 1984), 49–77, and "En Route to the Promised Land," in *We Are Leaving Mother Russia*, ed. Kerry M. Olitzky (Cincinnati: American Jewish Archives, 1990), 11–24; Zosa Szajkowski, "Sufferings of Jewish Emigrants to America in Transit through Germany," *Jewish Social Studies* 39 (1977): 105–16; and Jack Wertheimer, *Unwelcome Strangers: East European Jews in Imperial Germany* (New York: Oxford University Press, 1987), 13–15.

31. Carrie Davidson, *Out of Endless Yearnings: A Memoir of Israel Davidson* (New York: Bloch Publishing Company, 1946), 13.

32. Lutzky, 28.

33. Brinkmann, "Ort des Übergangs," 36, and "Travelling with Ballin," 481; and Michael R. Marrus, *The Unwanted: European Refugees in the Twentieth Century* (New York: Oxford University Press, 1985), 70–71, and 91–96.

34. US House, *Private Relief Bills Regarding Irregular Admission Documents*, 41.

35. Ibid., 87.

36. Ibid., 15.

37. Ibid., 51.

38. Ibid. That others avoided the naturalization process, or other interactions with government authorities, because of their illegal entry bears out this line of reasoning. Sidney Rabinovich's father, who crossed over from Canada illegally, never naturalized, though it bothered him not to be able to vote. Author's interview with Sidney Rabinovich, February 18, 2002. Similarly, M. Kusnetz, who also immigrated illegally to the United States from Canada, writes in her memoir that she did not want to give her employer personal data requested by the newly created Social Security Administration in the 1930s, fearing that her illegal entry would come to light. Autobiography of M. Kusnetz, American Autobiographies, Record Group 102, YIVO.

39. On these new "remote control" processes, see chapter 2, note 106.

40. US House, *Private Relief Bills Regarding Irregular Admission Documents*, 186.

41. Ibid., 184.

42. "Idishe imigrantn geratevet fun zinkendn shifl un vern arestirt ven zey viln zikh araynshugln keyn amerike" [Jewish immigrants rescued from sinking ship and arrested as they are trying to smuggle themselves into America], *Forverts*, May 14, 1931. The migrant Mordecai Freilich wrote the piece anonymously. See file Mordecai Freilich, Genealogy Collection, Record Group 126, YIVO. Thanks to Daniel Soyer for bringing this file to my attention.

43. Quoted in Matthew Frye Jacobson, *Barbarian Virtues: The United States Encounters Foreign Peoples at Home and Abroad, 1976–1917* (New York: Hill and Wang, 2000), 201. For a discussion of European and other immigrants' strategies of "passing" in order to cross the border in earlier eras, see Patrick Ettinger, *Imaginary Lines: Border Enforcement and the Origins of Undocumented Immigration, 1882–1930* (Austin: University of Texas Press, 2009), 111–18. For Chinese strategies of disguise and passing to get across the border during the exclusion era, see Erika Lee, "Enforcing the Borders: Chinese Exclusion along the US Borders with Canada and Mexico, 1882–1924," *Journal of Amerian History* 89, no. 1 (June 2002): 61–62.

44. Gayle Wald, *Crossing the Line: Racial Passing in Twentieth-Century U.S. Literature and Culture* (Durham: Duke University Press, 2000), 6. See also Elaine K. Ginsburg, ed. *Passing and the Fictions of Identity* (Durham: Duke University Press, 1996).

45. Judith Butler, *Gender Trouble* (New York: Routledge, 1990).

46. Some of the most important of such studies include Eric Lott, *Love and Theft, Blackface Minstrelsy and the American Working Class* (New York: Oxford University Press, 1993); David R. Roediger, *The Wages of Whiteness: Race and the Making of the American Working Class* (New York: Verso, 1991); and Alexander Saxton, *The Rise and Fall of the White Republic: Class, Politics and Mass Culture in Nineteenth-Century America* (London: Verso, 1990).

47. Michael Omi and Howard Winant, *Racial Formation in the United States: From the 1960s to the 1990s*, 2d ed. (New York: Routledge, 1994); Michael Alexander, *Jazz-Age Jews*

(Princeton: Princeton University Press, 2001), part III; Michael Rogin, *Blackface, White Noise: Jewish Immigrants in the Hollywood Melting Pot* (Berkeley: University of California Press, 1996).

48. Adam McKeown thus makes the case that the "liminality" of illegal Chinese immigrants crossing the border by fraudulent means followed them into their lives in America, barred as they were, with their fake identities, from "incorporation into American society . . . [T]he experience marked the Chinese as suspicious, illegitimate, and fraudulent, leaving them with the skeleton of a social identity." McKeown, "Ritualization of Regulation: The Enforcement of Chinese Exclusion in the United States and China," *American Historical Review* 108, no. 2 (April 2003): 402.

49. Isaac L. Smith to District Director, Immigration Service, Jacksonville, Florida, January 24, 1927, file 55166–31H, Entry 9, RG 85, NA.

50. Commissioner of New Orleans to Commissioner-General of Immigration, January 21, 1927, file 55166–31H, Entry 9, RG 85, NA.

51. "Smuggling Aliens Across Our Borders," *Saturday Evening Post*, August 1, 1925.

52. Patrol Inspector Henry Durant to Inspector in Charge, Niagara Falls, New York, September 25, 1924, file 53990–160B, Accession 60A600, RG 85, NA.

53. "Alien 'Gate Crashers' Still Pour in Over Our Frontiers," *New York Times*, June 19, 1927.

54. H. R. Landis to Commissioner General of Immigration, October 1, 1925, file 52730–40C, Entry 9, RG 85, NA.

55. "The Higher Bootlegging—Assisting Immigrants," *Literary Digest*, April 11, 1925.

56. "Alien 'Gate Crashers' Still Pour in Over Our Frontiers," *New York Times*, June 19, 1927.

57. Weiss Reports, February 4, 1925.

58. Weiss Reports, February 26, 1925.

59. Weiss Reports, February 26, 1925.

60. "Tales of Border Patrol Rival Those of Fiction," *Massena Observer* (New York), February [n.d.], 1927, located in file of newspaper clippings on activities of Border Patrol from late 1920s and early 1930s, file 55598–452, Entry 9, RG 85, NA.

61. Weiss Reports, January 24, 1925.

62. Weiss Reports, February 9, 1925.

63. Hearing of Gustav Kiene before Board of Special Inquiry, Ellis Island, March 2, 1927, file 55476–151B, Entry 9, RG 85, NA. For compelling analyses of similar interactions between Chinese immigrants and US immigration officials, see Estelle Lau, *Paper Families: Identity, Immigration Administration, and Chinese Exclusion* (Durham: Duke University Press, 2006); and McKeown, "Ritualization of Regulation," and *Melancholy Order: Asian Migration and the Globalization of Borders* (New York: Columbia University Press, 2008), esp. chap. 10.

64. Hearing of Gustav Kiene before Board of Special Inquiry, Ellis Island, March 2, 1927, file 55476–151B, Entry 9, RG 85, NA.

65. Inspector in Charge, Winnipeg, to Commissioner General of Immigration, January 11, 1924, file 53990–160A, Accession 60A600, RG 85, NA. On the highly developed systems of "coaching" for Chinese illegal immigrants, see McKeown, *Melancholy Order*, 277–81.

66. Hearing of Theodor Rosenberg before Board of Special Inquiry, Ellis Island, December 28, 1926, file 55476–151B, Entry 9, RG 85, NA.

67. Both historians and literary scholars have explored such tropes of the greenhorn's gaffes and the greenhorn's transformation into an American via language and clothing. See, e.g., Elizabeth Ewen, *Immigrant Women in the Land of Dollars: Life and Culture on the Lower East Side, 1890–1927* (New York: Monthly Review Press, 1985), especially chap. 4; and Laura Browder, *Slippery Characters: Ethnic Impersonators and American Identities* (Chapel Hill: University of North Carolina Press, 2000).

68. Author's interview with Martin Stein, January 17, 2002.

69. Martin Zielonka to Archibald Marx, March 21, 1923, microfilm reel 600b, Zielonka Correspondence, AJA.

70. Lutzky, 11.

71. Of course, as in the United States, there were also significant shifts in eastern Europe as to what "looking Jewish" might mean, in particular with the processes of urbanization and assimilation. Jews speaking the local languages and not adhering to traditional modes of dress were not necessarily identifiable in Poland or Russia any more than they were elsewhere.

72. Author's interview with Martin Stein, January 17, 2002.

73. Roth, *Wandering Jews*, 99–100.

74. Lutzky, 14.

75. US House, *Private Relief Bills Regarding Irregular Admission Documents*, 6.

76. Author's interview with Ethel Seid, January 27, 2002.

77. Report of M. A. Pitt, Immigrant Inspector, May 31, 1935, file 55879, Accession 58A734, RG 85, NA.

78. Autobiography of M. Kusnetz, American Autobiographies, Record Group 102, YIVO.

79. "Idishe imigrantn geratevet fun zinkendn shifl" [Jewish immigrants rescued from sinking ship], *Forverts*, May 14, 1931.

CHAPTER FIVE

1. For contemporary accounts of the passage of the law, see "History of Spectacular Battle Against Michigan Alien Registration Bill," *Detroit Jewish Chronicle*, December 11, 1931; and Maurice Sugar, "Michigan Passes the 'Spolansky Act,'" *Nation*, July 8, 1931. Thomas A. Klug also recounts the story of the law's passage in his article, "Labor Market Politics in Detroit: The Curious Case of the 'Spolansky Act' of 1931, *Michigan Historical Review 14* (Spring 1988): 1–32. See also Christopher H. Johnson, *Maurice Sugar: Law, Labor and the Left in Detroit, 1912–1950* (Detroit: Wayne State University Press, 1988), 118–19. The law is quoted in Arrowsmith v. Voorhies, 55 F.2d 310 (E.D. Michig. 1931).

2. "Ruling by Attorney-General Voorhies as to Legality and Constitutionality of Alien Registration Measure," *Detroit Jewish Chronicle*, May 29, 1931. Indeed, the paper also reported that a delegation had tried to meet with the governor to convince him not to sign the bill, but the governor cancelled the meeting.

3. "Sponsor Bill in New Jersey," *Detroit Jewish Chronicle*, June 12, 1931. The paper had also reported that twenty-one other states were about to sponsor such bills. "State is Enjoined from Enforcing Registration Bill; Hearing Before Three Judge Court Set for June 9," *Detroit Jewish Chronicle*, June 5, 1931.

4. Klug is an important exception to this scholarly neglect. However, his insightful article

about the battle over the registration law is written primarily as an investigation into local and regional labor history, rather than into larger questions surrounding immigration, foreignness, and Americanness during these years. Klug, "Labor Market Politics in Detroit."

5. There had been, in the eighteenth and nineteenth centuries, scattered attempts at and proposals for general registration of aliens. The Naturalization Act of 1798, e.g., contained a registration requirement for "free white aliens," but this provision apparently was never enforced and the law was repealed four years later. See Gerald L. Neuman, *Strangers to the Constitution: Immigrants, Borders, and Fundamental Law* (Princeton: Princeton University Press, 1996), 41. It was, however, really first in the era of mass restriction and governmental control that such proposals gained broad support among legislators and the public. See Edward Prince Hutchinson, *Legislative History of American Immigration Policy, 1798–1965* (Philadelphia: University of Pennsylvania Press, 1981), 540–41. There was one other pre–World War II alien registration policy that applied to all aliens, one instituted by Minnesota's Commission of Public Safety issued during World War I. But though also a registration measure, in practice this was a very different kind of policy from that implemented in Michigan. It was a temporary measure (not legislative but rather implemented by the commission), aimed not so much at flushing out illegal immigrants as at tracking those whose wartime loyalty might be in question. Moreover, while it required aliens to register, it did not require them to carry or show special identification. See Carl H. Chrislock, *Watchdog of Loyalty: The Minnesota Commission of Public Safety During World War I* (St. Paul: Minnesota Historical Society Press, 1991), chaps. 3 and 13.

6. See Max Kohler, "A Dangerous Project," in Max Kohler, *Immigration and Aliens in the United States* (New York: Bloch Publishing, 1936), 363–88; originally published as a pamphlet entitled "The Registration of Aliens, Voluntary or Compulsory, a Dangerous Project" (New York: League for American Citizenship, 1930).

7. James R. Barrett and David Roediger, "Inbetween Peoples: Race, Nationality and the 'New Immigrant' Working Class," *Journal of American Ethnic History* 16, no. 3 (Spring 1997): 3–44; Eric L. Goldstein, *The Price of Whiteness: Jews, Race, and American Identity* (Princeton: Princeton University Press, 2006), chap. 6; Matthew Frye Jacobson, *Whiteness of a Different Color: European Immigrants and the Alchemy of Race* (Cambridge: Harvard University Press, 1998); and David R. Roediger, *Working Toward Whiteness: How America's Immigrants Became White* (New York: Basic Books, 2005).

8. See, e.g., Ian F. Haney-López, *White by Law: The Legal Construction of Race* (New York: New York University Press, 1996); and Mae M. Ngai, *Impossible Subjects: Aliens and the Making of Modern America* (Princeton: Princeton University Press, 2004).

9. Eric Arnesen, "Whiteness and the Historians' Imagination," *International Labor and Working-Class History* 60 (Fall 2001): 3–32; and Eric Foner, "Response to Eric Arnesen," in Arnesen, "Whiteness and the Historians' Imagination," 57–60; and Thomas A. Guglielmo, *White on Arrival: Italians, Race, Color and Power in Chicago, 1890–1945* (New York: Oxford University Press, 2003).

10. Guglielmo, *White on Arrival*; Haney-López, *White by Law*; Ngai, *Impossible Subjects*; and Roediger, *Working Toward Whiteness*, 59–64.

11. Jacobson, *Whiteness of a Different Color*, 95.

12. Francisco Balderrama and Raymond Rodriguez, *Decade of Betrayal: Mexican Repatriation in the 1930s* (Albuquerque: University of New Mexico Press, 1995), 49–71, and 97–125;

Abraham Hoffman, *Unwanted Mexican Americans in the Great Depression: Repatriation Pressures, 1929–1939* (Tucson: University of Arizona Press, 1974), 33–35, and 120–21; George Sánchez, *Becoming Mexican American: Ethnicity, Culture, and Identity in Chicano Los Angeles, 1900–1945* (New York: Oxford University Press, 1993), chap. 10; and Zaragosa Vargas, *Proletarians of the North: A History of Mexican Industrial Workers in Detroit and the Midwest, 1917–1933* (Berkeley: University of California Press, 1999), chap. 5.

13. Mae M. Ngai's remarkable work, *Impossible Subjects: Aliens and the Making of Modern America*, on immigration policy in the era of the quota system is an important exception, for she examines both the discourses of alienness and of race, arguing that the quota laws and the ways the US government implemented them helped construct "a white American race, in which persons of European descent shared a common whiteness distinct from those deemed to be not white" (*Impossible Subjects*, 25), such as Mexicans and Asians. Nevertheless, she focuses primarily on how this process worked from the perspective of the state, leaving open for exploration the question of how foreignness and alienness took on new meanings for ethnic communities during this era. David R. Roediger's *Working Toward Whiteness: How America's Immigrants Became White* is another notable exception; he makes the case that the "new immigrants" of southern and eastern Europe continued to be in fraught relation to both whiteness and Americanness during the interwar period. I am indebted to his insightful reading of the dynamics of race and immigration during the era, though the extent to which the "new immigrants" continued to be defined as *alien*, and not only as "off-white," remains largely outside the realm of his analysis. See especially Roediger, *Working Toward Whiteness*, chap. 5. Thomas A. Guglielmo's impressive work, *White on Arrival: Italians, Race, Color and Power in Chicago, 1890–1945*, meanwhile, examines the ways Italian American communities fell under suspicion even while Italians were considered to be "white"; nevertheless, his work suggests that after the passage of the immigration quotas, immigration and foreignness in and of themselves largely ceased to be important issues in this regard.

14. Roediger similarly stresses that the path to whiteness for the "new immigrants" was not always obvious to historical actors at the time, however much it may seem clear in retrospect. Roediger, *Working Toward Whiteness*, 145.

15. Ngai makes a similar argument, though her focus is primarily on the increasingly common administrative practice of deportation rather than on alien registration. Ngai, *Impossible Subjects*, 57–64.

16. Mae Ngai, "The Architecture of Race in American Immigration Law: A Reexamination of the Immigration Act of 1924," *Journal of American History* (June 1999): 67–92.

17. Hutchinson, *Legislative History of American Immigration Policy*, 196–210; and Kohler, "Ameliorating the Quota Laws," in Kohler, *Immigration and Aliens*, 32–45.

18. Hutchinson, *Legislative History of American Immigration Policy*, 203 and 471. During this period, nonquota immigration also rose sharply, in part not only because of these limited successes in liberalizing the laws but also because of European immigrants' own increased tendency to naturalize, newly critical for those who wanted to bring over their close relatives but could only do so as citizens. See Ngai, *Impossible Subjects*, 66–67.

19. Roger Daniels, *Coming to America: A History of Immigration and Ethnicity in American Life* (New York: HarperCollins, 1990), 295.

20. See, e.g., "Shlogt imigrantn, ratevet amerike!" [Defeat immigrants, rescue America!], *Tog*,

December 10, 1931; and "Immigrants No Longer Wanted," *Detroit Jewish Chronicle*, August 21, 1931.

21. US Bureau of the Census, *Historical Statistics of the United States, Colonial Times to 1957* (Washington, DC: Government Printing Office, 1960), 65. The number of aliens cited at the time was often higher. Both Max Kohler ("Why Registration of Aliens is Inadvisable," in *Immigration and Aliens*) and the *Saturday Evening Post* ("Alien Guest Cards," January 24, 1931), for instance, invoked the figure of seven million.

22. In 1925, e.g., the *Detroit Jewish Chronicle* ("Another Professor on the Alien," *Detroit Jewish Chronicle*, December 18, 1925) quoted the writings of Harvard professor and well-known restrictionist Robert DeCourcy Ward: "We have long ago reached the saturation point where alien Immigration has brought about dangers to the very existence of our country. The thoughts of millions of people have been warped and twisted into evil shapes by the teachings of many of these aliens, who have not become Americanized in thought and act. Millions of them are foreign in sentiment and read only some one or more or the 1,200 papers printed in foreign language."

23. The subheading read: "Commissioner [General of Immigration] Hull Finds That the Immigration Law, If Strictly Enforced, Would Deport Many People Who Are Well Established in American Life" ("2,000,000 Aliens Are Here Without the Right to Stay," *New York Times*, July 26, 1925). For other estimates, see "Smuggled Aliens Are Still A Vast Problem," *New York Times*, April 22, 1928, which estimated that the number might be about a million. An article in 1930 similarly cited an estimate of "more than a million" illegal immigrants; "Asks Funds to End Alien Smuggling," *New York Times*, January 26, 1930.

24. "Preventive Medicine for Crime," *Saturday Evening Post*, May 28, 1932.

25. On Chinese illegal immigration to the United States in the era of the Chinese Exclusion Act of 1882, see Grace Delgado, *Making the Chinese Mexican: Global Migration, Localism, and Exclusion in the US-Mexico Borderlands* (Palo Alto: Stanford University Press, 2012), chap. 3; Estelle T. Lau, *Paper Families: Identity, Immigration Administration, and Chinese Exclusion* (Durham: Duke University Press, 2006); and Erika Lee, *At America's Gates: Chinese Immigration During the Exclusion Era, 1882–1943* (Chapel Hill: University of North Carolina Press, 2003). For Chinese migration during this era, including illegal immigration to the United States, in a global context, see Adam M. McKeown, *Melancholy Order: Asian Migration and the Globalization of Borders* (New York: Columbia University Press, 2008). On the broader history of illegal immigration to the United States, see Patrick Ettinger, *Imaginary Lines: Border Enforcement and the Origins of Undocumented Immigration, 1882–1930* (Austin: University of Texas Press, 2009).

26. "Alien Guest Cards," *Saturday Evening Post*, January 24, 1931.

27. Quoted in "Alien Guest Cards," *Saturday Evening Post*, January 24, 1931.

28. Ngai, *Impossible Subjects*, 60.

29. "President Hoover and Immigration," *Detroit Jewish Chronicle*, June 19, 1931,

30. "Doak the Deportation Chief," *Nation*, March 18, 1931.

31. "18 Aliens Seized at Finnish Dance," *New York Times*, February 16, 1931; "Doak the Deportation Chief," *Nation*, March 19, 1931; "The Week," *New Republic*, May 13, 1931; and Jane Perry Clark, *Deportation of Aliens from the United States to Europe* (New York: Columbia University Press, 1931), 325–26.

32. "Doak the Deportation Chief," *Nation*, March 19, 1931.

33. "Preventive Medicine for Crime," *Saturday Evening Post*, May 28, 1932.

34. Daniel Kanstroom, *Deportation Nation: Outsiders in American History* (Cambridge: Harvard University Press, 2007), 134–36, 158–59, and 165; and Ngai, *Impossible Subjects*, chap. 2. There were 256 deportations in 1900; 2,695 in 1910; 2,762 in 1920; and 16,631 in 1930. See Clark, *Deportation of Aliens*, 29.

35. US Senate Committee on Immigration, Hearings, *A Bill to Authorize the Issuance of Certificates of Admission to Aliens*, 71st Cong., 2d sess., February 21 and March 12, 1930, 21 (my italics.)

36. Louis Marshall, Address at a Luncheon Conference to Discuss Alien Registration and Deportation Bills at the Hotel Astor, New York, January 9, 1926, 14, folder K, box 136, Louis Marshall Papers, Jacob Rader Marcus Center of the American Jewish Archives, Cincinnati Campus, Hebrew Union College Jewish Institute of Religion (hereafter AJA).

37. Statement quoted in Kohler, "A Dangerous Project," 385.

38. Statement quoted in Kohler, "A Dangerous Project," 387.

39. Klug does a particularly thorough job of exploring the implications of the Michigan registration act for Detroit unions, workers, and employers. See his "Labor Market Politics in Detroit."

40. "Michigan Passes the 'Spolansky Act,'" *Nation*, July 8, 1931.

41. US Bureau of the Census, *Statistical Abstract of the United States* 53 (1931): 22.

42. Steve Babson, *Working Detroit: The Making of a Union Town* (Detroit: Wayne State University Press, 1986), 27.

43. *American Jewish Year Book* 31 (1929–30), 307. For a description of Detroit's Jewish neighborhoods in this period, see Sidney Bolkowsky, *Harmony and Dissonance: Voices of Jewish Identity in Detroit, 1914–1967* (Detroit: Wayne State University Press, 1991), 97–102.

44. For an insightful exploration of the politics of black-white relations in Detroit during this era, see Karen Miller, "The Color of Citizenship: Race and Politics in Detroit, 1916–1940" (PhD diss., University of Michigan, 2003). On the reactions to Ford's publication, see Neil Baldwin, *Henry Ford and the Jews: The Mass Production of Hate* (New York: PublicAffairs, 2002), chap. 8; Bolkowsky, *Harmony and Dissonance*, 80–82 and 101; Leonard Dinnerstein, *Antisemitism in America* (New York: Oxford University Press, 1994), 80–82; and Goldstein, *Price of Whiteness*, 126–27.

45. On the Ku Klux Klan in Detroit, see Baldwin, *Henry Ford and the Jews*, 93–94; and Bolkowsky, *Harmony and Dissonance*, 80 and 101. For a broader look at the Klan's success in urban areas, see Kenneth T. Jackson, *The Ku Klux Klan in the City, 1915–1930* (New York: Oxford University Press, 1967).

46. Clark, *Deportation of Aliens*, 262; and Klug, "Labor Market Politics in Detroit," 10. See also "Rum Running on the Detroit River," *Nation*, September 4, 1929.

47. Robert A. Rockaway, "The Notorious Purple Gang: Detroit's All-Jewish Prohibition-Era Mob," *Shofar* 20, no. 1 (Fall 2001): 113–30.

48. The *Nation* reported: "the United States Government has in the Detroit area 100 prohibition agents, twenty-five special prohibition agents, fifty regular customs officers, twenty special customs agents, 200 customs border patrolmen, 100 immigration officers, fifty coast

guardsmen—and fourteen small boats." "Rum Running on the Detroit River," *Nation*, September 4, 1929.

49. Earl [Coe?], Inspector in Charge, Port Huron, to Inspector in Charge, Detroit, January 9, 1924, file 53990–160a, Accession 60A600, Records of the US Immigration and Naturalization Service, Record Group 85 (citations to this record group hereafter as RG 85), National Archives Building, Washington, DC (hereafter NA).

50. Moreover, many employers started restricting hiring to citizens only. See Vargas, *Proletarians of the North*, 170. Particular suspicion about use of public resources fell on illegal immigrants. The *Detroit News* reported that local immigration authorities were investigating two thousand people—possible illegal immigrants receiving city relief—whose names were submitted by Detroit's Public Welfare Department; a similar number was already under investigation in Dearborn, and more investigations were soon to be undertaken in Flint, Pontiac, Hamtramck, and elsewhere. "Check Aliens Who Get Doles," *Detroit News*, July 4, 1931.

51. Babson, *Working Detroit*, 53; Nelson Lichtenstein, *Walter Reuther: The Most Dangerous Man in Detroit* (New York: Basic Books, 1995), 26; and Vargas, *Proletarians of the North*, 169–73. Karen Miller points out that in July 1930, Detroit's factories employed only 137,500 workers, 50,000 fewer than had been employed in July 1920, when the city was much smaller. See Miller, "Color of Citizenship," 147.

52. Johnson, *Maurice Sugar*, 116–18; and Miller, "Color of Citizenship," chap. 2.

53. Babson, *Working Detroit*, 53; and Johnson, *Maurice Sugar*, 116.

54. US House Special Committee to Investigate Communist Activities in the United States, Hearings, *Investigation of Communist Propaganda*, part 4:1, 71st Cong., 2d sess., July 25 and 26, 1930, 183.

55. Ibid., 175. Jacob Spolansky had worked for military intelligence during World War I and for the Department of Justice in Chicago from 1918 to 1924. He helped lead the raid for the Department of Justice on a Communist convention in Bridgman, Michigan, in 1922. In 1926 he was hired by "private interests" to help derail the Communist textile workers' strike in Passaic, New Jersey, and in 1927 was brought to Detroit by the National Metal Trades Association—which included most of the city's automobile-related interests, except Ford—to investigate communism and radicalism in the auto industry. See US House Special Committee to Investigate Communist Activities in the United States, Hearings, *Investigation of Communist Propaganda*, 174; Sugar, "Michigan Passes the 'Spolansky Act,'" *Nation*, July 8, 1931; and "Auto Bosses and Labor Spy Behind Michigan Alien Bill," *Daily Worker*, June 6, 1931. For Spolansky's own perspective, see his memoir, *The Communist Trail in America* (New York: Macmillan, 1951).

56. US House Special Committee to Investigate Communist Activities in the United States, Hearings, *Investigation of Communist Propaganda*, part 4:1; H.R. Rep. No. 2290, 71st Cont., 3d sess. (Washington, DC: Government Printing Office, 1931), 63.

57. Sugar, "Michigan Passes the 'Spolansky Act,'" *Nation*, July 8, 1931.

58. Ibid. Klug notes that at other historical moments, industrialists would not have been as inclined to see such antialien measures as in their interest, invested as they were in an open flow of labor. But in this anxious moment, anti-Communist activists persuaded a number of key industrialists to follow their lead, for working-class rebellion seemed a dangerously imminent prospect. Klug, "Labor Market Politics in Detroit," 19–22.

59. "Alien Registration Bill Is Passed," *Detroit News*, May 19, 1931; and "Prepare for Legal Battle against Alien Registration Bill; Governor Is Certain to Approve the Measure," *Detroit Jewish Chronicle*, May 22, 1931. The article reported that "Senator George G. Sadowsky [*sic*], Polish, of Detroit, bitterly condemned the bill, but he could only secure the co-operation of Senator Charles A. Roxborough, colored, of Detroit, and Senator James G. Bonine of Cassopolis, in opposition to the measure." Curiously, in 1935, George Sadowski, in his later position as US congressman from Michigan, sponsored a bill "To Exclude and Deport Alien Habitual Commuters," which focused on the daily traffic of working people coming over the Canadian border to labor in Detroit. See US House Committee on Immigration and Naturalization, Hearings, *To Exclude and Deport Alien Habitual Commuters*, 74th Cong., 2d sess., March 6, 7, 13, and 14, 1935.

60. "Ruling by Attorney-General Voorhies as to Legality and Constitutionality of Alien Registration Measure to Guide Governor Wilber M. Brucker's Action on Bill," *Detroit Jewish Chronicle*, May 29, 1931.

61. *American Jewish Year Book* 34 (1932–33), 285.

62. "Prepare for Legal Battle Against Alien Registration Bill; Governor Is Certain to Approve the Measure," *Detroit Jewish Chronicle*, May 22, 1931; and Klug, "Labor Market Politics in Detroit," 1–2.

63. "Ruling by Attorney-General Voorhies as to Legality and Constitutionality of Alien Registration Measure," *Detroit Jewish Chronicle*, May 29, 1931. Elsewhere, the paper quoted the mayor as saying, "I have received from nearly every racial group in the city strong pleas against the Cheeney Act." "State is Enjoined from Enforcing Registration Bill; Hearing Before Three Judge Court Set for June 9," *Detroit Jewish Chronicle*, June 5, 1931.

64. "State is Enjoined from Enforcing Registration Bill," *Detroit Jewish Chronicle*, June 5, 1931.

65. The *Detroit Jewish Chronicle* reported on and quoted extensively from these documents throughout its coverage. The court file for Arrowsmith v. Voorhies, 55 F.(2d) 310 (E.D. Michig. 1931) can be found in the holdings of the National Archives and Records Administration—Great Lakes Region (Chicago), Record Group 21.24.2.

66. "Alien Protest Suit in Court," *Detroit News*, July 1, 1931; and "Judges Denison, O'Brien and Simons Hear Constitutionality Arguments of Michigan Alien Registration Bill, *Detroit Jewish Chronicle*, July 3, 1931.

67. See, e.g., Max Kohler, "Un-American Character of Race Legislation," *Annals of the American Academy of Political and Social Science* 34 (September 1909): 55–73, and *Immigration and Aliens in the United States*; Charles Reznikoff, ed., *Louis Marshall, Champion of Liberty: Selected Papers and Addresses*, 2 vols. (Philadelphia: Jewish Publication Society of America, 1957), 1:422–500; and Lucy Salyer, *Laws Harsh as Tigers: Chinese Immigrants and the Shaping of Modern Immigration Law* (Chapel Hill: University of North Carolina Press, 1995), 159.

68. Haney-López, *White by Law*. Naturalization was also open to those of African descent as of 1870, but immigrants whose racial identity was questionable almost always sought to be classified as "white" in their bids to naturalize.

69. "State Fights Ban on Alien Registry," *Detroit News*, June 19, 1931; and "Law Listing Aliens Invalid," *Detroit News*, December 9, 1931.

70. Hoffman, *Unwanted Mexican Americans*, chap. 7; Vargas, *Proletarians of the North*, chap, 5; and Sánchez, *Becoming Mexican American*, chap. 10.

71. A collection of Kohler's writings on immigration issues can be found in Kohler, *Immigration and Aliens*.

72. See, e.g.,"35,000 Mexicans Leave California," *New York Times*, April 12, 1931; and "Hegira of Mexicans Bothers California," *New York Times*, April 19, 1931.

73. Vargas, *Proletarians of the North*, 181.

74. "State is Enjoined from Enforcing Registration Bill; Hearing Before Three Judge Court Set for June 9," *Detroit Jewish Chronicle*, June 5, 1931.

75. "President Hoover and Immigration," *Detroit Jewish Chronicle*, June 19, 1931.

76. The official was assistant US attorney Louis M. Hopping. "Theodore Levin Lauded on Manner in Which He Prepared His Case on the Alien Registration Bill," *Detroit Jewish Chronicle*, July 10, 1931.

77. "Theodore Levin Lauded on Manner in Which He Prepared His Case on the Alien Registration Bill," *Detroit Jewish Chronicle*, July 10, 1931.

78. "Fred M. Butzel's Attack on the Alien Registration Bill," *Detroit Jewish Chronicle*, June 5, 1931.

79. Ibid.

80. Ibid.

81. Max Kohler, "The Michigan Alien Registration Law," in Kohler, *Immigration and Aliens*, 389.

82. Ibid., 358–59.

83. See, e.g., "Shall Michigan Revert to Czarism?" *Detroit Jewish Chronicle*, May 22, 1931.

84. "Liberty on the Scaffold," *Detroit Jewish Chronicle*, June 5, 1931.

85. "Damned If They Do or If They Don't," *Detroit Jewish Chronicle*, June 5, 1931.

86. Kohler, "A Dangerous Project," 369, 384, 386.

87. "Alien Guest Cards," *Saturday Evening Post*, January 24, 1931.

88. Ibid.

89. The issuance of these identification cards led to some alarm by those who were against alien registration, who argued that the measure essentially served the same purpose. See, e.g., "An Act of Rank Injustice," *Detroit Jewish Chronicle*, June 22, 1928. Since 1929, there had also been a system of voluntary national registry that offered certificates of arrival (necessary for the naturalization process) to those immigrants who could prove they had been in the country since 1921 but were not able to procure proof of regular entry, either because they had entered illicitly before 1921 or because there was no proper record of their entry.

90. "Alien Guest Cards," *Saturday Evening Post*, January 24, 1931.

91. "Fred M. Butzel's Attack on the Alien Registration Bill," *Detroit Jewish Chronicle*, June 5, 1931.

92. "Alien Protest Suit in Court," *Detroit News*, July 1, 1931.

93. Sugar, "Michigan Passes the 'Spolansky Act,'" *Nation*, July 8, 1931.

94. Quoted in Sugar, "Michigan Passes the 'Spolansky Act,'" *Nation*, July 8, 1931.

95. "Di pasportn gzeyre" [The passport edict], *Fraye arbayter shtime*, June 19, 1931.

96. "Labor Department Order Calls for Identification System for Aliens; Denies it Leads to Registrations," *Detroit Jewish Chronicle*, June 22, 1928.

97. "Fred M. Butzel's Attack on the Alien Registration Bill," *Detroit Jewish Chronicle*, June 5, 1931.

98. In fact, as discussed in chapter 1, American Jews had sometimes feared that Jewish immigrants' right to naturalization might be threatened, particularly if those immigrants came to be seen as "Oriental" and thus nonwhite. See, e.g., the discussion of this issue in connection with court cases about Syrian immigrants' bids for citizenship in Goldstein, *Price of Whiteness*, 102–4.

99. "Fred M. Butzel's Attack on the Alien Registration Bill," *Detroit Jewish Chronicle*, June 5, 1931.

100. "Ruling by Attorney-General Voorhies as to Legality and Constitutionality of Alien Registration Measure," *Detroit Jewish Chronicle*, May 29, 1931.

101. "Judges Denison, O'Brien and Simons Hear Constitutionality Arguments of Michigan Alien Registration Bill," *Detroit Jewish Chronicle*, July 3, 1931.

102. "Theodore Levin Lauded on Manner in Which He Prepared His Case on the Alien Registration Bill," *Detroit Jewish Chronicle*, July 10, 1931.

103. "Capitalizing on Tragedy," *Detroit Jewish Chronicle*, June 19, 1931.

104. As Butzel put it, "It is on account of them [the alien members of the Communist party], I take it, that this registration bill was bootlegged through the Legislature" ("Fred M. Butzel's Attack on the Alien Registration Bill," *Detroit Jewish Chronicle*, June 5, 1931).

105. The division between leftists and the mainstream activists, however, was not always as clear as some of them insisted. Leftist Jewish labor lawyer Maurice Sugar, e.g., who was fiercely against the registration law, clearly saw the issue both as a constitutional one and as a class one. See Sugar, "Michigan Passes the 'Spolansky Act.'" For more on Sugar's activism, see Johnson, *Maurice Sugar*.

106. "State Hunger Marchers Ready; Demand Relief and No Registration," *Daily Worker*, May 22, 1931.

107. "The Michigan Slave Bill," *Daily Worker*, June 18, 1931.

108. "Michigan Workers Aroused Over Bill Hitting Foreign Born," *Daily Worker*, May 23, 1931.

109. For a thorough exploration of the Scottsboro trial, see James Goodman, *Stories of Scottsboro* (New York: Pantheon Books, 1994). On the trial's resonance among American Jews, see Hasia Diner, *In the Almost Promised Land: American Jews and Blacks, 1915–1935*, 2d ed. (Baltimore: Johns Hopkins University Press, 1995), 42–43, 98–99, and 114; and Goldstein, *Price of Whiteness*, 159.

110. "Workers of Detroit Rallying Against the Registration Bill and for Fight For Scottsboro 9," *Daily Worker*, June 5, 1931.

111. Olivier Zunz, *The Changing Face of Inequality: Urbanization, Industrial Development, and Immigrants in Detroit, 1880–1920* (Chicago: University of Chicago Press, 1982), chap. 14.

112. "Reds Denounce New Alien Law," *Detroit News*, June 20, 1931; and "Communist Rally to Hear Foster," *Detroit News*, June 19, 1931. Groups scheduled to participate included the Croatian Workers' Organization, the National Lithuanian Organization, the Russian Mutual Aid Society, the Finnish Educational Club, the Ukrainian Toilers, the League of Negro Rights, the Jewish Building Trades Union, and others.

113. "Organize to Fight Registration Bill at July 1 Hearing," *Detroit Jewish Chronicle*,

June 12, 1931; "Der tsarisher pasportn gezets" [The tsaristic passport law], *Morgn frayhayt,* June 18, 1931; and "In di arbeter organizatsiyes fun detroyt" [In the labor organizations of Detroit], *Morgn frayhayt,* June 19, 1931.

114. "Registration Bill Unconstitutional, Three Judges Rule," *Detroit Jewish Chronicle,* December 11, 1931. In December 1932 this decision was followed by the issuance of a permanent injunction; "Michigan Alien Law Nullified by Court," *New York Times,* December 20, 1932.

115. Arrowsmith v. Voorhies, 55 F.2d at 310 (E.D. Michig. 1931).

116. " 'Humanized' Laws for Aliens Urged," *New York Times,* March 2, 1936; and "Alien Listings Opposed," March 14, 1936.

117. A 1939 Pennsylvania alien registration law, e.g., was overturned in court: Hines v. Davidowitz, 312 U.S. at 52 (1941).

118. Alien Registration Act of June 28, 1940 (54 Stat. 670).

119. "Unnecessary Alien Registration," Letter to the Editor, *New York Times,* January 17, 1941.

120. With a few notable exceptions, American Jews did not protest the wartime internment of Japanese and Japanese Americans. On this issue, see Marc Dollinger, *Quest for Inclusion: Jews and Liberalism in Modern America* (Princeton and Oxford: Princeton University Press, 2000), 79–80, and 86–91; Ellen Eisenberg, *The First to Cry Down Injustice?: Western Jews and Japanese Removal During WWII* (Plymouth: Lexington Books, 2008); and Cheryl Greenberg, "Black and Jewish Responses to Japanese Internment," *Journal of American Ethnic History* 14, no. 2 (Winter 1995): 3–37.

121. Louis Adamic, "Aliens and Alien-Baiters," *Harpers,* November 1936; and Ngai, *Impossible Subjects,* 75–89. On some of the controversy engendered by the secretary of labor's use of such administrative discretion, see "Answers Charges of Helping Aliens," *New York Times,* September 15, 1940. Legislation passed in 1929 and 1939, as well as the 1940 registration law, also contained provisions that allowed some immigrants to legalize their status or avoid deportation. See Hutchinson, *Legislative History of American Immigration Policy,* 563–72; and Ngai, *Impossible Subjects,* 82.

CHAPTER SIX

1. Turkish Jew Gets First US Visa Under New Immigration Law," *Jewish Telegraphic Agency,* December 6, 1965, http://www.jta.org.

2. "Text of President's Speech on Immigration," *New York Times* (supplementary material from *New York Times* News Service and WQXR), October 4, 1965, http://www.nytimes.com.

3. Immigration Act of October 3, 1965 (79 Stat. 911).

4. Mae M. Ngai, *Impossible Subjects: Illegal Aliens and the Making of Modern America* (Princeton: Princeton University Press, 2004), 260–65; David Reimers, *Still the Golden Door: The Third World Comes to America* (New York: Columbia University Press, 1985), chaps. 4 and 5; Daniel J. Tichenor, *Dividing Lines: The Politics of Immigration Control in America* (Princeton: Princeton University Press, 2002), 219–20; and Aristide R. Zolberg, *A Nation by Design: Immigration Policy in the Fashioning of America* (New York: Russell Sage Foundation with Harvard University Press), 333–36.

5. "President Johnson Signs Immigration Bill in Ceremony at Statue of Liberty," *Jewish Telegraphic Agency*, October 4 1965, http://www.jta.org.

6. See, e.g., Keith Fitzgerald, *The Face of the Nation: Immigration, the State, and the National Identity* (Palo Alto: Stanford University Press, 1996), 213–17, and 224–27; Desmond King, *Making Americans: Immigration, Race, and the Origins of the Diverse Democracy* (Cambridge: Harvard University Press, 2000), chap. 8; Michael C. LeMay, *From Open Door to Dutch Door: An Analysis of U.S. Immigration Policy Since 1820* (Westport: Greenwood, 1987), 109–14; Cheryl Shanks, *Immigration and the Politics of American Sovereignty, 1890–1990* (Ann Arbor: University of Michigan Press, 2001), chap. 6; Tichenor, *Dividing Lines*, 205–16; and Zolberg, *Nation by Design*, 324–33.

7. Thomas Borstelmann, *The Cold War and the Color Line: American Race Relations in the Global Arena* (Cambridge: Harvard University Press, 2003); Mary Dudziak, *Cold War Civil Rights: Race and the Image of American Democracy* (Princeton: Princeton University Press, 2000); Fitzgerald, *Face of the Nation*, 224–25; Shanks, *Immigration and the Politics of American Sovereignty*, 144–45, and 164–66; Tichenor, *Dividing Lines*, 178–79; and Penny Von Eschen, *Race Against Empire: Black Americans and Anticolonialism, 1937–1957* (Ithaca: Cornell University Press, 1997).

8. Tichenor, *Dividing Lines*, 178–79.

9. Tichenor, *Dividing Lines*, 203–4; and Zolberg, *Nation by Design*, 312–13.

10. Ira Katznelson, "Strangers No Longer: Jews and Postwar American Political Culture," in *Divergent Jewish Cultures: Israel and America*, ed. Deborah Dash Moore and S. Ilan Troen (New Haven: Yale University Press, 2001), 304–17. See also Arthur Goren, "A 'Golden Decade' for American Jews: 1945–1955," *Studies in Contemporary Jewry* 8 (1992): 3–20.

11. On the intertwined history of race and housing, see Arnold R. Hirsch, *Making the Second Ghetto: Race and Housing in Chicago, 1940–1960* (Chicago: University of Chicago Press, 1998); Kenneth T. Jackson, *Crabgrass Frontier: The Suburbanization of the United States* (New York: Oxford University Press, 1985), 197–203, 207–13, 224–29, and 241–42; Stephen Grant Meyer, *As Long as They Don't Move Next Door: Segregation and Conflict in America's Neighborhoods* (Lanham: Rowman and Littlefield, 2000); and Thomas Sugrue, *The Origins of the Urban Crisis: Race and Inequality in Postwar Detroit* (Princeton: Princeton University Press, 2005). On Jews' and other white ethnics' inclusion in the white middle-class mainstream in postwar America, see Karen Brodkin, *How Jews Became White Folks and What that Says about Race in America* (New Brunswick: Rutgers University Press, 1998); Marc Dollinger, *Quest for Inclusion: Jews and Liberalism in Modern America* (Princeton: Princeton University Press, 2000), 129–30; Katznelson, "Strangers No Longer"; and Zolberg, *Nation by Design*, 295–301.

12. On American Jewish activism postwar as pursuing a universal liberal agenda, see Dollinger, *Quest for Inclusion*; and Stuart Svonkin, *Jews Against Prejudice: American Jews and the Fight for Civil Liberties* (New York: Columbia University Press, 1997).

13. Leonard Dinnerstein, *Antisemitism in America* (Oxford: Oxford University Press, 1994), chap. 8; and Dollinger, *Quest for Inclusion*, 143–44. For the argument that American Jews' ongoing postwar anxieties about anti-Semitism and the Jewish place in the nation was inextricably linked with their activism against discrimination more broadly, see Svonkin, *Jews Against Prejudice*.

14. Tichenor, *Dividing Lines*, 177.

15. The literature on this issue is voluminous. Significant entries into this scholarship include Shlomo Aronson, *Hitler, the Allies, and the Jews* (Cambridge: Cambridge University Press, 2004); Richard Breitman and Allen Kraut, *American Refugee Policy and European Jewry, 1933–1945* (Bloomington: Indiana University Press, 1987); Henry L. Feingold, *Bearing Witness: How America and Its Jews Responded to the Holocaust* (Syracuse: Syracuse University Press, 1995), and *The Politics of Rescue: The Roosevelt Administration and the Holocaust, 1938–1945* (New Brunswick: Rutgers University Press, 1970); Saul S. Friedman, *No Haven for the Oppressed: United States Policy toward Jewish Refugees, 1938–1945* (Detroit: Wayne State University Press, 1973); Theodore S. Hamerow, *Why We Watched: Europe, America and the Holocaust* (New York: W. W. Norton, 2008); Arthur Morse, *While Six Million Died: A Chronicle of American Apathy* (New York: Random House, 1968); and David S. Wyman, *The Abandonment of the Jews: America and the Holocaust* (New York: Pantheon Books, 1984), and *Paper Walls: America and the Refugee Crisis* (New York: Pantheon Books, 1985). For the argument that the United States and other democracies in fact had an extremely generous refugee policy, see William D. Rubinstein, *The Myth of Rescue: Why the Democracies Could Not Have Saved More Jews from the Nazis* (New York: Routledge, 1997).

16. For overviews of the United States's changing relationship to refugee policy after 1945, see Carl Bon Tempo, *Americans at the Gate: The United States and Refugees During the Cold War* (Princeton: Princeton University Press, 2008); and Gil Loescher and John A. Scanlan, *Calculated Kindness: Refugees and America's Half-Open Door, 1945 to the Present* (New York: Free Press, 1998).

17. Ngai, *Impossible Subjects*, 84–89.

18. Kelly Lytle Hernández, *Migra! A History of the US Border Patrol* (Berkeley: University of California Press, 2010), chap. 8; Ngai, *Impossible Subjects*, 148–50, 153–58, and 247–48; Tichenor, *Dividing Lines*, 193–94, and 201–2; and Zolberg, *Nation by Design*, 316–22.

19. Bon Tempo, *Americans at the Gate*, 15. For a discussion of the origins of the notion of "refugees" in a European context, see Michael R. Marrus, *The Unwanted: European Refugees in the Twentieth Century* (New York: Oxford University Press, 1985), esp. 3–11.

20. Bon Tempo, *Americans at the Gate*, 15; and Sheldon Morris Neuringer, *American Jewry and United States Immigration Policy, 1881–1953* (1969; reprint, New York: Arno Press, 1980), chap. 3.

21. Loescher and Scanlan, *Calculated Kindness*.

22. Harold Fields, "Closing Immigration Around the World," *American Journal of International Law* 26, no. 4 (1932): 671–99; Wyman, *Paper Walls*, 28, and 34; and Aristide R. Zolberg, "Global Movements, Global Walls: Responses to Migration, 1885–1925," in *Global History and Migrations*, ed. Wang Gungwu (New York: Westview Press, 1997), 297–303, and *Nation by Design*, 281.

23. Zolberg, *Nation By Design*, 278.

24. Feingold, *Bearing Witness*; Friedman, *No Haven for the Oppressed*, 139–54, and 203–4; and Rafael Medoff, *The Deafening Silence* (New York: Shapolsky, 1987).

25. *American Jewish Year Book* 41 (1939–40), 209–12; Breitman and Kraut, *American Refugee Policy*, 87–88; Dinnerstein, *Antisemitism in America*, chap. 6; Wyman, *Paper Walls*, 14–23; and Zolberg, *Nation by Design*, 275. For the history of Father Coughlin, see Alan Brinkley, *Voices of*

Protest: Huey Long, Father Coughlin, and the Great Depression (New York: Knopf, 1982), esp. chaps. 4–8.

26. Robert A. Divine, *American Immigration Policy, 1924–1952* (New Haven: Yale University Press, 1957), 97–98; and Zolberg, *Nation by Design*, 291.

27. Tichenor, *Dividing Lines*, 160.

28. Breitman and Kraut, *American Refugee Policy*, 30–39; Alan M. Kraut, Richard Breitman, and Thomas W. Imhoof, "The State Department, the Labor Department, and German Jewish Immigration, 1930–1940," *Journal of American Ethnic History* 3, no. 2 (Spring 1984): 5–38; Dinnerstein, *America and the Survivors of the Holocaust*, 2–3; Feingold, *Politics of Rescue*, 131–37; and Wyman, *Paper Walls*, 163, and *Abandonment of the Jews*, 124–37.

29. Wyman, *Paper Walls*, 5–7, and 13–14.

30. Tichenor, *Dividing Lines*, 158.

31. Breitman and Kraut, *American Refugee Policy*, 73–74; Divine, *American Immigration Policy*, 101; Tichenor, *Dividing Lines*, 164–65; and Wyman, *Paper Walls*, 75–98. Both Tichenor and Wyman point out that the enthusiasm with which Americans greeted a proposal to take in British children after the war started—later scuttled because of the difficulty of accomplishing this in the midst of hostilities—strongly suggests the anti-Jewish element in the resistance to the German children refugee bill, however much that bill was portrayed as one that would help children of different faiths. See Tichenor, *Dividing Lines*, 165; and Wyman, *Paper Walls*, 127–28.

32. Divine, *American Immigration Policy*, 96, and 98–99; and Zolberg, *Nation by Design*, 280.

33. Wyman, *Paper Walls*, 70; US Senate Committee on Immigration, *Deportation of Aliens: Hearings before a Subcommittee of the Committee on Immigration*, 76th Cong., 1st sess., March 21–23, 1939, 17–18, 34–35, 51–53, 60–61, 77, 88, 121–30, 192–93, and 206.

34. File 811.11, Box 56 (1939), Havana Consulate General, General Records, Department of State Records–Foreign Service Posts, Record Group 84, National Archives at College Park, College Park, Maryland (hereafter NA-MD).

35. Ibid.

36. "'DeLuxe Stowaway Passages' Sold in France," *New York Times*, December 26, 1938; and file 55879–688, Box 715, Accession 58A734, Records of the US Immigration and Naturalization Service, Record Group 85, National Archives Building, Washington, DC. The overstaying of visitors' visas is also evidenced by the private relief bills that granted such immigrants a change of status (e.g., House Committee on Immigration and Naturalization, Hearings on H.R. 7459, "A Bill for the Relief of Bettina Bernstein," 76th Cong., 3d sess., May 1, 1940), as well as the Displaced Persons legislation passed in 1948 and 1950 (see below) and later laws, which allowed a number of those who had entered as visitors to adjust their status to that of permanent residents. See Hutchinson, *Legislative History of American Immigration Policy*, 564–68.

37. Abraham Ascher, *A Community Under Siege: The Jews of Breslau under Nazism* (Palo Alto: Stanford University Press, 2007), 6.

38. Breitman and Kraut, *American Refugee Policy*, chap. 5; Max Paul Friedman, *Nazis and Good Neighbors: The United States Campaign Against the Germans of Latin America in World War II* (Cambridge: Cambridge University Press, 2003), 47 and 156; and Wyman, *Paper Walls*, 189–91. Relatedly, Friedman, *Nazis and Good Neighbors*, relates that many Germans in Latin

America who were deported, as enemy aliens, to the United States for internment were in fact German Jewish refugees.

39. See note 14, above.

40. Tichenor, *Dividing Lines*, 162; and Wyman, *Paper Walls*, 73, and 138–41.

41. Breitman and Kraut, *American Refugee Policy*, 48–50.

42. Tichenor, *Dividing Lines*, 161–62, and 167; and Zolberg, *Nation by Design*, 289–90. Neuringer cites a higher number of 157,000. Neuringer, *American Jewry and United States Immigration Policy*, 265–66.

43. *American Jewish Year Book* 48 (1946–47), 599.

44. Divine, *American Immigration Policy*, 110.

45. Dinnerstein, *America and the Survivors of the Holocaust*, 43; and Tichenor, *Dividing Lines*, 182.

46. Dinnerstein, *America and the Survivors of the Holocaust*, 7–8, and chaps. 4 and 5.

47. Dinnerstein, *America and the Survivors of the Holocaust*, 113; and Tichenor, *Dividing Lines*, 182.

48. Loescher and Scanlan, *Calculated Kindness*, 3; and Zolberg, *Nation By Design*, 305.

49. Hutchinson, *Legislative History of US Immigration Policy*, 270–71.

50. Dinnerstein, *America and Survivors of the Holocaust*, 133; Divine, *American Immigration Policy*, 113; Fitzgerald, *Face of the Nation*, 197; and Tichenor, *Dividing Lines*, 184–85.

51. Ed Gossett, "A New Fifth Column or the Refugee Racket" (Washington, DC: Government Printing Office, 1947), 4.

52. Ibid., 6.

53. Loescher and Scanlan, *Calculated Kindness*, 8–9; and Tichenor, *Dividing Lines*, 183.

54. Dinnerstein, *America and the Survivors of the Holocaust*, 117; and Divine, *American Immigration Policy*, 114–15.

55. Dinnerstein, *America and the Survivors of the Holocaust*, 120–61; and Loescher and Scanlan, *Calculated Kindness*, 9–11.

56. "Celler's View on Immigration," *Brooklyn Eagle*, March 30, 1947.

57. Ibid.

58. Displaced Persons Act of June 25, 1948 (62 Stat. 1009).

59. Loescher and Scanlan, *Calculated Kindness*, 22–23, and 211; and Tichenor, *Dividing Lines*, 186.

60. Fitzgerald, *Face of the Nation*, 196.

61. Dinnerstein, *America and the Survivors of the Holocaust*, 171.

62. Tichenor, *Dividing Lines*, 188.

63. "Veto Asked for DP Bill," *New York Times*, June 25, 1948.

64. Tichenor, *Dividing Lines*, 187; and Divine, *American Immigration Policy*, 128.

65. Dinnerstein, *America and the Survivors of the Holocaust*, 222–25; and Divine, *American Immigration Policy*, 131.

66. Displaced Persons Act of June 16, 1950 (64 Stat. 219); Dinnerstein, *America and the Survivors of the Holocaust*, 176–182, and 249–250; and Tichenor, *Dividing Lines*, 187–88.

67. Dinnerstein, *America and the Survivors of the Holocaust*, 251; and Tichenor, *Dividing Lines*, 188.

68. The bureaus of Immigration and Naturalization, which had existed as separate entities

within the Department of Labor, were joined together in 1933 to form the INS. In 1940, the INS was moved to the Department of Justice.

69. Dinnerstein, *America and Survivors of the Holocaust*, 223; and Divine, *American Immigration Policy*, 140.

70. Dinnerstein, *America and Survivors of the Holocaust*, 223.

71. Ibid., 189–90.

72. Ibid., 183–198, 221, and 233–42.

73. For the conflicts over specific documents and the definitions and ramifications of "misrepresentation," e.g., see Ann S. Petluck, United Service for New Americans, to James Mc-Tighe, Displaced Persons Commission, April 17, 1951, file "United Service for New Americans," Box 71, Records of the Legal Division, General Records Subject File, Records of the Displaced Persons Commission, Record Group 278 (citations to this record group hereafter as RG 278), NA-MD. For broader accusations about fraudulent documents, see Ed Suter to Harry Rosenfield, November 1, 1950, file "Screening," Box 69, Records of the Legal Division, General Records Subject File, RG 278, NA-MD.

74. Dinnerstein, *America and Survivors of the Holocaust*, 189, and 194–95.

75. Dinnerstein, *America and Survivors of the Holocaust*, 196; and "Half of DPs in US Called 'Illegal,'" *Washington Post*, February 4, 1950.

76. H.R. Rep. No. 356, 84th Cong., 1st sess. (March 3, 1955).

77. Ibid., 200.

78. Dinnerstein, *America and Survivors of the Holocaust*, 250.

79. Internal Security Act of August 23, 1950 (64 Stat. 987).

80. Dinnerstein, *America and Survivors of the Holocaust*, 231; and Divine, *American Immigration Policy*, 136–38. On McCarran's role in opposing a revised DP act more generally, see Dinnerstein, *America and the Survivors of the Holocaust*, chap. 9.

81. Dinnerstein, *America and Survivors of the Holocaust*, 251–52; Divine, *American Immigration Policy*, 162–63; and Tichenor, *Dividing Lines*, 189.

82. See, e.g., DPC correspondence about army counterintelligence (CIC) screening of visa applicants for their participation in "inimical organizations;" DPC officials observed that in similar cases Jews were treated with more suspicion of communist activity than non-Jews. Ed Suter to Harry Rosenfield, November 1, 1950, file "Screening," Box 69, Subject File, General Records, Records of the Legal Division, RG 278, NA-MD.

83. Tichenor, *Dividing Lines*, 183.

84. Dinnerstein, *America and Survivors of the Holocaust*, 182; Divine, *American Immigration Policy*, 129; and Fitzgerald, *Face of the Nation*, 199.

85. Dinnerstein, *America and the Survivors of the Holocaust*, 124. On this point see also David Reimers, "An Unintended Reform: The 1965 Immigration Act and Third World Immigration to the United States," *Journal of American Ethnic History* 3, no. 1 (Fall 1983): 11.

86. Bon Tempo, *At America's Gate*, 5, 59, and 86. Cubans fleeing to the United States after the revolution represent the most notable exception to the predominantly Eurocentric refugee policy that prevailed at the time. See Bon Tempo, *At America's Gate*, chap. 5.

87. Bon Tempo, *At America's Gate*, 3–5, 7–8, 44, 59–61, 85, and 97–104; Divine, *American Immigration Policy*, 145; Loescher and Scanlan, *Calculated Kindness*, 22–24, 73, and 211–13; Ngai, *Impossible Subjects*, 236; and Zolberg, *Nation by Design*, 323.

88. Tom Segev, *The Seventh Million: The Israelis and the Holocaust*, trans. Haim Watzman (New York: Hill and Wang, 1993), 40–41.

89. Yehuda Bauer, *Flight and Rescue: Brichah* (New York: Random House, 1970); Dinnerstein, *America and the Survivors of the Holocaust*, 110–11; Dalia Ofer, *Escaping the Holocaust: Illegal Immigration to the Land of Israel, 1939–1944* (New York: Oxford University Press, 1991); Segev, *Seventh Million*, 124–35; and Idith Zertal, *From Catastrophe to Power: The Holocaust Survivors and the Emergence of Israel* (Berkeley: University of California Press, 1998).

90. Segev, *Seventh Million*, 129–32; and Zertal, *From Catastrophe to Power*, 52–58, 82–92, and 239–54.

91. Bauer, *Flight and Rescue*, 128; and Zertal, *From Catastrophe to Power*, 210–11.

92. Bauer, *Flight and Rescue*, 138; Loescher and Scanlan, *Calculated Kindness*, 8; and Mayer Abramowitz, "The View from 82: The Bricha, A Secret Jewish Organization," *The Jewish Federations of North America*, http://www.jewishfederations.org/page.aspx?id=77354.

93. Eric L. Goldstein, *The Price of Whiteness: Jews, Race and American Identity* (Princeton: Princeton University Press, 2006), 192.

94. Karen Brodkin Sacks, "How Jews Became White Folks," in *Race*, ed. Steven Gregory and Roger Sanjek (New Brunswick: Rutgers University Press, 1994), 87.

95. Goldstein, *Price of Whiteness*, 192.

96. Hutchinson, *Legislative History of American Policy*, 564–65; and Ngai, *Impossible Subjects*, 84–87.

97. Ascher, *Community Under Siege*, 6.

98. Hutchinson, *Legislative History of American Immigration Policy*, 565; and Ngai, *Impossible Subjects*, 86–87.

99. Ngai, *Impossible Subjects*, 87.

100. Hutchinson, *Legislative History of American Immigration Policy*, 566–67.

101. INS *Annual Report* (1960), 98.

102. INS *Annual Report* (1960), 99; INS *Annual Report* (1961), 102; and INS *Annual Report* (1962), 107. The 1961 report indicates that 221 of the enacted bills were for the relief of Europeans (particularly from Italy and Poland), 100 for Asians, and 33 for North Americans.

103. H.R. Rep. No. 1682, 86th Cong., 2d sess. (1960); and Senate, Messages from the President–Approval of Bills, 86th Cong., 2d sess., *Cong. Rec.* 106, 12,370 (June 13, 1960).

104. "Langer Explains His Activities for Aliens," *Washington Post*, May 26, 1952.

105. "House Group Fights Deportation Fraud," *New York Times*, February 9, 1955.

106. "East European Aliens Pose Problems for US," *New York Times*, August 22, 1948; "Deportations Rise to 580,000 a Year," *New York Times*, May 6, 1951; "Reds Slip Into US, Congress Warned," *New York Times*, February 10, 1954. On the Canadian border, see "US Eyes Smuggling of Aliens," *New York Times*, September 20, 1953.

107. "Legislative Group," *Ohio Jewish Chronicle*, November 11, 1949.

108. Ngai, *Impossible Subjects*, 294; and Zolberg, *Nation by Design*, 257.

109. Hernández, *Migra!*, 31–32; Ngai, *Impossible Subjects*, 52–53; Tichenor, *Dividing Lines*, 167–75; and Zolberg, *Nation By Design*.

110. Hernández, *Migra!*, 89; Ngai, *Impossible Subjects*, 67–71; and George J. Sánchez, *Becoming Mexican American: Ethnicity, Culture and Identity in Chicano Los Angeles, 1900–1945* (New York: Oxford University Press, 1993), 57–59.

111. Ngai, *Impossible Subjects*, 70–71.

112. Francisco Balderrama and Raymond Rodriguez, *Decade of Betrayal: Mexican Repatriation in the 1930s* (Albuquerque: University of New Mexico Press, 1995), 49–71, and 97–125; Abraham Hoffman, *Unwanted Mexican Americans in the Great Depression: Repatriation Pressures, 1929–1939* (Tucson: University of Arizona Press, 1974), 33–35, and 120–21; Ngai, *Impossible Subjects*, 71–75; Sánchez, *Becoming Mexican American*, chap. 10; and Zaragosa Vargas, *Proletarians of the North: A History of Mexican Industrial Workers in Detroit and the Midwest, 1917–1933* (Berkeley: University of California Press, 1999), chap. 5.

113. Hernández, *Migra!*, 110; Ngai, *Impossible Subjects*, 163–65; and Tichenor, *Dividing Lines*, 224. On the broader history of the Bracero Program, see Kitty Calavita, *Inside the State: The Bracero Program, Immigration and the INS* (New York: Routledge, 1992); and Deborah Cohen, *Braceros: Migrant Citizens and Transnational Subjects in the Postwar United States and Mexico* (Chapel Hill: University of North Carolina Press, 2011).

114. Ngai, *Impossible Subjects*, 146–47.

115. Matthew García, "Intraethnic Conflict and the *Bracero* Program during World War II," in *American Dreaming, Global Realities: Rethinking US Immigration History*, ed. Donna Gabaccia and Vicki Ruiz (Chicago: University of Illinois Press, 2006), 407–8; and Ngai, *Impossible Subjects*, 148.

116. Ngai, *Impossible Subjects*, 147–48.

117. Ngai, *Impossible Subjects*, 147–48; and Zolberg, *Nation By Design*, 309.

118. "'Wetback' Influx Near Record," *New York Times*, November 22, 1953.

119. Tichenor, *Dividing Lines*, 201; and Ngai, *Impossible Subjects*, 149.

120. INS *Annual Report* (1953), 3.

121. Hernández, *Migra!*, 156–57.

122. Ngai, *Impossible Subjects*, 153.

123. Hernández, *Migra!*, 157.

124. Tichenor, *Dividing Lines*, 202; Ngai, *Impossible Subjects*, 155–56; and Zolberg, *Nation By Design*, 320–21.

125. Ngai, *Impossible Subjects*, 165–66; and Tichenor, *Dividing Lines*, 208–11.

126. Hernández, *Migra!*, 161–62.

127. Hernández, *Migra!*, 174–76, and 191–95; Ngai, *Impossible Subjects*, 158–61; and Zolberg, *Nation by Design*, 310. For a cogent examination of the range of tensions between Mexican American communities and braceros, see García, "Intraethnic Conflict and the *Bracero* Program."

128. Ngai, *Impossible Subjects*, 161–65; and Tichenor, *Dividing Lines*, 193, and 211.

129. Ngai, *Impossible Subjects*, 246–47, and 347n.64.

130. [Ugo] Carusi, "Rumor Versus Fact," *Monthly Review* 4, no. 9 (March 1947), 109.

131. Ngai, *Impossible Subjects*, 247–48.

132. "Letters to the Times: Deporting Aliens," *New York Times*, June 3, 1951.

133. Divine, *American Immigration Policy*, 166; Fitzgerald, *Face of the Nation*, 200; and Zolberg, *Nation By Design*, 311.

134. Immigration and Nationality Act of June 27, 1952 (66 Stat. 163).

135. Tichenor, *Dividing Lines*, 191.

136. "Alien Bill Scored by Jewish Leader," *New York Times*, June 12, 1952.

137. Coordinating Council for Amending the McCarran-Walter Act to "Congressman," June 24, 195, folder "Special Legislative File, Immigration, HR 4394, 87th Congress," container 478, Papers of Emanuel Celler, Library of Congress (hereafter Celler Papers).

138. Tichenor, *Dividing Lines*, 192.

139. "Efforts to Nullify the Evils of the McCarran-Walter Act," *Jewish Forum*, September 1953, 120.

140. "The Consequences of Our Immigration Policy," December 5, 1955, folder "Special Legislative File, Immigration H.R. 4394, 87th Congress," container 478, Celler Papers.

141. Bon Tempo, *Americans at the Gate*, 95; and "Kennedy Gets Plea on Immigration Law," *New York Times*, April 15, 1962.

142. "Celler Urges Major Revisions in Immigration and Nationality Act," press release, January 14, 1961, folder "Immigration-General-1961–62," container 492, Celler Papers.

143. "The Consequences of Our Immigration Policy," December 5, 1955, folder "Special Legislative File, Immigration H.R. 4394, 87th Congress," container 478, Celler Papers.

144. House of Representatives, Congressman Walter of Pennsylvania speaking in support of the Immigration and Nationality Act of 1952, 84th Cong., 1st sess., *Cong. Rec.* 101, pt. 2:2335 (March 2, 1955).

145. Harold Bennet to Emanuel Celler, January 27, 1955, folder "Special Legislative File, Immigration H.R. 4394, 87th Congress," container 478, Celler Papers.

146. *The Dan Smoot Report* 3, no. 6 (February 11, 1957), 6.

147. Herbert G. Moore, "The Plot Against the McCarran-Walter Act," *National Republic*, December 1952.

148. Zolberg, *Nation by Design*, 296.

149. Ngai, *Impossible Subjects*, 243; and Tichenor, *Dividing Lines*, 203–4.

150. Hubert H. Humphrey, *The Stranger at Our Gate: America's Immigration Policy* (New York: Public Affairs Committee, 1954); and Tichenor, *Dividing Lines*, 204.

151. Ngai, *Impossible Subjects*, 240.

152. John Higham, *Strangers in the Land: Patterns of American Nativism, 1865–1925*, 2d ed. (New York: Atheneum, [1955] 1977).

153. Ngai, *Impossible Subjects*, 246.

154. Bon Tempo, *Americans at the Gate*, 91; Tichenor, *Dividing Lines*, 212–15; and Zolberg, *Nation by Design*, 329.

155. Zolberg, *Nation by Design*, 331.

156. Bon Tempo, *Americans at the Gate*, 88.

157. Tichenor, *Dividing Lines*, 216; and Loescher and Scanlan, *Calculated Kindness*, 73.

158. Bon Tempo, *Americans at the Gate*, 97, and 101–5; and Loescher and Scanlan, *Calculated Kindness*, 211–13.

159. Ngai, *Impossible Subjects*, 261; and Zolberg, *Nation by Design*, 335.

160. Ngai, *Impossible Subjects*, 248–49; and Zolberg, *Nation by Design*, 318.

EPILOGUE

1. Aristide R. Zolberg, *A Nation by Design: Immigration Policy in the Fashioning of America* (New York: Russell Sage Foundation, 2006), 439–42.

2. For scholarship examining the extensive deportee "diaspora" created by US policies of deportation, see David Brotherton and Luis Barrios, *Banished to the Homeland: Dominican Deportees and Their Stories of Exile* (New York: Columbia University Press, 2011); and Daniel Kanstroom, *Aftermath: Deportation Law and the New American Diaspora* (New York: Oxford University Press, 2012). On the immigration prison system, see Mark Dow, *American Gulag: Inside U.S. Immigration Prisons* (Berkeley: University of California Press, 2005); and Dan Malone, "Immigration, Terror, and Secret Prisons," in *Keeping Out the Other: A Critical Introduction to Immigration Enforcement Today*, ed. David Brotherton and Philip Kretsedemas (New York: Columbia University Press, 2008), 44–62.

3. On the idea of "remote control" of immigration, see chapter 2, note 106.

4. Zolberg, *Nation by Design*, 13–14.